Java™ Performance Tuning

THE JAVA SERIES

Java™ Performance Tuning

Jack Shirazi

O'REILLY®

Beijing · Cambridge · Farnham · Köln · Paris · Sebastopol · Taipei · Tokyo

Java™ Performance Tuning

by Jack Shirazi

Copyright © 2000 O'Reilly & Associates, Inc. All rights reserved.
Printed in the United States of America.

Published by O'Reilly & Associates, Inc., 101 Morris Street, Sebastopol, CA 95472.

Editor: Mike Loukides

Production Editor: Emily Quill

Cover Designer: Hanna Dyer

Printing History:

      September 2000:   First Edition.

Library of Congress Cataloging-in-Publication Data

Shirazi, Jack
   Java performance tuning/Jack Shirazi.
     p. cm. – (Java series)
   ISBN 0-596-00015-4
    1. Java (Computer program language) I. Title. II. Java series (O'Reilly & Associates)

QA76.73.J38 S47 2000
005.13'3–dc21   00-062362

ISBN: 0-596-00015-4
[M]   [11/00]

Table of Contents

Preface

Performance has been an important issue with Java™ since the first version hit the Web years ago. Making those first interpreted programs run fast enough was a huge challenge for many developers. Since then, Java performance has improved enormously, and any Java program can now be made to run fast enough provided you avoid the main performance pitfalls.

This book provides all the details a developer needs to performance-tune any type of Java program. I give step-by-step instructions on all aspects of the performance-tuning process, right from early considerations such as setting goals, measuring performance, and choosing a compiler, to detailed examples on using profiling tools and applying the results to tune the code. This is not an entry-level book about Java, but you do not need any previous *tuning* knowledge to benefit from reading it.

Many of the tuning techniques presented in this book lead to an increased maintenance cost, so they should not be applied arbitrarily. Change your code only when a bottleneck has been identified, and never change the design of your application for minor performance gains.

Contents of This Book

Chapter 1 gives general guidelines on how to tune. If you do not yet have a tuning strategy, this chapter provides a methodical tuning process.

Chapter 2 covers the tools you need to use while tuning. Chapter 3 looks at the Java Development Kit™ (JDK, now Java SDK), including VMs and compilers.

Chapters 4 through 12 cover various techniques you can apply to Java code. Chapter 12 looks at tuning techniques specific to distributed applications.

Chapter 13 steps back from the low-level code-tuning techniques examined throughout most of the book and considers tuning at all other stages of the development process.

Chapter 14 is a quick look at some operating system–level tuning techniques.

Each chapter has a performance tuning checklist at its end. Use these lists to ensure that you have not missed any core tuning techniques while you are tuning.

Virtual Machine (VM) Versions

I have focused on the Sun VMs since there is enough variation within these to show interesting results. I have shown the time variation across different VMs for many of the tests. However, your main focus should be on the effects that tuning has on any one VM, as this identifies the usefulness of a tuning technique. Differences between VMs are interesting, but are only indicative and need to be verified for your specific application. Where I have shown the results of timed tests, the VM versions I have used are:

1.1.6

Version 1.1.x VMs do less VM-level work than later Java 2 VMs, so I have used a 1.1.x VM that includes a JIT. Version 1.1.6 was the earliest 1.1.x JDK that included enough optimizations to be a useful base. Despite many later improvements throughout the JDK, the 1.1.x VMs from 1.1.6 still show the fastest results for some types of tests. Version 1.1.6 supports running with and without a JIT. The default is with a JIT, and this is the mode used for all measurements in the book.

1.2

I have used the 1.2.0 JDK for the 1.2 tests. Java 2 VMs have more work to do than prior VMs because of additional features such as Reference objects, and 1.2.0 is the first Java 2 VM. Version 1.2 supports running with and without a JIT. The default is with a JIT, and this is the mode used for measurements labeled "1.2." Where I've labeled a measurement "1.2 no JIT," it uses the 1.2 VM in interpreted mode with the -Djava.compiler=NONE option to set that property.

1.3

I have used both the 1.3.0 full release and the 1.3 prerelease, as the 1.3 full release came out very close to the publication time of the book. Version 1.3 supports running in interpreted mode or with client-tuned HotSpot technology (termed "mixed" mode). Version 1.3 does not support a pure JIT mode. The default is the HotSpot technology, and this is the mode I've used for measurements labeled simply "1.3."

HotSpot 1.0

HotSpot 1.0 VM was run with the 1.2.0 JDK classes. Because HotSpot optimizations frequently do not kick in until after the program has run for a little while, I sometimes show measurements labeled "HotSpot 2nd Run." This set of measurements is the result from repeating the particular test within the same VM session, i.e., the VM does not exit between the first and second runs of the test.

Conventions Used in This Book

The following font conventions are used in this book:

Italic is used for:

- Pathnames, filenames, and program names

- Internet addresses, such as domain names and URLs

- New terms where they are defined

`Constant width` is used for:

- All Java code

- Command lines and options that should be typed verbatim

- Names and keywords in Java programs, including method names, variable names, and class names

`Constant width bold` is used for emphasis in some code examples.

Comments and Questions

The information in this book has been tested and verified, but you may find that features have changed (or you may even find mistakes!). You can send any errors you find, as well as suggestions for future editions, to:

O'Reilly & Associates, Inc.
101 Morris Street
Sebastopol, CA 95472
(800) 998-9938 (in the United States or Canada)
(707) 829-0515 (international/local)
(707) 829-0104 (fax)

You can also send messages electronically. To be put on the mailing list or request a catalog, send email to:

info@oreilly.com

To ask technical questions or comment on the book, send email to:

bookquestions@oreilly.com

There is a web site for the book, where examples, errata, and any plans for future editions are listed. You can access this site at:

http://www.oreilly.com/catalog/javapt/

For more information about this book and others, see the O'Reilly web site:

http://www.oreilly.com

Acknowledgments

A huge thank you to my wonderful wife Ava, for her unending patience with me. This book would have been considerably poorer without her improvements in clarity and consistency throughout. I am also very grateful to Mike Loukides and Kirk Pepperdine for the enormously helpful assistance I received from them while writing this book. Their many notes have helped to make this book much clearer and complete.

Thanks also to my reviewers, Patrick Killelea, Ethan Henry, Eric Brower, and Bill Venners, who provided many useful comments. They identified several errors and added good advice that makes this book more useful.

I am, of course, responsible for the final text of this book, including any erroors tthat rremain.

1

Introduction

The trouble with doing something right the first time is that nobody appreciates how difficult it was.

—Fortune

There is a general perception that Java programs are slow. Part of this perception is pure assumption: many people assume that if a program is not compiled, it must be slow. Part of this perception is based in reality: many early applets and applications *were* slow, because of nonoptimal coding, initially unoptimized Java Virtual Machines (VMs), and the overheads of the language.

In earlier versions of Java, you had to struggle hard and compromise a lot to make a Java application run quickly. More recently, there have been fewer reasons why an application should be slow. The VM technology and Java development tools have progressed to the point where a Java application (or applet, servlet, etc.) is not particularly handicapped. With good designs and by following good coding practices and avoiding bottlenecks, applications usually run fast enough. However, the truth is that the first (and even several subsequent) versions of a program written in any language are often slower than expected, and the reasons for this lack of performance are not always clear to the developer.

This book shows you why a particular Java application might be running slower than expected, and suggests ways to avoid or overcome these pitfalls and improve the performance of your application. In this book I've gathered several years of tuning experiences in one place. I hope you will find it useful in making your Java application, applet, servlet, and component run as fast as you need.

Throughout the book I use the generic words "application" and "program" to cover Java applications, applets, servlets, beans, libraries, and really any use of Java code. Where a technique can be applied only to some subset of these various types of Java programs, I say so. Otherwise, the technique applies across all types of Java programs.

Why Is It Slow?

This question is always asked as soon as the first tests are timed: "Where is the time going? I did not expect it to take this long." Well, the short answer is that it's slow because it has not been performance-tuned. In the same way the first version of the code is likely to have bugs that need fixing, it is also rarely as fast as it can be. Fortunately, performance tuning is usually easier than debugging. When debugging, you have to fix bugs throughout the code; in performance tuning, you can focus your effort on the few parts of the application that are the bottlenecks.

The longer answer? Well, it's true that there are overheads in the Java runtime system, mainly due to its virtual machine layer that abstracts Java away from the underlying hardware. It's also true that there are overheads from Java's dynamic nature. These overheads can cause a Java application to run slower than an equivalent application written in a lower-level language (just as a C program is generally slower than the equivalent program written in assembler). Java's advantages—namely, its platform-independence, memory management, powerful exception checking, built-in multithreading, dynamic resource loading, and security checks—add costs in terms of an interpreter, garbage collector, thread monitors, repeated disk and network accessing, and extra runtime checks.

For example, hierarchical method invocation requires an extra computation for every method call, because the runtime system has to work out which of the possible methods in the hierarchy is the actual target of the call. Most modern CPUs are designed to be optimized for fixed call and branch targets and do not perform as well when a significant percentage of calls need to be computed on the fly. On the other hand, good object-oriented design actually encourages many small methods and significant polymorphism in the method hierarchy. Compiler inlining is another frequently used technique that can significantly improve compiled code. However, this technique cannot be applied when it is too difficult to determine method calls at compile time, as is the case for many Java methods.

Of course, the same Java language features that cause these overheads may be the features that persuaded you to use Java in the first place. The important thing is that none of these overheads slows the system down too much. Naturally, "too much" is different depending on the application, and the users of the application usually make this choice. But the key point with Java is that a good round of performance tuning normally makes your application run as fast as you need it to run. There are already plenty of nontrivial Java applications, applets, and servlets that run fast enough to show that Java itself is not too slow. So if your application is not running fast enough, chances are that it just needs tuning.

The Tuning Game

Performance tuning is similar to playing a strategy game (but happily, you are usually paid to do it!). Your target is to get a better score (lower time) than the last score after each attempt. You are playing with, not against, the computer, the programmer, the design and architecture, the compiler, and the flow of control. Your opponents are time, competing applications, budgetary restrictions, etc. (You can complete this list better than I can for your particular situation.)

I once attended a customer who wanted to know if there was a "go faster" switch somewhere that he could just turn on and make the whole application go faster. Of course, he was not really expecting one, but checked just in case he had missed a basic option somewhere.

There isn't such a switch, but very simple techniques sometimes provide the equivalent. Techniques include switching compilers, turning on optimizations, using a different runtime VM, finding two or three bottlenecks in the code or architecture that have simple fixes, and so on. I have seen all of these give huge improvements to applications, sometimes a 20-fold speedup. Order-of-magnitude speedups are typical for the first round of performance tuning.

System Limitations and What to Tune

Three resources limit all applications:

- CPU speed and availability
- System memory
- Disk (and network) input/output (I/O)

When tuning an application, the first step is to determine which of these is causing your application to run too slowly.

If your application is CPU-bound, you need to concentrate your efforts on the code, looking for bottlenecks, inefficient algorithms, too many short-lived objects (object creation and garbage collection are CPU-intensive operations), and other problems, which I will cover in this book.

If your application is hitting system-memory limits, it may be paging sections in and out of main memory. In this case, the problem may be caused by too many objects, or even just a few large objects, being erroneously held in memory; by too many large arrays being allocated (frequently used in buffered applications); or by the design of the application, which may need to be reexamined to reduce its running memory footprint.

On the other hand, external data access or writing to the disk can be slowing your application. In this case, you need to look at exactly what you are doing to the disks that is slowing the application: first identify the operations, then determine the problems, and finally eliminate or change these to improve the situation.

For example, one program I know of went through web server logs and did reverse lookups on the IP addresses. The first version of this program was very slow. A simple analysis of the activity being performed determined that the major time component of the reverse lookup operation was a network query. These network queries do not have to be done sequentially. Consequently, the second version of the program simply multithreaded the lookups to work in parallel, making multiple network queries simultaneously, and was much, much faster.

In this book we look at the causes of bad performance. Identifying the causes of your performance problems is an essential first step to solving those problems. There is no point in extensively tuning the disk-accessing component of an application because we all know that "disk access is much slower than memory access" when, in fact, the application is CPU-bound.

Once you have tuned the application's first bottleneck, there may be (and typically is) another problem, causing another bottleneck. This process often continues over several tuning iterations. It is not uncommon for an application to have its initial "memory hog" problems solved, only to become disk-bound, and then in turn CPU-bound when the disk-access problem is fixed. After all, the application has to be limited by something, or it would take no time at all to run.

Because this bottleneck-switching sequence is normal—once you've solved the existing bottleneck, a previously hidden or less important one appears—you should attempt to solve only the *main* bottlenecks in an application at any one time. This may seem obvious, but I frequently encounter teams that tackle the main identified problem, and then instead of finding the next real problem, start applying the same fix everywhere they can in the application.

One application I know of had a severe disk I/O problem caused by using unbuffered streams (all disk I/O was done byte by byte, which led to awful performance). After fixing this, some members of the programming team decided to start applying buffering everywhere they could, instead of establishing where the next bottleneck was. In fact, the next bottleneck was in a data-conversion section of the application that was using inefficient conversion methods, causing too many temporary objects and hogging the CPU. Rather than addressing and solving this bottleneck, they instead created a large memory allocation problem by throwing an excessive number of buffers into the application.

A Tuning Strategy

Here's a strategy I have found works well when attacking performance problems:

1. Identify the main bottlenecks (look for about the top five bottlenecks, but go higher or lower if you prefer).

2. Choose the quickest and easiest one to fix, and address it (except for distributed applications where the top bottleneck is usually the one to attack: see the following paragraph).

3. Repeat from Step 1.

This procedure will get your application tuned the quickest. The advantage of choosing the "quickest to fix" of the top few bottlenecks rather than the absolute topmost problem is that once a bottleneck has been eliminated, the characteristics of the application change, and the topmost bottleneck may not even need to be addressed any longer. However, in distributed applications I advise you target the topmost bottleneck. The characteristics of distributed applications are such that the main bottleneck is almost always the best to fix and, once fixed, the next main bottleneck is usually in a completely different component of the system.

Although this strategy is simple and actually quite obvious, I nevertheless find that I have to repeat it again and again: once programmers get the bit between their teeth, they just love to apply themselves to the interesting parts of the problems. After all, who wants to unroll loop after boring loop when there's a nice juicy caching technique you're eager to apply?

You should always treat the actual identification of the cause of the performance bottleneck as a science, not an art. The general procedure is straightforward:

1. Measure the performance using profilers and benchmark suites, and by instrumenting code.

2. Identify the locations of any bottlenecks.

3. Think of a hypothesis for the cause of the bottleneck.

4. Consider any factors that may refute your hypothesis.

5. Create a test to isolate the factor identified by the hypothesis.

6. Test the hypothesis.

7. Alter the application to reduce the bottleneck.

8. Test that the alteration improves performance, and measure the improvement (include regression testing the affected code).

9. Repeat from Step 1.

Here's the procedure for a particular example:

1. Run the application through your standard profiler (measurement).

2. You find that the code spends a huge 11% of time in one method (identification of bottleneck).

3. Looking at the code, you find a complex loop and guess this is the problem (hypothesis).

4. You see that it is not iterating that many times, so possibly the bottleneck could be outside the loop (confounding factor).

5. You could vary the loop iteration as a test to see if that identifies the loop as the bottleneck. However, you instead try to optimize the loop by reducing the number of method calls it makes: this provides a test to identify the loop as the bottleneck and at the same time provides a possible solution. In doing this, you are combining two steps, Steps 5 and 7. Although this is frequently the way tuning actually goes, be aware that this can make the tuning process longer: if there is no speedup, it may be because your optimization did not actually make things faster, in which case you have neither confirmed nor eliminated the loop as the cause of the bottleneck.

6. Rerunning the profile on the altered application finds that this method has shifted its percentage time down to just 4%. This may still be a candidate bottleneck for further optimization, but nevertheless it's confirmed as the bottleneck and your change has improved performance.

7. (Already done, combined with Step 5).

8. (Already done, combined with Step 6).

Perceived Performance

It is important to understand that the user has a particular view of performance that allows you to cut some corners. The user of an application sees changes as part of the performance. A browser that gives a running countdown of the amount left to be downloaded from a server is seen to be faster than one that just sits there, apparently hung, until all the data is downloaded. People expect to see something happening, and a good rule of thumb is that if an application is unresponsive for more than three seconds, it is seen to be slow. Some Human Computer Interface authorities put the user-patience limit at just two seconds; an IBM study from the early '70s suggested people's attention began to wander after waiting for more than just one second. For performance improvements, it is also useful to know that users are not generally aware of response time improvements of less than 20%. This means that when tuning for user perception, you should not deliver any changes to the users until you have made improvements that add more than a 20% speedup.

A few long response times make a bigger impression on the memory than many shorter ones. According to Arnold Allen,* the perceived value of the average response time is not the average, but the 90th percentile value: the value that is greater than 90% of all observed response times. With a typical exponential distribution, the 90th percentile value is 2.3 times the average value. Consequently, so long as you reduce the variation in response times so that the 90th percentile value is smaller than before, you can actually increase the average response time, and the user will still perceive the application as faster. For this reason, you may want to target variation in response times as a primary goal. Unfortunately, this is one of the more complex targets in performance tuning: it can be difficult to determine exactly why response times are varying.

If the interface provides feedback and allows the user to carry on other tasks or abort and start another function (preferably both), the user sees this as a responsive interface and doesn't consider the application as slow as he might otherwise. If you give users an expectancy of how long a particular task might take and why, they often accept that this is as long as it has to take and adjust their expectations. Modern web browsers provide an excellent example of this strategy in practice. People realize that the browser is limited by the bandwidth of their connection to the Internet, and that downloading cannot happen faster than a given speed. Good browsers always try to show the parts they have already received so that the user is not blocked, and they also allow the user to terminate downloading or go off to another page at any time, even while a page is partly downloaded. Generally, it is not the browser that is seen to be slow, but rather the Internet or the server site. In fact, browser creators have made a number of tradeoffs so that their browsers appear to run faster in a slow environment. I have measured browser display of identical pages under identical conditions and found browsers that are actually faster at full page display, but seem slower because they do not display partial pages, or download embedded links concurrently, etc. Modern web browsers provide a good example of how to manage user expectations and perceptions of performance.

However, one area in which some web browsers have misjudged user expectation is when they give users a momentary false expectation that operations have finished when in fact another is to start immediately. This false expectation is perceived as slow performance. For example, when downloading a page with embedded links such as images, the browser status bar often shows reports like "20% of 34K," which moves up to "56% of 34K," etc., until it reaches 100% and indicates that the page

---

* *Introduction to Computer Performance Analysis with Mathematica* (Academic Press).

has finished downloading. However, at this point, when the user expects that all the downloading has finished, the status bar starts displaying "26% of 28K" and so on, as the browser reports separately on each embedded graphic as it downloads them. This causes frustration to users who initially expected the completion time from the first download report and had geared themselves up to do something, only to have to wait again (often repeatedly). A better practice would be to report on how many pages need to be downloaded as well as the current download status, giving the user a clearer expectation of the full download time.

Where there are varying possibilities for performance tradeoffs (e.g., resolution versus frame rate for animation, compression size versus speed of compression for compression utilities, etc.), the best strategy is to put the user in control. It is better to provide the option to choose between faster performance and better functionality. When users have made the choice themselves, they are often more willing to put up with actions taking longer in return for better functionality. When users do not have this control, their response is usually less tolerant.

This strategy also allows those users who have strong performance requirements to be provided for at their own cost. But it is always important to provide a reasonable default in the absence of any choice from the user. Where there are many different parameters, consider providing various levels of user-controlled tuning parameters, e.g., an easy set of just a few main parameters, a middle level, and an expert level with access to all parameters. This must, of course, be well documented to be really useful.

Threading to Appear Quicker

A lot of time (in CPU cycles) passes while the user is reacting to the application interface. This time can be used to anticipate what the user wants to do (using a background low priority thread), so that precalculated results are ready to assist the user immediately. This makes an application appear blazingly fast.

Similarly, ensuring that your application remains responsive to the user, even while it is executing some other function, makes it seem fast and responsive. For example, I always find that when starting up an application, applications that draw themselves on screen quickly and respond to repaint requests even while still initializing (you can test this by putting the window in the background and then bringing it to the foreground) give the impression of being much faster than applications that seem to be chugging away unresponsively. Starting different word-processing applications with a large file to open can be instructive, especially if the file is on the network or a slow (removable) disk. Some act very nicely, responding almost immediately while the file is still loading; others just hang unresponsively with windows only partially refreshed until the file is loaded; others don't even fully paint themselves until the file has finished loading. This illustrates what can happen if you do not use threads appropriately.

In Java, the key to making an application responsive is multithreading. Use threads to ensure that any particular service is available and unblocked when needed. Of course this can be difficult to program correctly and manage. Handling inter-thread communication with maximal responsiveness (and minimal bugs) is a complex task, but it does tend to make for a very snappily built application.

Streaming to Appear Quicker

When you display the results of some activity on the screen, there is often more information than can fit on a single screen. For example, a request to list all the details on all the files in a particular large directory may not fit on one display screen. The usual way to display this is to show as much as will fit on a single screen and indicate that there are more items available with a scrollbar. Other applications or other information may use a "more" button or have other ways of indicating how to display or move on to the extra information.

In these cases, you initially need to display only a partial result of the activity. This tactic can work very much in your favor. For activities that take too long and for which some of the results can be returned more quickly than others, it is certainly possible to show just the first set of results while continuing to compile more results in the background. This gives the user an apparently much quicker response than if you were to wait for all the results to be available before displaying them.

This situation is often the case for distributed applications. A well-known example is (again!) found in web browsers that display the initial screenful of a page as soon as it is available, without waiting for the whole page to be downloaded. The general case is when you have a long activity that can provide results in a stream, so that the results can be accessed a few at a time. For distributed applications, sending all the data is often what takes a long time; in this case, you can build streaming into the application by sending one screenful of data at a time. Also, bear in mind that when there is a really large amount of data to display, the user often views only some of it and aborts, so be sure to build in the ability to stop the stream and restore its resources at any time.

Caching to Appear Quicker

This section briefly covers the general principles of caching. Caching is an optimization technique I return to in several different sections of this book, when it is appropriate to the problem under discussion. For example, in the area of disk access, there are several caches that apply: from the lowest-level hardware cache up through the operating-system disk read and write caches, cached filesystems, and file reading and writing classes that provide buffered I/O. Some caches cannot be tuned at all; others are tuneable at the operating-system level or in Java. Where it is possible for a developer to take advantage of or tune a particular cache, I provide suggestions and approaches that cover the caching technique appropriate to that area of the application. In some cases where caches are not directly tuneable, it is still worth knowing the effect of using the cache in different ways and how this can affect performance. For example, disk hardware caches almost always apply a read-ahead algorithm: the cache is filled with the next block of data after the one just read. This means that reading backward through a file (in chunks) is not as fast as reading forward through the file.

Caches are effective because it is expensive to move data from one place to another or to calculate results. If you need to do this more than once to the same piece of data, it is best to hang on to it the first time and refer to the local copy in the future. This applies, for example, to remote access of files such as browser downloads. The browser caches locally on disk the file that was downloaded, to ensure that a subsequent access does not have to reach across the network to reread the file, thus making it much quicker to access a second time. It also applies, in a different way, to reading bytes from the disk. Here, the cost of reading one byte for operating systems is the same as reading a page (usually 4 or 8 KB), as data is read into memory a page at a time by the operating system. If you are going to read more than one byte from a particular disk area, it is better to read in a whole page (or all the data if it fits on one page) and access bytes through your local copy of the data.

General aspects of caching are covered in more detail in the section "Cached Access" in Chapter 11, *Appropriate Data Structures and Algorithms.* Caching is an important performance-tuning technique that trades space for time, and it should be used whenever extra memory space is available to the application.

Starting to Tune

Before diving into the actual tuning, there are a number of considerations that will make your tuning phase run more smoothly and result in clearly achieved objectives.

User Agreements

Any application must meet the needs and expectations of its users, and a large part of those needs and expectations is performance. Before you start tuning, it is crucial to identify the target response times for as much of the system as possible. At the outset, you should agree with your users (directly if you have access to them, or otherwise through representative user profiles, market information, etc.) what the performance of the application is expected to be.

The performance should be specified for as many aspects of the system as possible, including:

- Multiuser response times depending on the number of users (if applicable)

- Systemwide throughput (e.g., number of transactions per minute for the system as a whole, or response times on a saturated network, again if applicable)

- The maximum number of users, data, files, file sizes, objects, etc., the application supports

- Any acceptable and expected degradation in performance between minimal, average, and extreme values of supported resources

Agree on target values and acceptable variances with the customer or potential users of the application (or whoever is responsible for performance) before starting to tune. Otherwise, you will not know where to target your effort, how far you need to go, whether particular performance targets are achievable at all, and how much tuning effort those targets may require. But most importantly, without agreed targets, whatever you achieve tends to become the starting point.

The following scenario is not unusual: a manager sees horrendous performance, perhaps a function that was expected to be quick, but takes 100 seconds. His immediate response is, "Good grief, I expected this to take no more than 10 seconds." Then, after a quick round of tuning that identifies and removes a huge bottleneck, function time is down to 10 seconds. The manager's response is now, "Ah, that's more reasonable, but of course I actually meant to specify 3 seconds—I just never believed you could get down so far after seeing it take 100 seconds. Now you can start tuning." You do not want your initial achievement to go unrecognized (especially if money depends on it), and it is better to know at the outset what you need to reach. Agreeing on targets before tuning makes everything clear to everyone.

Setting Benchmarks

After establishing targets with the users, you need to set benchmarks. These are precise specifications stating what part of the code needs to run in what amount of time. Without first specifying benchmarks, your tuning effort is driven only by the target, "It's gotta run faster," which is a recipe for a wasted return. You must ask, "How much faster and in which parts, and for how much effort?" Your benchmarks should target a number of specific functions of the application, preferably from the user perspective (e.g., from the user pressing a button until the reply is returned, or the function being executed is completed).

You must specify target times for each benchmark. You should specify ranges: for example, best times, acceptable times, etc. These times are often specified in frequencies of achieving the targets. For example, you might specify that function A takes not more than 3 seconds to execute from user click to response received for 80% of executions, with another 15% of response times allowed to fall in the 3- to 5-second range, and 5% allowed to fall in the 5- to 10-second range. Note that the earlier section on user perceptions indicates that the user will see this function as having a 5-second response time (the 90th percentile value) if you achieve the specified ranges.

You should also have a range of benchmarks that reflect the contributions of different components of the application. If possible, it is better to start with simple tests so that the system can be understood at its basic levels, and then work up from these tests. In a complex application, this helps to determine the relative costs of subsystems and which components are most in need of performance-tuning.

The following point is critical: *Without clear performance objectives, tuning will never be completed.* This is a common syndrome on single or small group projects, where code keeps on being tweaked as better implementations or cleverer code is thought up.

Your general benchmark suite should be based on real functions used in the end application, but at the same time should not rely on user input, as this can make measurements difficult. Any variability in input times or any other part of the application should either be eliminated from the benchmarks or precisely identified and specified within the performance targets. There may be variability, but it must be controlled and reproducible.

The Benchmark Harness

There are tools for testing applications in various ways.* These tools focus mostly on testing the robustness of the application, but as long as they measure and report times, they can also be used for performance testing. However, because their focus tends to be on robustness testing, many tools interfere with the application's performance, and you may not find a tool you can use adequately or cost-effectively. If you cannot find an acceptable tool, the alternative is to build your own harness.

Your benchmark harness can be as simple as a class that sets some values and then starts the `main()` method of your application. A slightly more sophisticated harness might turn on logging and timestamp all output for later analysis. GUI-run

---

* You can search the Web for java+perf+test to find performance-testing tools. In addition, some Java profilers are listed in Chapter 15, *Further Resources.*

applications need a more complex harness and require either an alternative way to execute the graphical functionality without going through the GUI (which may depend on whether your design can support this), or a screen event capture and playback tool (several such tools exist*). In any case, the most important requirement is that your harness correctly reproduces user activity and data input and output. Normally, whatever regression-testing apparatus you have (and presumably are already using) can be adapted to form a benchmark harness.

The benchmark harness should not test the quality or robustness of the system. Operations should be normal: startup, shutdown, noninterrupted functionality. The harness should support the different configurations your application operates under, and any randomized inputs should be controlled; but note that the random sequence used in tests should be reproducible. You should use a realistic amount of randomized data and input. It is helpful if the benchmark harness includes support for logging statistics and easily allows new tests to be added. The harness should be able to reproduce and simulate all user input, including GUI input, and should test the system across all scales of intended use, up to the maximum numbers of users, objects, throughputs, etc. You should also validate your benchmarks, checking some of the values against actual clock time to ensure that no systematic or random bias has crept into the benchmark harness.

For the multiuser case, the benchmark harness must be able to simulate multiple users working, including variations in user access and execution patterns. Without this support for variations in activity, the multiuser tests inevitably miss many bottlenecks encountered in actual deployment and, conversely, do encounter artificial bottlenecks that are never encountered in deployment, wasting time and resources. It is critical in multiuser and distributed applications that the benchmark harness correctly reproduces user-activity variations, delays, and data flows.

Taking Measurements

Each run of your benchmarks needs to be under conditions that are as identical as possible; otherwise it becomes difficult to pinpoint why something is running faster (or slower) than in another test. The benchmarks should be run multiple times, and the full list of results retained, not just the average and deviation or the ranged percentages. Also note the time of day that benchmarks are being run and any special conditions that apply, e.g., weekend or after hours in the office. Sometimes the variation can give you useful information. It is essential that you always run an initial benchmark to precisely determine the initial times. This is important

---

* JDK 1.3 introduced a new `java.awt.Robot` class, which provides for generating native system-input events, primarily to support automated testing of Java GUIs.

because, together with your targets, the initial benchmarks specify how far you need to go and highlight how much you have achieved when you finish tuning.

It is more important to run all benchmarks under the same conditions than to achieve the end-user environment for those benchmarks, though you should try to target the expected environment. It is possible to switch environments by running all benchmarks on an identical implementation of the application in two environments, thus rebasing your measurements. But this can be problematic: it requires detailed analysis because different environments usually have different relative performance between functions (thus your initial benchmarks could be relatively skewed compared with the current measurements).

Each set of changes (and preferably each individual change) should be followed by a run of benchmarks to precisely identify improvements (or degradations) in the performance across all functions. A particular optimization may improve the performance of some functions while at the same time degrading the performance of others, and obviously you need to know this. Each set of changes should be driven by identifying exactly which bottleneck is to be improved and how much a speedup is expected. Using this methodology rigorously provides a precise target of your effort.

You need to verify that any particular change does improve performance. It is tempting to change something small that you are sure will give an "obvious" improvement, without bothering to measure the performance change for that modification (because "it's too much trouble to keep running tests"). But you could easily be wrong. Jon Bentley once discovered that eliminating code from some simple loops can actually slow them down.* If a change does not improve performance, you should revert back to the previous version.

The benchmark suite should not interfere with the application. Be on the lookout for artificial performance problems caused by the benchmarks themselves. This is very common if no thought is given to normal variation in usage. A typical situation might be benchmarking multiuser systems with lack of user simulation (e.g., user delays not simulated causing much higher throughput than would ever be seen; user data variation not simulated causing all tests to try to use the same data at the same time; activities artificially synchronized giving bursts of activity and inactivity; etc.). Be careful not to measure artificial situations, such as full caches with exactly the data needed for the test (e.g., running the test multiple times sequentially without clearing caches between runs). There is little point in performing tests that hit only the cache, unless this is the type of work the users will always perform.

---

* "Code Tuning in Context" by Jon Bentley, *Dr. Dobb's Journal*, May 1999. An empty loop in C ran slower than one that contained an integer increment operation.

When tuning, you need to alter any benchmarks that are quick (under five seconds) so that the code applicable to the benchmark is tested repeatedly in a loop to get a more consistent measure of where any problems lie. By comparing timings of the looped version with a single-run test, you can sometimes identify whether caches and startup effects are altering times in any significant way.

Optimizing code can introduce new bugs, so the application should be tested during the optimization phase. A particular optimization should not be considered valid until the application using that optimization's code path has passed quality assessment.

Optimizations should also be completely documented. It is often useful to retain the previous code in comments for maintenance purposes, especially as some kinds of optimized code can be more difficult to understand (and therefore to maintain).

It is typically better (and easier) to tune multiuser applications in single-user mode first. Many multiuser applications can obtain 90% of their final tuned performance if you tune in single-user mode and then identify and tune just a few major multiuser bottlenecks (which are typically a sort of give-and-take between single-user performance and general system throughput). Occasionally, though, there will be serious conflicts that are revealed only during multiuser testing, such as transaction conflicts that can slow an application to a crawl. These may require a redesign or rearchitecting of the application. For this reason, some basic multiuser tests should be run as early as possible to flush out potential multiuser-specific performance problems.

Tuning distributed applications requires access to the data being transferred across the various parts of the application. At the lowest level, this can be a packet sniffer on the network or server machine. One step up from this is to wrap all the external communication points of the application so that you can record all data transfers. Relay servers are also useful. These are small applications that just re-route data between two communication points. Most useful of all is a trace or debug mode in the communications layer that allows you to examine the higher-level calls and communication between distributed parts.

What to Measure

The main measurement is always wall-clock time. You should use this measurement to specify almost all benchmarks, as it's the real-time interval that is most appreciated by the user. (There are certain situations, however, in which system throughput might be considered more important than the wall-clock time; e.g., servers, enterprise transaction systems, and batch or background systems.)

The obvious way to measure wall-clock time is to get a timestamp using `System.currentTimeMillis()` and then subtract this from a later timestamp to determine the elapsed time. This works well for elapsed time measurements that are not short.* Other types of measurements have to be system-specific and often application-specific. You can measure:

- CPU time (the time allocated on the CPU for a particular procedure)
- The number of runnable processes waiting for the CPU (this gives you an idea of CPU contention)
- Paging of processes
- Memory sizes
- Disk throughput
- Disk scanning times
- Network traffic, throughput, and latency
- Transaction rates
- Other system values

However, Java doesn't provide mechanisms for measuring these values directly, and measuring them requires at least some system knowledge, and usually some application-specific knowledge (e.g., what is a transaction for your application?).

TIP   You need to be careful when running tests that have small differences in timings. The first test is usually slightly slower than any other tests. Try doubling the test run so that each test is run twice within the VM (e.g., rename `main()` to `maintest()`, and call `maintest()` twice from a new `main()`).

              There are almost always small variations between test runs, so always use averages to measure differences and consider whether those differences are relevant by calculating the variance in the results.

For distributed applications, you need to break down measurements into times spent on each component, times spent preparing data for transfer and from transfer (e.g., marshalling and unmarshalling objects and writing to and reading from a buffer), and times spent in network transfer. Each separate machine used on the networked system needs to be monitored during the test if any system parameters are to be included in the measurements. Timestamps must be synchronized across

---

* `System.currentTimeMillis()` can take up to half a millisecond to execute. Any measurement including the two calls needed to measure the time difference should be over an interval greater than 100 milliseconds to ensure that the cost of the `System.currentTimeMillis()` calls are less than 1% of the total measurement. I generally recommend that you do not make more than one time measurement (i.e., two calls to `System.currentTimeMillis()`) per second.

the system (this can be done by measuring offsets from one reference machine at the beginning of tests). Taking measurements consistently from distributed systems can be challenging, and it is often easier to focus on one machine, or one communication layer, at a time. This is usually sufficient for most tuning.

Don't Tune What You Don't Need to Tune

The most efficient tuning you can do is not to alter what works well. As they say, "If it ain't broke, don't fix it." This may seem obvious, but the temptation to tweak something just because you have thought of an improvement has a tendency to override this obvious statement.

The second most efficient tuning is to discard work that doesn't need doing. It is not at all uncommon for an application to be started with one set of specifications and to have some of the specifications change over time. Many times the initial specifications are much more generic than the final product. However, the earlier generic specifications often still have their stamps in the application. I frequently find routines, variables, objects, and subsystems that are still being maintained but are never used and never will be used, since some critical aspect of these resources is no longer supported. These redundant parts of the application can usually be chopped without any bad consequences, often resulting in a performance gain.

In general, you need to ask yourself exactly what the application is doing and why. Then question whether it needs to do it in that way, or even if it needs to do it at all. If you have third-party products and tools being used by the application, consider exactly what they are doing. Try to be aware of the main resources they use (from their documentation). For example, a zippy DLL (shared library) that is speeding up all your network transfers is using some resources to achieve that speedup. You should know that it is allocating larger and larger buffers before you start trying to hunt down the source of your mysteriously disappearing memory. Then you can realize that you need to use the more complicated interface to the DLL that restricts resource usage, rather than a simple and convenient interface. And you will have realized this before doing extensive (and useless) object profiling, because you would have been trying to determine why *your* application is being a memory hog.

When benchmarking third-party components, you need to apply a good simulation of exactly how you will use those products. Determine characteristics from your benchmarks and put the numbers into your overall model to determine if performance can be reached. Be aware that vendor benchmarks are typically useless for a particular application. Break your application down into a hugely simplified version for a preliminary benchmark implementation to test third-party components. You should make a strong attempt to include all the scaling necessary so that you are benchmarking a fully scaled usage of the components, not some reduced version that will reveal little about the components in full use.

Performance Checklist

- Specify the required performance.
  - — Ensure performance objectives are clear.
  - — Specify target response times for as much of the system as possible.
  - — Specify all variations in benchmarks, including expected response ranges (e.g., 80% of responses for X must fall within 3 seconds).
  - — Include benchmarks for the full range of scaling expected (e.g., low to high numbers of users, data, files, file sizes, objects, etc.).
  - — Specify and use a benchmark suite based on real user behavior. This is particularly important for multiuser benchmarks.
  - — Agree on all target times with users, customers, managers, etc., before tuning.

- Make your benchmarks long enough: over five seconds is a good target.
  - — Use elapsed time (wall-clock time) for the primary time measurements.
  - — Ensure the benchmark harness does not interfere with the performance of the application.
  - — Run benchmarks before starting tuning, and again after each tuning exercise.
  - — Take care that you are not measuring artificial situations, such as full caches containing exactly the data needed for the test.

- Break down distributed application measurements into components, transfer layers, and network transfer times.

- Tune systematically: understand what affects the performance; define targets; tune; monitor and redefine targets when necessary.
  - — Approach tuning scientifically: measure performance; identify bottlenecks; hypothesize on causes; test hypothesis; make changes; measure improved performance.
  - — Determine which resources are limiting performance: CPU, memory, or I/O.
  - — Accurately identify the causes of the performance problems before trying to tune them.

- — Use the strategy of identifying the main bottlenecks, fixing the easiest, then repeating.
- — Don't tune what does not need tuning. Avoid "fixing" nonbottlenecked parts of the application.
- — Measure that the tuning exercise has improved speed.
- — Target one bottleneck at a time. The application running characteristics can change after each alteration.
- — Improve a CPU limitation with faster code and better algorithms, and fewer short-lived objects.
- — Improve a system-memory limitation by using fewer objects or smaller long-lived objects.
- — Improve I/O limitations by targeted redesigns or speeding up I/O, perhaps by multithreading the I/O.

- Work with user expectations to provide the appearance of better performance.
  - — Hold back releasing tuning improvements until there is at least a 20% improvement in response times.
  - — Avoid giving users a false expectation that a task will be finished sooner than it will.
  - — Reduce the variation in response times. Bear in mind that users perceive the mean response time as the actual 90th percentile value of the response times.
  - — Keep the user interface responsive at all times.
  - — Aim to always give user feedback. The interface should not be dead for more than two seconds when carrying out tasks.
  - — Provide the ability to abort or carry on alternative tasks.
  - — Provide user-selectable tuning parameters where this makes sense.
  - — Use threads to separate out potentially blocking functions.
  - — Calculate "look-ahead" possibilities while the user response is awaited.
  - — Provide partial data for viewing as soon as possible, without waiting for all requested data to be received.
  - — Cache locally items that may be looked at again or recalculated.

- Quality-test the application after any optimizations have been made.
- Document optimizations fully in the code. Retain old code in comments.

2

Profiling Tools

If you only have a hammer,
you tend to see every problem as a nail.
—Abraham Maslow

Before you can tune your application, you need tools that will help you find the bottlenecks in the code. I have used many different tools for performance tuning, and so far I have found the commercially available profilers to be the most useful. You can easily find several of these, together with reviews of them, by searching the Web using java+optimi and java+profile, or checking the various computer magazines. These tools are usually available free for an evaluation period, and you can quickly tell which you prefer using. If your budget covers it, it is worth getting several profilers: they often have complementary features and provide different details about the running code. I have included a list of profilers in Chapter 15, *Further Resources*.

All profilers have some weaknesses, especially when you want to customize them to focus on particular aspects of the application. Another general problem with profilers is that they frequently fail to work in nonstandard environments. Nonstandard environments should be rare, considering Java's emphasis on standardization, but most profiling tools work at the VM level, and the JVMPI (Java Virtual Machine Profiler Interface) was only beginning to be standardized in JDK 1.2, so incompatibilities do occur. Even after the JVMPI standard is finalized, I expect there will be some nonstandard VMs you may have to use, possibly a specialized VM of some sort—there are already many of these.

When tuning, I normally use one of the commercial profiling tools, and on occasion where the tools do not meet my needs, I fall back on a variation of one of the custom tools and information extraction methods presented in this chapter.

Where a particular VM offers extra APIs that tell you about some running characteristics of your application, these custom tools are essential to access those extra APIs. Using a professional profiler and the proprietary tools covered in this chapter, you will have enough information to figure out where problems lie and how to resolve them. When necessary, you can successfully tune without a professional profiler, since the Sun VM does contain a basic profiler, which I cover in this chapter. However, this option is not ideal for the most rapid tuning.

NOTE   From JDK 1.2, Java specifies a VM-level interface, consisting of C function calls, which allows some external control over the VM. These calls provide monitoring and control over events in the VM, allowing an application to query the VM and to be notified about thread activity, object creation, garbage collection, method call stack, etc. These are the calls required to create a profiler. The interface is intended to standardize the calls to the VM made by a profiler, so any profiler works with any VM that supports the JVMPI standard. However, in JDK 1.2, the JVMPI is only experimental and subject to change.

In addition to Java-specific profilers, there are other more generic tools that can be useful for profiling:

- Network packet sniffers (both hardware and software types, e.g., *netstat*)

- Process and thread listing utilities (*top*, *ps* on Unix; the task manager and performance monitor on Windows)

- System performance measuring utilities (*vmstat, iostat, sar, top* on Unix; the task manager and performance monitor on Windows)

Measurements and Timings

When looking at timings, be aware that different tools affect the performance of applications in different ways. Any profiler slows down the application it is profiling. The degree of slowdown can vary from a few percent to a few hundred percent. Using `System.currentTimeMillis()` in the code to get timestamps is the only reliable way to determine the time taken by each part of the application. In addition, `System.currentTimeMillis()` is quick and has no effect on application timing (as long as you are not measuring too many intervals or ridiculously short intervals; see the discussion in "What to Measure" in Chapter 1, *Introduction*).

Another variation on timing the application arises from the underlying operating system. The operating system can allocate different priorities for different processes, and these priorities determine the importance the operating system applies to a particular process. This in turn affects the amount of CPU time allocated to a particular process compared to other processes. Furthermore, these priorities can change over the lifetime of the process. It is usual for server operating systems to gradually decrease the priority of a process over that process's lifetime. This means that the process will have shorter periods of the CPU allocated to it before it is put back in the runnable queue. An adaptive VM (like Sun's HotSpot) can give you the reverse situation, speeding up code shortly after it has started running (see "Faster VMs" in Chapter 3, *Underlying JDK Improvements*).

Whether or not a process runs in the foreground can also be important. For example, on a machine with the workstation version of Windows (most varieties including NT, 95, 98, and 2000), foreground processes are given maximum priority. This ensures that the window currently being worked on is maximally responsive. However, if you start a test and then put it in the background so that you can do something else while it runs, the measured times can be very different from the results you would get if you left that test running in the foreground. This applies even if you do not actually do anything else while the test is running in the background. Similarly, on server machines, certain processes may be allocated maximum priority (for example, Windows NT and 2000 server version, as well as most Unix server configured machines, allocate maximum priority to network I/O processes).

This means that to get pure absolute times, you need to run tests in the foreground on a machine with no other significant processes running, and use `System.currentTimeMillis()` to measure the elapsed times. Any other configuration implies some overhead added to timings, and you must be aware of this. As long as you are aware of any extra overhead, you can usually determine whether any particular measurement is relevant or not.

Most profiles provide useful relative timings, and you are usually better off ignoring the absolute times when looking at profile results. Be careful when comparing absolute times run under different conditions, e.g., with and without a profiler, in the foreground versus in the background, on a very lightly loaded server (for example, in the evening) compared to a moderately loaded one (during the day). All these types of comparisons can be misleading.

You also need to take into account cache effects. There will be effects from caches in the hardware, in the operating system, across various points in a network, and in the application. Starting the application for the first time on a newly booted system usually gives different timings as compared to starting for the first time on a system that has been running for a while, and these both give different timings compared to an application that has been run several times previously on the system. All these variations need to be considered, and a consistent test scenario used. Typically, you need to manage the caches in the application, perhaps explicitly emptying (or filling) them, for each test run to get repeatable results. The other caches are difficult to manipulate, and you should try to approximate the targeted running environment as closely as possible, rather than test each possible variation in the environment.

Garbage Collection

The Java runtime system normally includes a garbage collector.* Some of the commercial profilers provide statistics showing what the garbage collector is doing. You can also use the -verbosegc option with the VM. This option prints out time and space values for objects reclaimed and space recycled as the reclamations occur. The printout includes explicit synchronous calls to the garbage collector (using System.gc()) as well as asynchronous executions of the garbage collector, as occurs in normal operation when free memory available to the VM gets low.

NOTE   System.gc() does not necessarily force a synchronous garbage collection. Instead, the gc() call is really a hint to the runtime that now is a good time to run the garbage collector. The runtime decides whether to execute the garbage collection at that time and what type of garbage collection to run.

It is worth looking at some output from running with -verbosegc. The following code fragment creates lots of objects to force the garbage collector to work, and also includes some synchronous calls to the garbage collector:

```
package tuning.gc;
public class Test {
  public static void main(String[] args)
  {
    int SIZE = 4000;
    StringBuffer s;
    java.util.Vector v;

    //Create some objects so that the garbage collector
    //has something to do
    for (int i = 0; i < SIZE; i++)
    {
      s = new StringBuffer(50);
      v = new java.util.Vector(30);
      s.append(i).append(i+1).append(i+2).append(i+3);
    }
    s = null;
    v = null;
    System.out.println("Starting explicit garbage collection");
    long time = System.currentTimeMillis();
    System.gc();
```

---

* Some embedded runtimes do not include a garbage collector. All objects may have to fit into memory without any garbage collection for these runtimes.

```
        System.out.println("Garbage collection took " +
            (System.currentTimeMillis()-time) + " millis");

        int[] arr = new int[SIZE*10];
        //null the variable so that the array can be garbage collected
        time = System.currentTimeMillis();
        arr = null;
        System.out.println("Starting explicit garbage collection");
        System.gc();
        System.out.println("Garbage collection took " +
            (System.currentTimeMillis()-time) + " millis");
    }
}
```

When this code is run in Sun JDK 1.2 with the –verbosegc option,[*] you get:

```
<GC: need to expand mark bits to cover 16384 bytes>
<GC: managing allocation failure: need 1032 bytes, type=1, action=1>
<GC: 0 milliseconds since last GC>
<GC: freed 18578 objects, 658392 bytes in 26 ms, 78% free (658872/838856)>
  <GC: init&scan: 1 ms, scan handles: 12 ms, sweep: 13 ms, compact: 0 ms>
  <GC: 0 register-marked objects, 1 stack-marked objects>
  <GC: 1 register-marked handles, 31 stack-marked handles>
  <GC: refs: soft 0 (age >= 32), weak 0, final 2, phantom 0>
<GC: managing allocation failure: need 1032 bytes, type=1, action=1>
<GC: 180 milliseconds since last GC>
<GC: compactHeap took 15 ms, swap time = 4 ms, blocks_moved=18838>
<GC: 0 explicitly pinned objects, 2 conservatively pinned objects>
<GC: last free block at 0x01A0889C of length 1888>
<GC: last free block is at end>
<GC: freed 18822 objects, 627504 bytes in 50 ms, 78% free (658920/838856)>
  <GC: init&scan: 2 ms, scan handles: 11 ms, sweep: 16 ms, compact: 21 ms>
  <GC: 0 register-marked objects, 2 stack-marked objects>
  <GC: 0 register-marked handles, 33 stack-marked handles>
  <GC: refs: soft 0 (age >= 32), weak 0, final 0, phantom 0>
Starting explicit garbage collection
<GC: compactHeap took 9 ms, swap time = 5 ms, blocks_moved=13453>
<GC: 0 explicitly pinned objects, 5 conservatively pinned objects>
<GC: last free block at 0x019D5534 of length 211656>
<GC: last free block is at end>
<GC: freed 13443 objects, 447752 bytes in 40 ms, 78% free (657752/838856)>
  <GC: init&scan: 1 ms, scan handles: 12 ms, sweep: 12 ms, compact: 15 ms>
  <GC: 0 register-marked objects, 6 stack-marked objects>
  <GC: 0 register-marked handles, 111 stack-marked handles>
  <GC: refs: soft 0 (age >= 32), weak 0, final 0, phantom 0>
Garbage collection took 151 millis
...
```

---

[*] Note that –verbosegc can also work with applets by using java –verbosegc sun.applet. AppletViewer <URL>.

The actual details of the output are not standardized and likely to change between different VM versions as well as between VMs from different vendors. As a comparison, this is the output from the later garbage collector version using Sun JDK 1.3:

```
[GC 511K->96K(1984K), 0.0281726 secs]
[GC 608K->97K(1984K), 0.0149952 secs]
[GC 609K->97K(1984K), 0.0071464 secs]
[GC 609K->97K(1984K), 0.0093515 secs]
[GC 609K->97K(1984K), 0.0060427 secs]
Starting explicit garbage collection
[Full GC 228K->96K(1984K), 0.0899268 secs]
Garbage collection took 170 millis
Starting explicit garbage collection
[Full GC 253K->96K(1984K), 0.0884710 secs]
Garbage collection took 180 millis
```

As you can see, each time the garbage collector kicks in, it produces a report of its activities. Any one garbage collection reports on the times taken by the various parts of the garbage collector and specifies what the garbage collector is doing. Note that the internal times reported by the garbage collector are not the full time taken for the whole activity. In the examples, you can see the full time for one of the synchronous garbage collections, which is wrapped by print statements from the code fragment (i.e., those lines not starting with a < or [sign). However, these times include the times taken to output the printed statements from the garbage collector and are therefore higher times than those for the garbage collection alone. To see the pure synchronous garbage collection times for this code fragment, you need to run the program without the –verbosegc option.

In the previous examples, the garbage collector kicks in either because it has been called by the code fragment or because creating an object from the code fragment (or the runtime initialization) encounters a lack of free memory from which to allocate space for that object: this is normally reported as "managing allocation failure."

Some garbage-collector versions appear to execute their garbage collections faster than others. But be aware that this time difference may be an artifact: it can be caused by the different number of printed statements when using the –verbosegc option. When run without the –verbosegc option, the times may be similar. The garbage collector from JDK 1.2 executes a more complex scavenging algorithm than earlier JDK versions to smooth out the effects of garbage collection running in the background. (The garbage-collection algorithm is discussed briefly in Chapter 3. It cannot be tuned directly, but garbage-collection statistics can give you important information about objects being reclaimed, which helps you tune your application.) From JDK 1.2, the VM also handles many types of references that never existed in VM versions before 1.2. Overall, Java 2 applications do seem to have faster object recycling in application contexts than previous JDK versions.

It is occasionally worthwhile to run your application using the `-verbosegc` option to see how often the garbage collector kicks in. At the same time, you should use all logging and tracing options available with your application, so that the output from the garbage collector is set in the context of your application activities. It would be nice to have a consistent way to summarize the information generated with this verbose option, but the output depends on both the application and the VM, and I have not found a consistent way of producing summary information.

Method Calls

The main focus of most profiling tools is to provide a profile of method calls. This gives you a good idea of where the bottlenecks in your code are and is probably the most important way to pinpoint where to target your efforts. By showing which methods and lines take the most time, a good profiling tool can save you time and effort in locating bottlenecks.

Most method profilers work by sampling the call stack at regular intervals and recording the methods on the stack.* This regular snapshot identifies the method currently being executed (the method at the top of the stack) and all the methods below, to the program's entry point. By accumulating the number of hits on each method, the resulting profile usually identifies where the program is spending most of its time. This profiling technique assumes that the sampled methods are representative, i.e., if 10% of stacks sampled show method `foo()` at the top of the stack, then the assumption is that method `foo()` takes 10% of the running time. However, this is a sampling technique, and so it is not foolproof: methods can be missed altogether or have their weighting misrecorded if some of their execution calls are missed. But usually only the shortest tests are skewed. Any reasonably long test (i.e., over seconds, rather than milliseconds) will normally give correct results.

WARNING   This sampling technique can be difficult to get right. It is not enough to simply sample the stack. The profiler must also ensure that it has a coherent stack state, so the call must be synchronized across the stack activities, possibly by temporarily stopping the thread. The profiler also needs to make sure that multiple threads are treated consistently, and that the timing involved in its activities is accounted for without distorting the regular sample time. Also, too short a sample interval causes the program to become extremely slow, while too long an interval results in many method calls being missed and hence misrepresentative profile results being generated.

---

* A variety of profiling metrics, including the way different metrics can be used, are reported in the paper "A unifying approach to performance analysis in the Java environment," by Alexander, Berry, Levine, and Urquhart, in the *IBM Systems Journal*, Vol. 39, No. 1. This paper can be found at *http://www. research.ibm.com/journal/sj/391/alexander.html*. Specifically, see Table 4 in this paper.

The JDK comes with a minimal profiler, obtained by running a program using the java executable with the -Xrunhprof option (-prof before JDK 1.2, -Xprof with HotSpot). The result of running with this option is a file with the profile data in it. The default name of the file is *java.hprof.txt* (*java.prof* before 1.2). This filename can be specified by using the modified option, -Xrunhprof:file=<filename> (-prof:<filename> before 1.2). The output using these options is discussed in detail shortly.

Profiling Methodology

When using a method profiler, the most useful technique is to target the top five to ten methods and choose the quickest to fix. The reason for this is that once you make one change, the profile tends to be different the next time, sometimes markedly so. This way, you can get the quickest speedup for a given effort.

However, it is also important to consider what you are changing, so you know what your results are. If you select a method that is taking up 10% of the execution time, then if you halve the time that method takes, you have speeded up your application by 5%. On the other hand, targeting a method that takes up only 1% of execution time is going to give you a maximum of only 1% speedup to the application, no matter how much effort you put in to speed up that method.

Similarly, if you have a method that takes 10% of the time but is called a huge number of times so that each individual method call is quite short, you are less likely to speed up that method. On the other hand, if you can eliminate some significant fraction of the calling methods (the methods that call the method that takes 10% of the time), you might gain a good speedup in that way.

Let's look at the profile output from a short program that repeatedly converts some numbers to strings and also inserts them into a hash table:

```
package tuning.profile;
import java.util.*;

public class ProfileTest
{

  public static void main(String[] args)
  {
    //Repeat the loop this many times
    int repeat = 2000;

    //Two arrays of numbers, eight doubles and ten longs
    double[] ds = {Double.MAX_VALUE, -3.14e-200D,
      Double.NEGATIVE_INFINITY, 567.89023D, 123e199D,
      -0.000456D, -1.234D, 1e55D};
    long[] ls = {2283911683699007717L, -8007630872066909262L,
```

```
        4536503365853551745L, 548519563869L, 45L,
        Long.MAX_VALUE, 1L, -9999L, 7661314123L, 0L};

    //initializations
    long time;
    StringBuffer s = new StringBuffer();
    Hashtable h = new Hashtable();
    System.out.println("Starting test");
    time = System.currentTimeMillis();

    //Repeatedly add all the numbers to a stringbuffer,
    //and also put them into a hash table
    for (int i = repeat; i > 0; i--)
    {
        s.setLength(0);
        for (int j = ds.length-1; j >= 0; j--)
        {
            s.append(ds[j]);
            h.put(new Double(ds[j]), Boolean.TRUE);
        }
        for (int j = ls.length-1; j >= 0; j--)
        {
            s.append(ls[j]);
            h.put(new Long(ls[j]), Boolean.FALSE);
        }
    }
    time = System.currentTimeMillis() - time;
    System.out.println("  The test took " + time + " milliseconds");
    }
}
```

The relevant output from running this program with the JDK 1.2 method profiling option follows. (See the section "Java 2 "cpu=samples" Profile Output" for a detailed explanation of the 1.2 profiling option and its output.)

```
CPU SAMPLES BEGIN (total = 15813) Wed Jan 12 11:26:47 2000
rank   self  accum    count trace method
   1 54.79% 54.79%    8664    204 java/lang/FloatingDecimal.dtoa
   2 11.67% 66.46%    1846    215 java/lang/Double.equals
   3 10.18% 76.64%    1609    214 java/lang/FloatingDecimal.dtoa
   4  3.10% 79.74%     490    151 java/lang/FloatingDecimal.dtoa
   5  2.90% 82.63%     458    150 java/lang/FloatingDecimal.<init>
   6  2.11% 84.74%     333    213 java/lang/FloatingDecimal.<init>
   7  1.23% 85.97%     194    216 java/lang/Double.doubleToLongBits
   8  0.97% 86.94%     154    134 sun/io/CharToByteConverter.convertAny
   9  0.94% 87.88%     148    218 java/lang/FloatingDecimal.<init>
  10  0.82% 88.69%     129    198 java/lang/Double.toString
  11  0.78% 89.47%     123    200 java/lang/Double.hashCode
  12  0.70% 90.17%     110    221 java/lang/FloatingDecimal.dtoa
  13  0.66% 90.83%     105    155 java/lang/FloatingDecimal.multPow52
```

```
14  0.62% 91.45%      98    220 java/lang/Double.equals
15  0.52% 91.97%      83    157 java/lang/FloatingDecimal.big5pow
16  0.46% 92.44%      73    158 java/lang/FloatingDecimal.constructPow52
17  0.46% 92.89%      72    133 java/io/OutputStreamWriter.write
```

In this example, I have extracted only the top few lines from the profile summary table. The methods are ranked according to the percentage of time they take. Note that the trace does not identify actual method signatures, only method names. The top three methods take, respectively, 54.79%, 11.67%, and 10.18% of the time taken to run the full program.* The fourth method in the list takes 3.10% of the time, so clearly you need look no further than the top three methods to optimize the program. The methods ranked first, third, and fourth are the same method, possibly called in different ways. Obtaining the traces for these three entries from the relevant section of the profile output (trace 204 for the first entry, and traces 215 and 151 for the second and fourth entries), you get:

```
TRACE 204:
    java/lang/FloatingDecimal.dtoa(FloatingDecimal.java:Compiled method)
    java/lang/FloatingDecimal.<init>(FloatingDecimal.java:Compiled method)
    java/lang/Double.toString(Double.java:Compiled method)
    java/lang/String.valueOf(String.java:Compiled method)
TRACE 214:
    java/lang/FloatingDecimal.dtoa(FloatingDecimal.java:Compiled method)
TRACE 151:
    java/lang/FloatingDecimal.dtoa(FloatingDecimal.java:Compiled method)
    java/lang/FloatingDecimal.<init>(FloatingDecimal.java:Compiled method)
    java/lang/Double.toString(Double.java:132)
    java/lang/String.valueOf(String.java:2065)
```

In fact, both traces 204 and 151 are the same stack, but trace 151 provides line numbers for two of the methods. Trace 214 is a truncated entry, and is probably the same stack as the other two (these differences are one of the limitations of the JDK profiler, i.e., that information is sometimes lost).

So all three entries refer to the same stack: an inferred call from the StringBuffer to append a double, which calls String.valueOf(), which calls Double.toString(), which in turn creates a FloatingDecimal object. (<init> is the standard way to write a constructor call; <clinit> is the standard way to show a class initializer being executed. These are also the actual names for constructors and static initializers in the class file). FloatingDecimal is a class that is private to the java.lang package, which handles most of the logic involved in

---

* The samples that count towards a particular method's execution time are those where the method itself is executing at the time of the sample. If method foo() was calling another method when the sample was taken, that other method would be at the top of the stack instead of foo(). So you do not need to worry about the distinction between foo()'s execution time and the time spent executing foo()'s callees. Only the method at the top of the stack is tallied.

converting floating-point numbers. `FloatingDecimal.dtoa()` is the method called by the `FloatingDecimal` constructor that converts the binary floating-point representation of a number into its various parts of digits before the decimal point, after the decimal point, and the exponent. `FloatingDecimal` stores the digits of the floating-point number as an array of chars when the `FloatingDecimal` is created; no strings are created until the floating-point number is converted to a string.

Since this stack includes a call to a constructor, it is worth checking the object-creation profile to see whether you are generating an excessive number of objects: object creation is expensive, and a method that generates many new objects is often a performance bottleneck. (I show the object-creation profile and how to generate it in the later section "Object-Creation Profiling.") The object-creation profile shows that a large number of extra objects are being created, including a large number of `FDBigInt` objects that are created by the new `FloatingDecimal` objects.

Clearly, `FloatingDecimal.dtoa()` is the primary method to try to optimize in this case. Almost any improvement in this one method translates directly to a similar improvement in the overall program. However, normally only Sun can modify this method, and even if you want to modify it, it is long and complicated and takes an excessive amount of time to optimize unless you are already familiar with both floating-point binary representation and converting that representation to a string format.

Normally when tuning, the first alternative to optimizing `FloatingDecimal.dtoa()` is to examine the other significant bottleneck method, `Double.equals()`, which came second in the summary. Even though this entry takes up only 11.67% compared to over 68% for the `FloatingDecimal.dtoa()` method, it may be an easier optimization target. But note that while a small 10% improvement in the `FloatingDecimal.dtoa()` method translates into a 6% improvement for the program as a whole, the `Double.equals()` method needs to be speeded up to be more than twice as fast to get a similar 6% improvement for the full program.

The trace corresponding to this second entry in the summary example turns out to be another truncated trace, but the example shows the same method in 14th position, and the trace for that entry identifies the `Double.equals()` call as coming from the `Hashtable.put()` call. Unfortunately for tuning purposes, the `Double.equals()` method itself is already quite fast and cannot be optimized further.

When methods cannot be directly optimized, the next best choice is to reduce the number of times they are called or even avoid the methods altogether. (In fact, eliminating method calls is actually the better tuning choice, but is often considerably more difficult to achieve and so is not a first-choice tactic for optimization.)

The object-creation profile and the method profile together point to the FloatingDecimal class as being a huge bottleneck, so avoiding this class is the obvious tuning tactic here. In Chapter 5, *Strings*, I employ this technique, avoiding the default call through the FloatingDecimal class for the case of converting floating-point numbers to Strings, and I obtain an order-of-magnitude improvement. Basically, the strategy is to create a more efficient routine to run the equivalent conversion functionality, and then replacing the calls to the underperforming FloatingDecimal methods with calls to the more efficient optimized methods.

The best way to avoid the Double.equals() method is to replace the hash table with another implementation that stores double primitive data types directly rather than requiring the doubles to be wrapped in a Double object. This allows the == operator to make the comparison in the put() method, thus completely avoiding the Double.equals() call: this is another standard tuning tactic, where a data structure is replaced with a more appropriate and faster one for the task.

NOTE   The 1.1 profiling output is quite different and much less like a standard profiler's output. Running the 1.1 profiler with this program (details of this output are given in the section "JDK 1.1.x "–prof" and Java 2 "cpu=old" Profile Output") gives:

```
count callee caller time
21 java/lang/System.gc()V
     java/lang/FloatingDecimal.dtoa(IJI)V 760
8 java/lang/System.gc()V
     java/lang/Double.equals(Ljava/lang/Object;)Z 295
2 java/lang/Double.doubleToLongBits(D)J
     java/lang/Double.equals(Ljava/lang/Object;)Z 0
```

I have shown only the top four lines from the output. This output actually identifies both the FloatingDecimal.dtoa() and the Double.equals() methods as taking the vast majority of the time, and the percentages (given by the reported times) are listed as around 70% and 25% of the total program time for the two methods, respectively. Since the "callee" for these methods is listed as System.gc(), this also identifies that the methods are significantly involved in memory creation and suggests that the next tuning step might be to analyze the object-creation output for this program.

Java 2 "cpu=samples" Profile Output

The default profile output gained from executing with -Xrunhprof in Java 2 is not useful for method profiling. The default output generates object-creation statistics from the heap as the dump (output) occurs. By default, the dump occurs when the application terminates; you can modify the dump time by typing Ctrl-\ on Solaris and other Unix systems, or Ctrl-Break on Win32. To get a useful *method* profile, you need to modify the profiler options to specify method profiling. A typical call to achieve this is:

```
java -Xrunhprof:cpu=samples,thread=y <classname>
```

(Note that in a Windows command-line prompt, you need to surround the option with double quotes because the equals sign is considered a meta character.)

WARNING   Note that –Xrunhprof has an "h" in it. There seems to be an undocumented feature of the VM in which the option –Xrun<something> makes the VM try to load a shared library called <something>, e.g., using –Xrunprof results in the VM trying to load a shared library called "prof." This can be quite confusing if you are not expecting it. In fact, –Xrunhprof loads the "hprof" shared library.

The profiling option in JDK 1.2/1.3 can be pretty flaky. Several of the options can cause the runtime to crash (core dump). The output is a large file, since huge amounts of trace data are written rather than summarized. Since the profile option is essentially a Sun engineering tool, it has had limited resources applied to it, especially as Sun has a separate (not free) profile tool that Sun engineers would normally use. Another tool that Sun provides to analyze the output of the profiler is called *heap-analysis tool* (search *http://www.java.sun.com* for "HAT"). But this tool analyzes only the object-creation statistics output gained with the default profile output, and so is not that useful for method profiling (see "Object-Creation Profiling" for slightly more about this tool).

Nevertheless, I expect the free profiling option to stabilize and be more useful in future versions. The output when run with the options already listed (cpu=samples, thread=y) already results in fairly usable information. This profiling mode operates by periodically sampling the stack. Each unique stack trace provides a TRACE entry in the second section of the file; describing the method calls on the stack for that trace. Multiple identical samples are not listed; instead, the number of their "hits" are summarized in the third section of the file. The profile output file in this mode has three sections:

Section 1

A standard header section describing possible monitored entries in the file. For example:

```
WARNING!  This file format is under development, and is subject to
change without notice.

This file contains the following types of records:
```

```
THREAD START
THREAD END        mark the lifetime of Java threads

TRACE             represents a Java stack trace.  Each trace consists
                  of a series of stack frames.  Other records refer to
                  TRACEs to identify (1) where object allocations have
                  taken place, (2) the frames in which GC roots were
                  found, and (3) frequently executed methods.
```

Section 2

Individual entries describing monitored events, i.e., threads starting and terminating, but mainly sampled stack traces. For example:

```
THREAD START (obj=8c2640, id = 6, name="Thread-0", group="main")
THREAD END (id = 6)
TRACE 1:
    <empty>
TRACE 964:
    java/io/ObjectInputStream.readObject(ObjectInputStream.java:Compiled method)
    java/io/ObjectInputStream.inputObject(ObjectInputStream.java:Compiled method)
    java/io/ObjectInputStream.readObject(ObjectInputStream.java:Compiled method)
    java/io/ObjectInputStream.inputArray(ObjectInputStream.java:Compiled method)
TRACE 1074:
    java/io/BufferedInputStream.fill(BufferedInputStream.java:Compiled method)
    java/io/BufferedInputStream.read1(BufferedInputStream.java:Compiled method)
    java/io/BufferedInputStream.read(BufferedInputStream.java:Compiled method)
    java/io/ObjectInputStream.read(ObjectInputStream.java:Compiled method)
```

Section 3

A summary table of methods ranked by the number of times the unique stack trace for that method appears. For example:

```
CPU SAMPLES BEGIN (total = 512371) Thu Aug 26 18:37:08 1999
rank   self  accum   count trace method
   1 16.09% 16.09%   82426  1121 java/io/FileInputStream.read
   2  6.62% 22.71%   33926   881 java/io/ObjectInputStream.allocateNewObject
   3  5.11% 27.82%   26185   918 java/io/ObjectInputStream.inputClassFields
   4  4.42% 32.24%   22671   887 java/io/ObjectInputStream.inputObject
   5  3.20% 35.44%   16392   922 java/lang/reflect/Field.set
```

Section 3 is the place to start when analyzing this profile output. It consists of a table with six fields, headed rank, self, accum, count, trace, and method, as shown. These fields are used as follows:

rank

This column simply counts the entries in the table, starting with 1 at the top, and incrementing by 1 for each entry.

self

> The self field is usually interpreted as a percentage of the total running time spent in this method. More accurately, this field reports the percentage of samples that have the stack given by the trace field. Here's a one-line example:
>
> ```
> rank    self  accum    count trace method
>    1 11.55% 11.55%    18382    545 java/lang/FloatingDecimal.dtoa
> ```
>
> This example shows that stack trace 545 occurred in 18,382 of the sampled stack traces, and this is 11.55% of the total number of stack trace samples made. It indicates that this method was probably executing for about 11.55% of the application execution time, because the samples are at regular intervals. You can identify the precise trace from the second section of the profile output by searching for the trace with identifier 545. For the previous example, this trace was:
>
> ```
> TRACE 545: (thread=1)
>     java/lang/FloatingDecimal.dtoa(FloatingDecimal.java:Compiled method)
>     java/lang/FloatingDecimal.<init>(FloatingDecimal.java:Compiled method)
>     java/lang/Double.toString(Double.java:Compiled method)
>     java/lang/String.valueOf(String.java:Compiled method)
> ```
>
> This TRACE entry clearly identifies the exact method and its caller. Note that the stack is reported to a depth of four methods. This is the default depth: the depth can be changed using the depth parameter to the -Xrunhprof option, e.g., -Xrunhprof:depth=6,cpu=samples,....

accum

> This field is a running additive total of all the self field percentages as you go down the table: for the Section 3 example shown previously, the third line lists 27.82% for the accum field, indicating that the sum total of the first three lines of the self field is 27.82%.

count

> This field indicates how many times the unique stack trace that gave rise to this entry was sampled while the program ran.

trace

> This field shows the unique trace identifier from the second section of profile output that generated this entry. The trace is recorded only once in the second section no matter how many times it is sampled; the number of times that this trace has been sampled is listed in the count field.

method

> This field shows the method name from the top line of the stack trace referred to from the trace field, i.e., the method that was running when the stack was sampled.

This summary table lists only the method name and not its argument types. Therefore, it is frequently necessary to refer to the stack itself to determine the exact method, if the method is an overloaded method with several possible argument types. (The stack is given by the trace identifier in the `trace` field, which in turn references the trace from the second section of the profile output.) If a method is called in different ways, it may also give rise to different stack traces. Sometimes the same method call can be listed in different stack traces due to lost information. Each of these different stack traces results in a different entry in the third section of the profiler's output, even though the `method` field is the same. For example, it is perfectly possible to see several lines with the same `method` field, as in the following table segment:

```
rank   self  accum   count trace method
  95   1.1% 51.55%     110   699 java/lang/StringBuffer.append
 110   1.0% 67.35%     100   711 java/lang/StringBuffer.append
 128   1.0% 85.35%      99   332 java/lang/StringBuffer.append
```

When traces 699, 711, and 332 are analyzed, one trace might be `StringBuffer.append(boolean)`, while the other two traces could both be `StringBuffer.append(int)`, but called from two different methods (and so giving rise to two different stack traces and consequently two different lines in the summary example). Note that the trace does not identify actual method signatures, only method names. Line numbers are given if the class was compiled so that line numbers remain. This ambiguity can be a nuisance at times.

The profiler in this mode (`cpu=samples`) is useful enough to suffice when you have no better alternative. It does have an effect on real measured times, slowing down operations by variable amounts even within one application run. But it normally indicates major bottlenecks, although sometimes a little extra work is necessary to sort out multiple identical method-name references.

Using the alternative `cpu=times` mode, the profile output gives a different view of application execution. In this mode, the method times are measured from method entry to method exit, including the time spent in all other calls the method makes. This profile of an application gives a tree-like view of where the application is spending its time. Some developers are more comfortable with this mode for profiling the application, but I find that it does not directly identify bottlenecks in the code.

HotSpot and 1.3 "–Xprof" Profile Output

HotSpot does not support the standard Java 2 profiler detailed in the previous section; it supports a separate profiler using the –Xprof option. JDK 1.3 supports the HotSpot profiler as well as the standard Java 2 profiler detailed in the previous section. The HotSpot profiler has no further options available to modify its behavior; it works by sampling the stack every 10 milliseconds.

The output, printed to standard out, consists of a number of sections. Each section lists entries in order of the number of ticks counted while the method was executed. The various sections include methods executing in interpreted and compiled modes, and VM runtime costs as well:

Section 1

One-line header, for example:

```
Flat profile of 7.55 secs (736 total ticks): main
```

Section 2

A list of methods sampled while running in interpreted mode. The methods are listed in order of the total number of ticks counted while the method was at the top of the stack. For example:

```
Interpreted + native    Method
   3.7%    23  +    4      tuning.profile.ProfileTest.main
   2.4%     4  +   14      java.lang.FloatingDecimal.dtoa
   1.4%     3  +    7      java.lang.FDBigInt.<init>
```

Section 3

A list of methods sampled while running in compiled mode. The methods are listed in order of the total number of ticks counted while the method was at the top of the stack. For example:

```
Compiled + native   Method
  13.5%    99  +    0      java.lang.FDBigInt.quoRemIteration
   9.8%    71  +    1      java.lang.FDBigInt.mult
   9.1%    67  +    0      java.lang.FDBigInt.add
```

Section 4

A list of external (non-Java) method stubs, defined using the `native` keyword. Listed in order of the total number of ticks counted while the method was at the top of the stack. For example:

```
Stub + native    Method
   2.6%    11  +    8      java.lang.Double.doubleToLongBits
   0.7%     2  +    3      java.lang.StrictMath.floor
   0.5%     3  +    1      java.lang.Double.longBitsToDouble
```

Section 5

A list of internal VM function calls. Listed in order of the total number of ticks counted while the method was at the top of the stack. Not tuneable. For example:

```
Runtime stub + native   Method
   0.1%     1  +    0      interpreter_entries
   0.1%     1  +    0      Total runtime stubs
```

Section 6

Other miscellaneous entries not included in the previous sections:

```
Thread-local ticks:
    1.4%    10              classloader
    0.1%    1               Interpreter
   11.7%    86              Unknown code
```

Section 7

A global summary of ticks recorded. This includes ticks from the garbage collector, thread-locking overheads, and other miscellaneous entries:

```
Global summary of 7.57 seconds:
 100.0%   754              Received ticks
    1.9%    14              Received GC ticks
    0.3%    2               Other VM operations
```

The entries at the top of Section 3 are the methods that probably need tuning. Any method listed near the top of Section 2 should have been targeted by the HotSpot optimizer and may be listed lower down in Section 3. Such methods may still need to be optimized, but it is more likely that the methods at the top of Section 3 are what need optimizing. The ticks for the two sections are the same, so you can easily compare the time taken up by the top methods in the different sections and decide which to target.

JDK 1.1.x "–prof" and Java 2 "cpu=old" Profile Output

The JDK 1.1.x method-profiling output, obtained by running with the –prof option, is quite different from the normal 1.2 output. This output format is supported in Java 2, using the cpu=old variation of the –Xrunhprof option. This output file consists of four sections:

Section 1

The method profile table showing cumulative times spent in each method executed. The table is sorted on the first count field; for example:

```
callee caller time
29 java/lang/System.gc()V
        java/io/FileInputStream.read([B)I 10263
1 java/io/FileOutputStream.writeBytes([BII)V
        java/io/FileOutputStream.write([BII)V 0
```

Section 2

One line describing high-water gross memory usage. For example:

```
handles_used: 1174, handles_free: 339046, heap-used: 113960, heap-free: 21794720
```

The line reports the number of handles and the number of bytes used by the heap memory storage over the application's lifetime. A handle is an object reference. The number of handles used is the maximum number of objects that existed at any one time in the application (handles are recycled by the garbage collector, so over its lifetime the application could have used many more objects than are listed). The heap measurements are in bytes.

Section 3

Reports the number of primitive data type arrays left at the end of the process, just before process termination. For example:

```
sig  count    bytes  indx
[C     174    19060     5
[B       5    19200     8
```

This section has four fields. The first field is the primitive data type (array dimensions and data type given by letter codes listed shortly), the second field is the number of arrays, and the third is the total number of bytes used by all the arrays. This example shows 174 char arrays taking a combined space of 19,060 bytes, and 5 byte arrays taking a combined space of 19,200 bytes.

The reported data does not include any arrays that may have been garbage collected before the end of the process. For this reason, the section is of limited use. You could use the −noasyncgc option to try to eliminate garbage collection (if you have enough memory; you may also need −mx with a large number to boost the maximum memory available). If you do, also use −verbosegc so that if garbage collection is forced, you at least know that garbage collection has occurred and can get the basic number of objects and bytes reclaimed.

Section 4

The fourth section of the profile output is the per-object memory dump. Again, this includes only objects left at the end of the process just before termination, not objects that may have been garbage-collected before the end of the process. For example:

```
*** tab[267] p=4bba378 cb=1873248 cnt=219 ac=3 al=1103
  Ljava/util/HashtableEntry; 219 3504
  [Ljava/util/HashtableEntry; 3 4412
```

This dump is a snapshot of the actual object table. The fields in the first line of an entry are:

***tab[<index>]

The entry location as listed in the object table. The index is of no use for performance tuning.

p=<hex value>

Internal memory locations for the instance and class; of no use for performance tuning.

cb=<*hex value*>

    Internal memory locations for the instance and class; of no use for performance tuning.

cnt=<*integer*>

    The number of instances of the class reported on the next line.

ac=<*integer*>

    The number of instances of arrays of the class reported on the next line.

al=<*integer*>

    The total number of array elements for all the arrays counted in the previous (ac) field.

This first line of the example is followed by lines consisting of three fields: first, the class name prefixed by the array dimension if the line refers to the array data; next, the number of instances of that class (or array class); and last, the total amount of space used by all the instances, in bytes. So the example reports that there are 219 HashtableEntry instances taking a total of 3504 bytes between them,* and three HashtableEntry arrays having 1103 array indexes between them (which amounts to 4412 bytes between them, since each entry is a 4-byte object handle).

The last two sections, Sections 3 and 4, give snapshots of the object table memory and can be used in an interesting way: to run a garbage collection just before termination of your application. That leaves in the object table all the objects that are rooted† by the system and by your application (from static variables). If this snapshot shows significantly more objects than you expect, you may be referencing more objects than you realized.

The first section of the profile output is the most useful, consisting of multiple lines, each of which specifies a method and its caller, together with the total cumulative time spent in that method and the total number of times it was called from that caller. The first line of this section specifies the four fields in the profile table in this section: count, callee, caller, and time. They are detailed here:

count

    The total number of times the callee method was called from the caller method, accumulating multiple executions of the caller method. For

---

* A HashtableEntry has one int and three object handle instance variables, each of which takes 4 bytes, so each HashtableEntry is 16 bytes.

† Objects rooted by the system are objects the JVM runtime keeps alive as part of its runtime system. Rooted objects are generally objects that cannot be garbage collected because they are referenced in some way from other objects that cannot be garbage collected. The roots of these non-garbage-collectable objects are normally objects referenced from the stack, objects referenced from static variables of classes, and special objects the runtime system ensures are kept alive.

example, if `foo1()` calls `foo2()` 10 times every time `foo1()` is executed, and `foo1()` was itself called three times during the execution of the program, the count field should hold the value 30 for the callee-caller pair `foo2()-foo1()`. The line in the table should look like this:

```
30 x/y/Z.foo2()V x/y/Z.foo1()V 1263
```

(assuming the `foo*()` methods are in class `x.y.Z` and they both have a void return). The actual reported numbers may be less than the true number of calls: the profiler can miss calls.

callee

The method that was called `count` times in total from the `caller` method. The callee can be listed in other entries as the `callee` method for different `caller` methods.

caller

The method that called the `callee` method `count` times in total.

time

The cumulative time (in milliseconds) spent in the `callee` method, including time when the `callee` method was calling other methods (i.e., when the `callee` method was in the stack but not at the top, and so was not the currently executing method).

If each of the `count` calls in one line took exactly the same amount of time, then one call from caller to callee took `time` divided by `count` milliseconds.

This first section is normally sorted into `count` order. However, for this profiler, the time spent in methods tends to be more useful. Because the times in the `time` field include the total time that the callee method was anywhere on the stack, interpreting the output of complex programs can be difficult without processing the table to subtract subcall times. This format is different from the 1.2 output with `cpu=samples` specified, and is more equivalent to a 1.2 profile with `cpu=times` specified.

The lines in the profile output are unique for each callee-caller pair, but any one `callee` method and any one `caller` method can (and normally do) appear in multiple lines. This is because any particular method can call many other methods, and so the method registers as the caller for multiple callee-caller pairs. Any particular method can also be called by many other methods, and so the method registers as the callee for multiple callee-caller pairs.

The methods are written out using the internal Java syntax listed in Table 2-1.

Table 2-1. Internal Java Syntax for –prof Output Format

Internal Symbol	Java Meaning
/	Replaces the . character in package names (e.g., `java/lang/String` stands for `java.lang.String`)
B	`byte`
C	`char`
D	`double`
I	`int`
F	`float`
J	`long`
S	`short`
V	`void`
Z	`boolean`
[	One array dimension (e.g., `[[B` stands for a two-dimensional array of bytes, such as `new byte[3][4]`)
L<classname>;	A class (e.g., `Ljava/lang/String;` stands for `java.lang.String`)

There are free viewers, including source code, for viewing this format file:

- Vladimir Bulatov's HyperProf (search for HyperProf on the Web)

- Greg White's ProfileViewer (search for ProfileViewer on the Web)

- My own viewer (see the sidebar "ProfileStack: A Profile Viewer for Java 1.1")

The biggest drawback to the 1.1 profile output is that threads are not indicated at all. This means that it is possible to get time values for method calls that are longer than the total time spent in running the application, since all the call times from multiple threads are added together. It also means that you cannot determine from which thread a particular method call was made. Nevertheless, after re-sorting the section on the time field, rather than the count field, the profile data is useful enough to suffice as a method profiler when you have no better alternative.

One problem I've encountered is the limited size of the list of methods that can be held by the internal profiler. Technically, this limitation is 10,001 entries in the profile table, and there is presumably one entry per method. There are four methods that help you avoid the limitation by profiling only a small section of your code:

```
sun.misc.VM.suspendJavaMonitor()
sun.misc.VM.resumeJavaMonitor()
sun.misc.VM.resetJavaMonitor()
sun.misc.VM.writeJavaMonitorReport()
```

These methods also allow you some control over which parts of your application are profiled and when to dump the results.

ProfileStack: A Profile Viewer for Java 1.1

I have made my own viewer available, with source code. (Under the `tuning.`
`profview` package, the main class is `tuning.profview.ProfileStack` and
takes one argument, the name of the *prof* file. All classes from this book are
available by clicking the "Examples" link from this book's catalog page, *http://
www.oreilly.com/catalog/javapt/.*) My viewer analyzes the profile output file,
combines identical `callee` methods to give a list of its callers, and maps codes
into readable method names. The output to `System.out` looks like this:

```
time  count  localtime      callee
19650 2607   19354 int ObjectInputStream.read()
      Called by
      %      time  count    caller
      98.3   19335 46       short DataInputStream.readShort()
      1.1    227   1832     int DataInputStream.readUnsignedByte()
      0.2    58    462      int DataInputStream.readInt()
      0.1    23    206      int DataInputStream.readUnsignedShort()
      0.0    4     50       byte DataInputStream.readByte()
      0.0    1     9        boolean DataInputStream.readBoolean()
19342 387    19342 int SocketInputStream.socketRead(byte[],int,i
      Called by
      %      time  count    caller
      100.0  19342 4        int SocketInputStream.read(byte[],int,i
15116 3      15116 void ServerSocket.implAccept(Socket)
      Called by
      %      time  count    caller
      100.0  15116 3 Socket ServerSocket.accept()
```

Each main (nonindented) line of this output consists of a particular method
(`callee`) showing the cumulative time in milliseconds for all the callers of
that method, the cumulative count from all the callers, and the time actually
spent in the method itself (not in any of the methods that it called). This last
noncumulative time is found by identifying the times listed for all the callers
of the method and then subtracting the total time for all those calls from the
cumulative time for this method. Each main line is followed by several lines
breaking down all the methods that call this `callee` method, giving the percentage amongst them in terms of time, the cumulative time, the count of
calls, and the name of the `caller` method. The methods are converted into
normal Java source code syntax. The main lines are sorted by the time actually
spent in the method (the third field, `localtime`, of the nonindented lines).

Object-Creation Profiling

Unfortunately, the object-creation statistics available from the Sun JDK provide only very rudimentary information. Most profile tool vendors provide much better object-creation statistics, determining object numbers and identifying where particular objects are created in the code. My recommendation is to use a better (probably commercial) tool than the JDK profiler.

The heap-analysis tool (search *www.java.sun.com* for "HAT"), which can analyze the default profiling mode with Java 2, provides a little more information from the profiler output, but if you are relying on this, profiling object creation will require a lot of effort. To use this tool, you must use the binary output option to the profiling option:

```
java -Xrunhprof:format=b <classname>
```

I have used an alternate trick when a reasonable profiler is unavailable, cannot be used, or does not provide precisely the detail I need. This technique is to alter the `java.lang.Object` class to catch most nonarray object-creation calls. This is not a supported feature, but it does seem to work on most systems, because all constructors chain up to the `Object` class's constructor, and any explicitly created nonarray object calls the constructor in `Object` as its first execution point after the VM allocates the object on the heap. Objects that are created implicitly with a call to `clone()` or by deserialization do not call the `Object` class's constructor, and so are missed when using this technique.

Under the terms of the license granted by Sun, it is not possible to include or list an altered `Object` class with this book. But I can show you the simple changes to make to the `java.lang.Object` class to track object creation.

The change requires adding a line in the `Object` constructor to pass this to some object-creation monitor you are using. `java.lang.Object` does not have an explicitly defined constructor (it uses the default empty constructor), so you need to add one to the source and recompile. For any class other than `Object`, that is all you need to do. But there is an added problem in that `Object` does not have a superclass, and the compiler has a problem with this: the compiler cannot handle an explicit `super()` from the `Object` class, nor the use of this, without an explicit `super()` or `this()` call. In order to get around this restriction, you need to add a second constructor to `java.lang.Object`: a constructor that does nothing functional but does seem to satisfy the compiler.

NOTE   This trick works for the compiler that comes with the JDK; other compilers may be easier or more difficult to satisfy. It is specifically the compiler that has the problem. Generating the bytecodes without the extra constructor is perfectly legal.

Recursive calls to the `Object` constructor present an additional difficulty. You must ensure that when your monitor is called from the constructor, the `Object` constructor does not recursively call itself as it creates objects for your object-creation monitor. It is equally important to avoid recursive calls to the `Object` constructor at runtime initialization. The simplest way to handle all this is to have a flag on which objects are conditionally passed to the monitor from the `Object` constructor, and to have this flag in a simple class with no superclasses, so that classloading does not impose extra calls to superclasses.

So essentially, to change `java.lang.Object` so that it records object creation for each object created, you need to add something like the following two constructors to `java.lang.Object`:

```
public Object()
{
  this(true);
  if (tuning.profile.ObjectCreationMonitoringFlag.monitoring)
    tuning.profile.ObjectCreationMonitoring.monitor(this);
}
public Object(boolean b)
{
}
```

This code may seem bizarre, but then this technique uses an unsupported hack. You now need to compile your modified `java.lang.Object` and any object-monitoring classes (I find that compiling the object-monitoring classes separately before compiling the `Object` class makes things much easier). You then need to run tests with the new `Object` class* first in your (boot) classpath. The modified `Object` class must be before the real `java.lang.Object` in your classpath, otherwise the real one will be found first and used.

Once you have set the `tuning.profile.ObjectCreationMonitoringFlag.monitoring` variable to `true`, each newly created object is passed to the monitor during the creation call. (Actually, the object is passed immediately after it has been created by the runtime system but before any constructors have been executed, except for the `Object` constructor.) You should not set the `monitoring` variable to `true` before the core Java classes have loaded: a good place to set it to `true` is at the start of the application.

Unfortunately, this technique does not catch any of the arrays that are created: array objects do not chain through the `Object` constructor (although `Object` is their superclass), and so do not get monitored. But you typically populate arrays with objects (except for data type arrays such as `char` arrays), and the objects

---

* Different versions of the JDK require their `Object` classes to be recompiled separately; i.e., you cannot recompile the `Object` class for JDK 1.1.6 and then run that class with the 1.2 runtime.

populating the arrays are caught. In addition, objects that are created implicitly with a call to clone() or by deserialization do not call the Object class's constructor, and so these objects are also missed when using this technique. Deserialized objects can be included using a similar technique by redefining the ObjectInputStream class.

When I use this technique, I normally first get a listing of all the different object types that are created and the numbers of those objects that are created. Then I start to focus on a few objects. If you prefer, you can make the technique more focused by altering other constructors to target a specific hierarchy below Object. Or you could focus on particular classes within a more general monitoring class by filtering interesting hierarchies using instanceof. In addition, you can get the stack of the creation call for any object by creating an exception or filling in the stack trace of an existing exception (but not throwing the exception). As an example, I will define a monitoring class that provides many of the possibilities you might want to use for analysis. Note that to avoid recursion during the load, I normally keep my actual ObjectCreationMonitoringFlag class very simple, containing only the flag variable, and put everything else in another class with the monitor() method, i.e., the following defines the flag class:

```
package tuning.profile;
public class ObjectCreationMonitoringFlag
{
    public static boolean monitoring = false;
}
```

The next listed class, ObjectCreationMonitoring, provides some of the features you might need in a monitoring class, including those features previously mentioned. It includes a main() method that starts up the real application you wish to monitor and three alternative options. These report every object creation as it occurs (-v), a tally of object creations (-t), or a tally of object-creation stacks (-s; this option can take a long time).

If you run JDK 1.2* and have the recompiled Object class in a JAR file with the name *hack.jar* in the current directory, and also copy the *rt.jar* and *i18n.jar* files from under the *JDK1.2/jre/lib* (*JDK1.2\jre\lib*) directory to the current directory, then as an example you can execute the object-creation monitoring class on Windows like this (note that this is one long command line):

```
java -Xbootclasspath:hack.jar;rt.jar;i18n.jar
    tuning.profile.ObjectCreationMonitoring -t <real class and arguments>
```

---

* With JDK 1.3, there is a nicer prepend option to the bootclasspath, which allows you to execute using:

```
java -Xbootclasspath/p:hack.jar
    tuning.profile.ObjectCreationMonitoring -t <real class and arguments>
```

You might also need to add a -cp option to specify the location of the various non-core class files that are being run, or add to the -classpath list for JDK 1.1. The files listed in the -Xbootclasspath option can be listed with relative or absolute paths; they do not have to be in the current directory.

For Unix it looks like this (the main difference is the use of ";" for Windows and ":" for Unix):

```
java -Xbootclasspath:hack.jar:rt.jar:i18n.jar
    tuning.profile.ObjectCreationMonitoring -t <real class and arguments>
```

For JDK 1.1, the classpath needs to be set instead of the bootclasspath, and the *classes.zip* file from *JDK1.1.x/lib* needs to be used instead, so the command on Windows looks like:

```
java -classpath hack.jar;classes.zip tuning.profile.ObjectCreationMonitoring
    -t <real class and arguments>
```

For Unix it looks like this (again, the main difference is the use of ";" for Windows and ":" for Unix):

```
java -classpath hack.jar:classes.zip tuning.profile.ObjectCreationMonitoring
    -t <real class and arguments>
```

Using one of these commands to monitor the tuning.profile.ProfileTest class used in the earlier example from the section "Profiling Methodology" results in the following output:

```
Starting test
   The test took 3425 milliseconds
java.lang.FloatingDecimal      16000
java.lang.Double               16000
java.lang.StringBuffer         2
java.lang.Long                 20000
java.lang.FDBigInt             156022
java.util.Hashtable            1
java.util.Hashtable$Entry      18
java.lang.String               36002
```

To recap, that program repeatedly (2000 times) appends 8 doubles and 10 longs to a StringBuffer and inserts those numbers wrapped as objects into a hash table. The hash table requires 16,000 Doubles and 20,000 Longs, but beyond that, all other objects created are overheads due to the conversion algorithms used. Even the String objects are overheads: there is no requirement for the numbers to be converted to Strings before they are appended to the Stringbuffer. In Chapter 5, I show how to convert numbers and avoid creating all these intermediate objects. The resulting code produces faster conversions in every case.

Implementing the optimizations mentioned at the end of the section "Profiling Methodology" allows the program to avoid the FloatingDecimal class (and consequently the FDBigInt class too) and also to avoid the object wrappers for the doubles and longs. This results in a program that avoids all the temporary FloatingDecimal, Double, Long, FDBigInt, and String objects generated by the original version: over a quarter of a million objects are eliminated from the object-creation profile, leaving just a few dozen objects! So the order-of-magnitude improvement in speed attained is now more understandable.

The ObjectCreationMonitoring class used is listed here:

```
package tuning.profile;
import java.util.*;
import java.io.*;
import java.lang.reflect.*;

public class ObjectCreationMonitoring
{
  private static int MonitoringMode = 0;
  private static int StackModeCount = -1;
  public static final int VERBOSE_MODE = 1;
  public static final int TALLY_MODE = 2;
  public static final int GET_STACK_MODE = 3;

  public static void main(String args[])
  {
    try
    {
      //First argument is the option specifying which type of
      //monitoring: verbose; tally; or stack
      if(args[0].startsWith("-v"))
        //verbose - prints every object's class as it's created
        MonitoringMode = VERBOSE_MODE;
      else if(args[0].startsWith("-t"))
        //tally mode. Tally classes and print results at end
        MonitoringMode = TALLY_MODE;
      else if(args[0].startsWith("-s"))
      {
        //stack mode. Print stacks of objects as they are created
        MonitoringMode = GET_STACK_MODE;
        //support a limited number of stacks being generated
        //so that the running time can be shortened
        if(args[0].length() > 2)
          StackModeCount = Integer.parseInt(args[0].substring(2));
      }
      else
        throw new IllegalArgumentException(
          "First command line argument must be one of -v/-t/-s");
```

```java
      //Remaining arguments are the class with the
      //main() method, and its arguments
      String classname = args[1];
      String[] argz = new String[args.length-2];
      System.arraycopy(args, 2, argz, 0, argz.length);
      Class clazz = Class.forName(classname);

      //main has one parameter, a String array.
      Class[] mainParamType = {args.getClass()};
      Method main = clazz.getMethod("main", mainParamType);
      Object[] mainParams = {argz};

      //start monitoring
      ObjectCreationMonitoringFlag.monitoring = true;
      main.invoke(null, mainParams);
      //stop monitoring
      ObjectCreationMonitoringFlag.monitoring = false;
      if (MonitoringMode == TALLY_MODE)
        printTally();
      else if (MonitoringMode == GET_STACK_MODE)
        printStacks();
    }
  catch(Exception e)
  {
    e.printStackTrace();
  }
}

public static void monitor(Object o)
{
  //Disable object creation monitoring while we report
  ObjectCreationMonitoringFlag.monitoring = false;

  switch(MonitoringMode)
  {
    case 1: justPrint(o); break;
    case 2: tally(o); break;
    case 3: getStack(o); break;
    default:
      System.out.println(
        "Undefined mode for ObjectCreationMonitoring class");
      break;
  }

  //Re-enable object creation monitoring
  ObjectCreationMonitoringFlag.monitoring = true;
}
```

```
public static void justPrint(Object o)
{
  System.out.println(o.getClass().getName());
}


private static Hashtable Hash = new Hashtable();
public static void tally(Object o)
{
  //You need to print the tally from printTally()
  //at the end of the application
  Integer i = (Integer) Hash.get(o.getClass());
  if (i == null)
    i = new Integer(1);
  else
    i = new Integer(i.intValue() + 1);
  Hash.put(o.getClass(), i);
}
public static void printTally()
{
  //should really sort the elements in order of the
  //number of objects created, but I will just print them
  //out in any order here.
  Enumeration e = Hash.keys();
  Class c;
  String s;
  while(e.hasMoreElements())
  {
    c = (Class) e.nextElement();
    System.out.print(s = c.getName());
    for (int i = 31-s.length(); i >= 0; i--)
      System.out.print(' ');
    System.out.print("\t");
    System.out.println(Hash.get(c));
  }
}


private static Exception Ex = new Exception();
private static ByteArrayOutputStream MyByteStream =
    new ByteArrayOutputStream();
private static PrintStream MyPrintStream =
    new PrintStream(MyByteStream);
public static void getStack(Object o)
{
  if (StackModeCount > 0)
  StackModeCount--;
  else if (StackModeCount != -1)
      return;
  Ex.fillInStackTrace();
  MyPrintStream.flush();
  MyByteStream.reset();
```

```
      MyPrintStream.print("Creating object of type ");
      MyPrintStream.println(o.getClass().getName());
      //Note that the first two lines of the stack will be
      //getStack() and monitor(), and these can be ignored.
      Ex.printStackTrace(MyPrintStream);
      MyPrintStream.flush();
      String trace = new String(MyByteStream.toByteArray());
      Integer i = (Integer) Hash.get(trace);
      if (i == null)
        i = new Integer(1);
      else
        i = new Integer(i.intValue() + 1);
      Hash.put(trace, i);
  }

  public static void printStacks()
  {
    Enumeration e = Hash.keys();
    String s;
    while(e.hasMoreElements())
    {
      s = (String) e.nextElement();
      System.out.print("Following stack contructed ");
      System.out.print(Hash.get(s));
      System.out.println(" times:");
      System.out.println(s);
      System.out.println();
    }
  }

}
```

Monitoring Gross Memory Usage

The JDK provides two methods for monitoring the amount of memory used by the runtime system. The methods are freeMemory() and totalMemory() in the java.lang.Runtime class.

totalMemory() returns a long, which is the number of bytes currently allocated to the runtime system for this particular Java VM process. Within this memory allocation, the VM manages its objects and data. Some of this allocated memory is held in reserve for creating new objects. When the currently allocated memory gets filled and the garbage collector cannot allocate sufficiently more memory, the VM requests more memory to be allocated to it from the underlying system. If the underlying system cannot allocate any further memory, an OutOfMemoryError error is thrown. Total memory can go up and down; some Java runtimes can return sections of unused memory to the underlying system while still running.

`freeMemory()` returns a `long`, which is the number of bytes available to the VM to create objects from the section of memory it controls (i.e., memory already allocated to the runtime by the underlying system). The free memory increases when a garbage collection successfully reclaims space used by dead objects, and also increases when the Java runtime requests more memory from the underlying operating system. The free memory reduces each time an object is created, and also when the runtime returns memory to the underlying system.

It can be useful to monitor memory usage while an application runs: you can get a good feel for the hotspots of your application. You may be surprised to see steady decrements in the free memory available to your application when you were not expecting any change. This can occur when you continuously generate temporary objects from some routine; manipulating graphical elements frequently shows this behavior.

Monitoring memory with `freeMemory()` and `totalMemory()` is straightforward, and I include here a simple class that does this graphically. It creates three threads: one to periodically sample the memory, one to maintain a display of the memory usage graph, and one to run the program you are monitoring. Figure 2-1 shows a screen shot of the memory monitor after monitoring a run of the `ProfileTest` class defined earlier in the section "Profiling Methodology." The total memory allocation is flat because the class did not hold on to much memory at any one time. The free memory shows the typical sawtooth pattern of an application cycling through temporary objects: each upstroke is where the garbage collector kicked in and freed up the space being taken by the discarded dead objects.

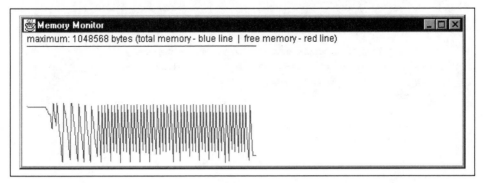

Figure 2-1. Memory monitoring the ProfileTest class

The monitor was run using the command:

```
java tuning.profile.MemoryMonitor tuning.profile.ProfileTest
```

Here are the classes for the memory monitor, together with comments:

```
package tuning.profile;
import java.awt.*;
```

```java
import java.awt.event.*;
import java.lang.reflect.*;

/*
 * Internal class to periodically sample memory usage
 */
class MemorySampler
  implements Runnable
{
  long[] freeMemory = new long[1000];
  long[] totalMemory = new long[1000];
  int sampleSize = 0;
  long max = 0;
  boolean keepGoing = true;

  MemorySampler()
  {
    //Start the object running in a separate maximum priority thread
    Thread t = new Thread(this);
    t.setDaemon(true);
    t.setPriority(Thread.MAX_PRIORITY);
    t.start();
  }

  public void stop()
  {
    //set to stop the thread when someone tells us
    keepGoing = false;
  }

  public void run()
  {
    //Just a loop that continues sampling memory values every
    //30 milliseconds until the stop() method is called.
    Runtime runtime = Runtime.getRuntime();
    while(keepGoing)
    {
      try{Thread.sleep(30);}catch(InterruptedException e){};
      addSample(runtime);
    }
  }

  public void addSample(Runtime runtime)
  {
    //Takes the actual samples, recording them in the two arrays.
    //We expand the arrays when they get full up.
    if (sampleSize >= freeMemory.length)
    {
      //just expand the arrays if they are now too small
```

```
          long[] tmp = new long[2 * freeMemory.length];
          System.arraycopy(freeMemory, 0, tmp, 0, freeMemory.length);
          freeMemory = tmp;
          tmp = new long[2 * totalMemory.length];
          System.arraycopy(totalMemory, 0, tmp, 0, totalMemory.length);
          totalMemory = tmp;
        }

        freeMemory[sampleSize] = runtime.freeMemory();
        totalMemory[sampleSize] = runtime.totalMemory();

        //Keep the maximum value of the total memory for convenience.
        if (max < totalMemory[sampleSize])
          max = totalMemory[sampleSize];
        sampleSize++;
    }
}


public class MemoryMonitor
  extends Frame
  implements WindowListener,Runnable
{
  //The sampler object
  MemorySampler sampler;

  //interval is the delay between calls to repaint the window
  long interval;
  static Color freeColor = Color.red;
  static Color totalColor = Color.blue;
  int[] xpoints = new int[2000];
  int[] yfrees = new int[2000];
  int[] ytotals = new int[2000];


  /*
   * Start a monitor and the graph, then start up the real class
   * with any arguments. This is given by the rest of the commmand
   * line arguments.
   */
  public static void main(String args[])
  {
    try
    {
      //Start the grapher with update interval of half a second
      MemoryMonitor m = new MemoryMonitor(500);

      //Remaining arguments are the class with
      //the main() method, and its arguments
```

```java
      String classname = args[0];
      String[] argz = new String[args.length-1];
      System.arraycopy(args, 1, argz, 0, argz.length);
      Class clazz = Class.forName(classname);

      //main has one parameter, a String array.
      Class[] mainParamType = {args.getClass()};
      Method main = clazz.getMethod("main", mainParamType);
      Object[] mainParams = {argz};

      //start real class
      main.invoke(null, mainParams);

      //Tell the monitor the application finished
      m.testStopped();
    }
    catch(Exception e)
    {
      e.printStackTrace();
    }
  }

public MemoryMonitor(long updateInterval)
{
    //Create a graph window and start it in a separate thread
    super("Memory Monitor");
    interval = updateInterval;

    this.addWindowListener(this);
    this.setSize(600,200);
    this.show();

    //Start the sampler (it runs itself in a separate thread)
    sampler = new MemorySampler();

    //and put myself into a separate thread
    (new Thread(this)).start();
}

public void run()
{
    //Simple loop, just repaints the screen every 'interval' milliseconds
    int sampleSize = sampler.sampleSize;
    for (;;)
    {
      try{Thread.sleep(interval);}catch(InterruptedException e){};
      if (sampleSize != sampler.sampleSize)
      {
```

```
      //Should just call repaint here
      //this.repaint();
      //but it doesn't always work, so I'll repaint in this thread.
      //I'm not doing anything else anyway in this thread.
      try{
        this.update(this.getGraphics());
      }
      catch(Exception e){e.printStackTrace();}
      sampleSize = sampler.sampleSize;
    }
  }
}

public void testStopped()
{
  //just tell the sampler to stop sampling.
  //We won't exit ourselves until the window is explicitly closed
  //so that our user can examine the graph at leisure.
  sampler.stop();
}

public void paint(Graphics g)
{
  //Straightforward - draw a graph for the latest N points of
  //total and free memory where N is the width of the window.
  try
  {
    java.awt.Dimension d = getSize();
    int width = d.width-20;
    int height = d.height - 40;
    long max = sampler.max;
    int sampleSize = sampler.sampleSize;
    if (sampleSize < 20)
      return;
    int free, total, free2, total2;
    int highIdx = width < (sampleSize-1) ? width : sampleSize-1;
    int idx = sampleSize - highIdx - 1;
    for (int x = 0 ; x < highIdx ; x++, idx++)
    {
      xpoints[x] = x+10;
      yfrees[x] = height -
        (int) ((sampler.freeMemory[idx] * height) / max) + 40;
      ytotals[x] = height -
        (int) ((sampler.totalMemory[idx] * height) / max) + 40;
    }
    g.setColor(freeColor);
    g.drawPolyline(xpoints, yfrees, highIdx);
    g.setColor(totalColor);
    g.drawPolyline(xpoints, ytotals, highIdx);
```

```
        g.setColor(Color.black);
        g.drawString("maximum: " + max +
          " bytes (total memory - blue line  |   free memory - red line)",
          10, 35);
      }
    catch (Exception e) {
      System.out.println("MemoryMonitor: " + e.getMessage());}
    }

  public void windowActivated(WindowEvent e){}
  public void windowClosed(WindowEvent e){}
  public void windowClosing(WindowEvent e) {System.exit(0);}
  public void windowDeactivated(WindowEvent e){}
  public void windowDeiconified(WindowEvent e){}
  public void windowIconified(WindowEvent e){}
  public void windowOpened(WindowEvent e) {}
  }
```

Client/Server Communications

To tune client/server or distributed applications, you need to identify all communications that occur during execution. The most important factors to look for are the number of transfers of incoming and outgoing data, and the amounts of data transferred. These elements affect performance the most. Generally, if the amount of data per transfer is less than about one kilobyte, the number of transfers is the factor that limits performance. If the amount of data being transferred is more than about a third of the network's capacity, the amount of data is the factor limiting performance. Between these two endpoints, either the amount of data or the number of transfers can limit performance, although in general, the number of transfers is more likely to be the problem.

As an example, websurfing with a browser typically hits both problems at different times. A complex page with many parts presented from multiple sites can take longer to display completely than one simple page with 10 times more data. Many different sites are involved in displaying the complex page; each site needs to have its server name converted to an IP address, which can take many network transfers,* and then each site needs to be connected to and downloaded from. The simple page needs only one name lookup and one connection, and this can make a huge difference. On the other hand, if the amount of data is large compared to the connection *bandwidth* (the speed of the Internet connection at the slowest link

---

* The DNS name lookup is often a hierarchical lookup that requires multiple DNS servers to chain a lookup request to resolve successive parts of the name. Although there is only one request as far as the browser is concerned, the actual request may require several server-to-server data transfers before the lookup is resolved.

between your client and the server machine), the limiting factor is that bandwidth, and so the complex page may display more quickly than the simple page.

Several generic tools are available for monitoring communication traffic, all aimed at system and network administrators (and quite expensive). I know of no general-purpose profiling tool targeted at *application*-level communications monitoring; normally, developers put their own monitoring capabilities into the application or use the trace mode in their third-party communications package, if they use one. (*snoop*, *netstat*, and *ndd* on Solaris are useful communication-monitoring tools. *tcpdump* and *ethereal* are freeware communication-monitoring tools.)

If you are using a third-party communications package, your first step in profiling is to make sure you understand how to use the full capabilities of its tracing mode. Most communications packages provide a trace mode to log various levels of communication details. Some let you install your own socket layer underlying the communications; this feature, though not usually present for logging purposes, can be quite handy for customizing communications tracing.

For example, RMI (remote method invocation), which comes as a communication standard with Java, has very basic call tracing enabled by setting the `java.rmi.server.logCalls` property to `true`, e.g., by starting the server class with:

```
java -Djava.rmi.server.logCalls=true <ServerClass> ...
```

The RMI framework also lets you install a custom RMI socket factory. This socket customization support is provided so that the RMI protocol is abstracted away from actual communication details, and it allows sockets to be replaced by alternatives such as nonsocket communications, or encrypted or compressed data transfers.

For example, here is the tracing from a small client/server RMI application. The client simply connects to the server and sets three attributes of a server object using RMI. The three attributes are a `boolean`, an `Object`, and an `int`, and the server object defines three remotely callable `set()` methods for setting the attributes:

```
Sun Jan 16 15:09:12 GMT+00:00 2000:RMI:RMI TCP Connection(3)-localhost/127.0.0.1:
[127.0.0.1: tuning.cs.ServerObjectImpl[0]: void setBoolean(boolean)]
Sun Jan 16 15:09:12 GMT+00:00 2000:RMI:RMI TCP Connection(3)-localhost/127.0.0.1:
[127.0.0.1: tuning.cs.ServerObjectImpl[0]: void setObject(java.lang.Object)]
Sun Jan 16 15:09:12 GMT+00:00 2000:RMI:RMI TCP Connection(3)-localhost/127.0.0.1:
[127.0.0.1: tuning.cs.ServerObjectImpl[0]: void setNumber(int)]
```

If you can install your own socket layer, you may also want to install a customized logging layer to provide details of the communication. An alternative way to trace communications is to replace the sockets (or other underlying communication classes) directly, providing your own logging. In the next section, I provide details for replacing socket-level communication for basic Java sockets.

In addition to Java-level logging, you should be familiar with system- and network-level logging facilities. The most ubiquitous of these is *netstat*. (*netstat* is a command-line utility; it's normally executed from a Unix shell or Windows command prompt.) For example, using *netstat* with the -s option provides a full dump of most network-related structures (cumulative readings since the machine was started). By filtering this, taking differences, and plotting various data, you get a good idea of the network traffic background and the extra load imposed by your application.

Using *netstat* with this application shows that connection, resolution of server object, and the three remote method invocations require four TCP sockets and 39 packets of data (frames) to be transferred. These include a socket pair opened from the client to the registry to determine the server location, and then a second socket pair between the client and the server. The frames include several handshake packets required as part of the RMI protocol, and other overhead that RMI imposes. The socket pair between the registry and server are not recorded, because the pair lives longer than the interval that measures differences recorded by *netstat*. However, some of the frames are probably communication packets between the registry and the server.

Another useful piece of equipment is a *network sniffer*. This is a hardware device you plug into the network line that views (and can save) all network traffic that is passed along that wire. If you absolutely must know every detail of what is happening on the wire, you may need one of these.

More detailed information on network utilities and tools can be found in system-specific performance tuning books (see Chapter 14, *Underlying Operating System and Network Improvements*, for more about system-specific tools and tuning tips).

Replacing Sockets

Occasionally, you need to be able to see what is happening to your sockets and to know what information is passing through them and the sizes of the packets being transferred. It is usually best to install your own trace points into the application for all communication external to the application; the extra overheads are generally small compared to network (or any I/O) overheads and can usually be ignored. The application can be deployed with these tracers in place but configured so as not to trace (until required).

However, the sockets are often used by third-party classes, and you cannot directly wrap the reads and writes. You could use a packet sniffer that is plugged into the network, but this can prove troublesome when used for application-specific purposes (and can be expensive). A more useful possibility I have employed is to wrap the socket I/O with my own classes. You can almost do this generically using the

SocketImplFactory, but if you install your own SocketImplFactory, there is no protocol to allow you to access the default socket implementation, so another way must be used. (You could add a SocketImplFactory class into java.net, which then gives you access to the default PlainSocketImpl class, but this is no more generic than the previous possibility, as it too cannot normally be delivered with an application.) My preferred solution, which is also not deliverable, is to wrap the sockets by replacing the java.net.Socket class with my own implementation. This is simpler than the previous alternatives and can be quite powerful. Only two methods from the core classes need changing, namely those that provide access to the input stream and output stream. You need to create your own input stream and output stream wrapper classes to provide logging. The two methods in Socket are getInputStream() and getOutputStream(), and the new versions of these look as follows:

```
public InputStream getInputStream() throws IOException {
    return new tuning.socket.SockInStreamLogger(this, impl.getInputStream());
}
public OutputStream getOutputStream() throws IOException {
    return new tuning.socket.SockOutStreamLogger(this, impl.getOutputStream());
}
```

The required stream classes are listed shortly. Rather than using generic classes, I tend to customize the logging on a per-application basis. I even tend to vary the logging implementation for different tests, slowly cutting out more superfluous communications data and headers, so that I can focus on a small amount of detail. Usually I focus on the number of transfers, the amount of data transferred, and the application-specific type of data being transferred. For a distributed RMI type communication, I want to know the method calls and argument types, and occasionally some of the arguments: the data is serialized and so can be accessed using the Serializable framework.

As with the customized Object class in the "Object-Creation Profiling" section, you need to ensure that your customized Socket class comes first in your (boot) classpath, before the JDK Socket version. The RMI example from the previous section results in the following trace when run with customized socket tracing. The trace is from the client only. I have replaced lines of data with my own interpretation (in bold) of the data sent or read:

```
Message of size 7 written by Socket
Socket[addr=jack/127.0.0.1,port=1099,localport=1092]
client-registry handshake
Message of size 16 read by Socket
Socket[addr=jack/127.0.0.1,port=1099,localport=1092]
client-registry handshake
Message of size 15 written by Socket
```

```
Socket[addr=jack/127.0.0.1,port=1099,localport=1092]
```
client-registry handshake: client identification
```
Message of size 53 written by Socket
Socket[addr=jack/127.0.0.1,port=1099,localport=1092]
```
client-registry query: asking for the location of the Server Object
```
Message of size 210 read by Socket
Socket[addr=jack/127.0.0.1,port=1099,localport=1092]
```
client-registry query: reply giving details of the Server Object
```
Message of size 7 written by Socket
Socket[addr=localhost/127.0.0.1,port=1087,localport=1093]
```
client-server handshake
```
Message of size 16 read by Socket
Socket[addr=localhost/127.0.0.1,port=1087,localport=1093]
```
client-server handshake
```
Message of size 15 written by Socket
Socket[addr=localhost/127.0.0.1,port=1087,localport=1093]
```
client-server handshake: client identification
```
Message of size 342 written by Socket
Socket[addr=localhost/127.0.0.1,port=1087,localport=1093]
```
client-server handshake: security handshake
```
Message of size 283 read by Socket
Socket[addr=localhost/127.0.0.1,port=1087,localport=1093]
```
client-server handshake: security handshake
```
Message of size 1 written by Socket
Socket[addr=jack/127.0.0.1,port=1099,localport=1092]
Message of size 1 read by Socket
Socket[addr=jack/127.0.0.1,port=1099,localport=1092]
Message of size 15 written by Socket
Socket[addr=jack/127.0.0.1,port=1099,localport=1092]
```
client-registry handoff
```
Message of size 1 written by Socket
Socket[addr=localhost/127.0.0.1,port=1087,localport=1093]
Message of size 1 read by Socket
Socket[addr=localhost/127.0.0.1,port=1087,localport=1093]
Message of size 42 written by Socket
Socket[addr=localhost/127.0.0.1,port=1087,localport=1093]
```
client-server rmi: set boolean request
```
Message of size 22 read by Socket
Socket[addr=localhost/127.0.0.1,port=1087,localport=1093]
```
client-server rmi: set boolean reply
```
Message of size 1 written by Socket
Socket[addr=localhost/127.0.0.1,port=1087,localport=1093]
Message of size 1 read by Socket
Socket[addr=localhost/127.0.0.1,port=1087,localport=1093]
Message of size 120 written by Socket
Socket[addr=localhost/127.0.0.1,port=1087,localport=1093]
```
client-server rmi: set Object request
```
Message of size 22 read by Socket
Socket[addr=localhost/127.0.0.1,port=1087,localport=1093]
```

```
client-server rmi: set Object reply
Message of size 45 written by Socket
Socket[addr=localhost/127.0.0.1,port=1087,localport=1093]
client-server rmi: set int request
Message of size 22 read by Socket
Socket[addr=localhost/127.0.0.1,port=1087,localport=1093]
client-server rmi: set int reply
```

Here is one possible implementation for the stream classes required by the altered
Socket class:

```java
package tuning.socket;
import java.io.InputStream;
import java.io.OutputStream;
import java.io.IOException;
import java.net.Socket;

public class SockStreamLogger
{
  public static boolean LOG_SIZE = false;
  public static boolean LOG_MESSAGE = false;

  public static void read(Socket so, int sz, byte[] buf, int off) {
    log(false, so, sz, buf, off); }
  public static void written(Socket so, int sz, byte[] buf, int off) {
    log(true, so, sz, buf, off); }
  public static void log(boolean isWritten, Socket so,
                         int sz, byte[] buf, int off)
  {
    if (LOG_SIZE)
    {
        System.err.print("Message of size ");
        System.err.print(sz);
        System.err.print(isWritten ? " written" : " read");
        System.err.print(" by Socket ");
        System.err.println(so);
    }
    if (LOG_MESSAGE)
      System.err.println(new String(buf, off, sz));
  }
}

public class SockInStreamLogger extends InputStream
{
  Socket s;
  InputStream in;
  byte[] one_byte = new byte[1];
  public SockInStreamLogger(Socket so, InputStream i){in = i; s = so;}
  public int available() throws IOException {return in.available();}
  public void close() throws IOException {in.close();}
```

```java
    public void mark(int readlimit) {in.mark(readlimit);}
    public boolean markSupported() {return in.markSupported();}
    public int read() throws IOException {
      int ret = in.read();
      one_byte[0] = (byte) ret;
      //SockStreamLogger.read(s, 1, one_byte, 0);
      return ret;
    }
    public int read(byte b[]) throws IOException {
      int sz = in.read(b);
      SockStreamLogger.read(s, sz, b, 0);
      return sz;
    }
    public int read(byte b[], int off, int len) throws IOException {
      int sz = in.read(b, off, len);
      SockStreamLogger.read(s, sz, b, off);
      return sz;
    }
    public void reset() throws IOException {in.reset();}
    public long skip(long n) throws IOException {return in.skip(n);}
}

public class SockOutStreamLogger extends OutputStream
{
    Socket s;
    OutputStream out;
    byte[] one_byte = new byte[1];
    public SockOutStreamLogger(Socket so, OutputStream o){out = o; s = so;}
    public void write(int b) throws IOException {
      out.write(b);
      one_byte[0] = (byte) b;
      SockStreamLogger.written(s, 1, one_byte, 0);
    }
    public void write(byte b[]) throws IOException {
      out.write(b);
      SockStreamLogger.written(s, b.length, b, 0);
    }
    public void write(byte b[], int off, int len) throws IOException {
      out.write(b, off, len);
      SockStreamLogger.written(s, len, b, off);
    }
    public void flush() throws IOException {out.flush();}
    public void close() throws IOException {out.close();}
}
```

Performance Checklist

- Use system- and network-level monitoring utilities to assist when measuring performance.

- Run tests on unloaded systems with the test running in the foreground.

  — Use `System.currentTimeMillis()` to get timestamps if you need to determine absolute times. Never use the timings obtained from a profiler as absolute times.

  — Account for all performance effects of any caches.

- Get better profiling tools. The better your tools, the faster and more effective your tuning.

  — Pinpoint the bottlenecks in the application: with profilers, by instrumenting code (putting in explicit timing statements), and by analyzing the code.

  — Target the top five to ten methods, and choose the quickest to fix.

  — Speed up the bottleneck methods that can be fixed the quickest.

  — Improve the method directly when the method takes a significant percentage of time and is not called too often.

  — Reduce the number of times a method is called when the method takes a significant percentage of time and is also called frequently.

- Use an object-creation profiler together with garbage-collection statistics to determine which objects are created in large amounts and which large objects are created.

  — See if the garbage collector executes more often than you expect.

  — Use the `Runtime.totalMemory()` and `Runtime.freeMemory()` methods to monitor gross memory usage.

- Check whether your communication layer has built-in tracing features.

  — Check whether your communication layer supports the addition of customized layers.

- Identify the number of incoming and outgoing transfers and the amounts of data transferred in distributed applications.

3

In this chapter:
• *Garbage Collection*
• *Replacing JDK Classes*
• *Faster VMs*
• *Better Optimizing Compilers*
• *Sun's Compiler and Runtime Optimizations*
• *Compile to Native Machine Code*
• *Native Method Calls*
• *Uncompressed ZIP/ JAR Files*

Underlying JDK Improvements

Throughout the progressive versions of Java, improvements have been made at all levels of the runtime system: in the garbage collector, in the code, in the VM handling of objects and threads, and in compiler optimizations. It is always worthwhile to check your own application benchmarks against each version (and each vendor's version) of the Java system you try out. Any differences in performance need to be identified and explained; if you can determine that a compiler from one version (or vendor) together with the runtime from another version (or vendor) speeds up your application, you may have the option of choosing the best of both worlds. Standard Java benchmarks tend to be of limited use in deciding which VMs provide the best performance for your application. You are always better off creating your own application benchmark suite for deciding which VM and compiler best suit your application.

The following sections identify some points to consider as you investigate different VMs, compilers, and JDK classes. If you control the target Java runtime environment, i.e., with servlet and other server applications, more options are available to you, and we will look at these extra options too.

Garbage Collection

The effects of the garbage collector can be difficult to determine accurately. It is worth including some tests in your performance benchmark suite that are specifically arranged to identify these effects. You can do this only in a general way, since the garbage collector is not under your control. The basic way to see what the garbage collector is up to is to run with the -verbosegc option. This prints out time and space values for objects reclaimed and space recycled. The printout includes explicit synchronous calls to the garbage collector (using System.gc()) as well as asynchronous executions of the garbage collector, as occurs in normal operation when free memory available to the VM gets low. You can try to force the VM to execute only synchronous garbage collections by using the -noasyncgc option to the Java executable (no longer available from JDK 1.2). This option does not actually stop the garbage-collector thread from executing: it still executes if the VM runs out of free memory (as opposed to just getting low on memory). Output from the garbage collector running with -verbosegc is detailed in "Garbage Collection" in Chapter 2, *Profiling Tools*.

The garbage collector usually works by freeing the memory that becomes available from objects that are no longer referenced or, if this does not free sufficient space, by expanding the available memory space by asking the operating system for more memory (up to a maximum specified to the VM with the -Xmx/-mx option). The garbage collector's space-reclamation algorithm tends to change with each version of the JDK.

Sophisticated generational garbage collectors, which smooth out the impact of the garbage collector, are now being used; HotSpot uses a state-of-the-art generational garbage collector. Analysis of object-oriented programs has shown that most objects are short-lived, fewer have medium lifespans, and very few objects are long-lived. Generational garbage collectors move objects through multiple spaces, each time copying live objects from one space to the next and reclaiming the space used by objects that are no longer alive. By concentrating on short-lived objects— the early spaces—and spending less time recycling space where older objects live, the garbage collector frees the maximum amount of space for the lowest impact.[*]

Because the garbage collector is different in different VM versions, the output from the -verbosegc option is also likely to change across versions, making it difficult to compare the effects of the garbage collectors across versions (not to mention between different vendors' VMs). But you should still attempt this comparison, as the effect of the garbage collector can make a difference to the application. Looking at garbage-collection output can tell you that parts of your application are causing significantly more work for the garbage collector, suggesting you may want to alter the flow of objects in those parts of the application. Garbage collection is also affected by the number of threads and whether objects are shared across threads. Expect to see improvements in threaded garbage collection over different VM versions.

---

[*] One book giving more details on garbage collection is *Inside the Java 2 Virtual Machine* by Bill Venners (McGraw-Hill). The garbage collection chapter is also available online at *http://www.artima.com*.

WARNING   A JDK bug seems to prevent the garbage collection of threads until
              the `Thread.stop()` method has been called on the terminated
              thread (this is true even though the `Thread.stop()` method has
              been deprecated in Java 2). This affects performance because the
              resources used by the thread are not released until the thread is gar-
              bage-collected. Ultimately, if you use many short-lived threads in
              your application, the system will run out of resources and will not
              supply any further threads. See Alan Williamson's article in the *Java
              Developer's Journal*, July 1999 and November 1999.

Garbage-collection times may be affected by the size of the VM memory. A larger
memory implies there will be more objects in the heap space before the garbage
collector needs to kick in. This in turn means that the process of sweeping dead
objects takes longer, as does the process of running through a larger object table.
Different VMs have optimal performance at different sizes of the VM, and the optimal size for any particular application-VM pairing must unfortunately be determined by trial and error.

Replacing JDK Classes

It is possible for you to replace JDK classes directly. Unfortunately, you can't
distribute these altered classes with any application or applet unless you have complete control of the target environment. Although you often do have this control
with in-house and enterprise-developed applications, most enterprises prefer not
to deploy alterations to externally built classes. The alterations then would not be
supported by the vendor (Sun in this case) and may violate the license, so contact
the vendor if you need to do this. In addition, altering classes in this way can be a
significant maintenance problem.[*]

The upshot is that you can easily alter JDK-supplied classes for development purposes, which can be useful for various reasons including debugging and tuning.
But if you need the functionality in your deployed application, you need to provide classes that are used instead of the JDK classes by redirecting method calls
into your own classes.

Replacing JDK classes indirectly in this way is a valid tuning technique. Some JDK
classes, such as `StreamTokenizer` (see "Strings Versus char Arrays" in Chapter 5,
Strings), are inefficient and can be replaced quite easily since you normally use
them in small, well-defined parts of a program. Other JDK classes, like `Date`,
`BigDecimal`, and `String` are used all over the place, and it can take a large effort

---

[*] If your application has its classes localized in one place on one machine, for example with servlets, you
   might consider deploying changes to the core classes.

to replace references with your own versions of these classes. The best way to replace these classes is to start from the design stage, so that you can consistently use your own versions throughout the application.

WARNING   In Version 1.3 of the JDK, many of the `java.lang.Math` methods were changed from `native` to call the corresponding methods in `java.lang.StrictMath`. `StrictMath` provides bitwise consistency across platforms; earlier versions of `Math` used the platform-specific native functions that were not identical across all platforms. Unfortunately, `StrictMath` calculations are somewhat slower than the corresponding native functions. My colleague Kirk Pepperdine, who first pointed out the performance problem to me, puts it this way: "I've now got a bitwise-correct but excruciatingly slow program." The potential workarounds to this performance issue are all ugly: using an earlier JDK version, replacing the JDK class with an earlier version, or writing your own class to manage faster alternative floating-point calculations.

For optimal performance, I recommend developing with your own versions of classes rather than the JDK versions whenever possible. This gives maximum tuning flexibility. However, this recommendation is clearly impractical in most cases. Given that, perhaps the single most significant class to replace with your own version is the `String` class. Most other classes can be replaced inside identified bottlenecks when required during tuning, without affecting other parts of the application. But `String` is used so extensively that replacing `String` references in one location tends to have widespread consequences, requiring extensive rewriting in many parts of the application. In fact, this observation also applies to other data type classes you use extensively (`Integer`, `Date`, etc.). But the `String` class tends to be the most often used of these classes. See Chapter 5 for details on why the `String` class can be a performance problem, and why you might need to replace it.

It is often impractical to replace the `String` classes where their internationalization capabilities are required. Because of this, you should logically partition the application's use of `Strings` to identify those aspects that require internationalization and those aspects that are really character processing, independent of language dependencies. The latter usage of `Strings` can be replaced more easily than the former. Internationalization-dependent `String` manipulation is difficult to tune, because you are dependent on internationalization libraries that are difficult to replace.

Many JDK classes provide generic capabilities (as you would expect from library classes), and so they are frequently more generic than what is required for your particular application. These generic capabilities often come at the expense of performance. For example, `Vector` is fine for generic `Objects`, but if you are using a `Vector` for only one type of object, then a custom version with an array and accessors of that type is faster, as you can avoid all the casts required to convert the generic Object back into your own type. Using Vector for basic data types (e.g., longs) is even worse, requiring the data type to be wrapped by an object to get it into the Vector. For example, building and using a LongVector class improves performance and readability by avoiding casts, Long wrappers, unwrapping, etc.:

```
public class LongVector
{
  long[] internalArray;
  int arraySize
  ...
  public void addElement(long l) {
  ...
  public long elementAt(int i) {
  ...
```

If you are using your own classes, you can extend them to have the specific functionality you require, with direct access to the internals of the class. Again using Vector as an example, if you want to iterate over the collection (e.g., to select a particular subset based on some criteria), you need to access the elements through the get() method for each element, with the significant overhead that that implies. If you are using your own (possibly derived) class, you can implement the specific action you want in the class, allowing your loop to access the internal array directly with the consequent speedup:

```
public class QueryVector extends MyVector
{
  public Object[] getTheBitsIWant{
    //Access the internal array directly rather than going through
    //the method accessors. This makes the search much faster
    Object[] results = new Object[10];
    for(int i = arraySize-1; i >= 0; i--)
      if (internalArray[i] ....
```

Finally, there are often many places where objects (especially collection objects) are used initially for convenience (e.g., Vector, because you did not know the size of the array you would need, etc.), and in a final version of the application can be replaced completely with presized arrays. A known-sized array (not a collection object) is the fastest way in Java to store and access elements of a collection.

Faster VMs

VM runtimes and Java compilers vary enormously over time and across vendors. More and more optimizations are finding their way into both VMs and compilers. Many possible compiler optimizations are considered in later sections of this chapter. In this section I focus on VM optimizations.

VM Speed Variations

Different VMs have different running characteristics. Some VMs are intended purely for development and are highly suboptimal in terms of performance. These VMs may have huge inefficiencies, even in such basic operations as casting between different numeric types. One development VM I used had this behavior; it provided the foundation of an excellent development environment (actually my preferred environment), but was all but useless for performance testing, as any data type manipulation other than with ints or booleans produced highly varying and misleading times.

It is important to run any tests involving timing or profiling in the same VM you plan to run the application. You should test your application in the current "standard" VMs if your target environment is not fully defined.

There is, of course, nothing much you can do about speeding up any one VM (short of upgrading the CPUs). But you should be aware of the different VMs available, whether or not you control the deployment environment of your application. If you control the target environment, you can choose your VM appropriately. If you do not control the environment on which your application runs, remember that performance is partly user expectation. If you tell your user that VM "A" gives such and such a performance for your application, but VM "B" gives this other much slower performance, then you at least inform your user community of the implications of their choice of VM. This could also possibly put pressure on vendors with slower VMs to improve them.

VMs with JIT Compilers

The basic bytecode interpreter VM executes by decoding and executing bytecodes. This is slow, and is pure overhead, adding nothing to the functionality of the application. A just-in-time (JIT) compiler in a virtual machine eliminates much of this overhead by doing the bytecode fetch and decode just once. The first time the method is loaded, the decoded instructions are converted into machine code native for the CPU the system is running on. After that, future invocations of a particular method no longer incur the interpreter overhead. However, a JIT must be fast at compiling to avoid slowing the runtime, so extensive optimizations within the compile phase are unlikely. This means that the compiled code is often not as fast as it could be. A JIT also imposes a significantly larger memory footprint to the process.

Without a JIT, you might have to optimize your bytecodes for a particular platform. Optimizing the bytecode for one platform can conceivably make that code run slower on another platform (though a speedup is usually reflected to some extent on all platforms). A JIT compiler can theoretically optimize the same code differently for different underlying CPUs, thus getting the best of all worlds.

In tests by Mark Roulo (*http://www.javaworld.com/javaworld/jw-09-1998/jw-09-speed. html*), he found that a good JIT speeded up the overhead of method calls from a best of 280 CPU clock cycles in the fastest non-JIT VM, to just 2 clock cycles in the JIT VM. In a direct comparison of method call times for this JIT VM compared to a compiled C++ program, the Java method call time was found to be just one clock cycle slower than the C++: fast enough for almost any application. However, object creation is not speeded up by anywhere near this amount, which means that with a JIT VM, object creation is relatively more expensive (and consequently more important when tuning) than with a non-JIT VM.

VM Startup Time

The time your application takes to start depends on a number of factors. First, there is the time taken by the operating system to start the executable process. This time is mostly independent of the VM, though the size of the executable and the size and number of shared libraries needed to start the VM process have some effect. But the main time cost is mapping the various elements into system memory. This time can be shortened by having as much as possible already in system memory. The most obvious way to have the shared libraries already in system memory is to have recently started a VM. If the VM was recently started, even for a short time, the operating system is likely to have cached the shared libraries in system memory, and so the next startup is quicker. A better but more complicated way of having the executable elements in memory is to have the relevant files mapped onto a memory resident filesystem; see the section "Cached Filesystems (RAM Disks, tmpfs, cachefs)" in Chapter 14, *Underlying Operating System and Network Improvements*, for more on how to manage this.

The second component in the startup time of the VM is the time taken to manage the VM runtime initializations. This is purely dependent on the VM system implementation. Interpreter VMs generally have faster startup times than the JIT VMs, because the JIT VMs need to manage extra compilations during the startup and initial classloading phases. Starting with JDK 1.3, Sun is trying to improve the startup time imposed by the VM. VMs are now already differentiated by their startup times; for example, the JDK 1.3 VM has a deliberately shortened startup time compared to JDK 1.2. HotSpot has the more leisurely startup time acceptable for long-running server processes. In the future you can expect to see VMs differentiated by their startup times even more.

Finally, the application architecture and class file configuration determine the last component of startup time. The application may require many classes and extensive initializations before the application is started, or it may be designed to start up as quickly as possible. It is useful to bear in mind the user perception of application startup when designing the application. For example, if you can create the startup window as quickly as possible and then run any initializations in the background without blocking windowing activity, the user will see this as a faster startup than if you waited for initializations to finish before creating the initial window. This design takes more work, but improves startup time.

The number of classes that need to be loaded before the application starts are part of the application initializations, and again the application design affects this time. In the later section "Uncompressed ZIP/JAR Files," I discuss the effects of class file configuration on startup time. The section "Analysis" in Chapter 13, *When to Optimize*, also has an example of designing an application to minimize startup time.

Other VM Optimizations

On the VM side, improvements are possible using JIT compilers to compile methods to machine code, using algorithms for code caching, applying intelligent analyses of runtime code, etc. Some bytecodes allow the system to bypass table lookups that would otherwise need to be executed. But these bytecodes take extra effort to apply to the VM. Using these techniques, an intelligent VM could skip some runtime steps after parts of the application have been resolved.

Generally, a VM with a JIT compiler gives a huge boost to a Java application, and is probably the quickest and simplest way to improve performance. The most optimistic predictions are that using optimizing compilers to generate bytecodes, together with VMs with intelligent JIT (re)compilers, will put Java performance on a par with or even better than an equivalent natively compiled C++ application. Theoretically, better performance is possible. Having a runtime environment adapt to the running characteristics of a program should, in theory at least, provide better performance than a statically compiled application. A similar argument runs in CPU design circles where dynamic rescheduling of instructions to take account of pipelining allows CPUs to process instructions out of order. But at the time of writing this book, we are not particularly close to proving this theory for the average Java application. The time available for a VM to do something other than the most basic execution and bytecode translation is limited. The following quote about dynamic scheduling in CPUs also applies to adaptive VMs:

> At runtime, the CPU knows almost everything, but it knows everything almost too late to do anything about it. (Tom R. Halfhill quoting Gerrit A. Slavenburg, "Inside IA-64," *Byte*, June 1998)

As an example of an "intelligent" VM, Sun's HotSpot VM is targeted precisely to this area of adaptive optimization. This VM includes some basic improvements (all of which are also present in VMs from other vendors) such as using direct pointers

instead of Java handles* (which may be a security issue), improved thread synchronization, a generational garbage collector, speedups to object allocation, and an
improved startup time (by not JIT-compiling methods initially). In addition to
these basic improvements, HotSpot includes adaptive optimization, which works as
follows: HotSpot runs the application initially in interpreted mode (as if there is
no JIT compiler present) while a profiler identifies the bottlenecks in the application. Then, an optimizing JIT compiler compiles into native machine code only
those hotspots in the application that are causing the bottlenecks. Because only a
small part of the application is targeted, the JIT compiler (which might in this case
be more realistically called an "after-a-while" compiler rather than a "just-in-time"
compiler) can spend extra time compiling those targeted parts of the application,
thus allowing more than the most basic compiler optimizations to be applied.

NOTE   Consider the example where 20% of the code accounts for 80% of
              the running application time. Here, a classic JIT compiler might
              improve the whole application by 30%: the application would now
              take 70% of the time it originally took.

              The HotSpot compiler ignores the nonbottlenecked code, instead
              focusing on getting the 20% of hotspot code to run twice as fast. The
              80% of application time is halved to just 40% of the original time.
              Adding in the remaining 20% of time means that the application
              now runs in 60% of the original time. These percentage figures are
              purely for illustration purposes.

              Note, however, that HotSpot can try too hard sometimes. For exam-
              ple, HotSpot can speculatively optimize on the basis of guessing the
              type of particular objects. If that guess turns out to be wrong,
              HotSpot has to deoptimize the code, which results in some very vari-
              able timings.

So far, I have no evidence that optimizations I have applied in the past (and
detailed in this book) have caused any problems after upgrading compilers and
VMs. However, it is important to note that the performance characteristics of your
application may change with different VMs and compilers, and not necessarily
always for the better. Be on the lookout for any problems a new compiler and VM
may bring, as well as the advantages. The technique of loading classes explicitly
from a new thread after application startup can conflict with a particular JIT VM's
caching mechanism and actually slow down the startup sequence of your application. I have no evidence for this; I am just speculating on possible conflicts.

---

* A handle is a pointer to a pointer. Java uses handles to ensure security, so that one object cannot gain
  direct access to another object without the security capabilities of Java being able to intervene.

Better Optimizing Compilers

Look out for Java code compilers that specifically target performance optimizations. These are increasingly available. (I suggest searching the Web for java+compile+optimi and checking in Java magazines. A list is also included in Chapter 15, *Further Resources*.) Of course, all compilers try to optimize code, but some are better than others. Some companies put a great deal of effort into making their compiler produce the tightest, fastest code, while others tend to be distracted by other aspects of the Java environment and put less effort into the compile phase.

There are also some experimental compilers around. For example, the JAVAR compiler (*http://www.extreme.indiana.edu/hpjava/*) is a prototype compiler that automatically parallelizes parts of a Java application to improve performance.

It is possible to write preprocessors to automatically achieve many of the optimizations you can get with optimizing compilers; indeed, you can think of an optimizing compiler as a preprocessor together with a basic compiler (though in many cases it is better described as a postprocessor and recompiler). However, writing such a preprocessor is a significant task. Even if you ignore the Java code parsing or bytecode parsing required,* any one preprocessor optimization can take months to create and verify. To get close to the full set of optimizations listed in the following sections could take years of development. Fortunately, it is not necessary for you to make that effort, because optimizing compiler vendors are making the effort for you.

What Optimizing Compilers Cannot Do

Optimizing compilers cannot change your code to use a better algorithm. If you are using an inefficient search routine, there may be hugely better search algorithms giving orders of magnitude speedups. But the optimizing compiler only tries to speed up the algorithm you are using (with a probable small incremental speedup). It is still important to profile applications to identify bottlenecks even if you intend to use an optimizing compiler.

It is important to start using an optimizing compiler from the early stages of development in order to tailor your code to its restrictions. More than one project I know of has found the cost of trying to integrate an optimizing compiler at a late stage of development too expensive. In these cases, it means restructuring core routines and many disparate method calls, and can even require some redesign to work around limitations imposed by being unable to correctly handle reflection

---

* Such parsing is a one-off task that can then be applied to any optimization. There are several free packages available for parsing class files, e.g., CFParse from the IBM alphaWorks site, *http://www.alphaworks. ibm.com.*

and runtime class resolution. Optimizing compilers have difficulty dealing with classes that cannot be identified at compile time (e.g., building a string at runtime and loading a class of that name). Basically, using `Class.forName()` is not (and cannot be) handled in any complete way, though several compilers try to manage as best they can. In short, managers with projects at a late stage of development are often reluctant to make extensive changes to either the development environment or the code. While code tuning can be targeted at bottlenecks and so normally affects only small sections of code, integrating an optimizing compiler can affect the entire project. If there are too many problems in this integration, most project managers decide that the potential risks outweigh the possible benefits and prefer to take the safe route of carrying on without the optimizing compiler.

What Optimizing Compilers Can Do

Compilers can apply many "classic" optimizations and a host of newer optimizations that apply specifically to object-oriented programs and languages with virtual machines. I list many optimizations in the following sections.

You can apply most classic compiler-optimization techniques by hand directly to the source. But usually you should not, as it makes the code more complicated to read and maintain. Individually, each of these optimizations improves performance only by small amounts. Collectively (as applied by a compiler across all the code), they can make a significant contribution to improving performance. This is important to remember: as you look at each individual optimization, in many cases the thought, "Well, that isn't going to make much difference," may cross your mind. This is correct. The power of optimizing compilers comes in applying many small optimizations automatically that would be annoying or confusing to apply by hand. The combination of all those small optimizations can add up to a big speedup.

Optimizing-compiler vendors claim to see significant speedups: up to 50% for many applications. Most applications in serious need of optimization are looking for speedups even greater than this, but don't ignore the optimizing compiler for that reason: it may be doubling the speed of your application for a relatively cheap investment. As long as you do not need to restructure much code to take advantage of them, optimizing compilers can give you the "biggest bang for your buck" after JIT VMs in terms of performance improvements.

The next sections list many of the well-known optimizations these compilers can apply. This list can help you when selecting optimizing compilers, and also can help if you decide you need to apply some of these optimizations by hand.

Remove unused methods and classes

When all application classes are known at compile time, an optimizing compiler can analyze the full runtime code-path tree, identifying all classes that can be used and all methods that can be called. Most method calls in Java necessarily invoke one of a limited set of methods, and by analyzing the runtime path, you can eliminate all but one of the possibilities. The compiler can then remove unused methods and classes. This can include removing superclass methods that have been overridden in a subclass and are never called in the superclass. The optimization makes for smaller download requirements for programs sent across a network and, more usefully, reduces the impact of method lookup at runtime by eliminating unused alternative methods.

Increase statically bound calls

An optimizing compiler can determine at compile time whether particular method invocations are necessarily polymorphic and so must have the actual method target determined at runtime, or whether the target for a particular method call can be identified at compile time. Many method calls that apparently need to have the target decided at runtime can, in fact, be uniquely identified (see the previous section). Once identified, the method invocation can be compiled as a static invocation, which is faster than a dynamic lookup. Static methods are statically bound in Java. The following example produces "in superclass" if method1() and method2() are static, but "in subclass" if method1() and method2() are not static:

```
public class Superclass {
  public static void main(String[] args) {(new Subclass()).method1();}
  public static void method1(){method2();}
  public static void method2(){System.out.println("in superclass ");}
}
class Subclass extends Superclass {
  public static void method2(){System.out.println("in subclass ");}
}
```

Cut dead code and unnecessary instructions, including checks for null

Section 14.9 of the Java specification requires compilers to carry out flow analysis on the code to determine the reachability of any section of code. The only valid unreachable code is the consequence of an `if` statement (see the later section "Dead code branches are eliminated"). Invalid unreachable code must be flagged as a compile error, but the valid code from an `if` statement is not a compile error and can be eliminated. The `if` statement test can also be eliminated if the boolean result is conclusively identified at compile time. In fact, this is a standard capability of almost all current compilers.

This flow analysis can be extended to determine if other sections and code branches that are syntactically valid are actually semantically unreachable. A typical example is testing for null. Some null tests can be eliminated by establishing that the variable has either definitely been assigned to or definitely never been assigned to before the test is reached. Similarly, some bytecode instructions that can be generated may be unnecessary after establishing the flow of control, and these can also be eliminated.

Use computationally cheaper alternatives (strength reduction)

An optimizing compiler should determine if there is a computationally cheaper alternative to a set of instructions and replace those slower instructions with the faster alternative.

The classic version of this technique, termed "strength reduction," replaces an operation with an equivalent operation that is faster. Consider the following lines of code:

```
x = x + 5;
y = x/2;
z = x * 4;
```

These lines can be replaced by faster operations without altering the meaning of any statements:

```
x += 5;     //Assignment in place is faster
y = x >> 1; //each right shift by one place is equivalent to dividing by 2
z = x << 2; //each left shift by one place is equivalent to multiplying by 2
```

These examples are the most common cases of strength reduction. All the shorthand arithmetic operators (++, --, +=, -=, *=, /=, |=, &=) are computationally faster than their nonshorthand expansions, and should be used (by the coder) or replaced (by the compiler) where appropriate.*

Replace runtime computations with compiled results

An optimizing compiler can identify code that requires runtime execution if bytecodes are directly generated, but can be replaced by computing the result of that code during the compilation phase. The result can then replace the code.

---

* One of the technical reviewers for this book, Ethan Henry, has pointed out to me that there is no actual guarantee that these strength reductions are more efficient in Java. This is true. However, they seem to work for at least some VMs. In addition, compilers producing native code (including JIT compilers) should produce faster code, as these techniques do work at the machine-code level.

This technique is applied by most compilers for the simple case of literal folding (see the later sections "Literal constants are folded" and "String concatenation is sometimes folded"). And it can be extended to other structures by adding some semantic input to the compiler. A simple example is:

```
String S_NINETY = "90";
int I_NINETY = Integer.parseInt(S_NINETY);
```

Although it is unlikely that anyone would do exactly this, similar kinds of initializations are used. An optimizing compiler that understood what `Integer.parseInt()` did could calculate the resulting `int` value and insert that result directly into the compiled file, thus avoiding the runtime calculation.

Remove unused fields

Analysis of the application can identify fields of objects that are never used, and these fields can then be removed. This makes the runtime take less memory and improves the speeds of both the object creation and the garbage collection of these objects. The type of analysis described in the earlier section "Remove unused methods and classes" improves the identification of unused fields.

Remove unnecessary parts of compiled files

Removing some unnecessary parts of compiled files is standard with most optimizing compilers. This option removes line number tables and local variable tables. The Java *.class* file structure allows extra information to be inserted, and some optimizing compilers make an effort to remove everything that is not necessary for runtime execution. This can be useful when it is important to minimize the size of the class files. Note that frequently, compilers with this capability can remove unnecessary parts of files that are already compiled, e.g., from third-party *.class* files you do not have the source for.

Reduce necessary parts of compiled files

Some optimizing compilers can reduce the necessary parts of compiled files. For example, the *.class* file includes a pool of constants (a structure containing various constants), and an optimizing compiler can minimize the size of the constant pool by combining and reducing entries.

Alter access control to speed up invocations

At least one optimizing compiler (the DashO optimizer by PreEmptive) provides the option to alter the access control to methods. The rationale for this is that any non-`public` method has access control on that method since it is access restricted, i.e., the runtime system must verify at some point that the caller to a method has access to calling that method. However, `public` methods require no such run-time checks. So the thinking is that any non-`public` method must have some overhead compared to an identical method declared as `public`.

The result is that the compiler supports normal compilation (so that any incorrect accesses are caught at the compilation stage), and the subsequent compiled class can have all its methods changed to `public`. This is, of course, a security risk.

Inline calls

Every optimizing compiler supports inlining. However, the degree of inlining supported can vary enormously, as different compilers are more or less aggressive about inlining (see the extended discussion in the later section "Optimizations Performed When Using the –O Option"). Inlining is the technique in which a method call is directly replaced with the code for that method; for example, the code as written may be:

```
private int method1() { return method2(); }
private int method2() { return 5; }
```

With inlining operating to optimize `method1()`, this code is compiled into the equivalent of:

```
//the call to method2() is replaced with the code in method2()
private int method1() { return 5; }
private int method2() { return 5; }
```

Remove dynamic type checks

Every compiler removes dynamic type checks when the compiler can establish they are unnecessary. The JDK compiler removes casts that are obviously unnecessary. For example, consider the following two lines of code:

```
Integer i = new Integer(3);
Integer j = (Integer) i;
```

The JDK compiler removes the obviously unnecessary cast here, and the code gets compiled as if the source was:

```
Integer i = new Integer(3);
Integer j = i;
```

This is very basic. A more sophisticated optimizing compiler can analyze a program far more intensively and eliminate further casting operations that the compiler can ascertain are always true. The `instanceof` operation is similar to casting (the test applied by `instanceof` differs from a class cast test, in that a cast on `null` always succeeds, but `null instanceof SomeClass` always returns `false`) and an optimizing compiler can also remove some tests involving `instanceof`.

Unroll loops

Loop unrolling makes the loop body larger by explicitly repeating the body statements while changing the amount by which the loop variable increases or decreases. This reduces the number of tests and iterations the loop requires to be completed. This is extensively covered in Chapter 7, *Loops and Switches*.

Code motion

Code motion moves calculations out of loops that need calculating only once. Consider the next code example:

```
for (int i = 0; i < z.length; i++)
  z[i] = x * Maths.abs(y);
```

The elements of an array are being assigned the same value each time, but the assignment expression is still calculating the value each time. Applying code motion, this code is automatically converted to:

```
int t1 = x * Maths.abs(y);
for (int i = 0; i < z.length; i++)
  z[i] = t1;
```

Another place where code motion is useful is in eliminating or reducing redundant tests (though compilers are usually less effective at this). Consider the following method:

```
public String aMethod(String first, String passed)
{
  StringBuffer copy = new StringBuffer(passed);
  if (first == null || first.length() == 0)
   return passed;
  else
  {
    ...//some manipulation of the string buffer to do something
    return copy.toString();
  }
}
```

This method creates an unnecessary new object if the `first` string is `null` or zero length. This should be recoded or bytecodes should be generated, so that the new object creation is moved to the `else` clause:

```
public String aMethod(String first, String passed)
{
  if (first == null || first.length() == 0)
   return passed;
  else
  {
    StringBuffer copy = new StringBuffer(passed);
    ...//some manipulation of the string buffer to do something
```

```
        return copy.toString();
    }
}
```

It would be nice, but difficult, for a compiler to apply this automatically, but this type of optimization probably needs to be applied manually. For the compiler to apply this sort of optimization, it needs to know that creating a new `StringBuffer` has no side effects, and so the creation can reasonably be moved to a different part of the code.

Both this technique and the next one are actually good coding practices.

Eliminate common subexpressions

Eliminating common subexpressions is similar to code motion. In this case, though, the compiler identifies an expression that is common to more than one statement and does not need to be calculated more than once. The following example uses the same calculation twice to map two pairs of variables:

```
z1 = x * Maths.abs(y) + x;
z2 = x * Maths.abs(y) + y;
```

After a compiler has analyzed this code to eliminate the common subexpression, the code becomes:

```
int t1 = x * Maths.abs(y);
z1 = t1 + x;
z2 = t1 + y;
```

Eliminate unnecessary assignments

An optimizing compiler should eliminate any unnecessary assignments. The following example is very simplistic:

```
int x = 1;
x = 2;
```

This should obviously be converted into one statement:

```
int x = 2;
```

Although you won't often see this type of example, it is not unusual for chained constructors to repeatedly assign to an instance variable in essentially the same way. An optimizing compiler should eliminate all extra unnecessary assignments.

Rename classes, fields, and methods

Some compilers rename classes, fields, and methods for various reasons, such as for obfuscating the code (making the code difficult to understand if it were decompiled). Renaming (especially to one-character names*) can make every-thing compiled much smaller, significantly reducing classloading times and net-work download times.

Reorder or change bytecodes

An optimizing compiler can reorder or change bytecode instructions to make methods faster. Normally, this reduces the number of instructions, but sometimes making an activity faster requires increasing the number of instructions. An exam-ple is where a switch statement is used with a list of unordered, nearly consecu-tive values for case statements. An optimizing compiler can reorder the case statements so that the values are in order, insert extra cases to make the values fully consecutive, and then use a faster switch bytecode to execute the switch statement. The optimization for switch statements is extensively covered in Chapter 7.

Generate information to help a VM

The Java bytecode specification provides support for optional extra information to be included with class files. This information can be VM-specific information: any VM that does not understand the codes must ignore them. Consequently, it is pos-sible that a particular compiler may be optimized (in the future) to generate extra information that allows particular VMs to run code faster. For example, it would be possible for the compiler to add extra information that tells the VM the opti-mal way in which a JIT should compile the code, thus removing some of the JIT workload (and overhead).

A more extreme example might be where a compiler generates optimized native code for several CPUs in addition to the bytecode for methods in the class file. This would allow a VM to execute the native code immediately if it were running on one of the supported CPUs. Unfortunately, this particular example would cause a security loophole, as there would be no guarantee to the VM that the natively compiled method was the equivalent of the bytecode-generated one.

Managing Compilers

All the optimizations previously listed are optimizations compilers should automat-ically handle. Unfortunately, you are not guaranteed that any particular compiler actually applies any single optimization. The only way I have found to be certain about the optimizations a particular compiler can make is to compile code with lines such as those shown previously, then decompile the bytecodes to see what comes out. There are several decompilers available on the Net: a web search for

---

* For example, the DashO optimizer renames everything possible to one-character names.

java+decompile should fetch a few. My personal favorite at the time of writing this is *jad* by Pavel Kouznetsov, which currently resides at *http://www.geocities.com/ SiliconValley/Bridge/8617/jad.html.*

Several Java compilers are targeted at optimizing bytecode, and several other compilers (including all mainstream ones) have announced the intention to roll more and more compiler optimizations into future versions of the compiler. This highlights another point: ensure that you have available your compiler's latest version. It may be that, for robustness reasons, you do not want to go into production with the very latest compiler, as that will have been less tested than an older version, and your own code will have been more thoroughly tested on the classes generated by the older compiler. Nevertheless, you should at least test whether the latest compiler gives your application a boost (using whatever standard benchmarks you choose to assess your application's performance).

Finally, the compiler you select to generate bytecode may not be the same compiler you use while developing code. You may even have different compilers for different parts of development and even for different optimizations (though this is unlikely). In any case, you need to be sure the deployed application is using the bytecodes generated by the specific compilers you have chosen for the final version. At times in large projects, I have seen some classes recompiled with the wrong compiler. This has occasionally resulted in some of these classes finding their way to the deployed version of the application.

This alternate recompilation does not affect the correctness of the application since all compilers should be generating correct bytecodes, which means that such a situation allows the application to pass all regression test suites. But you can end up with the production application not running as fast as you expect, and for reasons that are very difficult to track down.

Sun's Compiler and Runtime Optimizations

As you can see from the previous sections, knowing how the compiler alters your code as it generates bytecodes is important for performance tuning. Some compiler optimizations can be canceled out if you write your code so that the compiler cannot apply its optimizations. In this section, I cover what you need to know to get the most out of the compilation stage if you are using the JDK compiler (*javac*).

Optimizations You Get for Free

There are several optimizations that occur at the compilation stage without your needing to specify any compilation options. These optimizations are not necessarily required because of specifications laid down in Java. Instead, they have become standard compiler optimizations. The JDK compiler always applies them, and consequently almost every other compiler applies them as well. You should always determine exactly what your specific compiler optimizes as standard, from the documentation provided or by decompiling example code.

Literal constants are folded

This optimization is a concrete implementation of the ideas discussed in the "Replace runtime computations with compiled results" section earlier. In this implementation, multiple literal constants* in an expression are "folded" by the compiler. For example, in the following statement:

```
int foo = 9*10;
```

the 9*10 is evaluated to 90 before compilation is completed. The result is as if the line read:

```
int foo = 90;
```

This optimization allows you to make your code more readable without having to worry about avoiding runtime overheads.

String concatenation is sometimes folded

With the Java 2 compiler, string concatenations to literal constants are folded:

```
String foo = "hi Joe " + (9*10);
```

is compiled as if it read:

```
String foo = "hi Joe 90";
```

This optimization is not applied with JDK compilers prior to JDK 1.2. Some non-Sun compilers apply this optimization and some don't. The optimization applies where the statement can be resolved into literal constants concatenated with a literal string using the + concatenation operator. This optimization also applies to concatenation of two strings. In this last case, all compilers fold the two (or more) strings, as that action is required by the Java specification.

Constant fields are inlined

Primitive constant fields (those primitive data type fields defined with the final modifier) are inlined within a class and across classes, regardless of whether the classes are compiled in the same pass. For example, if class A has a public static final field, and class B has a reference to this field, the value from class A is inserted directly into class B, rather than a reference to the field in class A. Strictly

---

* Literals are data items that can be identified as numbers, double-quoted strings, and characters, e.g., 3, 44.5e-22F, 0xffee, "h", "hello", etc.

speaking, this is not an optimization, as the Java specification requires constant fields to be inlined. Nevertheless, knowing about it means you can take advantage of it.

For instance, if class A is defined as:

```
public class A
{
  public static final int VALUE = 33;
}
```

and class B is defined as:

```
public class B
{
  static int VALUE2 = A.VALUE;
}
```

then when class B is compiled, whether or not in a compilation pass of its own, it actually ends up as if it was defined as:

```
public class B
{
  static int VALUE2 = 33;
}
```

with no reference left to class A.

Dead code branches are eliminated

Another type of optimization automatically applied at the compilation stage is to cut out code that can never be reached because of a test in an `if` statement that can be completely resolved at compile time. The short discussion in the earlier section "Cut dead code and unnecessary instructions, including checks for null" is relevant to this section.

As an example, suppose classes A and B are defined (in separate files) as:

```
public class A
{
  public static final boolean DEBUG = false;
}

public class B
{
  static int foo()
  {
    if (A.DEBUG)
      System.out.println("In B.foo()");
    return 55;
  }
}
```

Then when class B is compiled, whether or not on a compilation pass of its own, it actually ends up as if it was defined as:

```
public class B
{
  static int foo()
  {
    return 55;
  }
}
```

No reference is left to class A, and no `if` statement is left. The consequence of this feature is to allow conditional compilation. Other classes can set a DEBUG constant in their own class the same way, or they can use a shared constant value (as class B used A.DEBUG in the earlier definition).

WARNING   A problem is frequently encountered with this kind of code. The constant value is set when the class with the constant, say class A, is compiled. Any other class referring to class A's constant takes the value that is currently set when that class is being compiled, and does not reset the value if A is recompiled. So you can have the situation when A is compiled with A.DEBUG set to false, then B is compiled and the compiler inlines A.DEBUG as false, possibly cutting dead code branches. Then if A is recompiled to set A.DEBUG to true, this does not affect class B; the compiled class B still has the value false inlined, and any dead code branches stay eliminated until class B is recompiled. You should be aware of this possible problem if you compile your classes in more than one compilation pass.

You should use this pattern for debug and trace statements, and assertion pre-conditions, postconditions, and invariants. There is more detail on this technique in "Conditional Error Checking" in Chapter 6, *Exceptions, Casts, and Variables*.

Optimizations Performed When Using the –O Option

The only *standard* compile-time option that can improve performance with the JDK compiler is the –O option. Note that –O (for Optimize) is a common option for compilers, and further optimizing options for other compilers often take the form –O1, –O2, etc. You should always check your compiler's documentation to find out what other options are available and what they do. Some compilers allow you to make the choice between optimizing the compiled code for speed or minimizing the size; there is often a tradeoff between these two aspects.

The standard –O option does not currently apply a variety of optimizations in the Sun JDK (up to JDK 1.2). In future versions it may do more. Currently, the option makes the compiler eliminate optional tables in the *.class* files, such as line number and local variable tables; this gives only a small performance improvement by making class files smaller and therefore quicker to load. You should definitely use this option if your class files are sent across a network.

But the main performance improvement of using the -O option comes from the compiler inlining methods. When using the -O option, the compiler considers inlining methods defined with any of the following modifiers: `private`, `static`, or `final`. Some methods, such as those defined as `synchronized`, are never inlined. If a method can be inlined, the compiler decides whether or not to inline it depending on its own unpublished considerations. These considerations seem mainly to be the simplicity of the method: in JDK 1.2 the compiler inlines only fairly simple methods. For example, one-line methods with no side effects, such as accessing or updating a variable, are invariably inlined. Methods that return just a constant are also inlined. Multiline methods are inlined if the compiler determines they are simple enough (e.g., a `System.out.println("blah")` followed by a `return` statement would get inlined).

Choosing simple methods to inline does have a rationale behind it. The larger the method being inlined, the more the code gets bloated with copies of the same code being inserted in many places. This has runtime costs in extra code being loaded and extra space taken by the runtime system. A JIT VM would also have the extra cost of having to compile more code. At some point, there is a decrease in performance from inlining too much code. In addition, some methods have side effects that can make them quite difficult to inline correctly.

The compiler applies its methodology for selecting methods to inline, irrespective of whether the target method is in a bottleneck: this is a machine-gun strategy of many little optimizations in the hope that some inline calls may improve the bottlenecks. A performance tuner applying inlining works the other way around, first finding the bottlenecks, then selectively inlining methods inside bottlenecks. This latter strategy can result in good speedups, especially in loop bottlenecks. This is because a loop can be speeded up significantly by removing the overhead of a repeated method call. If the method to be inlined is complex, you can often factor out parts of the method so that those parts can be executed outside the loop, gaining even more speedup.

I have not found any public document that specifies the actual decision-making process that determines whether or not a method is inlined. The only reference given is to Section 13.4.21 of *The Java Language Specification* that specifies only that binary compatibility with preexisting binaries must be maintained. It does specify that the package must be guaranteed to be kept together for the compiler to allow inlining across classes. The specification also states that the `final` keyword does not imply that a method can be inlined, as the runtime system may have a differently implemented method.

Why There Are Limits on Inlining

The compiler can inline only those methods that can be statically bound at compile time. To see why, consider the following example of class A and its subclass B, with two methods defined, foo1() and foo2(). The foo2() method is overridden in the subclass:

```
class A {
  public int foo1() {return foo2();}
  public int foo2() {return 5;}
}

public class B extends A {
  public int foo2() {return 10;}
}
```

If A.foo2() is inlined into A.foo1(), (new B()).foo1() incorrectly returns 5 instead of 10, because A is compiled incorrectly as if it read:

```
class A {
  public int foo1() {return 5;}
  public int foo2() {return 5;}
}
```

Any method that can be overridden at runtime cannot be validly inlined (it is a potential bug if it is). The Java specification states that final methods can be non-final at runtime, i.e., you can compile a set of classes with one class having a final method, but later recompile that class without the method as final (thus allowing subclasses to override it), and the other classes must run correctly. For this reason, not all final methods can be identified as statically bound at compile time, so not all final methods can be inlined. Some earlier compiler versions incorrectly inlined some final methods, and I have seen serious bugs caused by this.

Prior to JDK 1.2, the -O option used with the Sun compiler did inline methods across classes, even if they were not compiled in the same compilation pass. This behavior led to bugs.* From JDK 1.2, the -O option no longer inlines methods across classes, even if they are compiled in the same compilation pass.

Unfortunately, there is no way to directly specify which methods should be inlined, rather than relying on the compiler's internal workings. I guess that in the future, some compiler vendors will provide a mechanism that supports specifying which methods to inline, along with other preprocessor options. In the meantime, you

---

* Primarily methods that accessed private or protected variables were incorrectly inlined into other classes, leading to runtime authorization exceptions.

can implement a preprocessor (or use an existing one) if you require tighter control. Opportunities for inlining often occur inside bottlenecks (especially in loops), as discussed previously. Selective inlining by hand can give an order-of-magnitude speedup for some bottlenecks (and no speedup at all in others).

The speedup obtained purely from inlining is usually only a few percent: 5% is fairly common. Some optimizing compilers are very aggressive about inlining code. They apply techniques such as analyzing the entire program to alter and eliminate method calls in order to identify methods that can be coerced into being statically bound. Then these identified methods are inlined as much as possible according to the compiler's analysis. This technique has been shown to give a 50% speedup to some applications. Another inlining technique used is that by the HotSpot runtime, which aggressively inlines code after a bottleneck has been identified.

Performance Effects From Runtime Options

Some runtime options can help your application to run faster. These include:

*   Options that allow the VM to have a bigger footprint (-Xmx/-mx is the main one, which allows a larger heap space); but see the comments in the following paragraph.

*   -noverify, which eliminates the overhead of verifying classes at classload time (not available from 1.2).

Some options are detrimental to the application performance. These include:

*   The -Xrunhprof option, which makes applications run 10% to 1000% slower (-prof in 1.1).

*   Removing the JIT compiler (done with -Djava.compiler=NONE in JDK 1.2 and the -nojit option in 1.1).

*   -debug, which runs a slower VM with debugging enabled.

Increasing the maximum heap size beyond the default of 16 MB usually improves performance for applications that can use the extra space. However, there is a tradeoff in higher space-management costs to the VM (object table access, garbage collections, etc.), and at some point there is no longer any benefit in increasing the maximum heap size. Increasing the heap size actually causes garbage collection to take longer, as it needs to examine more objects and a larger space. Up to now, I have found no better method than trial and error to determine optimal maximum heap sizes for any particular application.

Beware of accidentally using the VM options detrimental to performance. I once had a customer who had a sudden 40% decrease in performance during tests. Their performance harness had a configuration file that set up how the VM could be run, and this was accidentally set to include the -prof option on the standard tests as well as for the profiling tests. That was the cause of the sudden performance decrease, but it was not discovered until time had been wasted checking software versions, system configurations, and other things.

Compile to Native Machine Code

If you know the target environments of your application, you have the option of taking your Java application and compiling it to a machine-code executable. There is a variety of these compilers already available for various target platforms, and the list continues to grow. (Check the computer magazines or follow the compiler links on good Java web sites. See also the compilers listed in Chapter 15.) These compilers can often work directly from the bytecode (i.e., the *.class* files) without the source code, so any third-party classes and beans you use can normally be included.

If you follow this option, a standard technique to remain multiplatform is to start the application from a batch file that checks the platform and installs (or even starts) the application binary appropriate for that platform, falling back to the standard Java runtime if no binary is available. Of course, the batch file also needs to be multiplatform, but then you could build it in Java.

But prepare to be disappointed with the performance of a natively compiled executable compared to the latest JIT-enabled runtime VMs. The compiled executable still needs to handle garbage collection, threads, exceptions, etc., all within the confines of the executable. These runtime features of Java do not necessarily compile efficiently into an executable. The performance of the executable may well depend on how much effort the compiler vendor has made in making those Java features run efficiently in the context of a natively compiled executable. The latest adaptive VMs have been shown to run some applications faster than running the equivalent natively compiled executable.

Advocates of the "compile to native executable" approach feel that the compiler optimizations will improve with time so that this approach will ultimately deliver the fastest applications. Luckily, this is a win-win situation for the performance of Java applications: try out both approaches if appropriate to you, and choose the one that works best.

There are also several translators that convert Java programs into C. I only include a mention of these translators for completeness, as I have not tried any of them. They presumably enable you to use a standard C compiler to compile to a variety of target platforms. However, most source code–to–source code translations between programming languages are suboptimal and do not usually generate fast code.

Native Method Calls

For that extra zing in your application (but probably not applet), try out calls to native code. Wave goodbye to 100% pure Java certification, and say hello to added complexity to your development environment and deployment procedure. (If you are already in this situation for reasons other than performance tuning, there is little overhead to taking this route in your project.)

A couple of examples I've seen where native method calls were used for performance reasons were intensive number-crunching for a scientific application and parsing large amounts of data in restricted time. In these and other cases, the runtime application environment at the time could not get to the required speed using Java. I should note that the latter parsing problem would now be able to run fast enough in pure Java, but the original application was built with quite an early version of Java. In addition, some number crunchers find that the latest Java runtimes and optimizing compilers give them sufficient performance in Java without resorting to any native calls.*

The JNI interface itself has its own overhead, which means that if a pure Java implementation comes close to the native call performance, the JNI overhead will probably cancel any performance advantages from the native call. However, on occasion the underlying system can provide an optimized native call that is not available from Java and cannot be implemented to work as fast in pure Java. In this kind of situation, JNI is useful for tuning.

Another case in which JNI can be useful is reducing the numbers of objects created, though this should be less common: you should normally be able to do this directly in Java. I once encountered a situation where JNI was needed to avoid excessive objects. This was with an application that originally required the use of a native DLL service. The vendor of that DLL ported the service to Java, which the application developers would have preferred using, but unfortunately the vendor neglected to tune the ported code. This resulted in the situation where a native call to a particular set of services produced just a couple dozen objects, but the Java-ported code produced nearly 10,000 objects. Apart from this difference, the speeds of the two implementations were similar.† However, the overhead in

---

* Serious number crunchers spend a large proportion of their time performance-tuning their code, whatever the language it is written in. To gain sufficient performance in Java, they of course need to intensively tune the application. But this is also true if the application is written in C or Fortran. The amount of tuning required is now, apparently, similar for these three languages. Further information can be found at *http://www.javagrande.org.*

† This increase in object creation normally results in a much slower implementation. However, in this particular case, the methods required synchronizing to a degree that gave a larger overhead than the object creation. Nevertheless, the much larger number of objects created by the untuned Java implementation needed reclaiming at some point, and this led to greater overhead in the garbage collection.

garbage collection caused a significant degradation in performance, which meant that the native call to the DLL was the preferred option.

If you are following the native function call route, there is little to say. You write your routines in C, plug them into your application using the `native` keyword as specified in the Java development kit, profile the resultant application, and confirm that it provides the required speedup. You can also use C (or C++ or whatever) profilers to profile the native code calls if it is complicated.

Other than this, the only recommendation that applies here is that if you are calling the native routines from loops, you should move the loops down into the native routines and pass the loop parameters to the routine as arguments. This usually produces faster implementations.

One other recommendation, which is not performance tuning–specific, is that it is usually good practice to provide a fallback methodology for situations when the native code cannot be loaded. This requires extra maintenance (two sets of code, extra fallback code) but is often worth the effort. You can manage the fallback at the time when the DLL library is being loaded by catching the exception when the load fails and providing an alternative path to the fallback code, either by setting boolean switches or by instantiating objects of the appropriate fallback classes as required.

Uncompressed ZIP/JAR Files

It is better to deliver your classes in a ZIP or JAR file than to deliver them one class at a time over the network or load them individually from separate files in the filesystem. This packaged delivery provides some of the benefits of clustering* (see "Clustering Files" in Chapter 14). The benefits gained from packaging class files come from reducing I/O overheads such as repeated file opening and closing, and possibly improving seek times.† Within the ZIP or JAR file, the classes should not be compressed unless network download time is a factor for the application. The best way to deliver local classes for performance reasons is in an uncompressed ZIP or JAR file. Coincidentally, that's how they're delivered with the JDK.

---

* "Clustering" is an unfortunately overloaded word, and is often used to refer to closely linked groups of server machines. In the context here, I use "clustering" to mean the close grouping of files.

† With operating system–monitoring tools, you can see the system temporarily stalling when the operating system issues a disk-cache flush if lots of files are closed close together in time. If you use a single packed file for all classes (and resources), you avoid this potential performance hit.

It is possible to further improve the classloading times by packing the classes into the ZIP/JAR file in the order in which they are loaded by the application. You can determine the loading order by running the application with the –verbose option, but note that this ordering is fragile: slight changes in the application can easily alter the loading order of classes. A further extension to this idea is to include your own classloader that opens the ZIP/JAR file itself and reads in all files sequentially, loading them into memory immediately. Perhaps the final version of this performance improvement route is to dispense with the ZIP/JAR filesystem: it is quicker to load the files if they are concatenated together in one big file, with a header at the start of the file giving the offsets and names of the contained files. This is similar to the ZIP filesystem, but it is better if you read the header in one block, and read in and load the files directly rather than going through the java.util.zip classes.

One further optimization to this classloading tactic is to start the classloader running in a separate (low-priority) thread immediately after VM startup.

Performance Checklist

Many of these suggestions apply only after a bottleneck has been identified:

- Test your benchmarks on each version of Java available to you (classes, compiler, and VM) to identify any performance improvements.

  — Test performance using the target VM or "best practice" VMs.

  — Include some tests of the garbage collector appropriate to your application, so that you can identify changes that minimize the cost of garbage collection in your application.

  — Run your application with both the –verbosegc option and with full application tracing turned on to see when the garbage collector kicks in and what it is doing.

  — Vary the –Xmx/–Xms option values to determine the optimal memory sizes for your application.

  — Avoid using the VM options that are detrimental to performance.

- Replace generic classes with more specific implementations dedicated to the data type being manipulated, e.g., implement a LongVector to hold longs rather than use a Vector object with Long wrappers.

  — Extend collection classes to access internal arrays for queries on the class.

  — Replace collection objects with arrays where the collection object is a bottleneck.

- Try various compilers. Look for compilers targeted at optimizing performance: these provide the cheapest significant speedup general to all runtime environments.

  — Use the –O option (but always check that it does not produce slower code).

  — Identify the optimizations a compiler is capable of so that you do not negate the optimizations.

  — Use a decompiler to determine precisely the optimizations generated by a particular compiler.

  — Consider using a preprocessor to apply some standard compiler optimizations more precisely.

  — Remember that an optimizing compiler can only optimize algorithms, not change them. A better algorithm is usually faster than an optimized slow algorithm.

  — Include optimizing compilers from the early stages of development.

  — Make sure that the deployed classes have been compiled with the correct compilers.

- Make sure that any loops using native method calls are converted so that the native call includes the loop instead of running the loop in Java. Any loop iteration parameters should be passed to the native call.

- Deliver classes in uncompressed format in ZIP or JAR files (unless network download is significant, in which case files should be compressed).

- Use a customized classloader running in a separate thread to load class files.

4.

Object Creation

> *The biggest difference between time and space is that you can't reuse time.*
>
> —Merrick Furst

"I thought that I didn't need to worry about memory allocation. Java is supposed to handle all that for me." This is a common perception, which is both true and false. Java handles low-level memory allocation and deallocation and comes with a garbage collector. Further, it prevents access to these low-level memory-handling routines, making the memory safe. So memory access should not cause corruption of data in other objects or in the running application, which is potentially the most serious problem that can occur with memory access violations. In a C or C++ program, problems of illegal pointer manipulations can be a major headache (e.g., deleting memory more than once, runaway pointers, bad casts). They are very difficult to track down and are likely to occur when changes are made to existing code. Java deals with all these possible problems and, at worst, will throw an exception immediately if memory is incorrectly accessed.

However, Java does not prevent you from using excessive amounts of memory nor from cycling through too much memory (e.g., creating and dereferencing many objects). Contrary to popular opinion, you can get memory leaks by holding on to objects without releasing references. This stops the garbage collector from reclaiming those objects, resulting in increasing amounts of memory being used.* In addition, Java does not provide for large numbers of objects to be created simultaneously (as you could do in C by allocating a large buffer), which eliminates one powerful technique for optimizing object creation.

---

* Ethan Henry and Ed Lycklama have written a nice article discussing Java memory leaks in the February 2000 issue of *Dr. Dobb's Journal*. This article is available online from the Dr. Dobb's web site, *http://www.ddj.com*.

When you're lost in a technical jungle...Ask Someone Who Knows™

Ever since Sun's initial release of Java™, developers have relied on *Java in a Nutshell* as their trusty guide. We've continued to track this important technology, and our Java Series provides a clear path for those on the hunt for dependable information.

As Java continues to grow, expanding and overlapping with other exciting new technologies such as Jini and XML, you can continue to trust O'Reilly to help cut through the hype and provide the insight, accuracy, and thoroughness of coverage you need.

So when you're hungry for information, sink your teeth into our Java Series for reliable, in-depth solutions to your meatiest technical problems.

Ask your favorite bookseller about O'Reilly Java books.

For more information go to **java.oreilly.com**
or call **800-998-9938**
or 707-829-0515

THE O'REILLY® JAVA SERIES

A DIFFERENT KIND of Animal

O'REILLY®
java.oreilly.com

Creating objects costs time and CPU effort for an application. Garbage collection and memory recycling cost more time and CPU effort. The difference in object usage between two algorithms can make a huge difference. In Chapter 5, *Strings*, I cover algorithms for appending basic data types to `StringBuffer` objects. These can be an order of magnitude faster than some of the conversions supplied with Java. A significant portion of the speedup is obtained by avoiding extra temporary objects used and discarded during the data conversions.*

Here are a few general guidelines for using object memory efficiently:

- Avoid creating objects in frequently used routines. Because these routines are called frequently, you will likely be creating objects frequently, and consequently adding heavily to the overall burden of object cycling. By rewriting such routines to avoid creating objects, possibly by passing in reusable objects as parameters, you can decrease object cycling.

- Try to presize any collection object to be as big as it will need to be. It is better for the object to be slightly bigger than necessary than to be smaller than it needs to be. This recommendation really applies to collections that implement size increases in such a way that objects are discarded. For example, `Vector` grows by creating a new larger internal array object, copying all the elements from and discarding the old array. Most collection implementations have similar implementations for growing the collection beyond its current capacity, so presizing a collection to its largest potential size reduces the number of objects discarded.

- When multiple instances of a class need access to a particular object in a variable local to those instances, it is better to make that variable a static variable rather than have each instance hold a separate reference. This reduces the space taken by each object (one less instance variable) and can also reduce the number of objects created if each instance creates a separate object to populate that instance variable.

- Reuse exception instances when you do not specifically require a stack trace (see "Exceptions" in Chapter 6, *Exceptions, Casts, and Variables*).

This chapter presents many other standard techniques to avoid using too many objects, and identifies some known inefficiencies when using some types of objects.

---

* Up to Java 1.3. Data-conversion performance is targeted by JavaSoft, however, so some of the data conversions may speed up after 1.3.

Object-Creation Statistics

Objects need to be created before they can be used, and garbage-collected when they are finished with. The more objects you use, the heavier this garbage-cycling impact becomes. General object-creation statistics are actually quite difficult to measure decisively, since you must decide exactly what to measure, what size to pregrow the heap space to, how much garbage collection impacts the creation process if you let it kick in, etc.

For example, on a medium Pentium II, with heap space pregrown so that garbage collection does not have to kick in, you can get around half a million to a million simple objects created per second. If the objects are very simple, even more can be garbage-collected in one second. On the other hand, if the objects are complex, with references to other objects, and include arrays (like `Vector` and `StringBuffer`) and nonminimal constructors, the statistics plummet to less than a quarter of a million created per second, and garbage collection can drop way down to below 100,000 objects per second. Each object creation is roughly as expensive as a *malloc* in C, or a *new* in C++, and there is no easy way of creating many objects together, so you cannot take advantage of efficiencies you get using bulk allocation.

There are already runtime systems that use generational garbage collection, minimize object-creation overhead, and optimize native-code compilation. By doing this they reach up to three million objects created and collected per second (on a Pentium II), and it is likely that the average Java system should improve to get closer to that kind of performance over time. But these figures are for basic tests, optimized to show the maximum possible object-creation throughput. In a normal application with varying size objects and constructor chains, these sorts of figures cannot be obtained or even approached. Also bear in mind that you are doing nothing else in these tests apart from creating objects. In most applications, you are usually doing something with all those objects, making everything much slower but significantly more useful. Avoidable object creation is definitely a significant overhead for most applications, and you can easily run through millions of temporary objects using inefficient algorithms that create too many objects. In Chapter 5, we look at an example that uses the `StreamTokenizer` class. This class creates and dereferences a huge number of objects while it parses a stream, and the effect is to slow down processing to a crawl. The example in Chapter 5 presents a simple alternative to using a `StreamTokenizer`, which is 100 times faster: a large percentage of the speedup is gained from avoiding cycling through objects.

Note that different VM environments produce different figures. If you plot object size against object-creation time for various environments, most plots are monotonically increasing, i.e., it takes more time to create larger objects. But there are discrepancies here too. For example, Netscape Version 4 running on Windows has the peculiar behavior that objects of size 4 and 12 ints are created fastest (refer to *http://www.javaworld.com/javaworld/jw-09-1998/jw-09-speed.html*). Also, note that JIT VMs actually have a worse problem with object creation relative to other VM activities, because JIT VMs can speed up almost every other activity, but object creation is nearly as slow as if the JIT compiler was not there.

Object Reuse

As we saw in the last section, objects are expensive to create. Where it is reasonable to reuse the same object, you should do so. You need to be aware of when not to call new. One fairly obvious situation is when you have already used an object and can discard it before you are about to create another object of the same class. You should look at the object and consider whether it is possible to reset the fields and then reuse the object, rather than throw it away and create another. This can be particularly important for objects that are constantly used and discarded: for example, in graphics processing, objects such as Rectangles, Points, Colors, and Fonts are used and discarded all the time. Recycling these types of objects can certainly improve performance.

Recycling can also apply to the internal elements of structures. For example, a linked list has nodes added to it as it grows, and as it shrinks, the nodes are discarded. Holding on to the discarded nodes is an obvious way to recycle these objects and reduce the cost of object creation.

Pool Management

Most container objects (e.g., Vectors, Hashtables) can be reused rather than created and thrown away. Of course, while you are not using the retained objects, you are holding on to more memory than if you simply discarded those objects, and this reduces the memory available to create other objects. You need to balance the need to have some free memory available against the need to improve performance by reusing objects. But generally, the space taken by retaining objects for later reuse is significant only for very large collections, and you should certainly know which ones these are in your application.

Note that when recycling container objects, you need to dereference all the elements previously in the container so that you don't prevent them from being garbage collected. Because there is this extra overhead in recycling, it may not always be worth recycling containers. As usual for tuning, this technique is best applied to ameliorate an object-creation bottleneck that has already been identified.

A good strategy for reusing container objects is to use your own container classes, possibly wrapping other containers. This gives you a high degree of control over

each collection object, and you can design these specifically for reuse. You can still
use a pool manager to manage your requirements, even without reuse-designed
classes. Reusing classes requires extra work when you've finished with a collection
object, but the effort is worth it when reuse is possible. The code fragment here
shows how you could use a vector pool manager:

```
//An instance of the vector pool manager.
public static VectorPoolManager vectorPoolManager =
    new VectorPoolManager(25);

...

public void someMethod()
{
  //Get a new Vector. We only use the vector to do some stuff
  //within this method, and then we dump the vector (i.e. it
  //is not returned or assigned to a state variable)
  //so this is a perfect candidate for reusing Vectors.
  //Use a factory method instead of 'new Vector()'
  Vector v = vectorPoolManager.getVector();

  ... //do vector manipulation stuff

  //and the extra work is that we have to explicitly tell the
  //pool manager that we have finished with the vector
  vectorPoolManager.returnVector(v);
}
```

Note that nothing stops the application from retaining a handle on a vector after
it has been returned to the pool, and obviously that could lead to a classic "inad-
vertent reuse of memory" bug. You need to ensure that handles to vectors are not
held anywhere: these Vectors should be used only internally within an application, not externally in third-party classes where a handle may be retained. The following class manages a pool of Vectors:

```
package tuning.reuse;

import java.util.Vector;

public class VectorPoolManager
{

  Vector[] pool;
  boolean[] inUse;
  public VectorPoolManager(int initialPoolSize)
  {
    pool = new Vector[initialPoolSize];
    inUse = new boolean[initialPoolSize];
    for (int i = pool.length-1; i>=0; i--)
    {
```

```
      pool[i] = new Vector();
      inUse[i] = false;
   }
}

public synchronized Vector getVector()
{
   for (int i = inUse.length-1; i >= 0; i--)
      if (!inUse[i])
      {
         inUse[i] = true;
         return pool[i];
      }

   //If we got here, then all the Vectors are in use. We will
   //increase the number in our pool by 10 (arbitrary value for
   //illustration purposes).
   boolean[] old_inUse = inUse;
   inUse = new boolean[old_inUse.length+10];
   System.arraycopy(old_inUse, 0, inUse, 0, old_inUse.length);

   Vector[] old_pool = pool;
   pool = new Vector[old_pool.length+10];
   System.arraycopy(old_pool, 0, pool, 0, old_pool.length);

   for (int i = old_pool.length; i < pool.length; i++)
   {
      pool[i] = new Vector();
      inUse[i] = false;
   }

   //and allocate the last Vector
   inUse[pool.length-1] = true;
   return pool[pool.length-1];
}

public synchronized void returnVector(Vector v)
{
   for (int i = inUse.length-1; i >= 0; i--)
      if (pool[i] == v)
      {
         inUse[i] = false;
         //Can use clear() for java.util.Collection objects
         //Note that setSize() nulls out all elements
         v.setSize(0);
         return;
      }
   throw new RuntimeException("Vector was not obtained from the pool: " + v);
}
}
```

Because you reset the Vector size to 0 when it is returned to the pool, all objects previously referenced from the vector are no longer referenced (the Vector. setSize() method nulls out all internal index entries beyond the new size to ensure no reference is retained). However, at the same time, you do not return any memory allocated to the Vector itself, because the Vector's current capacity is retained. A lazily initialized version of this class simply starts with zero items in the pool and sets the pool to grow by one or more each time.

(Many JDK collection classes, including java.util.Vector, have both a size and a capacity. The capacity is the number of elements the collection can hold before that collection needs to resize its internal memory to be larger. The size is the number of externally accessible elements the collection is actually holding. The capacity is always greater than or equal to the size. By holding spare capacity, elements can be added to collections without having to continually resize the underlying memory. This makes element addition faster and more efficient.)

ThreadLocals

The previous example of a pool manager can be used by multiple threads in a multithreaded application, although the getVector() and returnVector() methods first need to be defined as synchronized. This may be all you need to ensure that you reuse a set of objects in a multithreaded application. Sometimes though, there are objects you need to use in a more complicated way. It may be that the objects are used in such a way that you can guarantee you need only one object per thread, but any one thread must consistently use the same object. Singletons (see the "Canonicalizing Objects" section) that maintain some state information are a prime example of this sort of object.

In this case, you might want to use a ThreadLocal object. ThreadLocals have accessors that return an object local to the current thread. ThreadLocal use is best illustrated using an example; this one produces:

```
[This is thread 0, This is thread 0, This is thread 0]
[This is thread 1, This is thread 1, This is thread 1]
[This is thread 2, This is thread 2, This is thread 2]
[This is thread 3, This is thread 3, This is thread 3]
[This is thread 4, This is thread 4, This is thread 4]
```

Each thread uses the same access method to obtain a vector to add some elements. The vector obtained by each thread is always the same vector for that thread: the ThreadLocal object always returns the thread-specific vector. As the following code shows, each vector has the same string added to it repeatedly, showing that it is always obtaining the same thread-specific vector from the vector access method. (Note that ThreadLocals are only available from Java 2, but it is easy to create the equivalent functionality using a Hashtable: see the getVectorPriorToJDK12() method.)

```java
package tuning.reuse;

import java.util.*;

public class ThreadedAccess
  implements Runnable
{
  static int ThreadCount = 0;

  public void run()
  {
    //simple test just accesses the thread local vector, adds the
    //thread specific string to it, and sleeps for two seconds before
    //again accessing the thread local and printing out the value.
    String s = "This is thread " + ThreadCount++;
    Vector v = getVector();
    v.addElement(s);
    v = getVector();
    v.addElement(s);
    try{Thread.sleep(2000);}catch(Exception e){}
    v = getVector();
    v.addElement(s);
    System.out.println(v);
  }

  public static void main(String[] args)
  {
    try
    {
      //Four threads to see the multithreaded nature at work
      for (int i = 0; i < 5; i++)
      {
        (new Thread(new ThreadedAccess())).start();
        try{Thread.sleep(200);}catch(Exception e){}
      }
    }
    catch(Exception e){e.printStackTrace();}
  }

  private static ThreadLocal vectors = new ThreadLocal();
  public static Vector getVector()
  {
    //Lazily initialized version. Get the thread local object
    Vector v = (Vector) vectors.get();
    if (v == null)
    {
```

```
            //First time. So create a vector and set the ThreadLocal
            v = new Vector();
            vectors.set(v);
        }
        return v;
    }


    private static Hashtable hvectors = new Hashtable();
    /* This method is equivalent to the getVector() method,
     * but works prior to JDK 1.2 (as well as after).
     */
    public static Vector getVectorPriorToJDK12()
    {
        //Lazily initialized version. Get the thread local object
        Vector v = (Vector) hvectors.get(Thread.currentThread());
        if (v == null)
        {
            //First time. So create a vector and set the thread local
            v = new Vector();
            hvectors.put(Thread.currentThread(), v);
        }
        return v;
    }
}
```

Reusable Parameters

Reuse also applies when a constant object is returned for information. For example, the `preferredSize()` of a customized widget returns a `Dimension` object that is normally one particular dimension. But to ensure that the stored unchanging `Dimension` value does not get altered, you need to return a copy of the stored `Dimension`. Otherwise, the calling method accesses the original `Dimension` object and can change the `Dimension` values, thus affecting the original `Dimension` object itself.

Java provides a `final` modifier to fields that allows you to provide fixed values for the `Dimension` fields. Unfortunately, you cannot redefine an already existing class, so `Dimension` cannot be redefined to have `final` fields. The best solution in this case is that a separate class, `FixedDimension`, be defined with `final` fields (this cannot be a subclass of `Dimension`, as the fields can't be redefined in the subclass). This extra class allows methods to return the same `FixedDimension` object if applicable, or a new `FixedDimension` is returned (as happens with `Dimension`) if the method requires different values to be returned for different states. Of course, it is too late now for `java.awt` to be changed in this way, but the principle remains.

Note that making a field `final` does not make an object unchangeable. It only disallows changes to the field:

```
public class FixedDimension {
  final int height;
  final int width;
  ...
}


//Both the following fields are defined as final
public static final Dimension dim = new Dimension(3,4);
public static final FixedDimension fixedDim = new FixedDimension(3,4);


dim.width = 5;             //reassignment allowed
dim = new Dimension(3,5);//reassignment disallowed
fixedDim.width = 5;        //reassignment disallowed
fixedDim = new FixedDimension(3,5); //reassignment disallowed
```

An alternative to defining `preferredSize()` to return a fixed object is to provide a method that accepts an object whose values will be set, e.g., `preferred-Size(Dimension)`. The caller can then pass in a `Dimension` object, which would have its values filled in by the `preferredSize(Dimension)` method. The calling method can then access the values in the `Dimension` object. This same `Dimension` object can be reused for multiple components. This design pattern is beginning to be used extensively within the JDK. Many methods developed with JDK 1.2 and onward accept a parameter that is filled in, rather than returning a copy of the master value of some object. If necessary, backward compatibility can be retained by adding this method as extra, rather than replacing an existing method:

```
public static final Dimension someSize = new Dimension(10,5);
//original definition returns a new Dimension.
public Dimension someSize() {
  Dimension dim = new Dimension(0,0);
  someSize(dim);
  return dim;
}
//New method which fills in the Dimension details in a passed parameter.
public void someSize(Dimension dim) {
  dim.width = someSize.width;
  dim.width = someSize.height;
}
```

Canonicalizing Objects

Wherever possible, you should replace multiple objects with a single object (or just a few). For example, if you need only one `VectorPoolManager` object, it makes sense to provide a static variable somewhere that holds this. You can even enforce this by making the constructor private and holding the singleton in the class itself; e.g., change the definition of VectorPoolManager to:

```
public class VectorPoolManager
{
  public static final VectorPoolManager SINGLETON =
    new VectorPoolManager(10);
  Vector[] pool;
  boolean[] inUse;

  //Make the constructor private to enforce that
  //no other objects can be created.
  private VectorPoolManager(int initialPoolSize)
  {
  ...
}
```

An alternative implementation is to make everything static (all methods and both the instance variables in the VectorPoolManager class). This also ensures that only one pool manager can be used. My preference is to have a SINGLETON object for design reasons.*

This activity of replacing multiple copies of an object with just a few objects is often referred to as *canonicalizing* objects. The Booleans provide an existing example of objects that should have been canonicalized in the JDK. They were not, and no longer can be without breaking backward compatibility. For Booleans, only two objects need to exist, but by allowing a new Boolean object to be created (by providing public constructors), you lose canonicalization. The JDK should have enforced the existence of only two objects by keeping the constructors private. Note that canonical objects have another advantage in addition to reducing the number of objects created: they also allow comparison by identity. For example:

```
Boolean t1 = new Boolean(true);
System.out.println(t1==Boolean.TRUE);
System.out.println(t1.equals(Boolean.TRUE));
```

produces the output:

```
false
true
```

---

* The VectorPoolManager is really an object with behavior and state. It is not just a related group of functions (which is what class static methods are equivalent to). My colleague Kirk Pepperdine insists that this choice is more than just a preference. He states that holding on to an object as opposed to using statics provides more flexibility should you need to alter the use of the VectorPoolManager or provide multiple pools. I agree.

If `Booleans` had been canonicalized, all `Boolean` comparisons could be done by identity: comparison by identity is always faster than comparison by equality, because identity comparisons are simply pointer comparisons.*

You are probably better off not canonicalizing all objects that could be canonicalized. For example, the `Integer` class can (theoretically) have its instances canonicalized, but you need a map of some sort, and it is more efficient to allow multiple instances, rather than to manage a potential pool of four billion objects. However, the situation is different for particular applications. If you use just a few `Integer` objects in some defined way, you may find you are repeatedly creating the `Integer` objects with values 1, 2, 3, etc., and also have to access the `integerValue()` to compare them. In this case, you can canonicalize a few integer objects, improving performance in several ways: eliminating the extra `Integer` creations and the garbage collections of these objects when they are discarded, and allowing comparison by identity. For example:

```
public class IntegerManager
{
   public static final Integer ZERO = new Integer(0);
   public static final Integer ONE = new Integer(1);
   public static final Integer TWO = new Integer(2);
   public static final Integer THREE = new Integer(3);
   public static final Integer FOUR = new Integer(4);
   public static final Integer FIVE = new Integer(5);
   public static final Integer SIX = new Integer(6);
   public static final Integer SEVEN = new Integer(7);
   public static final Integer EIGHT = new Integer(8);
   public static final Integer NINE = new Integer(9);
   public static final Integer TEN = new Integer(10);
}

public class SomeClass
{
   public void doSomething(Integer i)
   {
     //Assume that we are passed a canonicalized Integer
     if (i == IntegerManager.ONE)
       xxx();
     else if(i == IntegerManager.FIVE)
       yyy();
     else ...
   }
   ...
}
```

---

* Deserializing `Booleans` would have required special handling to return the canonical `Boolean`. All canonicalized objects similarly require special handling to manage serialization. Java serialization supports the ability, when deserializing, to return specific objects in place of the object that is normally created by the default deserialization mechanism.

There are various other frequently used objects throughout an application that should be canonicalized. A few that spring to mind are the empty string, empty arrays of various types, and some dates.

String canonicalization

There can be some confusion about whether Strings are already canonicalized. There is no guarantee that they are, although the compiler can canonicalize Strings that are equal and are compiled in the same pass. The String.intern() method canonicalizes strings in an internal table. This is supposed to be, and usually is, the same table used by strings canonicalized at compile time, but in some earlier JDK versions (e.g., 1.0), it was not the same table. In any case, there is no particular reason to use the internal string table to canonicalize your strings unless you want to compare Strings by identity (see "String Comparisons and Searches" in Chapter 5). Using your own table gives you more control and allows you to inspect the table when necessary. To see the difference between identity and equality comparisons for Strings, including the difference that String.intern() makes, you can run the following class:

```
public class Test
{
  public static void main(String[] args)
  {
    System.out.println(args[0]); //see that we have the empty string

    //should be true
    System.out.println(args[0].equals(""));

    //should be false since they are not identical objects
    System.out.println(args[0] == "");

    //should be true unless there are two internal string tables
    System.out.println(args[0].intern() == "");
  }
}
```

This Test class, when run with the command line:

```
java Test ""
```

gives the output:

```
true
false
true
```

Changeable objects

Canonicalizing objects is best for read-only objects and can be troublesome for objects that change. If you canonicalize a changeable object and then change its state, then all objects that have a reference to the canonicalized object are still pointing to that object, but with the object's new state. For example, suppose you canonicalize a special Date value. If that object has its date value changed, all objects pointing to that Date object now see a different date value. This result may be desired, but more often it is a bug.

If you want to canonicalize changeable objects, one technique to make it slightly safer is to wrap the object with another one, or use your own (sub)class.* Then all accesses and updates are controlled by you. If the object is not supposed to be changed, you can throw an exception on any update method. Alternatively, if you want some objects to be canonicalized but with copy-on-write behavior, you can allow the updater to return a noncanonicalized copy of the canonical object.

Note that it makes no sense to build a table of millions or even thousands of strings (or other objects) if the time taken to test for, access, and update objects in the table is longer than the time you are saving canonicalizing them.

Weak references

One technique for maintaining collections of objects that can grow too large is the use of WeakReferences (from the java.lang.ref package in Java 2). If you need to maintain one or more pools of objects with a large number of objects being held, you may start coming up against memory limits of the VM. In this case, you should consider using WeakReference objects to hold on to your pool elements. Objects referred to by WeakReferences can be automatically garbage-collected if memory gets low enough (see the "Reference Objects" sidebar).

A WeakReference normally maintains references to elements in a table of canonicalized objects. If memory gets low, any of the objects referred to by the table and not referred to anywhere else in the application (except by other weak references) are garbage-collected. This does not affect the canonicalization because only those objects not referenced anywhere else are removed. The canonical object can be re-created when required, and this new instance is now the new canonical object: remember that no other references to the object exist, or the original could not have been garbage-collected.

For example, a table of canonical Integer objects can be maintained using WeakReferences. This example is not particularly useful: unlike the earlier example, in which Integer objects from 1 to 10 can be referenced directly with

---

* Beware that using a subclass may break the superclass semantics.

Reference Objects

In many ways, you can think of `Reference` objects as normal objects that have a private `Object` instance variable. You can access the private object (termed the *referent*) using the `Reference.get()` method. However, `Reference` objects differ from normal objects in one hugely important way. The garbage collector may be allowed to clear `Reference` objects when it decides space is low enough. Clearing the `Reference` object sets the referent to `null`. For example, say you assign an object to a `Reference`. Later you test to see if the referent is `null`. It could be `null` if, between the assignment and the test, the garbage collector kicked in and decided to reclaim space:

```
Reference ref = new WeakReference(someObject);
//ref.get() is someObject at the moment
//Now do something that creates lots of objects, making
//the garbage collector try to find more memory space
doSomething();

//now test if ref is null
if (ref.get() == null)
  System.out.println("The garbage collector deleted my ref");
else
  System.out.println("ref object is still here");
```

Note that the referent can be garbage-collected at any time, as long as there are no other strong references referring to it. (In the example, `ref.get()` can become `null` only if there are no other non-`Reference` objects referring to `someObject`.)

The advantage of `References` is that you can use them to hang on to objects that you want to reuse but are not needed immediately. If memory space gets too low, those objects not currently being used are automatically reclaimed by the garbage collector. This means that you subsequently need to create objects instead of reusing them, but that is preferable to having the program crash from lack of memory. (To delete the reference object itself when the referent is nulled, you need to create the reference with a `ReferenceQueue` instance. When the reference object is cleared, it is added to the `ReferenceQueue` instance and can then be processed by the application, e.g., explicitly deleted from a hash table in which it may be a key.)

—Continued—

There are three Reference types in Java 2. WeakReferences and SoftReferences differ essentially in the order in which the garbage collector clears them. Basically, the garbage collector does not clear WeakReference objects until all SoftReferences have been cleared. PhantomReferences (not addressed here) are not cleared automatically by the garbage collector and are intended for use in a different way.

The concept behind this differentiation is that SoftReferences are intended to be used for caches that may need to have memory automatically freed, and WeakReferences are intended for canonical tables that may need to have memory automatically freed.

The rationale is that caches normally take up more space and are the first to be reclaimed when memory gets low. Canonical tables are normally smaller, and developers prefer them not to be garbage-collected unless memory gets really low. This differentiation between the two reference types allows cache memory to be freed up first if memory gets low; only when there is no more cache memory to be freed does the garbage collector start looking at canonical table memory.

Java 2 comes with a java.util.WeakHashMap class that implements a hash table with keys held by weak references.

no overhead, thus providing a definite speedup for tests, the next example has overheads that would probably swamp any benefits of having canonical Integers. I present it only as a clear and simple example to illustrate the use of WeakReferences.

The example has two iterations: one sets an array of canonical Integer objects up to a value set by the command-line argument; a second loops through to access the first 10 canonical Integers. If the first loop is large enough (or the VM memory is constrained low enough), the garbage collector kicks in and starts reclaiming some of the Integer objects that are all being held by WeakReferences. The second loop then reaccesses the first 10 Integer objects. Earlier, I explicitly held on to five of these Integer objects (integers 3 to 7 inclusive) in variables so that they could not be garbage-collected, and so that the second loop would reset only the five reclaimed Integers. When running this test with the VM constrained to 4 MB:

```
java -Xmx4M  tuning.reuse.Test 100000
```

you get the following output:

```
Resetting integer 0
Resetting integer 1
Resetting integer 2
Resetting integer 8
Resetting integer 9
```

The example is defined here. Note the overheads. Even if the reference has not been garbage-collected, you have to access the underlying object and cast it to the desired type:

```
package tuning.reuse;

import java.util.*;
import java.lang.ref.*;

public class Test
{
  public static void main(String[] args)
  {
    try
    {
      Integer ic = null;
      int REPEAT = args.length > 0 ? Integer.parseInt(args[0]) : 10000000;

      //Hang on to the Integer objects from 3 to 7
      //so that they cannot be garbage collected
      Integer i3 = getCanonicalInteger(3);
      Integer i4 = getCanonicalInteger(4);
      Integer i5 = getCanonicalInteger(5);
      Integer i6 = getCanonicalInteger(6);
      Integer i7 = getCanonicalInteger(7);

      //Loop through getting canonical integers until there is not
      //enough space, and the garbage collector reclaims some.
      for (int i = 0; i < REPEAT; i++)
        ic = getCanonicalInteger(i);

      //Now just re-access the first 10 integers (0 to 9) and
      //the 0, 1, 2, 8, and 9 integers will need to be reset in
      //the access method since they will have been reclaimed
      for (int i = 0; i < 10; i++)
        ic = getCanonicalInteger(i);
      System.out.println(ic);
    }
    catch(Exception e){e.printStackTrace();}
  }

  private static Vector canonicalIntegers = new Vector();
  public static Integer getCanonicalInteger(int i)
  {
    //First make sure our collection is big enough
    if (i >= canonicalIntegers.size())
      canonicalIntegers.setSize(i+1);
```

```
//Now access the canonical value.
//This element contains null if the the value has never been set
//or a weak reference that may have been garbage collected
WeakReference ref = (WeakReference) canonicalIntegers.elementAt(i);
Integer canonical_i;

if (ref == null)
{
  //never been set, so create and set it now
  canonical_i = new Integer(i);
  canonicalIntegers.setElementAt(new WeakReference(canonical_i), i);
}
else if( (canonical_i = (Integer) ref.get()) == null)
{
  //has been set, but was garbage collected, so recreate and set it now
  //Include a print to see that we are resetting the Integer
  System.out.println("Resetting integer " + i);
  canonical_i = new Integer(i);
  canonicalIntegers.setElementAt(new WeakReference(canonical_i), i);
}
//else clause not needed, since the alternative is that the weak ref was
//present and not garbage collected, so we now have our canonical integer
return canonical_i;
  }


}
```

Enumerating constants

Another canonicalization technique often used is replacing constant objects with integers. For example, rather than use the strings "female" and "male", you should use a constant defined in an interface:

```
public interface GENDER
{
  public static final int FEMALE=1;
  public static final int MALE=2;
}
```

Used consistently, this enumeration can provide both speed and memory advantages. The enumeration requires less memory than the equivalent strings and makes network transfers faster. Comparisons are faster too, as the identity comparison can be used instead of the equality comparison. For example, you can use:

```
this.gender == FEMALE;
```

instead of:

```
this.gender.equals("female");
```

Avoiding Garbage Collection

The canonicalization techniques I've discussed are one way to avoid garbage collection: fewer objects means less to garbage-collect. Similarly, the pooling technique in that section also tends to reduce garbage-collection requirements, partly because you are creating fewer objects by reusing them, and partly because you deallocate memory less often by holding on to the objects you have allocated. Of course, this also means that your memory requirements are higher, but you can't have it both ways.

Another technique for reducing garbage-collection impact is to avoid using objects where they are not needed. For example, there is no need to create an extra unnecessary Integer to parse a String containing an int value, as in:

```
String string = "55";
int theInt = new Integer(string).intValue()
```

Instead, there is a static method available for parsing:

```
int theInt = Integer.parseInt(string);
```

Unfortunately, some classes do not provide static methods that avoid the spurious intermediate creation of objects. Until JDK Version 1.2, there were no static methods that allowed you to parse strings containing floating-point numbers to get doubles or floats. Instead, you needed to create an intermediate Double object and extract the value. (Even after JDK 1.2, an intermediate FloatingDecimal is created, but this is arguably due to good abstraction in the programming design.) When a class does not provide a static method, you can sometimes use a dummy instance to repeatedly execute instance methods, thus avoiding the need to create extra objects.

The primitive data types in Java use memory space that also needs reclaiming, but the overhead in reclaiming data-type storage is smaller: it is reclaimed at the same time as its holding object and so has a smaller impact. (Temporary primitive data types exist only on the stack and do not need to be garbage-collected at all: see the section "Variables" in Chapter 6 for more on this.) For example, an object with just one instance variable holding an int is reclaimed in one object reclaim, whereas if it holds an Integer object, the garbage collector needs to reclaim two objects.

Reducing garbage collection by using primitive data types also applies when you can hold an object in a primitive data-type format rather than another format. For example, if you have a large number of objects each with a String instance variable holding a number (e.g., "1492", "1997"), it is better to make that instance variable an int data type and store the numbers as ints, provided that the conversion overheads do not swamp the benefits of holding the values in this alternative format.

Similarly, you can use an int (or long) to represent a Date object, providing appropriate calculations to access and update the values, thus saving an object and the associated garbage overhead. Of course, you have a different runtime overhead instead, as those conversion calculations may take up more time.

A more extreme version of this technique is to use arrays to map objects: for example, see the section "Search Trees" in Chapter 11, *Appropriate Data Structures and Algorithms.* Towards the end of that example, one version of the class gets rid of node objects completely, using a large array to map and maintain all instances and instance variables. This leads to a large improvement in performance at all stages of the object life cycle. Of course, this technique is a specialized one that should not be used generically throughout your application, or you will end up with unmaintainable code. It should be used only when called for (and when it can be completely encapsulated). A simple example is for the class defined as:

```
class MyClass
{
  int x;
  boolean y;
}
```

This class has an associated collection class that seems to hold an array of MyClass objects, but that actually holds arrays of instance variables of the MyClass class:

```
class MyClassCollection
{
  int[] xs;
  boolean[] ys;
  public int getXForElement(int i) {return xs[i];}
  public boolean getYForElement(int i) {return ys[i];}
  //If possible avoid having to declare element access like the
  //following method:
  //public MyClass getElement(int i) {return new MyClass(xs[i], ys[i]);}
}
```

An extension of this technique flattens objects that have a one-to-one relationship. The classic example is a Person object that holds a Name object, consisting of first name and last name (and collection of middle names), and an Address object, with street, number, etc. This can be collapsed down to just the Person object, with all the fields moved up to the Person class. For example, the original definition consists of three classes:

```
public class Person {
  private Name name;
  private Address address;
}
```

```
class Name {
  private String firstName;
  private String lastName;
  private String[] otherNames;
}
class Address {
  private int houseNumber;
  private String houseName;
  private String streetName;
  private String town;
  private String area;
  private String greaterArea;
  private String country;
  private String postCode;
}
```

These three classes collapse into one class:

```
public class Person {
  private String firstName;
  private String lastName;
  private String[] otherNames;
  private int houseNumber;
  private String houseName;
  private String streetName;
  private String town;
  private String area;
  private String greaterArea;
  private String country;
  private String postCode;
}
```

This results in the same data and the same functionality (assuming that Addresses and Names are not referenced by more than one Person). But now you have one object instead of three for each Person. Of course, this violates the good design of an application and should not be used as standard, only when absolutely necessary.

Finally, here are some general recommendations that help to reduce the number of unnecessary objects being generated. These recommendations should be part of your standard coding practice, not just performance-related:

• Reduce the number of temporary objects being used, especially in loops. It is easy to use a method in a loop that has side effects such as making copies, or an accessor that returns a copy of some object you only need once.

• Use StringBuffer in preference to the String concatenation operator (+). This is really a special case of the previous point, but needs to be emphasized.

- Be aware of which methods alter objects directly without making copies and which ones return a copy of an object. For example, any `String` method that changes the string (such as `String.trim()`) returns a new `String` object, whereas a method like `Vector.setSize()` does not return a copy. If you do not need a copy, use (or create) methods that do not return a copy of the object being operated on.

- Avoid using generic classes that handle `Object` types when you are dealing with basic data types. For example, there is no need to use `Vector` to store `ints` by wrapping them in `Integers`. Instead, implement an `IntVector` class that holds the `ints` directly.

Initialization

All chained constructors are automatically called when creating an object with **new**. Chaining more constructors for a particular object causes extra overhead at object creation, as does initializing instance variables more than once. Be aware of the default values that Java initializes variables to:

- `null` for objects
- 0 for integer types of all lengths (`byte`, `char`, `short`, `int`, `long`)
- `0.0` for float types (`float` and `double`)
- `false` for `booleans`

There is no need to reinitialize these values in the constructor (although an optimizing compiler should be able to eliminate the extra redundant statement). Generalizing this point: if you can identify that the creation of a particular object is a bottleneck, either because it takes too long or because a great many of those objects are being created, you should check the constructor hierarchy to eliminate any multiple initializations to instance variables.

You can avoid constructors by unmarshalling objects from a serialized stream, because deserialization does not use constructors. However, serializing and deserializing objects is a CPU-intensive procedure and is unlikely to speed up your application. There is another way to avoid constructors when creating objects, namely by creating a `clone()` of an object. You can create new instances of classes that implement the `Cloneable` interface using the `clone()` method. These new instances do not call any class constructor, thus allowing you to avoid the constructor initializations. Cloning does not save a lot of time because the main overhead in creating an object is in the creation, not the initialization. However, when there are extensive initializations or many objects generated from a class with some significant initialization, this technique can help.

If you have followed the factory design pattern,* it is relatively simple to reimplement the original factory method to use a clone. For example, the original factory method can be defined similar to:

```
public static Something getNewSomething()
{
  return new Something();
}
```

The replaced implementation that uses cloning looks like:

```
private static Something MASTER_Something = new Something();
public static Something getNewSomething()
{
  return (Something) MASTER_Something.clone();
}
```

If you have not followed the factory design pattern, you may need to track down all calls that create a new instance of the relevant class and replace those calls. Note that the cloned object is still initialized, but the initialization is not the constructor initialization. Instead, the initialization consists of assigning exactly once to each instance variable of the new (cloned) object, using the instance variables of the object being cloned.

Java arrays all support cloning. This allows you to manage a similar trick when it comes to initializing arrays. But first let's see why you would want to clone an array for performance reasons.

When you create an array in code, using the curly braces to assign a newly created array to an array variable like this:

```
int[] array1 = {1,2,3,4,5,6,7,8,9};
```

you might imagine that the compiler creates an array in the compiled file, leaving a nice structure to be pulled in to memory. In fact, this is not what happens. The array is still created at runtime, with all the elements initialized then. Because of this, you should specify arrays just once, probably as a `static`, and assign that array as required. In most cases this is enough, and there is nothing further to improve on because the array is created just once. But sometimes you have a routine for which you want to create a new array each time you execute it. In this case,

---

* The factory design pattern recommends that object creation be centralized in a particular *factory method*. So instead of directly calling `new Something()` in the code to create an instance of the Something class, you call a method such as `SomethingFactory.getNewSomething()`, which creates and returns a new instance of the Something class. This is actually detrimental for performance, as there is the overhead of an extra method call for every object creation, but the pattern does provide more flexibility when it comes to tuning. My inclination is to use the factory pattern. If you identify a particular factory method as a bottleneck when performance-tuning, you can relatively easily inline that factory method using a preprocessor.

the complexity of the array determines how efficient the array creation is. If the array is quite complex, it is faster to hold a reference copy and clone that reference than it is to create a new array. For instance, the array example shown previously as `array1` is simple and therefore faster to create, as shown in that example. But the following more complex array, `array2`, is faster to create as a cloned array:

```
static int[] Ref_array1 = {1,2,3,4,5,6,7,8,9};
static int[][] Ref_array2 = {{1,2},{3,4},{5,6},{7,8}};

int[] array1 = {1,2,3,4,5,6,7,8,9};         //faster than cloning
int[] array1 = (int[]) Ref_array1.clone();  //slower than initializing

int[][] array2 = {{1,2},{3,4},{5,6},{7,8}}; //slower than cloning
int[][] array2 = (int[]) Ref_array2.clone();//faster than initializing
```

Early and Late Initialization

The final two sections of this chapter discuss two seemingly opposing tuning techniques. The first section, "Preallocating Objects," presents the technique of creating objects before they are needed. This technique is useful when a large number of objects need to be created at a time when CPU power is needed for other routines, and where those objects could feasibly be created earlier, at a time when there is ample spare CPU power.

The second section, "Lazy Initialization," presents the technique of delaying object creation until the last possible moment. This technique is useful for avoiding unnecessary object creation when only a few objects are used although many possible objects can be created.

In fact, these techniques represent two sides of the same coin: moving object creation from one time to another. Preallocating moves object creation to a time earlier than you would normally create those objects; lazy initialization moves object creation to a later time (or never).

Preallocating Objects

There may be situations in which you cannot avoid creating particular objects in significant amounts: perhaps they are necessary for the application and no reasonable amount of tuning has managed to reduce the object-creation overhead for them. If the creation time has been identified as a bottleneck, it is possible that you can still create the objects, but move the creation time to a part of the application when more spare cycles are available or there is more flexibility in response times.

The idea here is to choose another time to create some or all of the objects (perhaps in a partially initialized stage), and store those objects until they are needed. Again, if you have followed the factory design pattern, it is relatively simple to replace the `return new Something()` statement with an access to the collection of spare objects (presumably testing for a nonempty collection as well). If you have not followed the factory design pattern, you may need to track down all calls that create a new instance of the relevant class and replace them with a call to the factory method. For the real creation, you might want to spawn a background (low-priority) thread to churn out objects and add them into the storage collection until you run out of time, space, or necessity.

This is a variation of the "read-ahead" concept, and you can also apply this idea to:

- Classloading (obviously not for classes needed as soon as the application starts up): see "Uncompressed ZIP/JAR Files" in Chapter 3, *Underlying JDK Improvements.*

- Distributed objects: see Chapter 12, *Distributed Computing.*

- Reading in external data files.

Lazy Initialization

Lazy initialization means that you do not initialize objects until the first time they are used. Typically, this comes about when you are unsure of what initial value an instance variable might have but want to provide a default. Rather than initialize explicitly in the constructor (or class static initializer), it is left until access time for the variable to be initialized, using a test for `null` to determine if it has been initialized. For example:

```
public getSomething()
{
  if (something == null)
    something = defaultSomething();
  return something;
}
```

I find this kind of construct quite often in code (too often, in my opinion). I can only rarely see a justifiable reason for using lazy initialization. Not deciding where to initialize a variable correctly is more often a result of lazy design or lazy coding. The result can be many tests for `null` executing when you access your variables, and these `null` tests never go away: they are always performed, even after the variable has been initialized. In the worst case, this can impact performance badly, although generally the overhead is small and can be ignored. I always recommend avoiding the use of lazy initialization for general coding.

On the other hand, there are particular design situations in which it is appropriate to use lazy initialization. A good example is classloading, where classes are loaded dynamically as required. This is a specific design situation in which it is clear there will be a performance impact on running applications, but the design of the Java runtime merited this for the features that it brought.

Lazy initialization can be a useful performance-tuning technique. As usual, you should be tuning after functionality is present in your application, so I am not recommending using lazy initialization before the tuning stage. But there are places where you can change objects to be lazily initialized and make a large gain. Specifically, these are objects or variables of objects that may never be used. For example, if you need to make available a large choice of objects, of which only a few will actually be used in the application (e.g., based on a user's choice), then you are better off not instantiating or initializing these objects until they are actually used. An example is the char-to-byte encoding provided by the JDK. Only a few (usually one) of these are used, so you do not need to provide every type of encoding, fully initialized, to the application. Only the required encoding needs to be used.

When you have thousands of objects that need complex initializations but only a few will actually be used, lazy initialization provides a significant speedup to an application by avoiding exercising code that may never be run. A related situation in which lazy initialization can be used for performance tuning is when there are many objects that need to be created and initialized, and most of these objects will be used, but not immediately. In this case, it can be useful to spread out the load of object initialization so you don't get one large hit on the application. It may be better to let a background thread initialize all the objects slowly or to use lazy initialization to take many small or negligible hits, thus spreading the load over time. This is essentially the same technique as for preallocation of objects (see the previous section).

It is true that many of these kinds of situations should be anticipated at the design stage, in which case you could build lazy initialization into the application from the beginning. But this is quite an easy change to make (usually affecting just the accessors of a few classes), and so there is usually little reason to over-engineer the application prior to tuning.

Performance Checklist

Most of these suggestions apply only after a bottleneck has been identified:

- Establish whether you have a memory problem.

- Reduce the number of temporary objects being used, especially in loops.

  — Avoid creating temporary objects within frequently called methods.

  — Presize collection objects.

  — Reuse objects where possible.

  — Empty collection objects before reusing them. (Do not shrink them unless they are very large.)

  — Use custom conversion methods for converting between data types (especially strings and streams) to reduce the number of temporary objects.

  — Define methods that accept reusable objects to be filled in with data, rather than methods that return objects holding that data. (Or you can return immutable objects.)

  — Canonicalize objects wherever possible. Compare canonicalized objects by identity.

  — Create only the number of objects a class logically needs (if that is a small number of objects).

  — Replace strings and other objects with integer constants. Compare these integers by identity.

  — Use primitive data types instead of objects as instance variables.

  — Avoid creating an object that is only for accessing a method.

  — Flatten objects to reduce the number of nested objects.

  — Preallocate storage for large collections of objects by mapping the instance variables into multiple arrays.

  — Use `StringBuffer` rather than the string concatenation operator (+).

  — Use methods that alter objects directly without making copies.

  — Create or use specific classes that handle primitive data types rather than wrapping the primitive data types.

- Consider using a `ThreadLocal` to provide threaded access to singletons with state.

- Use the `final` modifier on instance-variable definitions to create immutable internally accessible objects.

- Use WeakReferences to hold elements in large canonical lookup tables. (Use SoftReferences for cache elements.)

- Reduce object-creation bottlenecks by targeting the object-creation process.

  — Keep constructors simple and inheritance hierarchies shallow.

  — Avoid initializing instance variables more than once.

  — Use the clone() method to avoid calling any constructors.

  — Clone arrays if that makes their creation faster.

  — Create copies of simple arrays faster by initializing them; create copies of complex arrays faster by cloning them.

- Eliminate object-creation bottlenecks by moving object creation to an alternative time.

  — Create objects early, when there is spare time in the application, and hold those objects until required.

  — Use lazy initialization when there are objects or variables that may never be used, or when you need to distribute the load of creating objects.

  — Use lazy initialization only when there is a defined merit in the design, or when identifying a bottleneck which is alleviated using lazy initialization.

5

Strings

Everyone has a logger and most of them are string pigs.

—Kirk Pepperdine

Strings have a special status in Java. They are the only objects with:

- Their own operators (+ and +=)

- A literal form (characters surrounded by double quotes, e.g., "hello")

- Their own externally accessible collection in the VM and class files (i.e., string pools, which provide uniqueness of String objects if the string sequence can be determined at compile time)

Strings are immutable and have a special relationship with StringBuffer objects. A String cannot be altered once created. Applying a method that looks like it changes the String (such as String.trim()) doesn't actually do so; instead, the method returns an altered copy of the String. Strings are also final, and so cannot be subclassed. These points have advantages and disadvantages so far as performance is concerned. For fast string manipulation, the inability to subclass String or access the internal char array can be a serious problem.

The Performance Effects of Strings

Let's first look at the advantages of the String implementation:

- Compilation creates unique strings. At compile time, strings are resolved as far as possible. This includes applying the concatenation operator and converting other literals to strings. So "hi7" and ("hi"+7) both get resolved at compile time to the same string, and are identical objects in the class string pool (see the discussion in "String concatenation is sometimes folded" in Chapter 3, *Underlying JDK Improvements*). Compilers differ in their ability to achieve this resolution. You can always check your compiler (e.g., by decompiling some statements involving concatenation) and change it if needed.

- Because `String` objects are immutable, a substring operation doesn't need to copy the entire underlying sequence of characters. Instead, a substring can use the same `char` array as the original string and simply refer to a different start point and endpoint in the `char` array. This means that substring operations are efficient, being both fast and conserving of memory; the extra object is just a wrapper on the same underlying `char` array with different pointers into that array.[*]

- `Strings` have strong support for internationalization. It would take a large effort to reproduce the internationalization support for an alternative class.

- The close relationship with `StringBuffers` allows `Strings` to reference the same `char` array used by the `StringBuffer`. This is a double-edged sword. For typical practice, when you use a `StringBuffer` to manipulate and append characters and data types, and then convert the final result to a `String`, this works just fine. The `StringBuffer` provides efficient mechanisms for growing, inserting, appending, altering, and other types of `String` manipulation. The resulting `String` then efficiently references the same `char` array with no extra character copying. This is very fast and reduces the number of objects being used to a minimum by avoiding intermediate objects. However, if the `StringBuffer` object is subsequently altered, the `char` array in that `StringBuffer` is copied into a new `char` array that is now referenced by the `StringBuffer`. The `String` object retains the reference to the previously shared `char` array. This means that copying overhead can occur at unexpected points in the application. Instead of the copying occurring at the `toString()` method call, as might be expected, any subsequent alteration of the `StringBuffer` causes a new `char` array to be created and an array copy to be performed. To make the copying overhead occur at predictable times, you could explicitly execute some method that makes the copying occur, such as `StringBuffer.setLength()`. This allows `StringBuffers` to be reused with more predictable performance.

The disadvantages of the `String` implementation are:

- Not being able to subclass `String` means that it is not possible to add behavior to `String` for your own needs.

- The previous point means that all access must be through the restricted set of currently available `String` methods, imposing extra overhead.

---

[*] Strings are implemented in the JDK as an internal `char` array with index offsets (actually a start offset and a character count). This basic structure is extremely unlikely to be changed in any version of Java.

- The only way to increase the number of methods allowing efficient manipulation of `String` characters is to copy the characters into your own array and manipulate them directly, in which case `String` is imposing an extra step and extra objects you may not need.

- char arrays are faster to process directly.

- The tight coupling with `StringBuffer` can lead to unexpectedly high memory usage. When `StringBuffer.toString()` creates a `String`, the current underlying array holds the string, regardless of the size of the array (i.e., the capacity of the `StringBuffer`). For example, a `StringBuffer` with a capacity of 10,000 characters can build a string of 10 characters. However, that 10-character `String` continues to use a 10,000-char array to store the 10 characters. If the `StringBuffer` is now reused to create another 10-character string, the `StringBuffer` first creates a new internal 10,000-char array to build the string with; then the new `String` also uses that 10,000-char array to store the 10 characters. Obviously, this process can continue indefinitely, using vast amounts of memory where not expected.

The advantages of `Strings` can be summed up as ease of use, internationalization support, and compatibility to existing interfaces. Most methods expect a `String` object rather than a `char` array, and `String` objects are returned by many methods. The disadvantage of `Strings` boils down to inflexibility. With extra work, most things you can do with `String` objects can be done faster and with less intermediate object-creation overhead by using your own set of `char` array manipulation methods.

For most performance tuning, you pinpoint a bottleneck and make localized changes to objects and methods that speed up that bottleneck. But `String` tuning often involves converting to `char` arrays, whereas you rarely come across `public` methods or interfaces that deal in `char` arrays. This makes it difficult to switch between `Strings` and `char` arrays in any localized way. The consequences are that you either have to switch back and forth between `Strings` and `char` arrays, or you have to make extensive modifications that can reach across many application boundaries. I have no easy solution for this problem. `String` tuning can get messy.

It is difficult to handle `String` internationalization capabilities using raw `char` arrays. But in many cases, internationalized `Strings` form a specific subset of `String` usage in an application, mainly in the user interface, and that subset of `Strings` rarely causes bottlenecks. You should differentiate between `Strings` that need internationalization and those that are simply processing characters, independent of language. These latter `Strings` can be replaced for tuning with `char` arrays.* Internationalization-dependent `Strings` are more difficult to tune, and I

---

* My editor summarized this succinctly with the statement, "Avoid using `String` objects if you don't intend to represent text."

provide some examples of tuning these later in the chapter. Note also that internationalized `Strings` can be treated as `char` arrays for some types of processing without any problems; see the "Line Filter Example" section later in this chapter.

Compile-Time Versus Runtime Resolution of Strings

For optimized use of `Strings`, you should know the difference between compile-time resolution of `Strings` and runtime creation. At compile time, `Strings` are resolved to eliminate the concatenation operator if possible. For example, the line:

```
String s = "hi " + "Mr. " + " " + "Buddy";
```

is compiled as if it read:

```
String s = "hi Mr. Buddy";
```

However, suppose you defined the `String` using a `StringBuffer`:

```
String s = (new StringBuffer()).append("hi ").
            append("Mr. ").append(" ").append("Buddy").toString();
```

Then the compiler cannot resolve the `String` at compile time. The result is that the `String` is created at runtime along with a temporary `StringBuffer`. The version that can be resolved at compile time is more efficient. It avoids the overhead of creating a `String` and an extra temporary `StringBuffer`, as well as avoiding the runtime cost of several method calls.

However, when an expression involving `String` concatenation cannot be resolved at compile time, the concatenation must execute at runtime. This causes extra objects to be generated. For example, consider the following method:

```
public String sayHi(String title, String name)
{
  return "hi " + title + " " + name;
}
```

The `String` generated by this method cannot be resolved at compile time because the variables can have any value. The compiler is free to generate code to optimize the `String` creation, but it does not have to. Consequently, the `String`-creation line could be compiled as:

```
return (new StringBuffer()).append("hi ").
  append(title).append(" ").append(name).toString();
```

This is optimal, creating only two objects. On the other hand, the compiler could also leave the line with the default implementation of the concatenation operator, which is equivalent to:

```
return "hi ".concat(title).concat(" ").concat(name);
```

This last implementation creates two intermediate `String` objects that are then thrown away, and these are generated every time the method is called.

So, when the `String` can be fully resolved at compile time, the concatenation operator is more efficient than using a `StringBuffer`. But when the `String` cannot be resolved at compile time, the concatenation operator is less efficient than using a `StringBuffer`.

One further point is that using the `String` constructor in a `String` definition forces a runtime string creation:

```
String s = new String("hi " + "Mr. " + " " + "Buddy");
```

is compiled as:

```
String s = new String("hi Mr. Buddy");
```

This line uses the compile-time resolved string as a parameter for the `String` constructor to create a new `String` object at runtime. The new `String` object is equal but not identical to the original string:

```
String s = new String("hi Mr. Buddy");
s == "hi Mr. Buddy";      //is false
s.equals("hi Mr. Buddy"); //is true
```

Conversions to Strings

Generally, the JDK methods that convert objects and data types to strings are suboptimal, both in terms of performance and the number of temporary objects used in the conversion procedure. In this section, we consider how to optimize these conversions.

Converting longs to Strings

Let's start by looking at conversion of `long` values. In the JDK, this is achieved with the `Long.toString()` method. Bear in mind that you typically add a converted value to a `StringBuffer` (explicitly, or implicitly with the + concatenation operator). So it would be nice to avoid the two intermediate temporary objects created while converting the `long`, i.e., the one `char` array inside the conversion method, and the returned `String` object that is used just to copy the `chars` into the `StringBuffer`.

Avoiding the temporary `char` array is difficult to do, because most fast methods for converting numbers start with the low digits in the number, and you cannot add to the `StringBuffer` from the low to the high digits unless you want all your numbers coming out backwards.

However, with a little work, you can get to a method that is fast and obtains the digits in order. The following code works by determining the magnitude of the number first, then successively stripping off the highest digit:

```java
//Up to radix 36
private static final char[] charForDigit = {
  '0','1','2','3','4','5','6','7','8','9','a','b','c','d','e','f','g','h',
  'i','j','k','l','m','n','o','p','q','r','s','t','u','v','w','x','y','z'
};

public static void append(StringBuffer s, long i)
{
  if (i < 0)
  {
    //convert negative to positive numbers for later algorithm
    if (i == Long.MIN_VALUE)
    {
      //cannot make this positive due to integer overflow,
      //so treat it specially
      s.append("-9223372036854775808");
      return;
    }
    //otherwise append the minus sign, and make the number positive
    s.append('-');
    i = -i;
  }
  //Get the magnitude of the int
  long mag = l_magnitude(i);
  long c;
  while ( mag > 1 )
  {
    //The highest digit
    c = i/mag;
    s.append(charForDigit[(int) c]);
    //remove the highest digit
    c *= mag;
    if ( c <= i)
      i -= c;
    //and go down one magnitude
    mag /= 10;
  }
  //The remaining magnitude is one digit large
  s.append(charForDigit[(int) i]);
}

private static long l_magnitude(long i)
{
    if (i < 10L) return 1;
    else if (i < 100L) return 10L;
    else if (i < 1000L) return 100L;
```

```
        else if (i < 10000L) return 1000L;
        else if (i < 100000L) return 10000L;
        else if (i < 1000000L) return 100000L;
        else if (i < 10000000L) return 1000000L;
        else if (i < 100000000L) return 10000000L;
        else if (i < 1000000000L) return 100000000L;
        else if (i < 10000000000L) return 1000000000L;
        else if (i < 100000000000L) return 10000000000L;
        else if (i < 1000000000000L) return 100000000000L;
        else if (i < 10000000000000L) return 1000000000000L;
        else if (i < 100000000000000L) return 10000000000000L;
        else if (i < 1000000000000000L) return 100000000000000L;
        else if (i < 10000000000000000L) return 1000000000000000L;
        else if (i < 100000000000000000L) return 10000000000000000L;
        else if (i < 1000000000000000000L) return 100000000000000000L;
        else return  1000000000000000000L;
    }
```

When compared to executing the plain `StringBuffer.append(long)`, the algorithm listed here takes at most 90% of the `StringBuffer` time (see Table 5-1) and creates two fewer objects (it can be even faster, but I'll leave the more complicated tuning to the next section). If you are writing out `long` values a large number of times, this is a useful speedup.

Table 5-1. Time Taken to Append a long to a StringBuffer

VM	1.2	1.3	HotSpot 1.0	1.1.6
JDK `long` conversion	100%	113%	227%	272%
Optimized `long` conversion	90%	103%	146%	133%

There are several things to note about possible variations of this algorithm. First, although the algorithm here is specifically radix 10 (decimal), it is easy to change to any radix. To do this, the reduction in magnitude in the loop has to go down by the radix value, and the `l_magnitude()` method has to be altered. For example, for radix 16, hexadecimal, the statement `mag = mag/10` becomes `mag = mag/16` and the magnitude method for radix 16 looks like:

```
    private static long l_magnitude16(long i)
    {
        if (i < 16L) return 1;
        else if (i < 256L) return 16L;
        else if (i < 4096L) return 256L;
        else if (i < 65536L) return 4096L;
        else if (i < 1048576L) return 65536L;
        else if (i < 16777216L) return 1048576L;
        else if (i < 268435456L) return 16777216L;
        else if (i < 4294967296L) return 268435456L;
        else if (i < 68719476736L) return 4294967296L;
```

```
    else if (i < 1099511627776L) return 68719476736L;
    else if (i < 17592186044416L) return 1099511627776L;
    else if (i < 281474976710656L) return 17592186044416L;
    else if (i < 4503599627370496L) return 281474976710656L;
    else if (i < 72057594037927936L) return 4503599627370496L;
    else if (i < 1152921504606846976L) return 72057594037927936L;
    else return 1152921504606846976L;
}
```

Second, because we are working through the digits in written order, this algorithm is suitable for writing directly to a stream or writer (such as a `FileWriter`) without the need for any temporary objects. This is potentially a large gain, enabling writes to files without generating intermediate temporary strings.

Finally, if you want formatting added in, the algorithm is again suitable, because you proceed through the number in written order, and also because you have the magnitude at the start. (You can easily create another method, similar to `magnitude()`, that returns the number of digits in the value.) You can put in a comma every three digits as the number is being written (or apply whatever internationalized format is required). This saves you having to write out the number first in a temporary object and then add formatting to it. For example, if you are using integers to fake fixed-place floating-point numbers, you can insert a point at the correct position without resorting to temporary objects.

Converting ints to Strings

While the previous `append()` version is suitable to use for `ints` by overloading, it is much more efficient to create another version specifically for `ints`. This is because `int` arithmetic is optimal and considerably faster than the `long` arithmetic being used. Although earlier versions of the JDK (before JDK 1.1.6) used an inefficient conversion procedure for `ints`, from 1.1.6 onward Sun targeted the conversion (for radix 10 integers only) and speeded it up by an order of magnitude. To better this already optimized performance, you need every optimization available.

There are three changes you can make to the `long` conversion algorithm already presented. First, you can change everything to use `ints`. This gives a significant speedup (more than a third faster than the `long` conversion). Second, you can inline the "magnitude" method. And finally, you can unroll the loop that handles the digit-by-digit conversion. In this case, the loop can be completely unrolled since there are at most 10 digits in an `int`.

The resulting method is a little long-winded:

```
public static void append(StringBuffer s, int i)
{
```

```
if (i < 0)
{
  if (i == Integer.MIN_VALUE)
  {
    //cannot make this positive due to integer overflow
    s.append("-2147483648");
    return this;
  }
  s.append('-');
  i = -i;
}
int mag;
int c;
if (i < 10)                    //one digit
  s.append(charForDigit[i]);
else if (i < 100)              //two digits
  s.append(charForDigit[i/10])
   .append(charForDigit[i%10]);
else if (i < 1000)             //three digits
  s.append(charForDigit[i/100])
   .append(charForDigit[(c=i%100)/10])
   .append(charForDigit[c%10]);
else if (i < 10000)            //four digits
  s.append(charForDigit[i/1000])
   .append(charForDigit[(c=i%1000)/100])
   .append(charForDigit[(c%100)/10])
   .append(charForDigit[c%10]);
else if (i < 100000)           //five digits
  s.append(charForDigit[i/10000])
   .append(charForDigit[(c=i%10000)/1000])
   .append(charForDigit[(c%1000)/100])
   .append(charForDigit[(c%100)/10])
   .append(charForDigit[c%10]);
else if (i < 1000000)          //six digits
  ... //I'm sure you get the idea
else if (i < 10000000)         //seven digits
  ... //so just keep doing the same, but more
else if (i < 100000000)        //eight digits
  ... //because my editor doesn't like wasting all this space
else if (i < 1000000000)       //nine digits
  ... //on unnecessary repetitions
else
  {
      //ten digits
      s.append(charForDigit[i/1000000000]);
      s.append(charForDigit[(c=i%1000000000)/100000000]);
      s.append(charForDigit[(c%100000000)/10000000]);
      s.append(charForDigit[(c%10000000)/1000000]);
      s.append(charForDigit[(c%1000000)/100000]);
```

```
        s.append(charForDigit[(c%=100000)/10000]);
        s.append(charForDigit[(c%=10000)/1000]);
        s.append(charForDigit[(c%=1000)/100]);
        s.append(charForDigit[(c%=100)/10]);
        s.append(charForDigit[c%10]);
    }
}
```

If you compare this implementation to executing `StringBuffer.append(int)`, the algorithm listed here runs in less time for all except the latest VM, and creates two fewer objects* (see Table 5-2). This is faster than the JDK optimized version, has a smaller impact on garbage creation, and has all the other advantages previously listed for the `long` conversion (i.e., it is easily generalized for other radix values, digits are iterated in order so you can write to a stream, and it is easier to alter for formatting without using temporary objects). Note that the `long` conversion method can also be improved using two of the three techniques we used for the `int` conversion method: inlining the magnitude method and unrolling the loop.

Table 5-2. Time Taken to Append an int to a StringBuffer

VM	1.2	1.3	HotSpot 1.0	1.1.6
JDK int conversion	100%	61%	89%	148%
Optimized int conversion	84%	60%	81%	111%

Converting bytes, shorts, chars, and booleans to Strings

You can use the `int` conversion method for `bytes` and `shorts` (using overloading). You can make `byte` conversion even faster using a `String` array as a lookup table for the 256 `byte` values. The conversion of `bytes` and `shorts` to `Strings` in the JDK appears not to have been tuned to as high a standard as radix 10 `ints` (up to JDK 1.3). This means that the `int` conversion algorithm shown previously, when applied to `bytes` and `shorts`, is significantly faster than the JDK conversions and does not produce any temporary objects.

When it comes to using the other data types, there is no need to handle `booleans` in any special way: the `Boolean.toString()` already uses canonical strings. And there is obviously nothing in particular that needs to be done for `chars` (apart from making sure you add them to strings as characters, not numbers).

---

* If the `StringBuffer.append(int)` used the algorithm shown here, it would be faster for all JDK versions measured in this chapter, since the characters could be added directly to the char buffer without going through the `StringBuffer.append(char)` method.

Converting floats to Strings

Converting floating-point numbers to strings turns out to be hideously under-optimized in every version of the JDK up to 1.3 (and maybe beyond). Looking at the JDK code and comments, it seems that no one has yet got around to tuning these conversions. Floating-point numbers can be converted using similar optimizations to the number conversions previously addressed. You need to check for and handle the special cases separately. You then scale the floats into an integer value and use the previously defined int conversion algorithm to convert to characters in order, ensuring that you format the decimal point at the correct position. The case of values between .001 and 10,000,000 are handled differently, because these are printed without exponent values; all other floats are printed with exponents. Finally, it would be possible to overload the float and double case, but it turns out that if you do this, the float does not convert as well (in correctness or speed), so it is necessary to duplicate the algorithms for the float and double cases.

Note that the printed values of floats and doubles are, in general, only representative of the underlying value. This is true both for the JDK algorithms and the conversions here. There are times when the string representation comes out differently for the two implementations, and neither is actually more accurate. The algorithm used by the JDK prints the minimum number of digits possible, while maintaining uniqueness of the printed value with respect to the other floating-point values adjacent to the value being printed. The algorithm presented here prints the maximum number of digits (not including trailing zeros) regardless of whether some digits are not needed to distinguish the number from other numbers. For example, the Float.MIN_VALUE is printed by the JDK as "1.4E-45", whereas the algorithm here prints it as "1.4285714E-45". Because of the limitations in the accuracy of numbers, neither printed representation is more or less accurate compared to the underlying floating-point number actually held in Float.MIN_VALUE (e.g., assigning both "1.46e-45F" and "1.45e-45F" to a float results in Float.MIN_VALUE being assigned). Note that the code that follows shortly uses the previously defined append() method for appending longs to StringBuffers. Also note that the dot character has been hardcoded as the decimal separator character here for clarity, but it is straightforward to change for internationalization.

This method of converting floats to strings has the same advantages as those mentioned previously for integral types, i.e., it is printed in digit order, no temporary objects are generated, etc. The double conversion (see the next section) is similar to the float conversion, with all the same advantages. In addition, both algorithms are several times faster than the JDK conversions.

Normally, when you print out floating-point numbers, you print in a defined format with a specified number of digits. The default floating-point `toString()` methods cannot format floating-point numbers; you must first create the string, then format it afterwards. The algorithm presented here could easily be altered to handle formatting floating-point numbers without using any intermediate strings. This algorithm is also easily adapted to handle rounding up or down; it already detects which side of the "half" value the number is on:

```
public static final char[] NEGATIVE_INFINITY =
      {'-','I','n','f','i','n','i','t','y'};
public static final char[] POSITIVE_INFINITY =
      {'I','n','f','i','n','i','t','y'};
public static final char[] NaN = {'N','a','N'};
private static final intfloatSignMask = 0x80000000;
private static final intfloatExpMask  = 0x7f800000;
private static final intfloatFractMask= ~(floatSignMask|floatExpMask);
private static final intfloatExpShift = 23;
private static final intfloatExpBias = 127;
//change dot to international character where this is used below
public static final char[] DOUBLE_ZERO = {'0','.','0'};
public static final char[] DOUBLE_ZERO2 = {'0','.','0','0'};
public static final char[] DOUBLE_ZERO0 = {'0','.'};
public static final char[] DOT_ZERO = {'.','0'};
private static final float[] f_magnitudes = {
 1e-44F, 1e-43F, 1e-42F, 1e-41F, 1e-40F,
 1e-39F, 1e-38F, 1e-37F, 1e-36F, 1e-35F, 1e-34F, 1e-33F, 1e-32F, 1e-31F, 1e-30F,
 1e-29F, 1e-28F, 1e-27F, 1e-26F, 1e-25F, 1e-24F, 1e-23F, 1e-22F, 1e-21F, 1e-20F,
 1e-19F, 1e-18F, 1e-17F, 1e-16F, 1e-15F, 1e-14F, 1e-13F, 1e-12F, 1e-11F, 1e-10F,
 1e-9F, 1e-8F, 1e-7F, 1e-6F, 1e-5F, 1e-4F, 1e-3F, 1e-2F, 1e-1F,
 1e0F, 1e1F, 1e2F, 1e3F, 1e4F, 1e5F, 1e6F, 1e7F, 1e8F, 1e9F,
 1e10F, 1e11F, 1e12F, 1e13F, 1e14F, 1e15F, 1e16F, 1e17F, 1e18F, 1e19F,
 1e20F, 1e21F, 1e22F, 1e23F, 1e24F, 1e25F, 1e26F, 1e27F, 1e28F, 1e29F,
 1e30F, 1e31F, 1e32F, 1e33F, 1e34F, 1e35F, 1e36F, 1e37F, 1e38F
};

public static void append(StringBuffer s, float d)
{
  //handle the various special cases
  if (d == Float.NEGATIVE_INFINITY)
    s.append(NEGATIVE_INFINITY);
  else if (d == Float.POSITIVE_INFINITY)
    s.append(POSITIVE_INFINITY);
  else if (d != d)
    s.append(NaN);
  else if (d == 0.0)
  {
    //can be -0.0, which is stored differently
    if ( (Float.floatToIntBits(d) & floatSignMask) != 0)
```

```
      s.append('-');
    s.append(DOUBLE_ZERO);
  }
  else
  {
    //convert negative numbers to positive
    if (d < 0)
    {
      s.append('-');
      d = -d;
    }
    //handle 0.001 up to 10000000 separately, without exponents
    if (d >= 0.001F && d < 0.01F)
    {
      long i = (long) (d * 1E12F);
      i = i%100 >= 50 ? (i/100) + 1 : i/100;
      s.append(DOUBLE_ZERO2);
      appendFractDigits(s, i,-1);
    }
    else if (d >= 0.01F && d < 0.1F)
    {
      long i = (long) (d * 1E11F);
      i = i%100 >= 50 ? (i/100) + 1 : i/100;
      s.append(DOUBLE_ZERO);
      appendFractDigits(s, i,-1);
    }
    else if (d >= 0.1F && d < 1F)
    {
      long i = (long) (d * 1E10F);
      i = i%100 >= 50 ? (i/100) + 1 : i/100;
      s.append(DOUBLE_ZERO0);
      appendFractDigits(s, i,-1);
    }
    else if (d >= 1F && d < 10F)
    {
      long i = (long) (d * 1E9F);
      i = i%100 >= 50 ? (i/100) + 1 : i/100;
      appendFractDigits(s, i,1);
    }
    else if (d >= 10F && d < 100F)
    {
      long i = (long) (d * 1E8F);
      i = i%100 >= 50 ? (i/100) + 1 : i/100;
      appendFractDigits(s, i,2);
    }
    else if (d >= 100F && d < 1000F)
    {
      long i = (long) (d * 1E7F);
      i = i%100 >= 50 ? (i/100) + 1 : i/100;
```

```
      appendFractDigits(s, i,3);
    }
    else if (d >= 1000F && d < 10000F)
    {
      long i = (long) (d * 1E6F);
      i = i%100 >= 50 ? (i/100) + 1 : i/100;
      appendFractDigits(s, i,4);
    }
    else if (d >= 10000F && d < 100000F)
    {
      long i = (long) (d * 1E5F);
      i = i%100 >= 50 ? (i/100) + 1 : i/100;
      appendFractDigits(s, i,5);
    }
    else if (d >= 100000F && d < 1000000F)
    {
      long i = (long) (d * 1E4F);
      i = i%100 >= 50 ? (i/100) + 1 : i/100;
      appendFractDigits(s, i,6);
    }
    else if (d >= 1000000F && d < 10000000F)
    {
      long i = (long) (d * 1E3F);
      i = i%100 >= 50 ? (i/100) + 1 : i/100;
      appendFractDigits(s, i,7);
    }
    else
    {
      //Otherwise the number has an exponent
      int magnitude = magnitude(d);
      long i;
      if (magnitude < -35)
        i = (long) (d*1E10F / f_magnitudes[magnitude + 45]);
      else
        i = (long) (d / f_magnitudes[magnitude + 44 - 9]);
      i = i%100 >= 50 ? (i/100) + 1 : i/100;
      appendFractDigits(s, i, 1);
      s.append('E');
      append(s,magnitude);
    }
  }
  return this;
}

private static int magnitude(float d)
{
  return magnitude(d,Float.floatToIntBits(d));
}
```

```
private static int magnitude(float d, int floatToIntBits)
{
  int magnitude =
    (int) ((((floatToIntBits & floatExpMask) >> floatExpShift)
                 - floatExpBias) * 0.301029995663981);

  if (magnitude < -44)
    magnitude = -44;
  else if (magnitude > 38)
    magnitude = 38;

  if (d >= f_magnitudes[magnitude+44])
  {
    while(magnitude < 39 && d >= f_magnitudes[magnitude+44])
      magnitude++;
    magnitude--;
    return magnitude;
  }
  else
  {
    while(magnitude > -45 && d < f_magnitudes[magnitude+44])
      magnitude--;
    return magnitude;
  }
}
private static void appendFractDigits(StringBuffer s, long i, int decimalOffset)
{
  long mag = magnitude(i);
  long c;
  while ( i > 0 )
  {
    c = i/mag;
    s.append(charForDigit[(int) c]);
    decimalOffset--;
    if (decimalOffset == 0)
      s.append('.'); //change to use international character
    c *= mag;
    if ( c <= i)
      i -= c;
    mag = mag/10;
  }
  if (i != 0)
    s.append(charForDigit[(int) i]);
  decimalOffset--;
  if (decimalOffset == 0)
    s.append(DOT_ZERO);
  else if (decimalOffset == -1)
    s.append('0');
}
```

The conversion times compared to the JDK conversions are shown in Table 5-3. Note that if you are formatting floats, the JDK conversion requires additional steps and so takes longer. However, the method shown here is likely to take even less time, as you normally print fewer digits that require fewer loop iterations.

Table 5-3. Time Taken to Append a float to a StringBuffer

VM	1.2	1.3	HotSpot 1.0	1.1.6
JDK float conversion	100%	85%	270%	128%
Optimized float conversion	26%	30%	95%	33%

Converting doubles to Strings

The double conversion is almost identical to the float conversion, except that the doubles extend over a larger range. The differences are the following constants used in place of the corresponding float constants:

```
private static final long  doubleSignMask = 0x8000000000000000L;
private static final long  doubleExpMask = 0x7ff0000000000000L;
private static final long  doubleFractMask= ~(doubleSignMask|doubleExpMask);
private static final int  doubleExpShift = 52;
private static final int  doubleExpBias = 1023;
//private static final double[] d_magnitudes = {
  //as f_magnitudes[] except doubles extending
  //from 1e-323D to 1e308D inclusive
  ...
}
```

The last section of the append() method is:

```
int magnitude = magnitude(d);
long i;
if (magnitude < -305)
  i = (long) (d*1E19 / d_magnitudes[magnitude + 324]);
else
  i = (long) (d / d_magnitudes[magnitude + 323 - 18]);
i = i%100 >= 50 ? (i/100) + 1 : i/100;
appendFractDigits(s, i, 1);
s.append('E');
append(s,magnitude);
```

and the magnitude methods are:

```
private static int magnitude(double d)
{
  return magnitude(d,Double.doubleToLongBits(d));
}
private static int magnitude(double d, long doubleToLongBits)
{
```

```
int magnitude =
  (int) ((((doubleToLongBits & doubleExpMask) >> doubleExpShift)
              - doubleExpBias) * 0.301029995663981);

if (magnitude < -323)
  magnitude = -323;
else if (magnitude > 308)
  magnitude = 308;

if (d >= d_magnitudes[magnitude+323])
{
  while(magnitude < 309 && d >= d_magnitudes[magnitude+323])
    magnitude++;
  magnitude--;
  return magnitude;
}
else
{
  while(magnitude > -324 && d < d_magnitudes[magnitude+323])
    magnitude--;
  return magnitude;
}
}
```

The conversion times compared to the JDK conversions are shown in Table 5-4. As with floats, formatting doubles with the JDK conversion requires additional steps and would consequently take longer, but the method shown here takes even less time, as you normally print fewer digits that require fewer loop iterations.

Table 5-4. Time Taken to Append a double to a StringBuffer

VM	1.2	1.3	HotSpot 1.0	1.1.6
JDK double conversion	100%	92%	129%	134%
Optimized double conversion	16%	16%	32%	23%

Converting Objects to Strings

Converting Objects to Strings is also inefficient in the JDK. For a generic object, the toString() method is usually implemented by calling any embedded object's toString() method, then combining the embedded strings in some way. For example, Vector.toString() calls toString() on all its elements, and combines the generated substrings with the comma character surrounded by opening and closing square brackets.

Although this conversion is generic, it usually creates a huge number of unnecessary temporary objects. If the JDK had taken the "printOn: aStream" paradigm from Smalltalk, the temporary objects used would be significantly reduced. This paradigm basically allows any object to be appended to a stream. In Java, it looks something like:

```
public String toString()
{
  StringBuffer s =new  StringBuffer();
  appendTo(s);
  return s.toString();
}

public void appendTo(StringBuffer s)
{
  //The real work of converting to strings. Any embedded
  //objects would have their 'appendTo()' methods called,
  //NOT their 'toString()' methods.
  ...
}
```

This implementation allows far fewer objects to be created in converting to strings. In addition, as StringBuffer is not a stream, this implementation becomes much more useful if you use a java.io.StringWriter and change the appendTo() method to accept any Writer, for example:

```
public String toString()
{
  java.io.StringWriter s =new  java.io.StringWriter();
  appendTo(s);
  return s.getBuffer().toString();
}

public void appendTo(java.io.Writer s)
{
  //The real work of converting to strings. Any embedded
  //objects would have their 'appendTo()' methods called,
  //NOT their 'toString()' methods.
  ...
}
```

This implementation allows the one appendTo() method to write out any object to any streamed writer object. Unfortunately, this implementation is not supported by the Object class, so you need to create your own framework of methods and interfaces to support this implementation. I find that I can use an Appendable interface with an appendTo() method, and then write toString() methods that check for that interface:

```
public interface Appendable
{
  public void appendTo(java.io.Writer s);
}
```

```java
public class SomeClass
  implements Appendable
{
  Object[] embeddedObjects;

  ...

  public String toString()
  {
    java.io.StringWriter s =new  java.io.StringWriter();
    appendTo(s);
    return s.getBuffer().toString();
  }
  public void appendTo(java.io.Writer s)
  {
    //The real work of converting to strings. Any embedded
    //objects would have their 'appendTo()' methods called,
    //NOT their 'toString()' methods.
    for (int i = 0; i<embeddedObjects.length; i++)
      if (embeddedObjects[i] instanceof Appendable)
        ( (Appendable) embeddedObjects[i]).appendTo(s);
      else
        s.write(embeddedObjects[i].toString());
  }
}
```

In addition, you can extend this framework even further to override the appending of frequently used classes such as **Vector**, allowing a more efficient conversion mechanism that uses fewer temporary objects:

```java
public class AppenderHelper
{
  final static String NULL = "null";
  final static String OPEN = "[";
  final static String CLOSE = "]";
  final static String MIDDLE = ", ";

  public void appendCheckingAppendable(Object o, java.io.Writer s)
  {
    //Use more efficient Appendable interface if possible,
    //and NULL string if appropriate
    if ((o = v.elementAt(0)) == null)
      s.write(NULL);
    else if (o instanceof Appendable)
      ( (Appendable) o).appendTo(s);
    else
      s.write(o.toString());
  }

  public void appendVector(java.util.Vector v, java.io.Writer s)
```

```
  {
    int size = v.size();
    Object o;

    //Write the opening bracket
    s.write(OPEN);

    if (size != 0)
    {
      //Add the first element
      appendCheckingAppendable(v.elementAt(0), s);
      //And add in each other element preceded by the MIDDLE separator
      for(int i = 1; i < size; i++);
      {
          s.append(MIDDLE);
          appendCheckingAppendable(v.elementAt(i), s);
      }
    }

    //Write the closing bracket
    s.append(CLOSE);
  }
}
```

If you add this framework to an application, you can support the notion of converting objects to string representations to a particular depth. For example, a `Vector` containing another `Vector` to depth two looks like this:

```
[1, 2, [3, 4, 5]]
```

But to depth one, it looks like this:

```
[1, 2, Vector@4444]
```

The default `Object.toString()` implementation in the JDK writes out strings for objects as:

```
return getClass().getName() + "@" + Integer.toHexString(hashCode());
```

The JDK implementation is inefficient for two reasons. First, the method creates an unnecessary intermediate string because it uses the concatenation operator twice. Second, the `Class.getName()` method (which is a `native` method) also creates a new string every time it is called: the class name is not cached. It turns out that if you reimplement this to cache the class name and avoid the extra temporary strings, your conversion is faster and uses fewer temporary objects. The two are related, of course: using fewer temporary objects means less object-creation overhead.

You can create a generic framework that converts the basic data types, while also supporting the efficient conversion of JDK classes (such as `Vector`, as well as

Integer, Long, etc.). With this framework in place, I find that performance is generally improved because the application uses more efficient conversion algorithms and reduces the number of temporary objects. In almost every respect, this framework is better than the simpler framework, which supports only the toString() method.

Strings Versus char Arrays

In one of my first programming courses, in the language C, our instructor made an interesting comment. He said, "C has lightning-fast string handling because it has no string type." He went on to explain this oxymoron by pointing out that in C, any null-terminated sequence of bytes can be considered a string: this convention is supported by all string-handling functions. The point is that since the convention is adhered to fairly rigorously, there is no need to use only the standard string-handling functions. Any string manipulation you want to do can be executed directly on the byte array, allowing you to bypass or rewrite any string-handling functions you need to speed up. Because you are not forced to run through a restricted set of manipulation functions, it is always possible to optimize code using your own hand-crafted functions. Furthermore, some string-manipulating functions operate directly on the original byte array rather than creating a copy of this array. This can be a source of bugs, but is another reason speed can be optimized.

In Java, the inability to subclass String or access its internal char array means you cannot use the techniques applied in C. Even if you could subclass String, this does not avoid the second problem: many other methods operate on or return copies of a String. Generally, there is no way to avoid using String objects for code external to your application classes. But internally, you can provide your own char array type that allows you to manipulate strings according to your needs.

As an example, let's look at a couple of simple text-parsing problems: first, counting the words in a body of text, and second, using a filter to select lines of a file based on whether they contain a particular string.

Word-Counting Example

Let's look at the typical Java approach to counting words in a text. I use the StreamTokenizer for the word count, as that class is tailor-made for this kind of problem.

The word count is fairly easy to implement. The only difficulty comes in defining what a word is and coaxing the StreamTokenizer to agree with that definition. To keep things simple, I define a word as any contiguous sequence of alphanumeric characters. This means that words with apostrophes and numbers with decimal points count as two words, but I'm more interested in the performance than the niceties of word definitions here, and I want to keep the implementation simple. The implementation looks like this:

```
public static void wordcount(String filename)
    throws IOException
{
    int count = 0;
    //create the tokenizer, and initialize it
    FileReader r = new FileReader(filename);
    StreamTokenizer rdr = new StreamTokenizer(r);
    rdr.resetSyntax();
    rdr.wordChars('a', 'z');    //words include any lowercase character
    rdr.wordChars('A', 'Z');    //words include any uppercase character
    rdr.wordChars('0','9');     //words include any digit
    //everything else is whitespace
    rdr.whitespaceChars(0, '0'-1);
    rdr.whitespaceChars('9'+1, 'A'-1);
    rdr.whitespaceChars('z'+1, '\uffff');
    int token;
    //loop getting each token (word) from the tokenizer
    //until we reach the end of the file
    while( (token = rdr.nextToken()) != StreamTokenizer.TT_EOF)
    {
        //If the token is a word, count it, otherwise it is whitespace
        if ( token == StreamTokenizer.TT_WORD)
            count++;
    }
    System.out.println(count + " words found.");
    r.close();
}
```

Now, for comparison, implement a more efficient version using char arrays. The word-count algorithm is relatively straightforward: test for sequences of alphanumerics and skip anything else. The only slight complication comes when you refill the buffer with the next chunk from the file. You need to avoid counting one word as two if it falls across the junction of the two reads into the buffer, but this turns out to be easy to handle. You simply need to remember the last character of the last chunk and skip any alphanumeric characters at the beginning of the next chunk if that last character was alphanumeric (i.e., continue with the word until it terminates). The implementation looks like this:

```
public static void cwordcount(String filename)
    throws IOException
{
    int count = 0;
    FileReader rdr = new FileReader(filename);
    //buffer to hold read in characters
    char[] buf = new char[8192];
    int len;
```

```
   int idx = 0;
   //initialize so that our 'current' character is in whitespace
   char c = ' ';
   //read in each chunk as much as possible,
   //until there is nothing left to read
   while( (len = rdr.read(buf, 0, buf.length)) != -1)
   {
      idx = 0;
      int start;
      //if we are already in a word, then skip the rest of it
      if (Character.isLetterOrDigit(c))
        while( (idx < len) && Character.isLetterOrDigit(buf[idx]) )
           {idx++;}
      while(idx < len)
      {
         //skip non alphanumeric
         while( (idx < len) && !Character.isLetterOrDigit(buf[idx]) )
            {idx++;}
         //skip word
         start = idx;
         while( (idx < len) && Character.isLetterOrDigit(buf[idx]) )
            {idx++;}
         if (start < len)
         {
            count++; //count word
         }
      }
      //get last character so we know whether to carry on a word
      c = buf[idx-1];
   }
   System.out.println(count + " words found.");
}
```

You can compare this implementation with the one using the `StreamTokenizer`. All tests use the same large text file for counting the words. I normalize to 100% the time taken by `StreamTokenizer` using JDK 1.2 with the JIT compiler (see Table 5-5). Interestingly, the test takes almost the same amount of time when I run using the `StreamTokenizer` without the JIT compiler running. Depending on the file I run with, sometimes the JIT VM turns out slower than the non-JIT VM with the `StreamTokenizer` test.

Table 5-5. Word Counter Timings Using wordcount or cwordcount Methods

VM	1.2	1.2 no JIT	1.3	HotSpot 1.0	1.1.6
wordcount	100%	104%	152%	199%	88%
cwordcount	0.7%	9%	1%	3%	0.6%

These results are already quite curious. When I run the test with the char array implementation, it takes 9% of the normalized time without the JIT running, and

0.7% of the time with the JIT turned on. I suspect the curious results and huge discrepancy may have something to do with `StreamTokenizer` being a severely underoptimized class, as well as being too generic a tool for this particular test.

Looking at object usage,* you find that the `StreamTokenizer` implementation winds through 1.2 million temporary objects, whereas the `char` array implementation uses only around 20 objects. Now you can understand the curious results. Object-creation differences of this order of magnitude impose a huge overhead on the `StreamTokenizer` implementation, explaining why the `StreamTokenizer` is so much slower than the `char` array implementation. The object-creation overhead also explains why both the JIT and non-JIT tests took similar times for the `StreamTokenizer`. Object creation requires similar amounts of time in both types of VM, and clearly the performance of the `StreamTokenizer` is limited by the number of objects it uses (see Chapter 4, *Object Creation*, for further details).

Line Filter Example

For the filter to select lines of a file, I'll use the simple `BufferedReader.readLine()` method. This contrasts with the previous methodology using a dedicated class (`StreamTokenizer`), which turned out to be extremely inefficient. The `readline()` method should present us with more of a performance-tuning challenge, since it is relatively much simpler and so should be more efficient.

The filter using `BufferedReader` and `String`s is easily implemented. I include an option to print only the count of matching lines:

```
public static void filter(String filter, String filename, boolean print)
  throws IOException
{
  count = 0;
  //just open the file
  BufferedReader rdr = new BufferedReader(new FileReader(filename));
  String line;
  //and read each line
  while( (line = rdr.readLine()) != null)
  {
    //choosing those lines that include the sought after string
    if (line.indexOf(filter) != -1)
    {
      count++;
      if (print)
        System.out.println(line);
```

---

* Object monitoring is easily done using the monitoring tools from Chapter 2, *Profiling Tools*: both the object-creation monitor detailed there, and also separately by using the `-verbosegc` option while adding an explicit `System.gc()` at the end of the test.

```
        }
    }
    System.out.println(count + " lines matched.");
    rdr.close();
}
```

Now let's consider how to handle this filter using `char` arrays. As in the previous example, you read into your `char` array using a `FileReader`. However, this example is a bit more complicated than the last word-count example. Here you need to test for a match against another `char` array, look for line endings, and handle reforming lines that are broken between `read()` calls in a more complete manner than for the word count.

Internationalization doesn't change this example in any obvious way. Both the `readLine()` implementation and the `char` array implementation stay the same whatever language the text contains.

NOTE   This statement about internationalization is slightly disingenuous. In fact, searches in some languages allow words to match even if they are spelled differently. For example, when searching for a French word that contains an accented letter, the user might expect a non-accented spelling to match. This is similar to searching for the word "color" and expecting to also match the British spelling "colour."

Such sophistication depends on how extensively the application supports this variation in spelling. The `java.text.Collator` class has four "strength" levels that support variations in the precision of word comparisons. Both implementations for the example in this section correspond to matches using the `Collator.IDENTICAL` strength together with the `Collator.NO_DECOMPOSITION` mode.

The full commented listing for the `char` array implementation is shown shortly. Looking at the code, it is clearly more complicated than using the `Buffered-Reader.readLine()`. Obviously you have to work a lot harder to get the performance you want. The result, though, is that some tests run as much as five times faster using the `char` array implementation (see Tables 5-6 and 5-7). The line lengths of the test files makes a big difference, hence the variation in results.* In addition, the `char` array implementation uses only 1% of the number of objects compared to the `BufferedReader.readLine()` implementation.

---

* The HotSpot VMs seem better able to optimize the `BufferedReader.readLine()` implementation. Consequently, there are a few long line measurements where the `BufferedReader.readLine()` implementation actually ran faster than the `char` array implementation. But while the HotSpot `BufferedReader.readLine()` implementation times are faster than the JIT times, the `char` array implementation times are significantly slower than the JIT VM times, indicating that HotSpot technology still has a little way to go to achieve its full potential.

Table 5-6. Filter Timings Using filter or cfilter method on a Short-Line File

VM	1.2	1.3	HotSpot 1.0	HotSpot 2nd Run[a]	1.1.6
filter	100%	52%	173%	49%	124%
cfilter	24%	35%	60%	30%	21%

[a] HotSpot timings are often significantly better if a test is repeated in the same VM session.

Table 5-7. Filter Timings Using filter or cfilter Method on a Long-Line File

VM	1.2	1.3	HotSpot 1.0	HotSpot 2nd Run[a]	1.1.6
filter	100%	99%	138%	96%	105%
cfilter	78%	106%	110%	99%	63%

[a] HotSpot timings are often significantly better if a test is repeated in the same VM session.

We have used the most straightforward implementation of the char array parsing. If you look in more detail at what you are doing, you can apply further optimizations and make the routine even faster (see, for example, Chapter 7, *Loops and Switches*, and Chapter 8, *I/O, Logging, and Console Output*).

Tuning like this takes effort, but you can see that it is possible to use char arrays to very good effect for most types of String manipulation. If you are an object purist, you may want to encapsulate the char array access. Otherwise, you may be content to expose external access through static methods. In any case, it is worth investing some time and effort to creating a usable char handling class. Usually this creation is a single, up-front effort. If the classes are well constructed, you can use them consistently within your applications, and this effort pays off handsomely when it comes to tuning (or, occasionally, the lack of a need to tune).

Here is the commented char array implementation that executes a line-by-line string-matching filter on a file:

```
public static void cfilter(String filter, String filename, boolean print)
  throws IOException
{
  count = 0;
  //use an OutputStreamWriter to write to System.out
  //so that we can write directly from the char array.
  OutputStreamWriter writer = print ? new OutputStreamWriter(System.out) : null;
  FileReader rdr = new FileReader(filename);
  char[] cfilter = new char[filter.length()];
  filter.getChars(0, cfilter.length, cfilter, 0);
  char[] buf = new char[8192];
  int len;
  int start = 0;     //start of the buffer for filling purposes
  int idx = 0;       //current index during parsing
  int startOfLine;   //the start of the current line
  int endOfLine;     //the end of the current line
```

```
    //read until there is nothing left
    while( (len = rdr.read(buf, start, buf.length-start)) != -1)
    {
      start = printMatchingLines(buf, 0, len, cfilter, writer);
    }
    //no more to read, but we may still have some lines left in the buffer
    if ((len > 0) && (start = printMatchingLines(buf,0,len,cfilter,writer)) != 0)
    {
      //unterminated line left
      if (indexOfChars(buf, 0, start, cfilter) != -1)
      {
        //Last unterminated line contains match
        printLine(buf, 0, start, writer);
      }
    }
    if (writer != null)
      writer.flush();
    System.out.println(count + " lines matched.");
}

public static int printMatchingLines(char[] buf, int idx, int len,
                   char[] filter, Writer writer)
    throws IOException
{
  int startOfLine;
  int endOfLine;
  while( idx < len )
  {
    //If there are no more matches in the buffer
    if ( (idx = indexOfChars(buf, idx, len, filter)) == -1)
    {
      //then reset the buffer, and return the buffer size
      return resetBuffer(buf, len);
    }
    //otherwise we found a match.
    //Find the beginning and end of the surrounding line
    else if ( (endOfLine = indexOfNewline(buf, idx, len)) == -1)
    {
      //unterminated line - possibly just because the buffer needs filling
      //further then reset the buffer, and return the buffer size
      return resetBuffer(buf, len);
    }
    else
    {
      //print the line
      startOfLine = lastIndexOfNewline(buf, idx, len);
      printLine(buf, startOfLine, endOfLine, writer);
      idx = endOfLine + 1;
    }
```

```
    }
    return resetBuffer(buf, len);
  }

  public static void printLine(char[] buf, int startOfLine,
                               int endOfLine, Writer writer)
    throws IOException
  {
    //print the line from startOfLine up to (including) endOfLine
    count++;
    if (writer != null)
    {
      writer.write(buf, startOfLine, endOfLine - startOfLine + 1);
      writer.write(NewLine);
      writer.flush();
    }
  }

  public static int resetBuffer(char[] buf, int len)
  {
    //copy from the start of the last line into the beginning of the buffer
    int startOfLine = lastIndexOfNewline(buf, len-1, len);
    System.arraycopy(buf, startOfLine, buf, 0, len-startOfLine);
    //and return the size of the buffer.
    return len-startOfLine;
  }

  public static int indexOfNewline(char[] buf, int startIdx, int len)
  {
    while((startIdx < len) && (buf[startIdx] != '\n') && (buf[startIdx] != '\r'))
      startIdx++;
    if ( (buf[startIdx] != '\n') && (buf[startIdx] != '\r') )
      return -1;
    else
      return startIdx-1;
  }

  public static int lastIndexOfNewline(char[] buf, int startIdx, int len)
  {
    while((startIdx > 0) && (buf[startIdx] != '\n') && (buf[startIdx] != '\r'))
      startIdx--;
    if ( (buf[startIdx] != '\n') && (buf[startIdx] != '\r') )
      return 0;
    else
      return startIdx+1;
  }

  public static int indexOfChars(char[] buf, int startIdx,
                                 int bufLen, char[] match)
```

```
{
  //Simple linear search
  int j;
  for (int i = startIdx; i < bufLen; i++)
  {
    if (matches(buf, i, bufLen, match))
      return i;
  }
  return -1;
}

public static boolean matches(char[] buf, int startIdx,
                              int bufLen, char[] match)
{
  if (startIdx + match.length > bufLen)
    return false;
  else
  {
    for(int j = match.length-1; j >= 0 ; j--)
      if(buf[startIdx+j] != match[j])
        return false;
    return true;
  }
}
```

The individual methods listed here are fairly basic. As with the JDK methods, I assume a line termination is indicated by a newline or return character. Otherwise, the main effort comes in writing efficient array-matching methods. In this example, I did not try hard to look for the very best array-matching algorithms. Instead, I used straightforward algorithms for clarity, since these are fast enough for the example. There are many sources describing more sophisticated array-matching algorithms; for example, the University of Rouen in France has a nice site listing "Exact String Matching Algorithms" at *http://www-igm.univ-mlv.fr/ ~lecroq/string/*.

String Comparisons and Searches

String comparison performance is highly dependent on both the string data and the comparison algorithm (this is really a truism about collections in general). The methods that come with the String class have a performance advantage in being able to directly access the underlying char collection. So if you need to make String comparisons, String methods usually provide better performance than your own methods, provided that you can make your desired comparison fit in with one of the String methods. Another necessary consideration is whether comparisons are case-sensitive or -insensitive, and I will consider this in more detail shortly.

To optimize for string comparisons, you need to look at the source of the comparison methods so you know exactly how they work. As an example, consider the `String.equals()` and `String.equalsIgnoreCase()` methods from the Java 2 distribution.

`String.equals(Object)` runs in a fairly straightforward way: it first checks for object identity, then for `null`, then for `String` type, then for same-size strings, and then character by character, running from the first characters to the last. Efficient and complete.

`String.equalsIgnoreCase(String)` is a little more complex. It checks for `null`, and then for strings being the same size (the `String` type check is not needed, since this method accepts only `String` objects). Then, using a case-insensitive comparison, `regionMatches()` is applied. `regionMatches()` runs a character-by-character test from the first character to the last, converting characters to uppercase before comparing them.

Immediately, you see that the more differences there are between the two strings, the faster these methods return. This behavior is common for collection comparisons, and the order of the comparison is crucial. In these two cases, the strings are compared starting with the first character, so the earlier the difference occurs, the faster the methods return. However, `equals()` returns faster if the two `String` objects are identical. It is unusual to check `Strings` by identity, but there are a number of situations where it is useful, for example, when you are using a set of canonical `Strings` (see Chapter 4, *Object Creation*). Another example is when an application has enough time during string input to `intern()`* the strings, so that later comparisons by identity are possible.

In any case, `equals()` returns immediately if the two strings are identical, but `equalsIgnoreCase()` does not even check for identity (which may be reasonable given what it does). This results in `equals()` running an order of magnitude faster than `equalsIgnoreCase()` if the two strings are identical; identical strings is the fastest test case resolvable for `equals()`, but the slowest case for `equalsIgnoreCase()`.

On the other hand, if the two strings are different in size, `equalsIgnoreCase()` has only two tests to make before it returns, whereas `equals()` makes four tests before it returns. This can make `equalsIgnoreCase()` run 20% faster than `equals()` for what may be the most common difference between strings.

---

* `String.intern()` returns the `String` object that is being stored in the internal VM string pool. If two `Strings` are equal, then their `intern()` results are identical; for example, if `s1.equals(s2)` is true, then `s1.intern() == s2.intern()` is also true.

There are more differences between these two methods. In almost every possible case of string data, `equals()` runs faster (often several times faster) than `equalsIgnoreCase()`. However, in a test against the words from a particular dictionary, I found that over 90% of the words were different in size from a randomly chosen word. When comparing the performance of these two methods for a comparison of a randomly chosen word against the entire dictionary, the total comparison time taken by each of the two methods was about the same. The many cases in which strings had different lengths compensated almost exactly for the slower comparison of `equalsIgnoreCase()` when the strings were similar or equal. This illustrates how the data and the algorithm interplay with each other to affect performance.

Even though `String` methods have access to the internal `chars`, it can be faster to use your own methods if there are no `String` methods appropriate for your test. You can build methods that are tailored to the data you have. One way to optimize an equality test is to look for ways to make the strings identical. An alternative that can actually be better for performance is to change the search strategy to reduce search time. For example, a linear search through a large array of `Strings` is slower than a binary search through the same size array if the array is sorted. This, in turn, is slower than a straight access to a hashed table. Note that when you are able and willing to deploy changes to JDK classes (e.g., for servlets), you can add methods directly to the `String` class. However, altering JDK classes can lead to maintenance problems.[*]

When case-insensitive searches are required, one standard optimization is to use a second collection containing all the strings uppercased. This second collection is used for comparisons, thus avoiding the need to repeatedly uppercase each character in the search methods. For example, if you have a hash table containing `String` keys, you need to iterate over all the keys to match keys case-insensitively. But, if you have a second hash table with all the keys uppercased, retrieving the key simply requires you to uppercase the element being searched for:

```
//The slow version, iterating through all the keys ignoring case
//until the key matches. (hash is a Hashtable)
public Object slowlyGet(String key)
{
  Enumeration e = hash.keys();
  String hkey;
  while(e.hasMoreElements())
  {
    if (key.equalsIgnoreCase(hkey = (String) e.getNext()))
      return hash.get(hkey);
```

---

[*] Several of my colleagues have emphasized their view that changes to the JDK sources lead to severe maintenance problems.

```
    }
    return null;
  }


  //The fast version assumes that a second hashtable was created
  //with all the keys uppercased. Access is straightforward.
  public Object quicklyGet(String key)
  {
    return uppercasedHash.get(key.toUppercase());
  }
```

However, note that `String.toUppercase()` (and `String.toLowercase()`) creates a complete copy of the `String` object with a new `char` array. Unlike `String.substring()`, `String.toUppercase()` has a processing time that is linearly dependent on the size of the string and also creates an extra object (a new `char` array). This means that repeatedly using `String.toUppercase()` (and `String.toLowercase()`) can impose a heavy overhead on an application. For each particular problem, you need to ensure that the extra temporary objects created and the extra processing overheads still provide a performance benefit rather than causing a new bottleneck in the application.

Sorting Internationalized Strings

One big advantage you get with `Strings` is that they are built (almost) from the ground up to support internationalization. This means that the Unicode character set is the lingua franca in Java. Unfortunately, because Unicode uses two-byte characters, many string libraries based on one-byte characters that can be ported into Java do not work so well. Most string-search optimizations use tables to assist string searches, but the table size is related to the size of the character set. For example, traditional Boyer-Moore string search takes much memory and a long initialization phase to use with Unicode.

Furthermore, sorting international `Strings` requires the ability to handle many kinds of localization issues, such as the sorted location for accented characters, characters that can be treated as character pairs, and so on. In these cases, it is difficult (and usually impossible) to handle the general case yourself. It is almost always easier to use the `String` helper classes Java provides, for example, the `java.text.Collator` class.*

---

* The code that handles this type of work didn't really start to get integrated in Java until 1.1, and did not start to be optimized until JDK 1.2. An article by Laura Werner of IBM in the February 1999 issue of the *Java Report*, "Efficient Text Searching in Java," covers the optimizations added to the `java.text.Collator` class for JDK 1.2. There is also a useful `StringSearch` class available at the IBM alphaWorks site (*http://www.alphaworks.ibm.com*).

The Boyer-Moore String-Search Algorithm

Boyer-Moore string search uses a table of characters to skip comparisons. Here's a simple example with none of the complexities. Assume you are matching "abcd" against a string. The "abcd" is aligned against the first four characters of the string. The fourth character of the string is checked first. If that fourth character is none of a, b, c, or d, the "abcd" can be skipped to be matched against the fifth to eighth characters, and the matching proceeds in the same way. If instead the fourth character of the string is b, the "abcd" can be skipped to align the b against the fourth character, and the matching proceeds as before. For optimum speed, this algorithm requires several arrays giving skip distances for each possible character in the character set. For more detail, see the Knuth book listed in Chapter 15, *Further Resources*, or the paper "Fast Algorithms for Sorting and Searching Strings," by Jon Bentley and Robert Sedgewick, Proceedings of the 8th Annual ACM-SIAM Symposium on Discrete Algorithms, January 1997. There is also a web site that describes a large number of string-searching algorithms at *http://www-igm.univ-mlv.fr/~lecroq/string/*.

Using the `java.text.CollationKey` object to represent each string is a standard optimization for repeated comparisons of internationalized `Strings`. You can use this when sorting an array of `Strings`, for example. `CollationKeys` perform more than twice as fast as using `java.text.Collator.compare()`. It is probably easiest to see how to use collation keys with a particular example. So let's look at tuning an internationalized `String` sort.

For this, I use a standard quicksort algorithm (the quicksort implementation can be found in "Finding the Index for Partially Matched Strings" in Chapter 11, *Appropriate Data Structures and Algorithms*). The only modification to the standard quicksort is that for each optimization, the quicksort needs to be adjusted to use the appropriate comparison method and the appropriate data type. For example, the generic quicksort that sorts an array of `Comparable` objects has the signature:

```
public static void quicksort(Comparable[] arr, int lo, int hi)
```

and uses the `Comparable.compareTo(Object)` method when comparing two `Comparable` objects. On the other hand, a generic quicksort that sorts objects based on a `java.util.Comparator` has the signature:

```
public static void quicksort(Object[] arr, int lo, int hi, Comparator c)
```

and uses the `java.util.Comparator.compare(Object, Object)` method when comparing any two objects. (See `java.util.Arrays.sort()` for a specific example.) In each case the underlying algorithm is the same. Only the comparison method changes (and in general the data type too, though not in these examples where the data type was Object).

The obvious first test, to get a performance baseline, is the straightforward internationalized sort:

```
public runsort() {
  quicksort(stringArray,0,stringArray.length-1, Collator.getInstance());
}
public static void quicksort(String[] arr, int lo, int hi, java.text.Collator c)
{
  ...
  int mid = ( lo + hi ) / 2;
  String middle = arr[ mid ]; //String data type
  ...
  //uses Collator.compare(String, String)
  if( c.compare(arr[ lo ], middle) > 0 )
  ...
}
```

I use a large dictionary of words for the array of strings, inserted in random order, and I use the same random order for each of the tests. The first test took longer than expected. Looking at the Collator class, I can see that it does a huge amount, and I cannot possibly bypass its internationalized support if I want to support internationalized strings.*

However, as previously mentioned, the Collator class comes with the java.util.CollationKey class specifically to provide for this type of speedup. It is simple to convert the sort in order to use this. You still need the Collator to generate the CollationKeys, so add a conversion method. The sort now looks like:

```
public runsort() {
  quicksort(stringArray,0,stringArray.length-1, Collator.getInstance());
}
public static void quicksort(String[] arr, int lo, int hi, Collator c)
{
  //convert to an array of CollationKeys
  CollationKey keys[] = new CollationKey[arr.length];
  for (int i = arr.length-1; i >= 0; i--)
    keys[i] = c.getCollationKey(arr[i]);

  //Run the sort on the collation keys
  quicksort_collationKey(keys, 0, arr.length-1);
```

---

* The kind of investment made in building such global support is beyond most projects; it is almost always much cheaper to buy the support. In this case, Taligent put a huge number of man years into the globalization you get for free with the JDK.

```
   //and unwrap so that we get our Strings in sorted order
   for (int i = arr.length-1; i >= 0; i--)
     arr[i] = keys[i].getSourceString();
 }
 public static void quicksort_collationKey(CollationKey[] arr, int lo, int hi)
 {
   ...
   int mid = ( lo + hi ) / 2;
   CollationKey middle = arr[ mid ];   //CollationKey data type
   ...
   //uses CollationKey.compareTo(CollationKey)
   if( arr[ lo ].compareTo(middle) > 0 )
   ...
 }
```

Normalizing the time for the first test to 100%, this test is much faster and takes
half the time (see Table 5-8). This is despite the extra cost imposed by a whole new
populated array of CollationKey objects, one for each string. Can it do better?
Well, there is nothing further in the java.text package that suggests so. Instead
look at the String class, and consider its implementation of the String.
compareTo() method. This is a simple lexicographic ordering, basically treating
the char array as a sequence of numbers and ordering sequence pairs as if there is
no meaning to the object being Strings. Obviously, this is useless for internationalized support, but it is much faster. A quick test shows that sorting the test String
array using the String.compareTo() method takes just 3% of time of the first
test, which seems much more reasonable.

But is this test incompatible with the desired internationalized sort? Well, maybe
not. Sort algorithms usually execute faster if they operate on a partially sorted
array. Perhaps using the String.compareTo() sort first might bring the array
considerably closer to the final ordering of the internationalized sort, and at a
fairly low cost. Testing this is straightforward:

```
public runsort() {
  quicksort(stringArray,0,stringArray.length-1, Collator.getInstance());
}
public static void quicksort(String[] arr, int lo, int hi, Collator c)
{
  //simple sort using String.compareTo()
  simple_quicksort(arr, lo, hi);

  //Full international sort on a hopefully partially sorted array
  intl_quicksort(arr, lo, hi, c);
}
public static void simple_quicksort(String[] arr, int lo, int hi)
{
  ...
  int mid = ( lo + hi ) / 2;
```

```
      String middle = arr[ mid ];   //uses String data type
      ...
      //uses String.compareTo(String)
      if( arr[ lo ].compareTo(middle) > 0 )
      ...
}
public static void intl_quicksort(String[] arr, int lo, int hi, Collator c)
{
   //convert to an array of CollationKeys
   CollationKey keys[] = new CollationKey[arr.length];
   for (int i = arr.length-1; i >= 0; i--)
      keys[i] = c.getCollationKey(arr[i]);

   //Run the sort on the collation keys
   quicksort_collationKey(keys, 0, arr.length-1);

   //and unwrap so that we get our Strings in sorted order
   for (int i = arr.length-1; i >= 0; i--)
      arr[i] = keys[i].getSourceString();
}
public static void quicksort_collationKey(CollationKey[] arr, int lo, int hi)
{
   ...
   int mid = ( lo + hi ) / 2;
   CollationKey middle = arr[ mid ]; //CollationKey data type
   ...
   //uses CollationKey.compareTo(CollationKey)
   if( arr[ lo ].compareTo(middle) > 0 )
   ...
}
```

This double-sorting implementation reduces the international sort time to a quarter of the original test time (see Table 5-8). Partially sorting the list first using a much simpler (and quicker) comparison test has doubled the speed of the total sort as compared to using only the CollationKeys optimization.

Table 5-8. Timings Using Different Sorting Strategies

Sort Using:	1.2	1.3	HotSpot 1.0	1.1.6
Collator	100%	55%	42%	1251%
CollationKeys	49%	25%	36%	117%
Sorted twice	22%	11%	15%	58%
String.compareTo( )	*3%*	*2%*	*4%*	*3%*

Of course, these optimizations have improved the situation only for the particular locale I have tested (my default locale is set for US English). However, running the test in a sampling of other locales (European and Asian locales), I find similar relative speedups. Without using locale-specific dictionaries, this locale variation test may not be fully valid. But the speedup will likely hold across all Latinized alpha-bets. You can also create a simple partial-ordering class-specific sort to some locales, which provides a similar speedup. For example, by duplicating the effect of using `String.compareTo()`, you can provide the basis for a customized partial sorter:

```
public class PartialSorter {
  String source;
  char[] stringArray;
  public Sorting(String s)
  {
    //retain the original string
    source = s;
    //and get the array of characters for our customized comparison
    stringArray = new char[s.length()];
    s.getChars(0, stringArray.length, stringArray, 0);
  }
  /* This compare method should be customized for different locales */
  public static int compare(char[] arr1, char[] arr2)
  {
    //basically the String.compareTo() algorithm
    int n = Math.min(arr1.length, arr2.length);
    for (int i = 0; i < n; i++)
    {
      if (arr1[i] != arr2[i])
        return arr1[i] - arr2[i];
    }
    return arr1.length - arr2.length;
  }
  public static void quicksort(String[] arr, int lo, int hi)
  {
    //convert to an array of PartialSorters
    PartialSorter keys[] = new PartialSorter[arr.length];
    for (int i = arr.length-1; i >= 0; i--)
      keys[i] = new PartialSorter(arr[i]);
    quicksort_mysorter(keys, 0, arr.length-1);
    //and unwrap so that we get our Strings in sorted order
    for (int i = arr.length-1; i >= 0; i--)
      arr[i] = keys[i].source;
  }
  public static void quicksort_mysorter(PartialSorter[] arr, int lo, int hi)
  {
    ...
    int mid = ( lo + hi ) / 2;
    PartialSorter middle = arr[ mid ]; //PartialSorter data type
    ...
    //Use the PartialSorter.compare() method to compare the char arrays
    if( compare(arr[ lo ].stringArray, middle.stringArray) > 0 )
    ...
  }
}
```

This `PartialSorter` class works similarly to the `CollationKey` class, wrapping a string and providing its own comparison method. The particular comparison method shown here is just an implementation of the `String.compareTo()` method. It is pointless to use it exactly as defined here, because object-creation overhead means that using the `PartialSorter` is twice as slow as using the `String.compareTo()` directly. But customizing the `PartialSorter.compare()` method for any particular locale is a reasonable task: remember, we are only interested in a simple algorithm that handles a partial sort, not the full intricacies of completely accurate locale-specific comparison.

Generally, you cannot expect to support internationalized strings and retain the performance of simple one-byte-per-character strings. But, as shown here, you can certainly improve the performance by some useful amounts.

Performance Checklist

Most of these suggestions apply only after a bottleneck has been identified:

- Logically partition your strings into those that require internationalization support (i.e., text) and those that don't.

  — Avoid internationalization where the `Strings` never require it.

- Avoid using the `StreamTokenizer`.

- Create and optimize your own framework to convert objects and primitives to and from strings.

- Use efficient methods of `String` that do not copy the characters of the string, e.g., `String.substring()`.

  — Avoid using inefficient methods of `String` that copy the characters of the string, e.g., `String.toUppercase()` and `String.toLowercase()`.

  — Use the string concatenation operator to create `Strings` at compile time.

  — Use `StringBuffers` to create `Strings` at runtime.

  — Specify when the underlying `char` array is copied when reusing `StringBuffers`.

- Improve access to the underlying `String char` array by copying the `chars` into your own array.

  — Manipulate characters in `char` arrays rather than using `String` and `StringBuffer` manipulation.

  — Reuse `char` arrays.

- Optimize the string comparison and search algorithm for the data being compared and searched.

  — Compare strings by identity.

  — Convert a comparison task to a (hash) table lookup.

  — Handle case-insensitive comparisons differently from case-sensitive comparisons.

  — Apply the standard performance optimization for case-insensitive access (maintaining a second collection with all strings uppercased).

  — Use `java.text.CollationKeys` rather than a `java.text.Collator` object to sort international strings.

  — Use `String.compareTo()` for string comparison where internationalization is unnecessary.

  — Partially sort (international) strings using a simple comparison algorithm before using the full (internationalized) comparison.

6

Exceptions, Casts, and Variables

For every complex problem, there is a solution that is simple, neat, and wrong.

—H. L. Mencken

Exceptions

In this section, we examine the cost of exceptions and consider ways to avoid that cost. First, we look at the costs associated with `try-catch` blocks, which are the structures you need to handle exceptions. Then, we go on to optimizing the use of exceptions.

The Cost of try-catch Blocks Without an Exception

`try-catch` blocks generally use no extra time if no exception is thrown, although some VMs may impose a slight penalty. The following test determines whether a VM imposes any significant overhead for `try-catch` blocks when the `catch` block is not entered. The test runs the same code twice, once with the `try-catch` entered for every loop iteration and again with just one `try-catch` wrapping the loop. Because we're testing the VM and not the compiler, you must ensure that your compiler has not optimized the test away; use an old JDK version to compile it if necessary. To determine that the test has not been optimized away by the compiler, you need to compile the code, then decompile it:

```
package tuning.exception;

public class TryCatchTimeTest
{
  public static void main(String[] args)
  {
    int REPEAT = (args.length == 0) ? 10000000 : Integer.parseInt(args[0]);
```

```java
    Object[] xyz = {new Integer(3), new Integer(10101), new Integer(67)};
    boolean res;
    long time = System.currentTimeMillis();
    res = try_catch_in_loop(REPEAT, xyz);
    System.out.println("try catch in loop took    " +
      (System.currentTimeMillis() - time));

    time = System.currentTimeMillis();
    res = try_catch_not_in_loop(REPEAT, xyz);
    System.out.println("try catch not in loop took " +
      (System.currentTimeMillis() - time));

    //Repeat the two tests several more times in this method
    //for consistency checking
    ...
}

public static boolean try_catch_not_in_loop(int repeat, Object[] o)
{
  Integer i[] = new Integer[3];
  try {
    for (int j = repeat; j > 0; j--)
    {
      i[0] = (Integer) o[(j+1)%2];
      i[1] = (Integer) o[j%2];
      i[2] = (Integer) o[(j+2)%2];
    }
    return false;
  }
  catch (Exception e) {return true;}
}

public static boolean try_catch_in_loop(int repeat, Object[] o)
{
  Integer i[] = new Integer[3];
  for (int j = repeat; j > 0; j--)
  {
    try {
      i[0] = (Integer) o[(j+1)%2];
      i[1] = (Integer) o[j%2];
      i[2] = (Integer) o[(j+2)%2];
    }
    catch (Exception e) {return true;}
  }
  return false;
}
}
```

Running this test in various VMs results in a 10% increase in the time taken by the looped `try-catch` test relative to the nonlooped test for some VMs. See Table 6-1.

Table 6-1. Extra Cost of the Looped try-catch Test Relative to the Nonlooped try-catch Test

VM	1.2	1.2 no JIT	1.3	HotSpot 1.0	1.1.6
Increase in time	~10%	None	~10%	~10%	None

The Cost of try-catch Blocks with an Exception

Throwing an exception and executing the `catch` block has a significant overhead. This overhead seems to be due mainly to the cost of getting a snapshot of the stack when the exception is created (the snapshot allows the stack trace to be printed). The cost is large: exceptions should not be thrown as part of the normal code path of your application unless you have factored it in. Generating exceptions is one place where good design and performance go hand in hand. You should throw an exception only when the condition is truly exceptional. For example, an end-of-file condition is not an exceptional condition (all files end) unless the end-of-file occurs when more bytes are expected.* Generally, the performance cost of throwing an exception is equivalent to several hundred lines of simple code executions.

WARNING   If your application is implemented to throw an exception during the normal flow of the program, you must not avoid the exception during performance tests. Any time costs coming from throwing exceptions must be included in performance testing, or the test results will be skewed from the actual performance of the application after deployment.

To find the cost of throwing an exception, compare two ways of testing whether an object is a member of a class: trying a cast and catching the exception if the cast fails, versus using `instanceof`. In the code that follows, I have highlighted the lines that run the alternative tests:

```
package tuning.exception;

public class TryCatchCostTest
{
  public static void main(String[] args)
  {
    Integer i = new Integer(3);
    Boolean b = new Boolean(true);
```

---

* There are exceptions to the rule. For example, in "Exception-Terminated Loops" in Chapter 7, *Loops and Switches*, the cost of one exception thrown is less than the cost of repeatedly making a test in the loop, though this is seen only if the number of loop iterations is large enough.

```
    int REPEAT = 5000000;
    int FACTOR = 1000;
    boolean res;

    long time = System.currentTimeMillis();
    for (int j = REPEAT*FACTOR; j > 0 ; j--)
      res = test1(i);
    time = System.currentTimeMillis() - time;
    System.out.println("test1(i) took " + time);

    time = System.currentTimeMillis();
    for (int j = REPEAT; j > 0 ; j--)
      res = test1(b);
    time = System.currentTimeMillis() - time;
    System.out.println("test1(b) took " + time);

    //and the same timed test for test2(i) and test2(b),
    //iterating REPEAT*FACTOR times
    ...
  }

  public static boolean test1(Object o)
  {
    try {
      Integer i = (Integer) o;
      return false;
    }
    catch (Exception e) {return true;}
  }

  public static boolean test2(Object o)
  {
    if (o instanceof Integer)
      return false;
    else
      return true;
  }
}
```

The results of this comparison show that if `test2()` (using `instanceof`) takes one time unit, `test1()` with the `ClassCastException` thrown takes over 5000 time units in JDK 1.2 (see Table 6-2). On this time scale, `test1()` without the exception thrown takes eight time units: this time reflects the cost of making the cast and assignment. You can take the eight time units as the base time to compare exactly the same method executing with two different instances passed to it. Even for this comparison, the cost of executing `test1()` with an instance of the wrong type (where the exception is thrown) is at least 600 times more expensive than when the instance passed is of the right type.

Table 6-2. Extra Cost of try-catch Blocks When Exceptions Are Thrown

Relative Times for	1.2	1.2 no JIT	1.3	HotSpot 1.0	1.1.6
test1(b)/test2(b)	~5000	~75	~150	~400	~4000
test1(b)/test1(i)	~600	~150	~2000	~1750	~500
test2(b)/test2(i)	1	~2	~12	~4	1

NOTE   For VMs not running a JIT, the relative times for test2() are different depending on the object passed. test2() takes one time unit when returning true but, curiously, two to twelve time units when returning false. This curious difference for a false result indicates that the instanceof operator is faster when the instance's class correctly matches the tested class. A negative instanceof test must also check whether the instance is from a subclass or interface of the tested type before it can definitely return false. Given this, it is actually quite interesting that with a JIT, there is no difference in times between the two instanceof tests.

Because it is impossible to add methods to classes that are compiled (as opposed to classes you have the source for and can recompile), there are necessarily places in Java code where you have to test for the type of object. Where this type of code is unavoidable, you should use instanceof, as shown in test2(), rather than a speculative class cast. There is no maintenance disadvantage in using instanceof, nor is the code any clearer or easier to alter by avoiding its use. I strongly advise you to avoid the use of the speculative class cast, however. It is a real performance hog and ugly as well.

Using Exceptions Without the Stack Trace Overhead

You may decide that you definitely require an exception to be thrown, despite the disadvantages. If the exception is thrown explicitly (i.e., using a throw statement rather than a VM-generated exception such as the ClassCastException or ArrayIndexOutOfBoundsException), you can reduce the cost by reusing an exception object rather than creating a new one. Most of the cost of throwing an exception is incurred in actually creating the new exception, which is when the stack trace is filled in. Reusing an existing exception object without resetting the stack trace avoids the exception-creation overhead. Throwing and catching an existing exception object is two orders of magnitude faster than doing the same with a newly created exception object:

```
public static Exception REUSABLE_EXCEPTION = new Exception();
...

  //Much faster reusing an existing exception
  try {throw REUSABLE_EXCEPTION;}
  catch (Exception e) {...}
```

```
//This next try-catch is 50 to 100 times slower than the last
try {throw new Exception();}
catch (Exception e) {...}
```

The sole disadvantage of reusing an exception instance is that the instance does not have the correct stack trace, i.e., the stack trace held by the exception object is the one generated when the exception object was created.* However, this disadvantage can be important for some situations when the trace is important, so be careful. This technique can easily lead to maintenance problems.

Conditional Error Checking

During development, you typically write a lot of code that checks the arguments passed into various methods for validity. This kind of checking is invaluable during development and testing, but it can lead to a lot of overhead in the finished application. Therefore, you need a technique for implementing error checks that can optionally be removed during compilation. The most common way to do this is to use an if block:

```
public class GLOBAL_CONSTANTS {
  public static final boolean ERROR_CHECKING_ON = true;
  ...
}


//and code in methods of other classes includes an if block like
if (GLOBAL_CONSTANTS.ERROR_CHECKING_ON)
{
  //error check code of some sort
  ...
```

This technique allows you to turn off error checking by recompiling the application with the ERROR_CHECKING_ON variable set to false. Doing this recompilation actually eliminates all if blocks completely, due to a feature of the compiler (see the section "Dead code branches are eliminated" in Chapter 3, *Underlying JDK Improvements*). Setting the value to false without recompilation also works, but avoids only the block, not the block entry test. In this case, the if statement is still executed, but the block is not entered. This still causes some performance impact: an extra test for almost every method call is significant, so it is better to recompile.†

---

* To get the exception object to hold the stack trace that is current when it is thrown, rather than created, you must use the fillInStackTrace() method. Of course, this is what causes the large overhead that you are trying to avoid.

† However, this technique cannot eliminate all types of code blocks. For example, you cannot use this technique to eliminate try-catch blocks from the code they surround. You can achieve that level of control only by using a preprocessor. My thanks to Ethan Henry for pointing this out.

Casts

Casts also have a cost. Casts that can be resolved at compile time can be eliminated by the compiler (and are eliminated by the JDK compiler). Consider the two lines:

```
Integer i = new Integer(3);
Integer j = (Integer) i;
```

These two lines get compiled as if they were written as:

```
Integer i = new Integer(3);
Integer j = i;
```

On the other hand, casts not resolvable at compile time must be executed at runtime. But note that an `instanceof` test cannot be fully resolved at compile time:

```
Integer integer = new Integer(3);
if (integer instanceof Integer)
  Integer j = integer;
```

The test in the `if` statement here cannot be resolved by most compilers, because `instanceof` can return `false` if the first operand (`integer`) is `null`. (A more intelligent compiler might resolve this particular case by determining that `integer` was definitely not `null` for this code fragment, but most compilers are not that sophisticated.)

Primitive data type casts (`ints`, `bytes`, etc.) are quicker than object data type casts because there is no test involved, only a straightforward data conversion. But a primitive data type cast is still a runtime operation and has an associated cost.

Object type casts basically confirm that the object is of the required type. It appears that a VM with a JIT compiler is capable of reducing the cost of some casts to practically nothing. The following test, when run under JDK 1.2 without a JIT, shows object casts as having a small but measurable cost. With the JIT compiler running, the cast has no measurable effect (see Table 6-3):

```
package tuning.exception;

public class CastTest
{
  public static void main(String[] args)
  {
    Integer i = new Integer(3);
    int REPEAT = 500000000;
    Integer res;

    long time = System.currentTimeMillis();
    for (int j = REPEAT; j > 0 ; j--)
      res = test1(i);
    time = System.currentTimeMillis() - time;
```

```
      System.out.println("test1(i) took " + time);

      time = System.currentTimeMillis();
      for (int j = REPEAT; j > 0 ; j--)
        res = test2(i);
      time = System.currentTimeMillis() - time;
      System.out.println("test2(i) took " + time);

      ... and the same test for test2(i) and test1(i)
    }

  public static Integer test1(Object o)
  {
    Integer i = (Integer) o;
    return i;
  }

  public static Integer test2(Integer o)
  {
    Integer i = (Integer) o;
    return i;
  }
 }
```

Table 6-3. The Extra Cost of Casts

VM	1.2	1.2 no JIT	1.3	HotSpot 1.0	1.1.6
Increase in time	None	>10%	>20%	~5%	None

However, the cost of an object type cast is not constant: it depends on the depth of the hierarchy and whether the casting type is an interface or a class. Interfaces are generally more expensive to use in casting, and the further back in the hierarchy (and ordering of interfaces in the class definition), the longer the cast takes to execute. Remember, though: never change the design of the application for minor performance gains.

It is best to avoid casts whenever possible, for example by creating and using type-specific collection classes instead of using generic collection classes. Rather than use a standard List to store a list of Strings, you gain better performance by creating and using a StringList class. You should always try to type the variable as precisely as possible. In Chapter 9, *Sorting*, you can see that by rewriting a sort implementation to eliminate casts, the sorting time can be halved.

If a variable needs casting several times, cast once and save the object into a temporary variable of the cast type. Use that temporary instead of repeatedly casting; avoid the following kind of code:

```
if (obj instanceof Something)
  return ((Something)obj).x + ((Something)obj).y + ((Something)obj).z;
  ...
```

Instead, use a temporary:*

```
if (obj instanceof Something)
{
  Something something = (Something) obj;
  return something.x + something.y + something.z;
}
...
```

The revised code is also more readable. In tight loops, you may need to evaluate the cost of repeatedly assigning values to a temporary variable (see Chapter 7).

Variables

Local (temporary) variables and method-argument variables are the fastest variables to access and update. Local variables remain on the stack, so they can be manipulated directly; the manipulation of local variables depends on both the VM and underlying machine implementation. Heap variables (static and instance variables) are manipulated in heap memory through the Java VM-assigned bytecodes that apply to these variables. There are special bytecodes for accessing the first four local variables and parameters on a method stack. Arguments are counted first; then, if there are less than four passed arguments, local variables are counted. For nonstatic methods, `this` always takes the first slot. `longs` and `doubles` each take two slots. Theoretically, this means that methods with no more than three parameters and local variables combined (four for `static` methods) should be slightly faster than equivalent methods with a larger number of parameters and local variables. This also means that any variables allocated the special bytecodes should be slightly faster to manipulate. In practice, I have found any effect is small or negligible, and it is not worth the effort involved to limit the number of arguments and variables.

Instance and static variables can be up to an order of magnitude slower to operate on when compared to method arguments and local variables. You can see this clearly with a simple test comparing local and static loop counters:

```
package tuning.exception;

public class VariableTest2
{
  static int cntr;
  public static void main(String[] args)
  {
    int REPEAT = 500000000;
```

---

* This is a special case of common subexpression elimination. See "Eliminate common subexpressions" in Chapter 3.

```
int tot = 0;
long time = System.currentTimeMillis();
for (int i = -REPEAT; i < 0; i++)
  tot += i;
time = System.currentTimeMillis() - time;
System.out.println("Loop local took " + time);

tot = 0;
time = System.currentTimeMillis();
for (cntr = -REPEAT; cntr < 0; cntr++)
  tot += cntr;
time = System.currentTimeMillis() - time;
System.out.println("Loop static took " + time);


  }
}
```

Running this test results in the second loop taking several times longer than the first loop (see Table 6-4).

Table 6-4. The Cost of Nonlocal Loop Variables Relative to Local Variables

Times Relative to Loop Local Variables	1.2	1.2 no JIT	1.3	HotSpot 1.0	1.1.6
Static variable time/ local variable time	500%	191%	149%	155%	785%
Static array element/ local variable time	503%	307%	359%	232%	760%

If you are making many manipulations on an instance or static variable, it is better to execute them on a temporary variable, then reassign to the instance variable at the end. This is true for instance variables that hold arrays as well. Arrays also have an overhead, due to the range checking Java provides. So if you are manipulating an element of an array many times, again you should probably assign it to a temporary variable for the duration. For example, the following code fragment repeatedly accesses and updates the same array element:

```
for(int i = 0; i < Repeat; i++)
  countArr[0]+=i;
```

You should replace such repeated array element manipulation with a temporary variable:

```
int count = countArr[0];
for(int i = 0; i < Repeat; i++)
  count+=i;
countArr[0]=count;
```

This kind of substitution can also apply to an array object:

```
static int[] Static_array = {1,2,3,4,5,6,7,8,9};

public static int manipulate_static_array() {
   //assign the static variable to a local variable, and use that local
   int[] arr = Static_array;
   ...

//or even
public static int manipulate_static_array() {
   //pass the static variable to another method that manipulates it
   return manipulate_static_array(Static_array);}
public static int manipulate_static_array(int[] arr) {
   ...
```

Array-element access is typically two to three times as expensive as accessing non-array elements (see *http://www.javaworld.com/javaworld/jw-09-1998/jw-09-speed.html*). This expense is probably due to the range checking and null pointer checking (for the array itself) done by the VM. The VM JIT compiler manages to eliminate almost all the overhead in the case of large arrays. But in spite of this, you can assume that array-element access is going to be slower than plain-variable access in almost every Java environment (this also applies to array element updates). See "Initialization" in Chapter 4, *Object Creation*, for techniques to improve performance when initializing arrays.

ints are normally the fastest variable type to operate on. longs and doubles can take longer to access and update than other variables because they are twice the basic storage length for Java (which is four bytes). *The Java Language Specification* allows longs and doubles to be stored in more than one action. The specification allows the actual manipulation of longs and doubles to be implementation- and processor-dependent, so you cannot assume longs and doubles always take longer. If you have one specific target environment, you can test it to determine its implementation. Note that because of the specification, longs and doubles are the only data types that can be corrupted by simultaneous assignment from multiple threads (see "Atomic Access and Assignment" in Chapter 10, *Threading*, for more details).

When executing arithmetic with the primitive data types, ints are undoubtedly the most efficient. shorts, bytes, and chars are all widened to ints for almost any type of arithmetic operation. They then require a cast back if you want to end up with the data type you started with. For example, adding two bytes produces an int and requires a cast to get back a byte. longs are usually less efficient. Floating-point arithmetic seems to be the worst.

Note that temporary variables of primitive data types (i.e., not objects) can be allocated on the stack, which is usually implemented using a faster memory cache local to the CPU. Temporary objects, however, must be created from the heap (the object reference itself is allocated on the stack, but the object must be in the heap). This means that operations on any object are invariably slower than on any of the primitive data types for temporary variables. Also, as soon as variables are discarded at the end of a method call, the memory from the stack can immediately be reused for other temporaries. But any temporary objects remain in the heap until garbage collection reallocates the space. The result is that temporary variables using primitive (nonobject) data types are better for performance.

One other way to speed up applications is to access public instance variables rather than use accessor methods (getters and setters). Of course, this breaks encapsulation, so it is bad design in most cases. The JDK uses this technique in a number of places (e.g., `Dimension` and `GridBagConstraints` in `java.awt` have `public` instance variables; in the case of `Dimension`, this is almost certainly for performance reasons). Generally, you can use this technique without too much worry if you are passing an object that encapsulates a bunch of parameters (such as `GridBagConstraints`); in fact, this makes for an extensible design. If you really want to ensure that the object remains unaltered when passed, you can set the instance variables to be `final` (so long as it is one of your application-defined classes).

Method Parameters

As I said at the beginning of the last section, method parameters are low-cost, and you normally don't need to worry about the cost of adding extra method parameters. But it is worth being alert to situations in which there are parameters that could be added but have not. This is a simple tuning technique that is rarely considered. Typically, the parameters that could be added are arrays and array lengths. For example, when parsing a `String` object, it is common not to pass the length of the string to methods, because each method can get the length using the `String.length()` method. But parsing tends to be intensive and recursive, with lots of method calls. Most of those methods need to know the length of the string. Although you can eliminate multiple calls within one method by assigning the length to a temporary variable, you cannot do that when many methods need that length. Passing the string length as a parameter is almost certainly cheaper than repeated calls to `String.length()`.

Similarly, you typically access the elements of the string one at a time using `String.charAt()`. But again, it is better for performance purposes to copy the `String` object into a `char` array, and then pass this array through your methods (see Chapter 5, *Strings*). To provide a possible performance boost, try passing extra values and arrays to isolated groups of methods. As usual, you should do this only when a bottleneck has been identified, not throughout an implementation.

Finally, you can reduce the number of objects used by an application by passing an object into a method, which then fills in the object's fields. This is almost always more efficient than creating new objects within the method. See "Reusable Parameters" in Chapter 4 for a more detailed explanation of this technique.

Performance Checklist

Most of these suggestions apply only after a bottleneck has been identified:

- Include all error-condition checking in blocks guarded by `if` statements.
- Avoid throwing exceptions in the normal code path of your application.
    - Check if a `try-catch` in the bottleneck imposes any extra cost.
    - Use `instanceof` instead of making speculative class casts in a `try-catch` block.
    - Consider throwing exceptions without generating a stack trace by reusing a previously created instance.
    - Include any exceptions generated during the normal flow of the program when running performance tests.
- Minimize casting.
    - Avoid casts by creating and using type-specific collection classes.
    - Use temporary variables of the cast type, instead of repeatedly casting.
    - Type variables as precisely as possible.
- Use local variables rather than instance or static variables for faster manipulation.
    - Use temporary variables to manipulate instance variables, static variables, and array elements.
    - Use `int`s in preference to any other data type.
    - Avoid `long` and `double` instance or static variables.
    - Use primitive data types instead of objects for temporary variables.
- Consider accessing instance variables directly rather than through accessor methods. But note that this breaks encapsulation.
- Add extra method parameters when that would allow a method to avoid additional method calls.

7

Loops and Switches

> *I have made this letter longer than usual because I lack the time to make it shorter.*
>
> —Blaise Pascal

Programs spend most of their time in loops. There are many optimizations that can speed up loops:

- Take out of the loop any code that does not need to be executed on every pass. This includes assignments, accesses, tests, and method calls that need to run only once.

- Method calls are more costly than the equivalent code without the call, and by repeating method calls again and again, you just add overhead to your application. Move any method calls out of the loop, even if this requires rewriting. Inline method calls in loops when possible.

- Array access (and assignment) always has more overhead than temporary variable access because the VM performs bounds-checking for array-element access. Array access is better done once (and assigned to a temporary) outside the loop rather than repeated at each iteration. For example, consider this next loop:

```
for(int i = 0; i < Repeat; i++)
  countArr[0]+=10;
```

The following loop optimizes the last loop using a temporary variable to execute the addition within the loop. The array element is updated outside the loop. This optimized loop is significantly better (twice as fast) than the original loop:

```
count = countArr[0];
for(int i = 0; i < Repeat; i++)
  count+=10;
countArr[0]=count;
```

- Comparison to 0 is faster than comparisons to most other numbers. The VM has optimizations for comparisons to the integers –1, 0, 1, 2, 3, 4, and 5. So rewriting loops to make the test a comparison against 0 may be faster.* This alteration typically reverses the iteration order of the loop from counting up (0 to max) to counting down (max to 0). For example, `for` loops are usually coded:

```
for(int i = 0; i < Repeat; i++)
```

Both of these functionally identical `for` loops are faster:

```
for(int i = Repeat-1; i >= 0; i--)
for(int i = Repeat; --i >= 0 ; )
```

- Avoid using a method call in the loop termination test. The overhead is significant. I often see loops like this when iterating through collections such as Vectors and Strings:

```
for(int i = 0; i < collection.size(); i++) //or collection.length()
```

This next loop factors out the maximum iteration value and is faster:

```
int max = v.size(); //or int max = s.length();
for(int i = 0; i < max; i++)
```

- Using `int` data types for the index variable is faster than using any other numeric data types. The VM is optimized to use `ints`. Operations on `bytes`, `shorts`, and `chars` are normally carried out with implicit casts to and from `ints`. The loop:

```
for(int i = 0; i < Repeat; i++)
```

is faster than using any of the other numeric data types:

```
for(long i = 0; i < Repeat; i++)
for(double i = 0; i < Repeat; i++)
for(char i = 0; i < Repeat; i++)
```

- `System.arraycopy()` is faster than using a loop for copying arrays in any destination VM except where you are guaranteed that the VM has a JIT. In the latter case, using your own `for` loop may be slightly faster. I recommend using `System.arraycopy()` in either case, since even when the `for` loop is executing in a JIT VM, it is only slightly faster.

- When tests need to be made within a loop, try to use the fastest tests. For example, convert equality comparisons to identity comparisons whenever possible. The following uses an equality comparison:

```
Integer one = new Integer(1);
    ...
```

---

* The latest VMs try to optimize the standard `for(int i = 0; i < Repeat; i++)` expression, so rewriting the loop may not produce faster code. Only non-JIT VMs and HotSpot showed improvements by rewriting the loop. Note that HotSpot does not generate native code for any method executed only once or twice.

```
for (...)
   if (integer.equals(one))
```

This comparison is better replaced with an identity comparison:

```
for (...)
   if (integer == CANONICALIZED_INTEGER_ONE)
```

Clearly, for this substitution to work correctly, the objects being compared must be matched by identity. You may be able to achieve this by canonicalizing your objects (see "Canonicalizing Objects" in Chapter 4, *Object Creation*). You can compare `Strings` by identity if you `String.intern()` them to ensure you have a unique `String` object for every sequence of characters, but obviously there is no performance gain if you have to do the interning within the loop or in some other time-critical section of the application. Similarly, the `java.util.Comparator` and `Comparable` interfaces provide a nice generic framework. But they impose a heavy overhead in requiring a method call for every comparison and may be better avoided in special situations (see Chapter 9, *Sorting*). One test I sometimes see is for a `Class`:

```
if (obj.getClass().getName().equals("foo.bar.ClassName"))
```

It is more efficient to store an instance of the class in a static variable and test directly against that instance (there is only one instance of any class):

```
//In class initialization
public static final Class FOO_BAR_CLASSNAME = Class.forName("foo.bar.ClassName");
...
//and in the method
if (obj.getClass() == FOO_BAR_CLASSNAME)
```

Note that `foo.bar.ClassName.class` is a valid construct to refer to the `foo.bar.ClassName` class object. However, the compiler generates a static method that calls `Class.forName()` and replaces the `foo.bar.ClassName.class` construct with a call to that static method. So it is better to use the `FOO_BAR_CLASSNAME` static variable as suggested, rather than:

```
if (obj.getClass() == foo.bar.ClassName.class)
```

- When several boolean tests are made together in one expression in the loop, try to phrase the expression so that it "short-circuits" (see the later sidebar "Short-Circuit Operators") as soon as possible by putting the most likely case first. Ensure that by satisfying earlier parts of the expression, you do not cause the later expressions to be evaluated. For example, the following expression tests whether an integer is either in the range 4 to 8 or is the smallest integer:

```
if (someInt == Integer.MIN_VALUE || (someInt > 3 && someInt < 9))
   ... //condition1
else
   ... //condition2
```

Short-Circuit Operators

The || and && boolean operators are "short-circuit" operators. Their left side is evaluated first, and their right side is not evaluated at all if the result of the left side produces a conclusive result for the expression. Specifically, the conditional-And operator, &&, evaluates its right side only if the result of its left operand is true. The conditional-Or operator, ||, evaluates its right side only if the result of its left operand is false.

These operators differ from the logical And and Or operators, & and |, in that these latter logical boolean operators always evaluate both of their arguments. The following example illustrates the differences between these two types of logical operators by testing both boolean And operators:

```
boolean b, c;
  b = c = true;
  //Left hand side makes the expression true
  if( (b=true) || (c=false) ) //is always true
    System.out.println(b + " " + c);
  b = c = true;
  if( (b=true) | (c=false) ) //is always true
    System.out.println(b + " " + c);
```

Here is the output this code produces:

```
true true
true false
```

The first test evaluates only the left side; the second test evaluates both sides even though the result of the right side is not needed to determine the result of the full boolean expression.

Suppose that the integers passed to this expression are normally in the range of 4 to 8. Suppose also that if they are not in that range, the integers passed are most likely to be values larger than 8. In this case, the given ordering of tests is the worst possible ordering for the expression. As the expression stands, the most likely result (integer in the 4 to 8 range) and the second most likely result (integer larger than 8) both require all three boolean tests in the expression to be evaluated. Let's try an alternative phrasing of the test:

```
if (someInt > 8 || (someInt < 4 && someInt != Integer.MIN_VALUE))
... //condition2
else
... //condition1
```

This rephrasing is functionally identical to the original. But it requires only two tests to be evaluated to process the most likely case, where the integer is in the 4 to 8 range; and only one test is required to be evaluated for the second most likely case, where the integer is larger than 8.

Avoid the use of reflection within loops (i.e., methods and objects in the `java.lang.reflect` package). Using reflection to execute a method is much slower than direct execution (as well as being bad style). When reflection functionality is necessary within a loop, change any implementation so that you can achieve the same effect using interfaces and type overloading. Note that it is not just the resolution of a method that causes overhead when using reflection. Invoking method calls using `Method.invoke()` is also more expensive than using the plain method call. Handling method references can be complicated, especially with VMs supporting natively compiled code. It can be necessary to manage artificial stack frames that impose overhead to the method calls.

Java.io.Reader Converter

In the `java.io` package, the `Reader` (and `Writer`) classes provide character-based I/O (as opposed to byte-based I/O). The `InputStreamReader` provides a bridge from byte to character streams. It reads bytes and translates them into characters according to a specified character encoding. If no encoding is specified, a default converter class is provided. For applications that spend a significant amount of time in reading, it is not unusual to see the `convert()` method of this encoding class high up on a profile of how the application time is spent.

It is instructive to examine how this particular conversion method functions and to see the effect of a tuning exercise. Examining the bytecodes of the `convert()` method* where most of the time is being spent, you can see that the bytecodes correspond to the following method (the `Exception` used is different; I have just used the generic `Exception` class):

```
public int convert(byte input[], int byteStart, int byteEnd,
                   char output[], int charStart, int charEnd)
  throws Exception
{
  int charOff = charStart;
  for(int byteOff = byteStart; byteOff < byteEnd;)
  {
    if(charOff >= charEnd)
      throw new Exception();
    int i1 = input[byteOff++];
    if(i1 >= 0)
```

---

* The convert method is a method in one of the `sun.*` packages, so the source code is not available. I have chosen the convert method from the default class used in some ASCII environments, the ISO 8859_1 conversion class.

```
            output[charOff++] = (char)i1;
        else
            output[charOff++] = (char)(256 + i1);
    }


    return charOff - charStart;
}
```

Basically, the method takes a byte array (input) and converts the elements from byteStart to byteEnd of that array into characters. The conversion of bytes to chars is straightforward, consisting of mapping positive byte values to the same char value, and mapping negative byte values to the char with value (byte value + 256). These chars are put into the passed char array (output) from indexes charStart to charEnd.

It doesn't seem that there is too much scope for tuning. There is the obvious first test, which is performed every time through the loop. You can certainly move that. But let's start by trying to tune the data conversion itself. First, be sure that casts on data types are efficient. It's only a quick test to find out. Add a static char array to the class, which contains just char values 0 to 127 at elements 0 to 127 in the array. Calling this array MAP1, test the following altered method:

```
public int convert(byte input[], int byteStart, int byteEnd,
                   char output[], int charStart, int charEnd)
    throws Exception
{
    int charOff = charStart;
    for(int byteOff = byteStart; byteOff < byteEnd;)
    {
        if(charOff >= charEnd)
            throw new Exception();
        int i1 = input[byteOff++];
        if(i1 >= 0)
            output[charOff++] = MAP1[i1];
        else
            output[charOff++] = (char)(256 + i1);
    }


    return charOff - charStart;
}
```

On the basis of the original method taking a normalized 100.0 seconds in test runs, this alternative takes an average of 111.8 seconds over a set of test runs. Well, that says that casts are not so slow, but it hasn't helped make this method any faster. However, the second cast involves an addition as well, and perhaps you can do better here. Unfortunately, there is no obvious way to use a negative value as an index into the array without executing some offset operation, so you won't gain time. For completeness, test this (with an index offset given by i1+128) and find that the average time is at the 110.7-second mark. This is not significantly better than the last test and definitely worse than the original.

TIP   Array-lookup speeds are highly dependent on the processor and the memory-access instructions available from the processor. The lookup speed is also dependent on the compiler taking advantage of the fastest memory-access instructions available. It is possible that other processors, VMs, or compilers will produce lookups faster than the cast.

But you have gained an extra option from these two tests. It is now clear that you can map all the `bytes` to `chars` through an array. Perhaps you can eliminate the test for positiveness applied to the `byte` (i.e., `if(i1 >= 0)`) and use a `char` array to map all the `bytes` directly. And indeed you can. Use the index conversion from the second test (an index offset given by i1+128), with a static `char` array that contains just `char` values 128 to 255 at elements 0 to 127 in the array, and `char` values 0 to 127 at elements 128 to 255 in the array.

The method now looks like:

```
public int convert(byte input[], int byteStart, int byteEnd,
                   char output[], int charStart, int charEnd)
  throws Exception
{
  int charOff = charStart;
  for(int byteOff = byteStart; byteOff < byteEnd;)
  {
    if(charOff >= charEnd)
      throw new Exception();
    int i1 = input[byteOff++];
    output[charOff++] = MAP3[128 + i1];
  }

  return charOff - charStart;
}
```

You have eliminated one boolean test each time through the loop at the expense of using a slightly more expensive data-conversion method (array access rather than the cast). The average test result is now slightly faster than before, but still over the 100 seconds (some VMs show a speedup at this stage, but not the JDK 1.2 VM).

Cleaning up the method slightly, you can see that the temporary variable, i1, which was previously required for the test, is no longer needed. Being an assiduous tuner and clean coder, you eliminate it and retest so that you have a new baseline to start from. Astonishingly (to me at least), this speeds the test up measurably. The average test time is now still slightly above 100 seconds (again, some VMs do show a speedup at this stage, greater than before, but not the JDK 1.2 VM). There was a definite overhead from the redundant temporary variable in the loop: a lesson to keep in mind for general tuning.

It may be worth testing to see if an int array performs better than the char array (MAP3) previously used, since ints are the faster data type. And indeed, changing the type of this array and putting a char cast in the loop improves times so that you are now very slightly, but consistently, faster than 100 seconds for JDK 1.2. Not all VMs are faster at this stage, though all are close to the 100-second mark. For example, JDK 1.1.6 shows timings slightly larger than 100 seconds. More to the point, after this effort, you have not really managed a speedup consistent enough or good enough to justify the time spent on this tuning exercise.

Now I'm out of original ideas, but we have yet to apply the standard optimizations. Start* by eliminating expressions from the loop that do not need to be repeatedly called, and move the other boolean test (the one for the out-of-range Exception) out of the loop. The method now looks like this (MAP5 is the int array mapping for bytes to chars):

```
public int convert(byte input[], int byteStart, int byteEnd,
                   char output[], int charStart, int charEnd)
  throws Exception
{
  int max = byteEnd;
  boolean throwException = false;
  if ( byteEnd-byteStart > charEnd-charStart )
  {
    max = byteStart+(charEnd-charStart);
    throwException = true;
  }

  int charOff = charStart;
  for(int byteOff = byteStart; byteOff < max;)
  {
    output[charOff++] = (char) MAP5[input[byteOff++]+128];
  }
  if(throwException)
    throw new Exception();

  return charOff - charStart;
}
```

I am taking the trouble to make the method functionally identical to the original. The original version filled in the array until the actual out-of-range exception is

---

* Although the tuning optimizations I've tried so far have not provided a significant speedup, I will continue tuning with the most recent implementation discussed, instead of starting again from the beginning. There is no particular reason why I should not restart from the original implementation.

encountered, so I do the same. If you throw the exception as soon as you establish the index is out of range, the code will be slightly more straightforward. Other than that, the loop is the same as before, but without the out-of-range test and without the temporary assignment. The average test result is now a very useful 83.3 seconds. You've shaved off nearly a fifth of the time spent in this loop. This is mainly down to eliminating a test that was originally being run through on each loop iteration. This speedup applied to all VMs tested (many had a better speedup, i.e., a lower relative time to the 100-second mark).

Loop unrolling is another standard optimization that eliminates some more tests. Let's partially unroll the loop and see what sort of a gain we get. In practice, the optimal amount of loop unrolling corresponds to the way the application uses the convert() method, for example, the size of the typical array that is being converted. But in any case, we use a particular example of 10 loop iterations to see the effect.

TIP   Optimal loop unrolling depends on a number of factors, including the underlying operating system and hardware. Loop unrolling is ideally achieved by way of an optimizing compiler rather than by hand. HotSpot interacts with manual loop unrolling in a highly variable way: sometimes HotSpot makes the unoptimized loop faster, sometimes the manually unrolled loop comes out faster. An example can be seen in Tables 8-1 and 8-2, which show HotSpot producing both faster *and* slower times for the same manually unrolled loop, depending on the data being processed. These two tables show the results from the same optimized program being run against files with long lines (Table 8-1) and files with short lines (Table 8-2). Of all the VMs tested, only the HotSpot VM produces inconsistent results, with a speedup when processing the long-line files but a slowdown when processing the short-line files (the last two lines of each table show the difference between the original loop and the manually unrolled loop).

The method now looks like this:

```
public int convert(byte input[], int byteStart, int byteEnd,
                   char output[], int charStart, int charEnd)
  throws Exception
{
  //Set the maximum index of the input array to wind to
  int max = byteEnd;
  boolean throwException = false;
  if ( byteEnd-byteStart > charEnd-charStart )
  {
    //If the byte arry length is larger than the char array length
    //then we will throw an exception when we get to the adjusted max
    max = byteStart+(charEnd-charStart);
```

```
      throwException = true;
    }

    //charOff is the 'current' index into 'output'
    int charOff = charStart;

    //Check that we have at least 10 elements for our
    //unrolled part of the loop
    if (max-byteStart > 10)
    {
      //shift max down by 10 so that we have some elements
      //left over before we run out of groups of 10
      max -= 10;
      int byteOff = byteStart;
      //The loop test only tests every 10th test compared
      //to the normal loop. All the increments are done in
      //the loop body. Each line increments the byteoff by 1
      //until it's incremented by 10 after 10 lines. Then the test
      //checks that we are still under max - if so then loop again.
      for(; byteOff < max;)
      {
        output[charOff++] = (char) MAP5[input[byteOff++]+128];
        output[charOff++] = (char) MAP5[input[byteOff++]+128];
        output[charOff++] = (char) MAP5[input[byteOff++]+128];
        output[charOff++] = (char) MAP5[input[byteOff++]+128];
        output[charOff++] = (char) MAP5[input[byteOff++]+128];
        output[charOff++] = (char) MAP5[input[byteOff++]+128];
        output[charOff++] = (char) MAP5[input[byteOff++]+128];
        output[charOff++] = (char) MAP5[input[byteOff++]+128];
        output[charOff++] = (char) MAP5[input[byteOff++]+128];
        output[charOff++] = (char) MAP5[input[byteOff++]+128];
      }

      //We exited the loop because the byteoff went over the max.
      //Fortunately we kept back 10 elements so that we didn't go
      //too far past max. Now add the 10 back, and go into the
      //normal loop for the last few elements.
      max += 10;
      for(; byteOff < max;)
      {
        output[charOff++] = (char) MAP5[input[byteOff++]+128];
      }
    }
    else
    {
      //If we're in this conditional, then there aren't even
      //10 elements to process, so obviously we don't want to
      //do the unrolled part of the method.
      for(int byteOff = byteStart; byteOff < max;)
```

```
    {
      output[charOff++] = (char) MAP5[input[byteOff++]+128];
    }
  }
  //Finally if we indicated that the method needed an exception
  //thrown, we do it now.
  if(throwException)
    throw new Exception();

  return charOff - charStart;
}
```

The average test result is now a very good 72.6 seconds. You've now shaved off over one quarter of the time compared to the original loop (in JDK 1.2; other VMs give an even larger speedup, some taking down to 60% of the time of the original loop). It is worth repeating that this is mainly a result of eliminating tests that were originally run in each loop iteration. For tight loops (i.e., loops that have a small amount of actual work that needs to be executed on each iteration), the overhead of tests is definitely significant.

It is also important during the tuning exercise to run the various improvements under different VMs, and determine that the improvements are generally applicable. My tests indicate that these improvements are generally valid for all runtime environments. (One development environment with a very slow VM—an order of magnitude slower than the Sun VM without JIT—showed only a small improvement. However, it is not generally a good idea to base performance tests on development environments.)

For a small Java program that does simple filtering or conversion of data from text files, this `convert()` method could take 40% of the total program time. Improving this one method as shown can shave 10% from the time of the whole program, which is a good gain for a relatively small amount of work (it took me longer to write this section than to tune the `convert()` method).

Exception-Terminated Loops

This is a technique for squeezing out the very last driblet of performance from loops. With this technique, instead of testing on each loop iteration to see whether the loop has reached its normal termination point, you use an exception generated at the end of the loop to halt the loop, thus avoiding the extra test on each run through the loop.

I include this technique here mainly because it is a known performance-tuning technique, but I do not recommend using it, as I feel it is bad programming practice (the phrase "enough rope to hang yourself" springs to mind). I'll illustrate the technique with some straightforward examples. The full class for testing the examples is listed later, after I discuss the test results. The tests themselves are very simple. Basically, each test runs two varieties of loops. The first variety runs a standard for loop as you normally write it:

```
for (int loopvar = 0; loopvar < someMax; loopvar++)
```

The second variety misses out the termination test in the for loop, thus making the loop infinite. But these latter loops are put inside a try-catch block to catch an exception that terminates the loop:

```
try
{
  for (int loopvar = 0; ; loopvar++)
  ... //exception is thrown when loop needs to terminate
}
catch(Exception e) {}
```

The three tests I use are:

- A loop that executes integer divisions. The unterminated variety throws an ArithmeticException when a division by zero occurs to terminate the loop.

- A loop that initializes an array of integers. The unterminated variety throws an ArrayIndexOutOfBoundsException when the index of the array grows too large.

- A loop that enumerates a Vector. The unterminated variety throws a NoSuchElementException when there are no more elements to enumerate.

I found the results of my test runs (summarized in Table 7-1) to be variable due to variations in memory allocation, disk paging, and garbage collection. The VMs using HotSpot technology could show quite variable behavior. The plain JDK 1.2 VM had a huge amount of trouble reclaiming memory for the later tests, even when I put in pauses and ran explicit garbage-collection calls more than once. For each set of tests, I tried to increase the number of loop iterations until the timings were over one second. For the memory-based tests, it was not always possible to achieve times of over a second: paging or out-of-memory errors were encountered.

Table 7-1. Speedup Using Exception-Driven Loop Termination

Speedups	1.2	1.2 no JIT	1.3	HotSpot 1.0	1.1.6
Integer division	~2%	~5%	None[a]	~10%	~2%
Assignment to loop	None	~75%	~10%	~30%	None
Vector enumeration	None	~10%	~20%	None[b]	~10%

[a] The timings varied enormously as the test was repeated within a VM. There was no consistent speedup.
[b] The exception-driven case was 40% faster initially. After the first test, HotSpot successfully optimized the normal loop to make it much faster, but failed to optimize the exception-driven loop.

In all test cases, I found that the number of iterations for each test was quite important. When I could run the test consistently, there was usually a loop iteration value above which the exception-terminated loop ran faster. One test run output (without JIT) follows:

```
Division loop with no exceptions took 2714 milliseconds
Division loop with an exception took 2604 milliseconds
Division loop with an exception took 2574 milliseconds
Division loop with no exceptions took 2714 milliseconds
Assignment loop with no exceptions took 1622 milliseconds
Assignment loop with an exception took 1242 milliseconds
Assignment loop with an exception took 1222 milliseconds
Assignment loop with no exceptions took 1622 milliseconds
Enumeration loop with no exceptions took 42632 milliseconds
Enumeration loop with an exception took 32386 milliseconds
Enumeration loop with an exception took 31536 milliseconds
Enumeration loop with no exceptions took 43162 milliseconds
```

It is completely conceivable (and greatly preferable) that a compiler or runtime system automatically optimizes loops like this to give the fastest alternative. On some Java systems, try-catch blocks may have enough extra cost associated with them to make this technique slower. Because of the differences in systems, and also because I believe exception-terminated code is difficult to read and likely to lead to bugs and maintenance problems if it proliferates, I prefer to steer clear of this technique.

The actual improvement (if any) in performance depends on the test case that runs in the loop and the code that is run in the body of the loop. The basic consideration is the ratio of the time taken in the loop test compared to the time taken in the body of the loop. The simpler the loop-body execution is compared to the termination test, the more likely that this technique will give a useful effect. This technique works because the termination test iterated many times can have a higher cost than producing and catching an Exception once. Here is the class used for testing, with comments. It is very simple, and the exception-terminated loop technique used is clearly illustrated. Look for the differences between the no_exception methods and the with_exception methods:

```java
package tuning.loop;

public class ExceptionDriven
{
  //Use a default size for the number of iterations
  static int SIZE = 1000000;

  public static void main(String args[])
  {
    //Allow an argument to set the size of the loop.
```

```
    if (args.length != 0)
      SIZE = Integer.parseInt(args[0]);

    //Run the two tests twice each to ensure there were no
    //initialization effects, reversing the order on the second
    //run to make sure one test does not affect the other.
    no_exception1(); with_exception1();
    with_exception1(); no_exception1();

    //Execute the array assignment tests only if there is no second
    //argument to allow for large SIZE values on the first test
    //that would give out of memory errors in the second test.
    if (args.length > 1)
      return;
    no_exception2(); with_exception2();
    with_exception2(); no_exception2();
    no_exception3(); with_exception3();
    with_exception3(); no_exception3();
  }
  public static void no_exception1()
  {
    //Standard loop.
    int result;
    long time = System.currentTimeMillis();
    for (int i = SIZE; i > 0 ; i--)
      result = SIZE/i;
    System.out.println("Division loop with no exceptions took " +
      (System.currentTimeMillis()-time) + " milliseconds");
  }
  public static void with_exception1()
  {
    //Non-standard loop with no test for termination using
    //the ArithmeticException thrown at division by zero to
    //terminate the loop.
    int result;
    long time = System.currentTimeMillis();
    try
    {
      for (int i = SIZE; ; i--)
      result = SIZE/i;
    }
    catch (ArithmeticException e) {}
    System.out.println("Division loop with an exception took " +
      (System.currentTimeMillis()-time) + " milliseconds");
  }
  public static void no_exception2()
  {
    //Create the array, get the time, and run the standard loop.
    int array[] = new int[SIZE];
```

```java
    long time = System.currentTimeMillis();
    for (int i = 0; i < SIZE ; i++)
      array[i] = 3;
    System.out.println("Assignment loop with no exceptions took " +
      (System.currentTimeMillis()-time) + " milliseconds");

    //Garbage collect so that we don't run out of memory for
    //the next test. Set the array variable to null to allow
    //the array instance to be garbage collected.
    array = null;
    System.gc();
  }
  public static void with_exception2()
  {
    //Create the array, get the time, and run a non-standard
    //loop with no test for termination using the
    //ArrayIndexOutOfBoundsException to terminate the loop.
    int array[] = new int[SIZE];
    long time = System.currentTimeMillis();
    try
    {
    for (int i = 0; ; i++)
      array[i] = 3;
    }
    catch (ArrayIndexOutOfBoundsException e) {}
    System.out.println("Assignment loop with an exception took " +
      (System.currentTimeMillis()-time) + " milliseconds");

    //Garbage collect so that we don't run out of memory for
    //the next test. Set the array variable to null to allow
    //the array instance to be garbage collected.
    array = null;
    System.gc();
  }
  public static void no_exception3()
  {
    //Create the Vector, get the time, and run the standard loop.
    java.util.Vector vector = new java.util.Vector(SIZE);
    vector.setSize(SIZE);
    java.util.Enumeration enum = vector.elements();
    Object nothing;
    long time = System.currentTimeMillis();
    for ( ; enum.hasMoreElements(); )
      nothing = enum.nextElement();
    System.out.println("Enumeration loop with no exceptions took " +
      (System.currentTimeMillis()-time) + " milliseconds");

    //Garbage collect so that we don't run out of memory for
    //the next test. We need to set the variables to null to
    //allow the instances to be garbage collectable.
```

```
      enum = null;
      vector = null;
      System.gc();
    }
    public static void with_exception3()
    {
      //Create the Vector, get the time, and run a non-standard
      //loop with no termination test using the
      //java.util.NoSuchElementException to terminate the loop.
      java.util.Vector vector = new java.util.Vector(SIZE);
      vector.setSize(SIZE);
      java.util.Enumeration enum = vector.elements();
      Object nothing;
      long time = System.currentTimeMillis();
      try
      {
        for ( ; ; )
          nothing = enum.nextElement();
      }
      catch (java.util.NoSuchElementException e) {}
      System.out.println("Enumeration loop with an exception took " +
        (System.currentTimeMillis()-time) + " milliseconds");

      //Garbage collect so that we don't run out of memory for
      //the next test. We need to set the variables to null to
      //allow the instances to be garbage collectable.
      enum = null;
      vector = null;
      System.gc();
    }
  }
```

Switches

The Java bytecode specification allows a switch statement to be compiled into one of two different bytecodes. One compiled switch type works as follows:

> Given a particular value passed to the switch block to be compared, the passed value is successively compared against the value associated with each case statement in order. If, after testing all cases, no statements match, then the default label is matched. When a case statement that matches is found, the body of that statement and all subsequent case bodies are executed (until one body exits the switch statement, or the last one is reached).

The operation of this switch statement is equivalent to holding an ordered collection of values that are compared to the passed value, one after the other in order, until a match is determined. This means that the time taken for the switch to find the case that matches depends on how many `case` statements there are and where in the list the matched case is. If no cases match, and the `default` must be used, that always takes the longest matching time.

The other `switch` bytecode works for `switch` statements where the case values all lie in a particular range (or can be made to lie in a particular range). It works as follows:

> Given a particular value passed to the `switch` block to be compared, the passed value is tested to see if it lies in the range. If it does not, the `default` label is matched; otherwise, the offset of the case is calculated and the corresponding case is matched directly. The body of that matched label and all subsequent `case` bodies are executed (until one body exits the `switch` statement, or the last one is reached).

For this latter `switch` bytecode, the time taken for the `switch` statement to match the `case` is constant. The time is not dependent on the number of `cases` in the switch, and if no `cases` match, the time to carry out the matching and go to the `default` is still the same. This `switch` statement operates as an ordered collection with `switch` value first being checked to see if it is a valid index into the ordered collection, and then that value is used as the index to arrive immediately at the matched location.

Clearly, the second type of `switch` statement is faster than the first. Sometimes compliers can add dummy `cases` to a `switch` statement, converting the first type of `switch` into the second (faster) kind. (A compiler is not obliged to use the second type of `switch` bytecode at all, but generally it does if it can easily be used.) You can determine which `switch` a particular statement has been compiled into using `javap`, the disassembler available with the JDK. Using the `-c` option so that the code is disassembled, examine the method that contains the `switch` statement. It contains either a "tableswitch" bytecode identifier, or a "lookupswitch" bytecode identifier. The `tableswitch` keyword is the identifier for the faster (second) type of `switch`.

If you identify a bottleneck that involves a `switch` statement, do not leave the decision to the compiler. You are better off constructing `switch` statements that use contiguous ranges of `case` values, ideally by inserting dummy `case` statements to specify all the values in the range, or possibly by breaking up the `switch` into multiple `switches` that each use contiguous ranges. You may need to apply both of these optimizations as in the next example.

Our `tuning.loop.SwitchTest` class provides a repeated test on three methods with `switch` statements, and one other array-access method for comparison. The first method, `switch1()`, contains some noncontiguous values for the `cases`, with each returning a particular integer value. The second method, switch2(), converts the single switch statement in switch1() into four switch statements, with some of those four switch statements containing extra dummy cases to make each switch statement contain a contiguous set of cases. This second method, switch2(), is functionally identical to switch1().

The third method, switch3(), replaces the cases with a contiguous set of cases, integers 1 to 13. This method is not directly comparable to the first two methods; it is present as a control test. The fourth method, switch4(), is functionally identical to switch3(), but uses an array access instead of the switch statement, essentially doing in Java code what the compiler implicitly does in bytecodes for switch3(). I run two sets of tests. The first set passes in a different integer for each call to the switches. This means that most of the time, the default label is matched. The second set of tests always passes in the integer 8 to the switches. The results are shown in Table 7-2 for various VMs. "Varying" and "constant" refer to the value passed to the switch statement. Tests labeled varying passed different integers for each iteration of the test loop; tests labeled constant passed the integer 8 for each iteration of the loop.

Table 7-2. Speedup Using Exception-Driven Loop Termination

		1.2	1.3	HotSpot 1.0	HotSpot 2nd Run[a]	1.1.6
1	switch1 varying	100%	55%	208%	29%	109%
2	switch2 varying	12%	53%	218%	27%	12%
3	switch3 varying	23%	79%	212%	36%	23%
4	switch4 varying	9%	36%	231%	15%	9%
5	switch1 constant	41%	33%	195%	30%	45%
6	switch2 constant	17%	42%	207%	30%	15%
7	switch3 constant	20%	48%	186%	24%	20%
8	switch4 constant	6%	42%	200%	12%	6%

[a] HotSpot is tuned for long-lived server applications, and so applies its optimizations after the first run of the test indicates where the bottlenecks are.

There is a big difference in optimizations gained depending on whether the VM has a JIT or uses HotSpot technology. The times are all relative to the JDK 1.2 "switch1 varying" case. From the variation in timings, it is not clear whether the HotSpot technology fails to compile the handcrafted switch in an optimal way, or whether it does optimally compile all the switch statements but adds overheads that cancel some of the optimizations.

For the JIT results, the first and second lines of output show the speedup you can get by recrafting the switch statements. Here, both switch1() and switch2() are using the default for most of the tests. In this situation, switch1() requires

13 failed comparisons before executing the `default` statement. `switch2()`, on the other hand, checks the value against the range of each of its four `switch` statements, then immediately executes the `default` statement.

The first and third lines of output show the worst-case comparison between the two types of `switch` statements. In this test, `switch1()` almost always fails all its comparison tests. On the other hand, `switch3()`, with the contiguous range, is much faster than `switch1()` (JIT cases only). This is exactly what is expected, as the average case for `switch1()` here consists of 13 failed comparisons followed by a `return` statement. The average case for `switch3()` in this test is only a pair of checks followed by a `return` statement. The two checks are that the integer is smaller than or equal to 13, and larger than or equal to 1. Both checks fail in most of the calls for this "varying" case.

Even when the case statement in `switch1()` is always matched, the fifth and sixth lines show that `switch2()` can be faster (though again, not with HotSpot). In this test, the matched statement is about halfway down the list of `cases` in `switch1()`, so the seven or so failed comparisons for `switch1()` compared to two range checks for `switch2()` translate into `switch2()` being more than twice as fast as `switch1()`.

In each set of tests, `switch2()`, which is functionally identical to `switch1()`, is faster. The output for `switch4()` is included for comparison, and it turns out to be faster than the functionally identical `switch3()`, thus indicating that it is worth considering dispensing with the `switch` tests completely when you can convert the `switch` to an array access. In this example, the `switch` merely returns an integer, so the conversion to an array access is feasible; in general, it may be difficult to convert a set of body statements into an array access and subsequent processing:

```
package tuning.loop;

public class SwitchTest
{
  //Use a default size for the loop of 1 million iterations
  static int SIZE = 10000000;

  public static void main(String args[])
  {
    //Allow an argument to set the size of the loop.
    if (args.length != 0)
      SIZE = Integer.parseInt(args[0]);
    int result = 0;
    //run tests looking mostly for the default (switch
    //test uses many different values passed to it)
    long time = System.currentTimeMillis();
    for (int i = SIZE; i >=0 ; i--)
      result += switch1(i);
```

```
    System.out.println("Switch1 took " +
      (System.currentTimeMillis()-time) + " millis to get " + result);

    //and the same code to test timings on switch2(),
    //switch3() and switch4()
    ...

    //run tests using one particular passed value (8)
    result = 0;
    time = System.currentTimeMillis();
    for (int i = SIZE; i >=0 ; i--)
      result += switch1(8);
    System.out.println("Switch1 took " +
      (System.currentTimeMillis()-time) + " millis to get " + result);

    //and the same code to test timings on switch2(),
    //switch3() and switch4()
    ...
  }

public static int switch1(int i)
{
  //This is one big switch statement with 13 case statements
  //in no particular order.
  switch(i)
  {
    case 318: return 99;
    case 320: return 55;
    case 323: return -1;
    case 14: return 6;
    case 5: return 8;
    case 123456: return 12;
    case 7: return 15;
    case 8: return 29;
    case 9: return 11111;
    case 123457: return 12345;
    case 112233: return 6666;
    case 112235: return 9876;
    case 112237: return 12;
    default: return -1;
  }
}
public static int switch2(int i)
{
  //In this method we break up the 13 case statements from
  //switch1() into four almost contiguous ranges. Then we
  //add in a few dummy cases so that the four ranges are
  //definitely contiguous. This should ensure that the compiler
  //will generate the more optimal tableswitch bytcodes
  switch(i)
```

```java
  {
    case 318: return 99;
    case 319: break;        //dummy
    case 320: return 55;
    case 321: break;        //dummy
    case 322: break;        //dummy
    case 323: return -1;
  }
  switch(i)
  {
    case 5: return 8;
    case 6: break;          //dummy
    case 7: return 15;
    case 8: return 29;
    case 9: return 11111;
    case 10: break;         //dummy
    case 11: break;         //dummy
    case 12: break;         //dummy
    case 13: break;         //dummy
    case 14: return 6;
  }
  switch(i)
  {
    case 112233: return 6666;
    case 112234: break;         //dummy
    case 112235: return 9876;
    case 112236: break;         //dummy
    case 112237: return 12;
  }
  switch(i)
  {
    case 123456: return 12;
    case 123457: return 12345;
    default: return -1;
  }
}
public static int switch3(int i)
{
  switch(i)
  {
    //13 contiguous case statements as a kind of fastest control
    case 1: return 99;
    case 2: return 55;
    case 3: return -1;
    case 4: return 6;
    case 5: return 8;
    case 6: return 12;
    case 7: return 15;
    case 8: return 29;
    case 9: return 11111;
```

```
        case 10: return 12345;
        case 11: return 6666;
        case 12: return 9876;
        case 13: return 12;
        default: return -1;
    }
  }
  final static int[] RETURNS = {
      99, 55, -1, 6, 8, 12, 15, 29,
      11111, 12345, 6666, 9876, 12
    };
  public static int switch4(int i)
  {
    //equivalent to switch3(), but using an array lookup
    //instead of a switch statement.
    if (i < 1 || i > 13)
      return -1;
    else
      return RETURNS[i-1];
  }
}
```

Recursion

Recursive algorithms are used because they're often clearer and more elegant than the alternatives, and therefore have a lower maintenance cost than the equivalent iterative algorithm. However, recursion often (but not always) has a cost to it; recursive algorithms are frequently slower. So it is useful to understand the costs associated with recursion, and how to improve the performance of recursive algorithms when necessary.

Recursive code can be optimized by a clever compiler (as is done with some C compilers), but only if presented in the right way (typically, it needs to be tail-recursive: see the sidebar "Tail Recursion"). For example, Jon Bentley* found that a functionally identical recursive method was optimized by a C compiler if he did not use the ?: conditional operator (using if statements instead). However, it was *not* optimized if he did use the ?: conditional operator. He also found that recursion can be very expensive, taking up to 20 times longer for some operations that are naturally iterative. Bentley's article also looks briefly at optimizing partial match searching in ternary search trees by transforming a tail recursion in the search into an iteration. See Chapter 11, *Appropriate Data Structures and Algorithms*, for an example of tuning a ternary search tree, including an example of converting a recursive algorithm to an iterative one.

---

* "The Cost of Recursion," *Dr. Dobb's Journal*, June 1998.

Tail Recursion

A tail-recursive function is a recursive function for which each recursive call to itself is a reduction of the original call. A *reduction* is the situation where a problem is converted into a new problem that is simpler, and the solution of that new problem is exactly the solution of the original problem, with no further computation necessary. This is a subtle concept, best illustrated with a simple example. I will take the factorial example used in the text. The original recursive solution is:

```
public static long factorial1(int n)
{
  if (n < 2) return 1L;
  else return n*factorial1(n-1);
}
```

This is not tail-recursive, since each call to itself does not provide the solution to the original problem. Instead, the recursive call provides a partial solution that must be multiplied by a number to get the final result. If you consider the operating stack of the VM, each recursive call must be kept on the stack, as each call is incomplete until the next call above on the stack is returned. So factorial1(20) goes on the stack and stays there until factorial1(19) returns. factorial1(19) goes above factorial1(20) on the stack and stays there until factorial1(18) returns, etc.

The tail-recursive version of this function requires two functions: one to set up the recursive call (to keep compatibility), and the actual recursive call. This looks like:

```
public static long factorial1a(int n)
{
  //NOT recursive. Sets up the tail-recursive call to factorial1b()
  if (n < 2) return 1L;
  else return factorial1b(n, 1L);
}

public static long factorial1b(int n, long result)
{
  //No need to consider n < 2, as factorial1a handles that
  if (n == 2) return 2L*result;
  else return factorial1b(n-1, result*n);
}
```

—Continued—

I have changed the recursive call to add an extra parameter, which is the partial result, built up as you calculate the answer. The consequence is that each time you return the recursive call, the answer is the full answer to the function, since you are holding the partial answer in a variable. Considering the VM stack again, the situation is vastly improved. Because the recursive method returns a call to itself each time, with no further operations needed (i.e., the recursive caller actually exits with the call to recurse), there is no need to keep any calls on the stack except for the current one. factorial1b(20,1) is put on the stack, but this exits with a call to factorial1b(19,20), which replaces the call to factorial1b(20,1) on the stack (since it has exited). This in turn is replaced by the call to factorial1b(18,380), which in turn is replaced by the call to factorial1b(17,6840), and so on, until factorial1b(2, ...) returns just the result.

Generally, the advice for dealing with methods that are naturally recursive (because that is the natural way to code them for clarity) is to go ahead with the recursive solution. You only need to spend time counting the cost (if any) when your profiling shows that this particular method call is a bottleneck in the application. At that stage, it is worth pursuing alternative implementations or avoiding the method call completely with a different structure.

In case you need to tune a recursive algorithm or convert it into an iterative one, I provide some examples here. I start with an extremely simple recursive algorithm for calculating factorial numbers, as this illustrates several tuning points:

```
public static long factorial1(int n)
{
  if (n < 2) return 1L;
  else return n*factorial1(n-1);
}
```

I have limited the function to long values, which means that you cannot use the function beyond factorial 20, as that overflows the long data type. This is to keep the function simple for this illustration.

Since this function is easily converted to a tail-recursive version, it is natural to test the tail-recursive version to see if it performs any better. For this particular function, the tail-recursive version does not perform any better, which is not typical. Here, the factorial function consists of a very simple fast calculation, and the extra function call overhead in the tail-recursive version is enough of an overhead that it negates the benefit that is normally gained. (Note that the HotSpot 1.0 VM does manage to optimize the tail-recursive version to be faster than the original, after the compiler optimizations have had a chance to be applied. See Table 7-3.)

Let's look at other ways this function can be optimized. Start with the classic conversion for recursive to iterative and note that the factorial method contains just one value which is successively operated on, to give a new value (the result), along with a parameter specifying how to operate on the partial result (the current input to the factorial). A standard way to convert this type of recursive method is to replace the parameters passed to the method with temporary variables in a loop. In this case, you need two variables, one of which is passed into the method and can be reused. The converted method looks like:

```
public static long factorial2(int n)
{
  long result = 1;
  while(n>1)
  {
    result *= n--;
  }
  return result;
}
```

Measuring the performance, you see that this method calculates the result in 88% of the time taken by the original recursive `factorial1()` method (using the JDK 1.2 results.* See Table 7-3).

Table 7-3. Timings of the Various Factorial Implementations

	1.2	1.2 no JIT	1.3	HotSpot 1.0 2nd Run	1.1.6
factoral1 (original recursive)	100%	572%	152%	137%	101%
factoral1a (tail recursive)	110%	609%	173%	91%	111%
factorial2 (iterative)	88%	344%	129%	177%	88%
factoral3 (dynamically cached)	46%	278%	71%	74%	46%
factoral4 (statically cached)	41%	231%	67%	57%	40%
factoral3 (dynamically cached with cache size of 21 elements)	4%	56%	11%	8%	4%

The recursion-to-iteration technique as illustrated here is general, and another example in a different domain may help make this generality clear. Consider a linked list, with singly linked nodes consisting of a next pointer to the next node, and a value instance variable holding (in this case) just an integer. A simple linear search method to find the first node holding a particular integer looks like:

```
Node find_recursive(int i)
{
  if (node.value == i)
```

---

* HotSpot optimized the recursive version sufficiently to make it faster than the iterative version.

```
      return node;
   else if(node.next != null)
      node.next.find_recursive(i);
   else
      return null;
}
```

To convert this to an iterative method, use a temporary variable to hold the "current" node, and reassign that variable with the next node in the list at each iteration. The method is clear, and its only drawback compared to the recursive method is that it violates encapsulation (this one method directly accesses the instance variable of each node object):

```
Node find_iterative(int i)
{
   Node node = this;
   while(node != null)
   {
      if (node.value == i)
         return node;
      else
         node = node.next;
   }
   return null;
}
```

Before looking at general techniques for converting other types of recursive methods to iterative ones, I will revisit the original factorial method to illustrate some other techniques for improving the performance of recursive methods.

To test the timing of the factorial method, I put it into a loop to recalculate `factorial(20)` many times. Otherwise, the time taken is too short to be reliably measured. When this situation is close to the actual problem, a good tuning technique is to cache the intermediate results. This technique can be applied when some recursive function is repeatedly being called and some of the intermediate results are repeatedly being identified. This technique is simple to illustrate for the factorial method:

```
public static final int CACHE_SIZE = 15;
public static final long[] factorial3Cache = new long[CACHE_SIZE];

public static long factorial3(int n)
{
   if (n < 2) return 1L;
   else if (n < CACHE_SIZE)
   {
      if (factorial3Cache[n] == 0)
         factorial3Cache[n] = n*factorial3(n-1);
      return factorial3Cache[n];
```

```
    }
    else return n*factorial3(n-1);
}
```

With the choice of 15 elements for the cache, the `factorial3()` method takes 46% of the time taken by `factorial1()`. If you choose a cache with 21 elements, so that all except the first call to `factorial3(20)` is simply returning from the cache with no calculations at all, the time taken is just 4% of the time taken by `factorial1()` (using the JDK 1.2 results: see Table 7-3).

In this particular situation, you can make one further improvement, which is to compile the values at implementation and hardcode them in:

```
public static final long[] factorial4Cache = {
  1L, 1L, 2L, 6L, 24L, 120L, 720L, 5040L, 40320L, 362880L, 3628800L,
  39916800L, 479001600L, 6227020800L, 87178291200L};
public static final int CACHE_SIZE = factorial4Cache.length;
public static long factorial4(int n)
{
  if (n < CACHE_SIZE)
    return factorial4Cache[n];
  else return n*factorial4(n-1);
}
```

This is a valid technique that applies when you can identify and calculate partial solutions that can be included with the class at compilation time.*

Recursion and Stacks

The techniques for converting recursive method calls to iterative ones are suitable only for methods that take a single search path at every decision node when navigating through the solution space. For more complex recursive methods that evaluate multiple paths from some nodes, you can convert a recursive method into an iterative method based on a stack. This is best illustrated with an example. I'll use here the problem of looking for all the files with names ending in some particular string.

The following method runs a recursive search of the filesystem, printing all non-directory files that end in a particular string:

```
public static String FS = System.getProperty("file.separator");
public static void filesearch1(String root, String fileEnding)
{
  File f = new File(root);
```

---

* My editor points out that a variation on hardcoded values, used by state-of-the-art high-performance mathematical functions, is a partial table of values together with an interpolation method to calculate intermediate values.

```
    String[] filelist = f.list();
    if (filelist == null)
      return;
    for (int i = filelist.length-1; i >= 0; i--)
    {
      f = new File(root, filelist[i]);
      if (f.isDirectory())
        filesearch1(root+FS+filelist[i], fileEnding);
      else if(filelist[i].toUpperCase().endsWith(fileEnding))
        System.out.println(root+ls+filelist[i]);
    }
  }
```

To convert this into an iterative search, it is not sufficient to use an extra variable to hold the current directory. At any one directory, there are several possible directories underneath, all of which must be held onto and searched, and you cannot reference them all from a plain variable. Instead, you can make that variable into a collection object. The standard object to use is a stack. With this hint in mind, the method converts quite easily:

```
public static void filesearch2(String root, String fileEnding)
{
  Stack dirs = new Stack();
  dirs.push(root);
  File f;
  int i;
  String[] filelist;
  while(!dirs.empty())
  {
    f = new File(root = (String) dirs.pop());
    filelist = f.list();
    if (filelist == null)
      continue;
    for (i = filelist.length-1; i >= 0; i--)
    {
      f = new File(root, filelist[i]);
      if (f.isDirectory())
        dirs.push(root+FS+filelist[i]);
      else if(filelist[i].toUpperCase().endsWith(fileEnding))
        System.out.println(root+ls+filelist[i]);
    }
  }
}
```

In fact, the structures of the two methods are almost the same. This second iterative version has the main part of the body wrapped in an extra loop that terminates when the extra variable holding the stack becomes empty. Otherwise, instead of the recursive call, the directory is added to the stack.

In the cases of these particular search methods, the time-measurement comparison shows that the iterative method actually takes 5% longer than the recursive method. This is due to the iterative method having the overhead of the extra stack object to manipulate, whereas filesystems are generally not particularly deep (the ones I tested on were not), so the recursive algorithm is not particularly inefficient. This illustrates that a recursive method is not always worse than an iterative one.

TIP   Note that the methods here were chosen for illustration, using an easily understood problem that could be managed iteratively and recursively. Since the I/O is actually the limiting factor for these methods, there would not be much point in actually making the optimization shown.

For this example, I eliminated the I/O overheads, as they would have swamped the times and made it difficult to determine the difference between the two implementations. To do this, I mapped the filesystem into memory using a simple replacement of the `java.io.File` class. This stored a snapshot of the filesystem in a hash table. (Actually, only the full pathname of directories as keys, and their associated string array list of files as values, need be stored.)

This kind of trick—replacing classes with another implementation to eliminate extraneous overheads—is quite useful when you need to identify exactly where times are going.

Performance Checklist

Most of these suggestions apply only after a bottleneck has been identified:

- Make the loop do as little as possible.

  — Remove from the loop any execution code that does not need to be executed on each pass.

  — Move any code that is repeatedly executed with the same result, and assign that code to a temporary variable before the loop ("code motion").

  — Avoid method calls in loops when possible, even if this requires rewriting or inlining.

  — Multiple access or update to the same array element should be done on a temporary variable and assigned back to the array element when the loop is finished.

  — Avoid using a method call in the loop termination test.

  — Use `int` data types preferentially, especially for the loop variable.

  — Use `System.arraycopy()` for copying arrays.

- — Try to use the fastest tests in loops.
- — Convert equality comparisons to identity comparisons when possible.
- — Phrase multiple boolean tests in one expression so that they "short circuit" as soon as possible.
- — Eliminate unneeded temporary variables from loops.
- — Try unrolling the loop to various degrees to see if this improves speed.
- Rewrite any `switch` statements to use a contiguous range of `case` values.
- Identify if a recursive method can be made faster.
  - — Convert recursive methods to use iteration instead.
  - — Convert recursive methods to use tail recursion.
  - — Try caching recursively calculated values to reduce the depth of recursion.
  - — Use temporary variables in place of passed parameters to convert a recursive method using a single search path into an iterative method.
  - — Use temporary stacks in place of passed parameters to convert a recursive method using multiple search paths into an iterative method.

8

I/O, Logging, and Console Output

I/O, I/O, it's off to work we go.

—Ava Shirazi

I/O to the disk or the network is hundreds to thousands of times slower than I/O to computer memory. Disk and network transfers are expensive activities, and are two of the most likely candidates for performance problems. Two standard optimization techniques for reducing I/O overhead are buffering and caching.

For a given amount of data, I/O mechanisms work more efficiently if the data is transferred using a few large chunks of data, rather than many small chunks. Buffering groups data into larger chunks, improving the efficiency of the I/O by reducing the number of I/O operations that need to be executed.

Where some objects or data are accessed repeatedly, caching those objects or data can replace an I/O call with a hugely faster memory access (or replace a slow network I/O call with faster local disk I/O). For every I/O call that is avoided because an item is accessed from a cache, you save a large chunk of time equivalent to executing hundreds or thousands of simple operations.*

There are some other general points about I/O at the system level that are worth knowing. First, I/O buffers throughout the system typically use a read-ahead algorithm for optimization. This normally means that the next few chunks are read from disk into a low-level buffer somewhere. Consequently, reading sequentially

---

* Caching usually requires intercepting a simple attempt to access an object and replacing that simple access with a more complex routine that accesses the object from the cache. Caching is easier to implement if the application has been designed with caching in mind from the beginning, by grouping external data access. If the application is not so designed, you may still be lucky, as there are normally only a few points of external access from an application that allow you to add caching easily.

forward through a file is usually faster than other orders, such as reading back to front through a file or random access of file elements.

The next point is that at the system level, most operating systems support mmap(), memcntl(), and various shared-memory options. Using these can improve I/O performance dramatically, but they also increase complexity. Portability is also compromised, though not as much as you might think. If you need to use these sorts of features and also maintain portability, you may want to start with the latest Perl distribution. Perl has been ported to a large number of systems (at the time of writing, about twice as many systems as Java), and these features are mapped consistently to system-level features in all ports. Since the Perl source is available, it is possible to extract the relevant system-independent mappings for portability purposes.

In the same vein, when simultaneously using multiple open file handles to I/O devices (sockets, files, pipes, etc.), Java requires you to use either polling across the handles, which is system-intensive; a separate thread per handle, which is also system-intensive; or a combination of these two, which in any case is bad for performance. However, almost all operating systems support an efficient multiplexing function call, often called select() or sometimes poll(). This function provides a way to ask the system in one request if any of the (set of) open handles are ready for reading or writing. Again, Perl provides a standardized mapping for this function if you need hints on maintaining portability. For efficient complex I/O performance, this is probably the largest single missing piece of functionality in Java.

WARNING   Java does provide nonblocking I/O by means of polling. Polling means that every time you want to read or write, you first test whether there are bytes to read or space to write. If you cannot read or write, you go into a loop, repeatedly testing until you can perform the desired read/write operation. Polling of this sort is extremely system-intensive, especially because in order to obtain good performance, you must normally put I/O into the highest-priority thread. Polling solutions are usually more system-intensive than multi-threaded I/O and do not perform as well. Multiplexed I/O, as obtained with the select() system call, provides far superior performance to both. Polling does not scale. If you are building a server, you are well advised to add support for the select() system call.

Here are some other general techniques to improve I/O performance:

- Execute I/O in the background. Decoupling the application processes from the I/O operations means that, ideally, your application does not spend time waiting for I/O. In practice, it can be difficult to completely decouple the I/O, but usually some reads can be anticipated and some writes can be run asynchronously without the program requiring immediate confirmation of success.

- Avoid executing I/O in loops. Try to replace multiple smaller I/O calls with a few larger I/O calls. Because I/O is a slow operation, executing in a loop means that the loop is normally bottlenecked on the I/O call.

- When actions need to be performed while executing I/O, try to separate the I/O from those actions to minimize the number of I/O operations that need to be executed. For example, if a file needs to be parsed, instead of reading a bit, parsing a bit, and repeating until finished, it can be quicker to read in the whole file and then parse the data in memory.

- If you repeatedly access different locations within the same set of files, you can optimize performance by keeping the files open and navigating around them instead of repeatedly opening and closing the files. This often requires using random-access classes (e.g., `RandomAccessFile`) rather than the easier sequential-access classes (e.g., `FileReader`).

- Preallocate files to avoid the operating-system overhead that comes from allocating files. This can be done by creating files of the expected size, filled with any character (0 is conventional). The bytes can then be overwritten (e.g., with the `RandomAccessFile` class).

- Using multiple files simultaneously can improve performance because of disk parallelism and CPU availability during disk reads and writes. However, this technique needs to balanced against the cost of extra opens and closes and the extra resources required by multiple open streams. Sequentially opening and closing multiple files is usually bad for performance (e.g., when loading unpacked class files from the filesystem into the Java runtime).

Replacing System.out

Typically, an application generates output to `System.out` or `System.err`, if only for logging purposes during development. It is important to realize that this output can affect performance. Any output not present in the final deployed version of the application should be turned off during performance tests; otherwise, your performance results can get skewed. This is also true for any other I/O: to disk, pipes, other processes, or the network.

It is best to include a framework for logging output in your design. You want a framework that centralizes all your logging operations and lets you enable or disable certain logging features (perhaps by setting a "debug level"). You may want to implement your own logging class, which decides whether to send output at all and where to send it. The Unix *syslog* utility provides a good starting point for designing such a framework. It has levels of priority (emergency, alert, critical, error, warning, notice, info, debug) and other aspects that are useful to note.

If you are already well into development without this kind of framework, but need a quick fix for handling unnecessary output, it is still possible to replace System. out and System.err.

It is simple to replace the print stream in System.out and System.err. You need an instance of a java.io.PrintStream or one of its subclasses, and you can use the System.setOut() and System.setErr() methods to replace the current PrintStream instances. It is useful to retain a reference to the original print-stream objects you are replacing, since these retain access to the console. For example, the following class simply eliminates all output sent to System.out and System.err if TUNING is true; otherwise, it sends all output to the original destination. This class illustrates how to implement your own redirection classes:

```
package tuning.console;

public class PrintWrapper
   extends java.io.PrintStream
{
   java.io.PrintStream wrappedOut;
   public static boolean TUNING = false;

   public static void install()
   {
     System.setOut(new PrintWrapper(System.out));
     System.setErr(new PrintWrapper(System.err));
   }

   public PrintWrapper(java.io.PrintStream out)
   {
     super(out);
     wrappedOut = out;
   }

   public boolean checkError() {return wrappedOut.checkError();}
   public void close() {wrappedOut.close();}
   public void flush() {wrappedOut.flush();}
   public void print(boolean x) {if (!TUNING) wrappedOut.print(x);}
   public void print(char x) {if (!TUNING) wrappedOut.print(x);}
   public void print(char[] x) {if (!TUNING) wrappedOut.print(x);}
   public void print(double x) {if (!TUNING) wrappedOut.print(x);}
   public void print(float x) {if (!TUNING) wrappedOut.print(x);}
   public void print(int x) {if (!TUNING) wrappedOut.print(x);}
   public void print(long x) {if (!TUNING) wrappedOut.print(x);}
   public void print(Object x) {if (!TUNING) wrappedOut.print(x);}
   public void print(String x) {if (!TUNING) wrappedOut.print(x);}
   public void println() {if (!TUNING) wrappedOut.println();}
   public void println(boolean x) {if (!TUNING) wrappedOut.println(x);}
   public void println(char x) {if (!TUNING) wrappedOut.println(x);}
```

```
    public void println(char[] x) {if (!TUNING) wrappedOut.println(x);}
    public void println(double x) {if (!TUNING) wrappedOut.println(x);}
    public void println(float x) {if (!TUNING) wrappedOut.println(x);}
    public void println(int x) {if (!TUNING) wrappedOut.println(x);}
    public void println(long x) {if (!TUNING) wrappedOut.println(x);}
    public void println(Object x) {if (!TUNING) wrappedOut.println(x);}
    public void println(String x) {if (!TUNING) wrappedOut.println(x);}
    public void write(byte[] x, int y, int z) {
       if (!TUNING) wrappedOut.write(x,y,z);}
    public void write(int  x) {if (!TUNING) wrappedOut.write(x);}
}
```

Logging

Logging always degrades performance. The penalty you pay depends to some extent on how logging is done. One possibility is using a final static variable to enable logging, as in the following code:

```
public final static boolean LOGGING = true;
...
if (LOGGING)
  System.out.println(...);
```

This code allows you to remove the logging code during compilation. If the LOGGING flag is set to **false** before compilation, the compiler eliminates the debugging code.* This approach works well when you need a lot of debugging code during development but don't want to carry the code into your finished application. You can use a similar technique for when you do want logging capabilities during deployment, by compiling with logging features but setting the boolean at runtime.

An alternative technique is to use a logging object:

```
public class LogWriter {
  public static LogWriter TheLogger = sessionLogger();
  ...
}
...
LogWriter.TheLogger.log(...)
```

This technique allows you to specify various LogWriter objects. Examples include a null log writer that has an empty log() method, a file log writer that logs to file, a sysout log writer logging to System.out, etc. Using this technique allows logging

---

* See "Conditional Error Checking" in Chapter 6, *Exceptions, Casts, and Variables*, and "Dead code branches are eliminated" in Chapter 3, *Underlying JDK Improvements*.

to be turned on after an application has started. It can even install a new type of log writer after deployment, which can be useful for some applications. However, be aware that any deployed logging capabilities should not do too much logging (or even decide whether to log too often), or performance will suffer.

Personally, I prefer to deploy an application with a simple set of logging features still in place. But I first establish that the logging features do not slow down the application.

From Raw I/O to Smokin' I/O

So far we have looked only at general points about I/O and logging. Now we look at an example of tuning I/O performance. The example consists of reading lines from a large file. This section was inspired from an article from Sun Engineering,[*] though I go somewhat further along the tuning cycle.

The initial attempt at file I/O might be to use the `FileInputStream` to read through a file. Note that `DataInputStream` has a `readLine()` method (now deprecated because it is byte-based rather than char-based, but ignore that for the moment), so you wrap the `FileInputStream` with the `DataInputStream`, and run. The code looks like:

```
DataInputStream in = new DataInputStream(new FileInputStream(file));
while ( (line = in.readLine()) != null)
{
  doSomethingWith(line);
}
in.close();
```

For these timing tests, I use two different files, a 1.8-MB file with about 20,000 lines (long lines), and a one-third of a megabyte file with about 34,000 lines (short lines). I will test using several VMs to show the variations across VMs and the challenges in improving performance across different runtime environments. To make comparisons simpler, I report the times as normalized to 100% for the JDK 1.2 VM with JIT. The long-line case and the short-line case will be normalized separately. Tests are averages across at least three test runs. For the baseline test, I have the following chart (see Tables 8-1 and 8-2 for full results). Note that the HotSpot results are those for the second run of tests, after HotSpot has had a chance to apply its optimizations.

---

[*] "Java Performance I/O Tuning," *Java Developer's Journal*, Volume 2, Issue 11. See *http://www. JavaDevelopersJournal.com*.

Normalized read times on	Long Lines				Short Lines			
	1.2	1.3	HotSpot	1.1.6	1.2	1.3	HotSpot	1.1.6
Unbuffered input stream	100%a	86%	84%	69%	100%a	84%	94%	67%

a The short-line 1.2 and long-line 1.2 cases have been separately normalized to 100%. All short-line times are relative to the short-line 1.2, and all long-line times are relative to the long-line 1.2.

The first test in absolute times is really dreadful, because you are executing I/O one byte at a time. This performance is the result of using a plain FileInput-Stream without buffering the I/O, because the process is completely I/O-bound. For this reason, I expected the absolute times of the various VMs to be similar, since the CPU is not the bottleneck. But curiously, they are varied. Possibly the underlying native call implementation may be different between 1.1.6 and 1.2, but I am not interested enough to spend time deciding why there should be differences for the unbuffered case. After all, no one uses unbuffered I/O. Everyone knows you should buffer your I/O (except when memory is really at a premium, like in an embedded system).

So let's immediately move to wrap the FileInputStream with a BufferedInput-Stream.* The code has only slight changes, in the constructor:

```
//DataInputStream in = new DataInputStream(new FileInputStream(file));
DataInputStream in = new DataInputStream(
    new BufferedInputStream(new FileInputStream(file)));
while ( (line = in.readLine()) != null)
{
   doSomethingWith(line);
}
in.close();
```

However, the times are already faster by an order of magnitude, as you can see in the following chart:

Normalized read times on	Long Lines				Short Lines			
	1.2	1.3	HotSpot	1.1.6	1.2	1.3	HotSpot	1.1.6
Unbuffered input stream	100%a	86%	84%	69%	100%a	84%	94%	67%
Buffered input stream	5%	3%	2%	9%	8%	3%	4%	12%

a The short-line 1.2 and long-line 1.2 cases have been separately normalized to 100%. All short-line times are relative to the short-line 1.2, and all long-line times are relative to the long-line 1.2.

---

* Buffering I/O does not require the use of buffered class. You can buffer I/O directly from the FileInputStream class and other low-level classes by passing arrays to the read() and write() methods. This means you need to handle buffer overflows yourself.

The lesson is clear, if you haven't already had it drummed home somewhere else: buffered I/O performs much better than unbuffered I/O. Having established that buffered I/O is better than unbuffered, you renormalize your times on the buffered I/O case so that you can compare any improvements against the normal case.

So far, we have used only the default buffer, which is a 2048-byte buffer (contrary to the JDK 1.1.6 documentation, which states it is 512 bytes; always check the source on easily changeable things like this). Perhaps a larger buffer would be better. Let's try 8192 bytes:

```
//DataInputStream in = new DataInputStream(new FileInputStream(file));
//DataInputStream in = new DataInputStream(
//    new BufferedInputStream(new FileInputStream(file)));
DataInputStream in = new DataInputStream(
    new BufferedInputStream(new FileInputStream(file), 8192));
while ( (line = in.readLine()) != null)
{
  doSomethingWith(line);
}
in.close();
```

Normalized read times on	Long Lines				Short Lines			
	1.2	1.3	HotSpot	1.1.6	1.2	1.3	HotSpot	1.1.6
Unbuffered input stream	1951%	1684%	1641%	1341%	1308%	1101%	1232%	871%
Buffered input stream	100%[a]	52%	45%	174%	100%[a]	33%	54%	160%
8K buffered input stream	102%	50%	48%	225%	101%	31%	54%	231%

[a] The short-line 1.2 and long-line 1.2 cases have been separately normalized to 100%. All short-line times are relative to the short-line 1.2, and all long-line times are relative to the long-line 1.2.

The variations are large, but there is a mostly consistent pattern. The 8K buffer doesn't seem to be significantly better than the default. I find this exception curious enough to do some further testing. One variation in testing is to repeat the test several times in the same VM process. Sometimes this can highlight obscure differences. Doing this, I find that if I repeat the test in the same JDK 1.2 VM process, the second test run is consistently faster for the 8K buffered stream. The entry for this second time is 75%. I cannot identify why this happens, and I do not want to get sidetracked debugging the JDK just now, so we'll move on with the tuning process.

Let's get back to the fact that we are using a deprecated method, readLine(). You should really be using Readers instead of InputStreams, according to the Java docs, for full portability, etc. Let's move to Readers, and what it costs us:

```
//DataInputStream in = new DataInputStream(new FileInputStream(file));
//DataInputStream in = new DataInputStream(
```

```
//    new BufferedInputStream(new FileInputStream(file)));
//DataInputStream in = new DataInputStream(
//    new BufferedInputStream(new FileInputStream(file), 8192));
BufferedReader in = new BufferedReader(new FileReader(file));
while ( (line = in.readLine()) != null)
{
  doSomethingWith(line);
}
in.close();
```

Normalized read times on	Long Lines				Short Lines			
	1.2	1.3	HotSpot	1.1.6	1.2	1.3	HotSpot	1.1.6
Buffered input stream	100%a	52%	45%	174%	100%a	33%	54%	160%
8K buffered input stream	102%	50%	48%	225%	101%	31%	54%	231%
Buffered reader	47%	43%	41%	43%	111%	39%	45%	127%

a The short-line 1.2 and long-line 1.2 cases have been separately normalized to 100%. All short-line times are relative to the short-line 1.2, and all long-line times are relative to the long-line 1.2.

These results tell us that someone at Sun spent time optimizing Readers. You can reasonably use Readers in most situations where you would have used an InputStream. Some situations can show a performance decrease, but generally there is a performance increase.

Now let's get down to some real tuning. So far we have just been working from bad coding to good working practice. The final version so far uses buffered Reader classes for I/O, as recommended by Sun. Can we do better? Well of course, but now let's get down and get dirty. You know from general tuning practices that creating objects is overhead you should try to avoid. Up until now, we have used the readLine() method, which returns a string. Suppose you work on that string and then discard it, as is the typical situation. You would do better to avoid the String creation altogether. Also, if you want to process the String, then for performance purposes you are better off working directly on the underlying char array. Working on char arrays is quicker, since you can avoid the String method overhead (or, more likely, the need to copy the String into a char array buffer to work on it). See Chapter 5, *Strings*, for more details on this technique.

Basically, this means that you need to implement the readLine() functionality with your own buffer, while passing the buffer to the method that does the string processing. The following implementation uses its own char array buffer. It reads in characters to fill the buffer, then runs through the buffer looking for ends of lines. Each time the end of a line is found, the buffer, together with the start and end index of the line in that buffer, is passed to the doSomething() method for processing. This implementation avoids both the String-creation overhead and the subsequent String-processing overhead, but these are not included in any timings here. The only complication comes when you reach the end of the buffer, and you need to fill it with the next chunk from the file, but you also need to retain the line fragment from the end of the last chunk. It is unlikely your 8192-char chunk will end exactly on an end of line, so there are almost always some characters left to be carried over to the next chunk. To handle this, simply copy the characters to the beginning of the buffer and read in the next chunk into the buffer starting from after those characters. The commented code looks like this:

```java
public static void myReader(String string)
    throws IOException
{
    //Do the processing myself, directly from a FileReader
    //But don't create strings for each line, just leave it
    //as a char array
    FileReader in = new FileReader(string);
    int defaultBufferSize = 8192;
    int nextChar = 0;
    char[] buffer = new char[defaultBufferSize];

    char c;
    int leftover;
    int length_read;
    int startLineIdx = 0;

    //First fill the buffer once before we start
    int nChars = in.read(buffer, 0, defaultBufferSize);
    boolean checkFirstOfChunk = false;

    for(;;)
    {
        //Work through the buffer looking for end of line characters.
        //Note that the JDK does the eol search as follows:
        //It hardcodes both of the characters \r and \n as end
        //of line characters, and considers either to signify the
        //end of the line. In addition, if the end of line character
        //is determined to be \r, and the next character is \n,
        //it winds past the \n. This way it allows the reading of
        //lines from files written on any of the three systems
        //currently supported (Unix with \n, Windows with \r\n,
        //and Mac with \r), even if you are not running on any of these.
        for (; nextChar < nChars; nextChar++)
        {
            if (((c = buffer[nextChar]) == '\n') || (c == '\r'))
            {
                //We found a line, so pass it for processing
                doSomethingWith(buffer, startLineIdx, nextChar-1);
```

```
      //And then increment the cursors. nextChar is
      //automatically incremented by the loop,
      //so only need to worry if 'c' is \r
      if (c == '\r')
      {
        //need to consider if we are at end of buffer
        if (nextChar == (nChars - 1) )
          checkFirstOfChunk = true;
        else if (buffer[nextChar+1] == '\n')
          nextChar++;
      }
      startLineIdx = nextChar + 1;
    }
  }

  leftover = 0;
  if (startLineIdx < nChars)
  {
    //We have some characters left over at the end of the chunk.
    //So carry them over to the beginning of the next chunk.
    leftover = nChars - startLineIdx;
    System.arraycopy(buffer, startLineIdx, buffer, 0, leftover);
  }
  do
  {
    length_read = in.read(buffer, leftover,
          buffer.length-leftover );
  } while (length_read == 0);
  if (length_read > 0)
  {
    nextChar -= nChars;
    nChars = leftover + length_read;
    startLineIdx = nextChar;
    if (checkFirstOfChunk)
    {
      checkFirstOfChunk = false;
      if (buffer[0] == '\n')
      {
        nextChar++;
        startLineIdx = nextChar;
      }
    }
  }
  else
  { /* EOF */
    in.close();
    return;
  }
}
}
```

The following chart shows the new times:

Normalized read times on	Long Lines				Short Lines			
	1.2	**1.3**	**HotSpot**	**1.1.6**	**1.2**	**1.3**	**HotSpot**	**1.1.6**
Buffered input stream	100%[a]	52%	45%	174%	100%[a]	33%	54%	160%
Buffered reader	47%	43%	41%	43%	111%	39%	45%	127%
Custom-built reader	26%	37%	36%	15%	19%	28%	26%	14%

[a] The short-line 1.2 and long-line 1.2 cases have been separately normalized to 100%. All short-line times are relative to the short-line 1.2, and all long-line times are relative to the long-line 1.2.

All the timings are the best so far, and most are significantly better than before.[*] You can try one more thing: performing the byte-to-char conversion. The code comes from Chapter 7, *Loops and Switches*, in which we looked at this conversion in detail. The changes are straightforward. Change the FileReader to FileInput-Stream and add a byte array buffer of the same size as the char array buffer:

```
//    FileReader in = new FileReader(string);
//this last line becomes
     FileInputStream in = new FileInputStream(string);
     int defaultBufferSize = 8192;
     //and add the byte array buffer
     byte[] byte_buffer = new byte[defaultBufferSize];
```

You also need to change the read() calls to read into the byte buffer, adding a convert() call after these. The first read() is changed like this:

```
//First fill the buffer once before we start
//  this next line becomes a byte read followed by convert() call
//  int nChars = in.read(buffer, 0, defaultBufferSize);
     int nChars = in.read(byte_buffer, 0, defaultBufferSize);
     convert(byte_buffer, 0, nChars, buffer, 0, nChars, MAP3);
```

The second read() in the main loop is also changed, but the conversion isn't done immediately here. It's done just after the number of characters, nChars, is set, a few lines later:

```
//       length_read = in.read(buffer, leftover,
//                buffer.length-leftover );
//becomes
          length_read = in.read(byte_buffer, leftover,
               buffer.length-leftover);
```

---

[*] Note that the HotSpot timings are, once again, for the second run of the repeated tests. No other VMs exhibited consistent variations between the first and second run tests. See Tables 8-1 and 8-2 for the full set of results.

```
  } while (length_read == 0);
  if (length_read > 0)
  {
    nextChar -= nChars;
    nChars = leftover + length_read;
    startLineIdx = nextChar;
    //And add the conversion here
    convert(byte_buffer, leftover, nChars, buffer,
        leftover, nChars, MAP3);
```

Measuring the performance with these changes, the times are now significantly better in almost every case, as shown in the following chart:

Normalized read times on	Long Lines				Short Lines			
	1.2	1.3	HotSpot	1.1.6	1.2	1.3	HotSpot	1.1.6
Buffered input stream	100%[a]	52%	45%	174%	100%[a]	33%	54%	160%
Custom-built reader	26%	37%	36%	15%	19%	28%	26%	14%
Custom reader and converter	12%	18%	17%	10%	9%	21%	53%	8%

[a] The short-line 1.2 and long-line 1.2 cases have been separately normalized to 100%. All short-line times are relative to the short-line 1.2, and all long-line times are relative to the long-line 1.2.

Only the HotSpot short-line case is worse.* All the times are now under one second, even on a slow machine. Subsecond times are notoriously variable, although in my tests the results were fairly consistent.

We have, however, hardcoded in the ISO 8859_1 type of byte-to-char conversion, rather than supporting the generic case (where the conversion type is specified as a property). But this conversion represents a common class of character-encoding conversions, and you could fall back on the method used in the previous test where the conversion is specified differently (in the System property file.encoding). Often, you will read from files you know and whose format you understand and can predict. In those case, building in the appropriate encoding is not a problem.

Using a buffered reader is adequate for most purposes. But we have seen that it is possible to speed up I/O even further if you're willing to spend the effort. Avoiding the creation of intermediate Strings gives you a good gain. This is true for both reading and writing, and allows you to work on the char arrays directly. Working directly on char arrays is usually better for performance, but is also more

---

* This shows that HotSpot is quite variable with its optimizations. HotSpot sometimes makes an unoptimized loop faster, and sometimes the manually unrolled loop comes out faster. Tables 8-1 and 8-2 show HotSpot producing both faster *and* slower times for the same manually unrolled loop, depending on the data being processed (i.e., short lines or long lines).

work. In specialized cases, you might want to consider taking control of every aspect of the I/O right down to the byte-to-char encoding, but for this you need to consider how to maintain compatibility with the JDK.

Tables 8-1 and 8-2 summarize all the results from these experiments.

Table 8-1. Timings of the Long-Line Tests Normalized to the JDK 1.2 Buffered Input Stream Test

	1.2	1.2 no JIT	1.3	HotSpot 1.0	HotSpot 2nd Run	1.1.6
Unbuffered input stream	1951%	3567%	1684%	1610%	1641%	1341%
Buffered input stream	100%	450%	52%	56%	45%	174%
8K buffered input stream	102%	477%	50%	45%	48%	225%
Buffered reader	47%	409%	43%	74%	41%	43%
Custom-built reader	26%	351%	37%	81%	36%	15%
Custom reader and converter	12%	69%	18%	77%	17%	10%

Table 8-2. Timings of the Short-Line Tests Normalized to the JDK 1.2 Buffered Input Stream Test

	1.2	1.2 no JIT	1.3	HotSpot 1.0	HotSpot 2nd Run	1.1.6
Unbuffered input stream	1308%	2003%	1101%	1326%	1232%	871%
Buffered input stream	100%	363%	33%	50%	54%	160%
8K buffered input stream	101%	367%	31%	41%	54%	231%
Buffered reader	111%	554%	39%	149%	45%	127%
Custom-built reader	19%	237%	28%	94%	26%	14%
Custom reader and converter	9%	56%	21%	80%	53%	8%

Serialization

Objects are serialized in a number of situations in Java. The two main reasons to serialize objects are to transfer objects and to store them.

There are several ways to improve the performance of serialization and deserialization. First, fields that are transient do not get serialized, saving both space and time. You can consider implementing readObject() and writeObject() (see java.io.Serializable documentation) to override the default serialization routine; it may be that you can produce a faster serialization routine for your specific objects. If you need this degree of control, you are better off using the java.io.Externalizable interface (the reason is illustrated shortly). Overriding the default serialization routine in this way is generally only worth doing for large or frequently serialized objects. The tight control this gives you may also be necessary to correctly handle canonicalized objects (to ensure objects remain canonical when deserializing them).

To transfer objects across networks, it is worth compressing the serialized objects. For large amounts of data, the transfer overhead tends to swamp the costs of compressing and decompressing the data. For storing to disk, it is worth serializing multiple objects to different files rather than to one large file. The granularity of access to individual objects and subsets of objects is often improved as well.

It is also possible to serialize objects in a separate thread for storage and network transfers, letting the serialization execute in the background. For objects whose state can change between serializations, consider using transaction logs or change-logs (logs of the differences in the objects since they were last fully serialized) rather than reserializing the whole object. This works much like the way full and incremental backups work. You need to maintain the changes somewhere, of course, so it makes the objects more complicated, but this complexity can have a really good payback in terms of performance: consider how much faster an incremental backup is compared to a full backup.

It is worthwhile to spend some time on a basic serialization tuning exercise. I chose a couple of fairly simple objects to serialize, but they are representative of the sorts of issues that crop up in serialization:

```
class Foo1 implements Serializable
{
  int one;
  String two;
  Bar1[] four;

  public Foo1()
  {
    two = new String("START");
    one = two.length();
    four = new Bar1[2];
    four[0] = new Bar1();
    four[1] = new Bar1();
  }
}

class Bar1 implements Serializable
{
  float one;
  String two;
  public Bar1()
  {
```

```
        two = new String("hello");
        one = 3.14F;
    }
}
```

Note that I have given the objects default initial values for the tuning tests. The defaults assigned to the various String variables are forced to be unique for every object by making them new Strings. Without doing this, the compiler assigns the identical String to every object. That alters the timings: only one String is written on output, and when created on input, all other String references reference the same string by identity. (Java serialization can maintain relative identity of objects for objects that are serialized together.) Using identical Strings would make the serialization tests quicker, and would not be representative of normal serializations.

NOTE   Test measurements are easily skewed by rewriting previously written objects. Previously written objects are not converted and written out again; instead, only a reference to the original object is written. Writing this reference can be faster than writing out the object again. The speed is even more skewed on reading, since only one object gets created. All the other references refer to the same uniquely created object.

Early in my career, I was set the task of testing the throughput of an object database. The first tests registered a fantastically high throughput until we realized we were storing just a few objects once, and all the other objects we thought we were storing were only references to those first few.

The Foo objects each contain two Bar objects in an array, to make the overall objects slightly more representative of real-world objects. I'll make a baseline using the standard serialization technique:

```
if (toDisk)
    OutputStream ostream = new FileOutputStream("t.tmp");
else
    OutputStream ostream = new ByteArrayOutputStream();
ObjectOutputStream wrtr = new ObjectOutputStream(ostream);

long time = System.currentTimeMillis();
//write objects: time only the 3 lines for serialization output
wrtr.writeObject(lotsOfFoos);
wrtr.flush();
wrtr.close();
System.out.println("Writing time: " +
        (System.currentTimeMillis()-time));

if (toDisk)
```

```
    InputStream istream = new FileInputStream("t.tmp");
else
    InputStream istream = new ByteArrayInputStream(
        ((ByteArrayOutputStream) ostream).toByteArray());
ObjectInputStream rdr = new ObjectInputStream(istream);

time = System.currentTimeMillis();
//read objects: time only the 2 lines for serialization input
Foo1[] allFoos = (Foo1[]) rdr.readObject();
rdr.close();
System.out.println("Reading time: " +
        (System.currentTimeMillis()-time));
```

As you can see, I provide for running tests either to disk or purely in memory. This allows you to break down the cost into separate components. The actual values revealed that 95% of the time is spent in the serialization. Less than 5% is the actual write to disk (of course, the relative times are system-dependent, but these results are probably representative).

TIP	When measuring, I used a pregrown `ByteArrayOutputStream` so that there were no effects from allocating the `byte` array in memory. Furthermore, to eliminate extra memory copying and garbage-collection effects, I reused the same `ByteArrayOutputStream`, and indeed the same `byte` array from that `ByteArrayOutputStream` object for reading. The `byte` array is accessible by subclassing `ByteArrayOutputStream` and providing an accessor to the `ByteArrayOutputStream.buf` instance variable.

The results of this first test for JDK 1.2* are:

	Writing (serializing)	**Reading (deserializing)**
Standard serialization	100%	175%

I have normalized the baseline measurements to 100% for the `byte` array output (i.e., serializing the collection of Foos). On this scale, the reading (deserializing) takes 175%. This is not what I expected, because I am used to the idea that "writing" takes longer than "reading." Thinking about exactly what is happening, you can see that for the serialization you take the data in some objects and write that data out to a stream of bytes, which basically accesses and converts objects into bytes. But for the deserializing, you access elements of a byte array and convert these to other object and data types, including creating any required objects. Added to the fact that the serializing procedures are much more costly than the

---

* Table 8-3 lists the full results of tests with a variety of VMs. I have used the 1.2 results for discussion in this section, and the results are generally applicable to the other VMs tested.

actual (disk) writes and reads, and it is now understandable that deserialization is likely to be the more intensive, and consequently slower, activity.

Considering exactly what the `ObjectInputStream` and `ObjectOutputStream` must do, I realize that they are accessing and updating internal elements of the objects they are serializing, without knowing beforehand anything about those objects. This means there must be a heavy usage of the `java.reflect` package, together with some internal VM access procedures (since the serializing can reach private and protected fields and methods).* All this suggests that you should improve performance by taking explicit control of the serializing.

TIP   Alert readers might have noticed that `Foo` and `Bar` have constructors that initialize the object, and may be wondering if deserializing could be speeded up by changing the constructors to avoid the unnecessary overhead there. In fact, the deserialization uses internal VM access to create the objects without going through the constructor, similar to cloning the objects. Although the `Serializable` interface requires serializable objects to have no-arg constructors, deserialized objects do not actually use that (or any) constructor.

To start with, the `Serializable` interface supports two methods that allow classes to handle their own serializing. So the first step is to try these methods. Add the following two methods to `Foo`:

```
private void writeObject(java.io.ObjectOutputStream out)
    throws IOException
{
    out.writeUTF(two);
    out.writeInt(one);
    out.writeObject(four);
}
private void readObject(java.io.ObjectInputStream in)
    throws IOException, ClassNotFoundException
{
    two = in.readUTF();
    one = in.readInt();
    four = (Bar2[]) in.readObject();
}
```

`Bar` needs the equivalent two methods:

```
private void writeObject(java.io.ObjectOutputStream out)
    throws IOException
{
```

---

* The actual code is difficult and time-consuming to work through. It was written in parts as one huge iterated/recursed switch, probably for performance reasons.

```
    out.writeUTF(two);
    out.writeFloat(one);
}
private void readObject(java.io.ObjectInputStream in)
    throws IOException, ClassNotFoundException
{
    two = in.readUTF();
    one = in.readFloat();
}
```

The following chart shows the results of running the test with these methods
added to the classes:

	Writing (serializing)	Reading (deserializing)
Standard serialization	100%	175%
Customized read/writeObject() in Foo and Bar	125%	148%

We have improved the reads but made the writes worse. I expected an improvement for both, and I cannot explain why the writes are worse (other than perhaps
that the ObjectOutputStream class may have suboptimal performance for this
method overriding feature). Instead of analyzing what the ObjectOutputStream
class may be doing, let's try further optimizations.

Examining and manipulating objects during serialization takes more time than the
actual conversion of data to or from streams. Considering this, and looking at the
customized serializing methods, you can see that the Foo methods simply pass control back to the default serializing mechanism to handle the embedded Bar
objects. It may be worth handling the serializing more explicitly. For this example,
I'll break encapsulation by accessing the Bar fields directly (although going
through accessors and updators or calling serialization methods in Bar would not
make much difference in time here). I redefine the Foo serializing methods as:

```
private void writeObject(java.io.ObjectOutputStream out)
    throws IOException
{
    out.writeUTF(two);
    out.writeInt(one);
    out.writeUTF(four[0].two);
    out.writeFloat(four[0].one);
    out.writeUTF(four[1].two);
    out.writeFloat(four[1].one);
}
private void readObject(java.io.ObjectInputStream in)
    throws IOException, ClassNotFoundException
{
    two = in.readUTF();
```

```
        one = in.readInt();
        four = new Bar3[2];
        four[0] = new Bar3();
        four[1] = new Bar3();
        four[0].two = in.readUTF();
        four[0].one = in.readFloat();
        four[1].two = in.readUTF();
        four[1].one = in.readFloat();
    }
```

The Foo methods now handle serialization for both Foo and the embedded Bar objects, so the equivalent methods in Bar are now redundant. The following chart illustrates the results of running the test with these altered methods added to the classes (Table 8-3 lists the full results of tests with a variety of VMs):

	Writing (serializing)	Reading (deserializing)
Standard serialization	100%	175%
Customized read/writeObject() in Foo and Bar	125%	148%
Customized read/writeObject() in Foo handling Bar	31%	59%

Now this gives a clearer feel for the costs of dynamic object examination and manipulation.

Given the overheads the serializing I/O classes incur, it has now become obvious that the more serializing you handle explicitly, the better off you are. This being the case, the next step is to ask the objects explicitly to serialize themselves, rather than going through the ObjectInputStream and ObjectOutputStream to have them in turn ask the objects to serialize themselves.

The readObject() and writeObject() methods must be defined as private according to the Serializable interface documentation, so they cannot be called directly. You must either wrap them in another public method or copy the implementation to another method so you can access them directly. But in fact, java.io provides a third alternative. The Externalizable interface also provides support for serializing objects using ObjectInputStream and Object-OutputStream. But Externalizable defines two public methods rather than the two private methods required by Serializable. So you can just change the names of the two methods: readObject(ObjectInputStream) becomes readExternal(ObjectInput), and writeObject(ObjectOutputStream) becomes writeExternal(ObjectOutput). You must also redefine Foo as implementing Externalizable instead of Serializable. All of these are simple changes, but to be sure that nothing untoward has happened as a consequence, rerun the tests (as good tuners should for any changes, even minor ones). The following chart shows the new test results.

	Writing (serializing)	Reading (deserializing)
Standard serialization	100%	175%
Customized read/writeObject() in Foo handling Bar	31%	59%
Foo made Externalizable, using last methods renamed	28%	46%

Remarkably, the times are significantly faster. This probably reflects the improvement you get from being able to compile and execute a line such as:

```
((Externalizable) someObject).writeExternal(this)
```

in the ObjectOutputStream class, rather than having to go through java. reflect and the VM internals to reach the private writeObject() method. This example also shows that you are better off making your classes Externalizable rather than Serializable if you want to control your own serializing.

WARNING   The drawback to controlling your own serializing is a significantly higher maintenance cost, as any change to the class structure also requires changes to the two Externalizable methods (or the two methods supported by Serializable). In some cases (as in the example presented in this tuning exercise), changes to the structure of one class actually require changes to the Externalizable methods of another class. The example presented here requires that if the structure of Bar is changed, the Externalizable methods in Foo must also be changed to reflect the new structure of Bar. Here, you can avoid the dependency between the classes by having the Foo serialization methods call the Bar serialization methods directly. But the general fragility of serialization, when individual class structures change, still remains.

You changed the methods in the first place to provide public access to the methods in order to access them directly. Let's continue with this task. Now, for the first time, you will change actual test code, rather than anything in the Foo or Bar classes. The new test looks like:

```
if (toDisk)
    OutputStream ostream = new FileOutputStream("t.tmp");
else
    OutputStream ostream = new ByteArrayOutputStream();
ObjectOutputStream wrtr = new ObjectOutputStream(ostream);

//The old version of the test just ran the next
//commented line to write the objects
//wrtr.writeObject(lotsOfFoos);

long time = System.currentTimeMillis();
```

```
//This new version writes the size of the array,
//then each object explicitly writes itself
//time these five lines for serialization output
wrtr.writeInt(lotsOfFoos.length);
for (int i = 0; i < lotsOfFoos.length ; i++)
  lotsOfFoos[i].writeExternal(wrtr);
wrtr.flush();
wrtr.close();
System.out.println("Writing time: " +
    (System.currentTimeMillis()-time));

if (toDisk)
  InputStream istream = new FileInputStream("t.tmp");
else
  InputStream istream = new ByteArrayInputStream(
    ((ByteArrayOutputStream) ostream).toByteArray());
ObjectInputStream rdr = new ObjectInputStream(istream);

//The old version of the test just ran the next
//commented line to read the objects
//Foo1[] allFoos = (Foo1[]) rdr.readObject();

time = System.currentTimeMillis();
//This new version reads the size of the array and creates
//the array, then each object is explicitly created and
//reads itself. read objects - time these ten lines to
//the close() for serialization input
int len = rdr.readInt();
Foo[] allFoos = new Foo[len];
Foo foo;
for (int i = 0; i < len ; i++)
{
  foo = new Foo();
  foo.readExternal(rdr);
  allFoos[i] = foo;
}
rdr.close();
System.out.println("Reading time: " +
    (System.currentTimeMillis()-time));
```

This test bypasses the serialization overhead completely. You are still using the
ObjectInputStream and ObjectOutputStream classes, but really only to write
out basic data types, not for any of their object-manipulation capabilities. If you
didn't require those specific classes because of the required method signatures,
you could have happily used DataInputStream and DataOutputStream classes
for this test. The following chart shows the test results.

	Writing (serializing)	Reading (deserializing)
Standard serialization	100%	175%
Foo made Externalizable, using last methods renamed	28%	46%
Foo as last test, but read/write called directly in test	8%	36%

If you test serializing to and from the disk, you find that the disk I/O now takes nearly one-third of the total test times. Because disk I/O is now a significant portion of the total time, the CPU is now underworked and you can even gain some speedup by serializing in several threads, i.e., you can evenly divide the collection into two or more subsets and have each subset serialized by a separate thread (I leave that as an exercise for you).

Note that since you are now explicitly creating objects by calling their constructors, the instance variables in Bar are being set twice during deserialization, once at the creation of the Bar instance in Foo.readExternal(), and again when reading in the instance variable values and assigning those values. Normally you should move any Bar initialization out of the no-arg constructor to avoid redundant assignments.

Is there any way of making the deserializing faster? Well, not significantly, if you need to read in all the objects and use them all immediately. But more typically, you need only some of the objects immediately. In this case, you can use lazily initialized objects to speed up the deserializing phase (see also "Lazy Initialization" in Chapter 4, *Object Creation*). The idea is that instead of combining the read with the object creation in the deserializing phase, you decouple these two operations. So each object reads in just the bytes it needs, but does not convert those bytes into objects or data until that object is actually accessed. To test this, add a new instance variable to Foo to hold the bytes between reading and converting to objects or data. You also need to change the serialization methods. I will drop support for the Serializable and Externalizable interfaces, since we are now explicitly requiring the Foo objects to serialize and deserialize themselves, and I'll add a second stream to store the size of the serialized Foo objects. Foo now looks like:

```
class Foo1 implements Serializable
{
  int one;
  String two;
  Bar1[] four;
  byte[] buffer;

  //empty constructor to optimize deserialization
  public Foo5(){}
  //And constructor that creates initialized objects
  public Foo5(boolean init)
```

```
{
  this();
  if (init)
    init();
}
public void init()
{
  two = new String("START");
  one = two.length();
  four = new Bar5[2];
  four[0] = new Bar5();
  four[1] = new Bar5();
}


//Serialization method
public void writeExternal(MyDataOutputStream out, DataOutputStream outSizes)
  throws IOException
{
  //Get the amount written so far so that we can determine
  //the extra we write
  int size = out.written();

  //write out the Foo
  out.writeUTF(two);
  out.writeInt(one);
  out.writeUTF(four[0].two);
  out.writeFloat(four[0].one);
  out.writeUTF(four[1].two);
  out.writeFloat(four[1].one);

  //Determine how many bytes I wrote
  size = out.written() - size;

  //and write that out to our second stream
  outSizes.writeInt(size);
}
public void readExternal(InputStream in, DataInputStream inSizes)
  throws IOException
{
  //Determine how many bytes I consist of in serialized form
  int size = inSizes.readInt();

  //And read me into a byte buffer
  buffer = new byte[size];
  int len;
  int readlen = in.read(buffer);

  //be robust and handle the general case of partial reads
  //and incomplete streams
  if (readlen == -1)
    throw new IOException("expected more bytes");
```

```
        else
          while(readlen < buffer.length)
          {
            len = in.read(buffer, readlen, buffer.length-readlen);
            if (len < 1)
              throw new IOException("expected more bytes");
            else
              readlen += len;
          }
      }


      //This method does the deserializing of the byte buffer to a 'real' Foo
      public void convert()
        throws IOException
      {
        DataInputStream in = new DataInputStream(new ByteArrayInputStream(buffer));
        two = in.readUTF();
        one = in.readInt();
        four = new Bar5[2];
        four[0] = new Bar5();
        four[1] = new Bar5();
        four[0].two = in.readUTF();
        four[0].one = in.readFloat();
        four[1].two = in.readUTF();
        four[1].one = in.readFloat();
        buffer = null;
      }
    }
```

As you can see, I have chosen to use `DataInputStreams` and `DataOutput-Streams`, since they are all that's needed. In addition, I use a subclass of `DataOutputStream` called `MyDataOutputStream`. This class adds only one method, `MyDataOutputStream.written()`, to provide access to the `DataOutputStream.written` instance variable so you have access to the number of bytes written. The timing tests are essentially the same as before, except that you change the stream types and add a second stream for the sizes of the serialized objects (e.g., to file *t2.tmp*, or a second pair of byte-array input and output streams). The following chart shows the new times:

	Writing (serializing)	Reading (deserializing)
Standard serialization	100%	175%
Foo as last test, but read/write called directly in test	8%	36%
Foo lazily initialized	20%	7%

We have lost out on the writes because of the added complexity, but improved the reads considerably. The cost of the `Foo.convert()` method has not been factored in, but the strategy illustrated here is for cases where you need to run only that convert method on a small subset of the deserialized objects, and so the extra overhead should be small. This technique works well when transferring large groups of objects across a network.

For the case in which you need only a few objects out of many serialized objects that have been stored on disk, another strategy is available that is even more efficient. The strategy uses techniques similar to the example just shown. One file (the data file) holds the serialized objects. A second file (the index file) holds the offset of the starting byte of each serialized object in the first file. For serializing, the only difference to the example is that when writing out the objects, the full `DataOutputStream.written` instance variable is added to the index file as the `writeExternal()` method is entered, instead of writing the difference between successive values of `DataOutputStream.written`. A moment's thought should convince you that this provides the byte offset into the data file.

With this technique, deserializing is straightforward. You enter the index file and skip to the correct index for the object you want in the data file (e.g., for the object at array index 54, skip 54 × 4 = 216 bytes from the start of the index file). The serialized `int` at that location holds the byte offset into the data file, so you deserialize that `int`. Then you enter the data file, skipping to the specified offset, and deserialize the object there. (This is also the first step in building your own database: the next steps are normally to waste time and effort before realizing that you can more easily buy a database that does most of what you want.) This "index file–plus–data file" strategy works best if you leave the two files open and skip around the files, rather than repeatedly opening and closing the files every time you want to deserialize an object. The strategy illustrated in this paragraph does not work as well for transferring serialized objects across a network. For network transfers, a better strategy is to limit the objects being transferred to only those that are needed.[*] Table 8-3 shows the tunings of the serialization tests, normalized to the JDK 1.2 standard serialization test. Each entry is a pair giving write/read timings. The test name in brackets refers to the method name executed in the `tuning.io.SerializationTest` class.

---

[*] You could transfer index files across the network, then use those index files to precisely identify the objects required and limit transfers to only those identified objects.

Table 8-3. Timings (in write/read pairs) of the Serialization Tests with Various VMs

	1.2	1.2 no JIT	1.3	HotSpot 1.0
Standard serialization (test1a)	100%/ 175%	393%/ 366%	137%/ 137%	127%/ 219%
Customized write/readObject() in Foo and Bar (test2a)	125%/ 148%	326%/ 321%	148%/ 161%	160%/ 198%
Customized write/readObject() in Foo handling Bar (test3a)	31%/ 59%	113%/ 162%	47%/ 63%	54%/ 83%
Foo made Externalizable, using last methods renamed (test4a)	28%/ 46%	104%/ 154%	32%/ 47%	33%/ 50%
Foo as last test, but write/read called directly in test (test4c)	8%/ 36%	35%/ 106%	6%/ 21%	7%/ 26%
Foo lazily initialized (test5a)	20%/ 7%	54%/ 12%	19%/ 4%	14%/ 11%

Clustering Objects and Counting I/O Operations

Clustering is a technique that takes advantage of locality (usually on the disk) to improve performance. It is useful when you have objects stored on disk and can arrange where objects are in reference to each other. For example, suppose you store serialized objects on disk, but need to have fast access to some of these objects. The most basic example of clustering is arranging the serialization of the objects in such a way as to selectively deserialize them to get exactly the subset of objects you need, in as few disk accesses, file openings, and object deserializations as possible.

Suppose you want to serialize a table of objects. Perhaps they cannot all fit into memory at the same time, or they are persistent, or there are other reasons for serialization. It may be that of the objects in the table, 10% are accessed frequently, while the other 90% are only infrequently accessed and the application can accept slight delays on accessing these less frequently required objects. In this scenario, rather than serializing the whole table, you may be better off serializing the 10% of frequently used objects into one file (which can be deserialized in one long call), and the other 90% into one or more other files with an object table index allowing individual objects to be read in as needed.

Alternatively, it may be that objects are grouped in some way in your application so that whenever one of the table objects is referenced, this also automatically requires certain other related objects. In this case, you want to cluster these groups of objects so they are deserialized together.

If you need to manage objects on disk for persistency, sharing, memory, or whatever reason, you should consider using an object-storage system (such as an object database). The serialization provided with Java is very basic and provides little in the way of simple systemwide customization. For example, if you have a collection of objects on disk, typically you want to read into memory the collection down to one or two levels (i.e., only the collection elements, not any objects held in the instance variables of the collection elements). With serialization, you get the *transitive closure** of the collection in general, which is almost certainly much more than you want. Serialization supports reading to certain levels in only a very rudimentary way: basically, it says you have to do the reading yourself, but it gives you the hooks that let you customize on a per-class basis. The ability to tune to this level of granularity is really what you need for any sort of disk-based object storage beyond the most basic. And you usually do get those extra tuning capabilities in various object-storage systems.

At a lower level, you should be aware that the system reads in data from the disk one page at a time (page size is system-dependent, normally 4 or 8 KB). This means that if you cluster data (of whatever type) on the disk so that the data that needs to be together is physically close together on disk, then the reading of that data into memory is also speeded up. Typically, the most control you have over clustering objects is by putting data into the same file near to each other, and hoping that the filesystem is not too fragmented. Defragmenting the disks on occasion can help.

Clustering should reduce the number of disk I/O operations you need to execute. Consequently, measuring the number of disk I/O operations that are executed is essential to determine if you have clustered usefully.† The simplest technique to measure I/O is to monitor the number of reads, writes, opens, and closes that are performed. This gets complicated by using different I/O classes wrapped one around the other. But you can always find the lowest-level class that is actually doing the I/O (usually one of `FileInputStream`, `FileOutputStream`, and `RandomAccessFile` in the `java.io` package). You can determine all actual methods that execute I/O fairly easily if you have the JDK source: simply find all source files with the word "native." If you look in `java.io` for these and look at the actual method names of the native methods, you will find that in almost every case, the only classes applicable to you are the `FileInputStream`, `FileOutputStream`, and `RandomAccessFile` classes. Now the difficult part is wrapping these calls so that you can monitor them. Native methods that are declared `private` are straightforward to handle: just redefine the `java.io` class to count the times they are called

---

* The transitive closure is the set of all objects reachable from any one object, i.e., an object and its data variables and their data variables, etc.

† Ultimately, it is the number of low-level I/O operations that matter. But if you reduce the high-level I/O operations, the low-level ones are generally reduced by the same proportion. The Java read/write/open/close operations at the "native" level are also the OS read/write/open/close operations for all the Java runtimes I've investigated.

internally. Native methods that are protected or have no access modifier are similarly handled: just ensure you do the same redefinition for subclasses and package members. But the methods defined with the public modifier need to be tracked for any classes that call these native methods, which can be difficult and tiresome, but not impossible.

The simplest alternative would be to use the debug interface to count the number of hits on the method. Unfortunately, you cannot set a breakpoint on a native method, so this is not possible.

The result is that it takes some effort to identify every I/O call in an application. If you have consistently used your own I/O classes, the java.io buffered classes, and the java.io Reader and Writer classes, it may be enough to wrap the I/O calls to FileOutputStream and FileInputStream from these classes. If you have done nonstandard things, you need to put in more effort.

One other way to determine how many I/O operations you have used is to execute Runtime.getRuntime().traceMethodCalls(true) before the test starts, capture the method trace, and filter out the native calls you have identified. Unfortunately, this is optional functionality in the JDK (Java specifies that the traceMethodCalls() method must exist in Runtime, but it does not have to do anything), so you are lucky if you use a system that supports it. The only one I am aware of is the Symantec development environment, and in that case, you have to be in the IDE and running in debug mode. Running the Symantec VM outside the IDE does not seem to enable this feature. Some profilers (see also Chapter 2, *Profiling Tools*) may also help to produce a trace of all I/O operations.

I would recommend that all basic I/O calls have logging statements next to them, capable of reporting the amount of I/O performed (both the number of I/O operations and the number of bytes transferred). I/O is typically so costly that one null call or if statement (when logging is not turned on) is not at all significant for each I/O performed. On the other hand, it is incredibly useful to be able to determine at any time whether I/O is causing a performance problem. Typically, I/O performance depends on the configuration of the system and on resources outside the application. So if an unusual configuration causes I/O to be dramatically more expensive, this can be easily missed in testing and difficult to determine (especially remotely) unless you have an I/O-monitoring capability built into your application.

Compression

A colleague of mine once installed a compression utility on his desktop machine that compressed the entire disk. The utility worked as a type of disk driver: accesses to the disk went through the utility, and every read and write was decompressed or compressed transparently to the rest of the system, and to the user. My colleague was expecting the system to run slower, but needed the extra disk space and was willing to put up with a slower system.

What he actually found was that his system ran faster! It turned out that the major bottleneck to his system was disk throughput, and by making most files smaller (averaging half the previous size), everything was moving between memory and disk much quicker. The CPU had plenty of spare cycles necessary to handle the compression-decompression procedures because it was waiting for disk transfers to complete.

This illustrates how the overhead of compression can be outweighed by the benefits of reducing I/O. The system described obviously had a disk that was relatively too slow in comparison to the CPU processing power. But this is quite common. Disk throughput has not improved nearly as fast as CPUs have increased in speed, and this divergent trend is set to continue for some time. The same is true for networks. Although networks do tend to have a huge jump in throughput with each generation, this jump tends to be offset by the much larger volumes of data being transferred. Furthermore, network-mounted disks are also increasingly common, and the double performance hit from accessing a disk over a network is surely a prime candidate for increasing speed using compression.

On the other hand, if a system has a fully loaded CPU, adding compression can make things worse. This means that when you control the environment (servers, servlets, etc.), you can probably specify precisely, by testing, whether or not to use compression in your application to improve performance. When the environment is unknown, the situation is more complex. One suggestion is to write I/O wrapper classes that handle compressed and uncompressed I/O automatically on the fly. Your application can then test whether any particular I/O destination has better performance using compression, and then automatically use compression when called for.

One final thing to note about compressed data is that it is not always necessary to decompress the data in order to work with it. As an example, if you are using 2-Ronnies compression,* the text "Hello. Have you any eggs? No, we haven't any eggs" is compressed into "LO. F U NE X? 9, V FN NE X."

---

* "The Two Ronnies" was a British comedy show that featured very inventive comedy sketches, many based on word play. One such sketch involved a restaurant scene where all the characters spoke only in letters and numbers, joining the letters up in such a way that they sounded like words. The mapping for some of the words to letters was as follows:

have ↔ F	you ↔ U	any ↔ NE	eggs ↔ X	hello ↔ LO	no ↔ 9
yes ↔ S	we ↔ V	have ↔ F	haven't ↔ FN	ham ↔ M	and ↔ N

Now, if I want to search the text to see if it includes the phrase "any eggs," I do not actually need to decompress the compressed text. Instead, I compress the search string "any eggs" using 2-Ronnies compression into "NE X", and I can now use that compressed search string to search directly on the compressed text.

When applied to objects or data, this technique requires some effort. You need to ensure that any small data chunk compresses in the same way both on its own and as part of a larger volume of data containing that data chunk. If this is not the case, you may need to break objects and searchable data into fields that are individually compressed.

There are several advantages to this technique of searching directly against compressed data:

- There is no need to decompress a large amount of data.

- Searches are actually quicker because the search is against a smaller volume of data.

- More data can be held in memory simultaneously (since it is compressed), which can be especially important for searching through large volumes of disk stored data.

It is rarely possible to search for compressed substrings directly in compressed data because of the way most compression algorithms use tables covering the whole dataset. However, this scheme has been used to selectively query for data locations. For this usage, unique data keys are compressed separately from the rest of the data. A pointer is stored next to the compressed key. This produces a compressed index table that can be searched without decompressing the keys. The compression algorithm is separately applicable for each key. This scheme allows compressed keys to be searched directly to identify the location of the corresponding data.

Performance Checklist

Most of these suggestions apply only after a bottleneck has been identified:

- Ensure that performance tests are run with the same amount of I/O as the expected finished application. Specifically, turn off any extra logging, tracing, and debugging I/O.

- Use `Runtime.traceMethodCalls()`, when supported, to count I/O calls.

  — Redefine the I/O classes to count I/O calls if necessary.

  — Include logging statements next to all basic I/O calls in the application.

- Parallelize I/O by splitting data into multiple files.

- Execute I/O in a background thread.

- Avoid the filesystem file-growing overhead by preallocating files.

- Try to minimize the number of I/O calls.

  — Buffer to reduce the number of I/O operations by increasing the amount of data transfer each I/O operation executes.

  — Cache to replace repeated I/O operations with much faster memory or local disk access.

  — Avoid or reduce I/O calls in loops.

  — Replace `System.out` and `System.err` with customized `PrintStream` classes to control console output.

  — Use logger objects for tight control in specifying logging destinations.

  — Try to eliminate duplicate and unproductive I/O statements.

  — Keep files open and navigate around them rather than repeatedly opening and closing the files.

- Consider optimizing the Java `byte-to-char` (and `char-to-byte`) conversion.

- Handle serializing explicitly, rather than using default serialization mechanisms.

  — Use transient fields to avoid serialization.

  — Use the `java.io.Externalizable` interface if overriding the default serialization routines.

  — Use change-logs for small changes, rather than reserializing the whole object.

  — Minimize the work done in the no-arg constructor.

  — Consider partitioning objects into multiple sets and serializing each set concurrently in different threads.

  — Use lazy initialization to move or spread the deserialization overhead to other times.

  — Consider indexing an object table for selective access to stored serialized objects.

  — Optimize network transfers by transferring only the data and objects needed, and no more.

— Cluster serialized objects that are used together by putting them into the same file.

— Put objects next to each other if they are required together.

— Consider using an object-storage system (such as an object database) if your object-storage requirements are at all sophisticated.

- Use compression when the overhead of compression is outweighed by the benefit of reducing I/O.

— Avoid compression when the system has a heavily loaded CPU.

— Consider using "intelligent" I/O classes that can decide to use compression on the fly.

— Consider searching directly against compressed data without decompressing.

Sorting

Avoiding Unnecessary Sorting Overhead

The JDK system provides sorting methods in `java.util.Arrays` (for arrays of objects) and in `java.util.Collections` (for objects implementing the `Collection` interfaces). These sorts are usually adequate for all but the most specialized applications. To optimize a sort, you can normally get enough improvement by reimplementing a standard sort (such as quicksort) as a method in the class being sorted. Comparisons of elements can then be made directly, without calling generic comparison methods. Only the most specialized applications usually need to search for specialized sorting algorithms.

As an example, here is a simple class with just an `int` instance variable, on which you need to sort:

```
public class Sortable
  implements Comparable
{
  int order;
  public Sortable(int i){order = i;}
  public int compareTo(Object o){return order - ((Sortable) o).order;}
  public int compareToSortable(Sortable o){return order - o.order;}
}
```

I can use the `Arrays.sort()` to sort this, but as I want to make a direct comparison with exactly the same sorting algorithm as I tune, I use an implementation of a standard quicksort. (This implementation is not shown here; for an example, see the quicksort implementation in "Finding the Index for Partially Matched Strings" in Chapter 11, *Appropriate Data Structures and Algorithms*.) The only modification to the standard quicksort will be that for each optimization, the quicksort is adjusted

237

to use the appropriate comparison method and data type. For example, a generic quicksort that sorts an array of Comparable objects is implemented as:

```
public static void quicksort(Comparable[] arr, int lo, int hi)
{
  ...
  int mid = ( lo + hi ) / 2;
  Comparable middle = arr[ mid ]; //Comparable data type
  ...
  //uses Comparable.compareTo(Object)
  if(arr[ lo ].compareTo(middle) > 0 )
  ...
}
```

To start with, I use a quicksort that takes an array of Objects. The comparisons are made using the Comparator.compareTo() method, so every Object in the array must implement the Comparable interface. Since every object is a Comparable, why don't I specify a Comparable[] instead of an Object[] in the quicksort signature? I use an Object[] signature initially, to illustrate why it is faster to use a Comparable[] signature. java.util.Arrays.sort() has an Object[] as its argument rather than a Comparable[] because it needs to support any array type, and Java doesn't let you cast a generic array to a more specific array type. That is, you cannot use:

```
Object[] arr = new Object[10];
... //fill the array with Comparable objects
//The following line does not compile
Arrays.sort( (Comparable[]) arr); //NOT valid Java code, invalid cast
```

This means that if you specify a sort with the signature that accepts only a Comparable[] object array, then you actually have to create a new Comparable array and copy all your objects to that array. And it is often the case that your array is already in an Object array, hence the more generic (but slower) support in the JDK. Another option for the JDK would be to have a second copy of the identical sort method in java.util.Arrays, except that the second sort would specify Comparable[] in the signature and have no casts in the implementation. This has not been done in java.util.Arrays up to JDK 1.3, but may be in the future.

Back to the example. The first quicksort with the Object[] signature gives a baseline at 100%. I am sorting a randomized array of Sortable objects, using the same randomized order for each test. Switching to a quicksort that specifies an array of Comparable objects (which means you avoid casting every object for each comparison) is faster for every VM I tested (see Table 9-1). You can modify the quicksort even further to cater specifically to Sortable objects, so that you call the Sortable.compareToSortable() method directly. This avoids yet another cast, the cast in the `Sortable.compareTo()` method, and therefore reduces the time even further.

Table 9-1. Timings of the Various Sorting Tests Normalized to the Initial JDK 1.2 Test

	1.2	1.2 no JIT	1.3	HotSpot 1.0	HotSpot 2nd Run
Quicksort(Object[])	100%	322%	47%	56%	42%
Quicksort(Comparable[])	64%	242%	43%	51%	39%
Quicksort(Sortable[])	45%	204%	42%	39%	28%
Quicksort(Sortable[]) using field access	40%	115%	30%	28%	28%
Arrays.sort()	109%	313%	57%	87%	57%

The last quicksort accepting a `Sortable[]` array looks like:

```
public static void quicksort(Sortable[] arr, int lo, int hi)
{
  ...
  int mid = ( lo + hi ) / 2;
  Sortable middle = arr[ mid ]; //Sortable data type
  ...
  //uses Sortable.compareToSortable(Sortable)
  if(arr[ lo ].compareToSortable(middle) > 0 )
  ...
```

You can make one further improvement, which is to access the `Sortable.order` fields directly from the quicksort. The final modified quicksort looks like:

```
public static void quicksort(Sortable[] arr, int lo, int hi)
{
  ...
  int mid = ( lo + hi ) / 2;
  Sortable middle = arr[ mid ]; //Sortable data type
  ...
  //uses Sortable.order field for direct comparison
  //if(arr[ lo ].order - middle.order > 0 ) -- same as next line
  if(arr[ lo ].order > middle.order )
  ...
```

This last quicksort gives a further improvement in time (see Table 9-1). Overall, this tuning example shows that by avoiding the casts by implementing a standard sort algorithm and comparison method specifically for a particular class, you can more than double the speed of the sort with little effort. For comparison, I have included in Table 9-1 the timings for using the `Arrays.sort()` method, applied to the same randomized list of `Sortable` objects used in the example. The `Arrays.sort()` method uses a merge sort that performs better on a partially sorted list. Merge sort was chosen for `Arrays.sort()` because, although quicksort provides better performance on average, the merge sort provides sort stability. A stable sort does not alter the order of elements that are equal based on the comparison method used.[*]

For more specialized and optimized sorts, there are books (including Java-specific ones) covering various sort algorithms, and a variety of sort implementations available on the Web. The computer literature is full of articles providing improved sorting algorithms for specific types of data, and you may need to run a search to find specialized sorts for your particular application. A good place to start is with the classic reference *The Art of Computer Programming* by Donald Knuth.

In the case of nonarray elements such as linked-list structures, a recursive merge sort is the best sorting algorithm and can be faster than a quicksort on arrays with the same dataset. Note that the JDK `Collections.sort()` methods are suboptimal for linked lists. The `Collections.sort(List)` method converts the list into an array before sorting it, which is the wrong strategy to sort linked lists, as shown in an article by John Boyer.[†] Boyer also shows that a binary search on a linked list is significantly better than a linear search if the cost of comparisons is more than about two or three node traversals, as is typically the case.

If you need your sort algorithm to run faster, optimizing the comparisons in the sort method is a good place to start. This can be done in several ways:

- Eliminating casts by specifying data types more precisely.

- Modifying the comparison algorithm to be quicker.

- Replacing the objects with wrappers that compare faster (e.g., `java.text. CollationKeys`). These are best used when the comparison method requires a calculation for each object being compared, and that calculation can be cached.

- Eliminating methods by accessing fields directly.

- Partially presorting the array with a faster partial sort, followed by the full sort.

Only when the performance is still short of your target do you need to start looking for alternatives. Several of the techniques listed here have been applied in the earlier example, and also in the internationalized string sorting example in "Sorting Internationalized Strings" in Chapter 5, *Strings*.

---

[*] The standard quicksort algorithm also has very bad worst-case performance. There are quicksort variations that improve the worst-case performance.

[†] "Sorting and Searching Linked Lists in Java," *Dr. Dobb's Journal*, May 1998.

An Efficient Sorting Framework

The sorting methods provided by the JDK are perfectly adequate for most situations, and when they fall short, the techniques illustrated in the previous section often speed things up as much as is required. However, if you work on a project where varied and flexible sorting capabilities are needed, sorting is one area of performance tuning where it is sensible to create a framework early during the development cycle. A good sorting framework should allow you to change sorting-algorithm and comparison-ordering methods in a generic way, without having to change too much in the application.

Providing support for arbitrary sorting algorithms is straightforward: just use sorting interfaces. There needs to be a sorting interface for each type of object that can be sorted. Arrays and collection objects should be supported by any sorting framework, along with any other objects that are specific to your application. Here are two interfaces that define sorting objects for arrays and collections:

```
import java.util.Comparator;
import java.util.Collection;

public interface ArraySorter
{
  public void sort(Comparator comparator, Object[] arr);
  public void sort(Comparator comparator, Object[] arr,
       int startIndex, int length);
  public void sortInto(Comparator comparator, Object[] source,
       int sourceStartIndex, int length,
       Object[] target, int targetStartIndex);
}

public interface CollectionSorter
{
  public Object[] sort(Comparator comparator, Collection c);
  public void sortInto(Comparator comparator, Collection c,
       Object[] target, int targetStartIndex);
}
```

Individual classes that implement the interfaces are normally stateless, and hence implicitly thread-safe. This allows you to specify singleton sorting objects for use by other objects. For example:

```
public class ArrayQuickSorter
  implements ArraySorter
{
  public static final ArrayQuickSorter SINGLETON = new ArrayQuickSorter();

  //protect the constructor so that external classes are
  //forced to use the singleton
```

```
    protected ArrayQuickSorter(){}

    public void sortInto(Comparator comparator, Object[] source,
      int sourceStartIndex, int length, Object[] target, int targetStartIndex)
    {
      //Only need the target - quicksort sorts in place.
      if ( !(source == target && sourceStartIndex == targetStartIndex) )
        System.arraycopy(source, sourceStartIndex, target,
            targetStartIndex, length);
      this.sort(comparator, target, targetStartIndex, length);
    }

    public void sort(Comparator comparator, Object[] arr)
    {
      this.sort(comparator, arr, 0, arr.length);
    }

    public void sort(Comparator comparator, Object[] arr,
        int startIndex, int length)
    {
      //quicksort algorithm implementation using Comparator.compare(Object, Object)
      ...
    }
```

This framework allows you to change the sort algorithm simply by changing the sort object you use. For example, if you use a quicksort but realize that your array is already partially sorted, simply change the sorter instance from `ArrayQuick-Sorter.SINGLETON` to `ArrayInsertionSorter.SINGLETON`.

However, we are only halfway to an efficient framework. Although the overall sorting structure is here, you have not supported generic optimizations such as optimized comparison wrappers (e.g., as with `java.text.CollationKey`). For generic support, you need the `Comparator` interface to have an additional method that checks whether it supports optimized comparison wrappers (which I will now call `ComparisonKeys`). Unfortunately, you cannot add a method to the `Comparator` interface, so you have to use the following subinterface:

```
    public interface KeyedComparator
      extends Comparator
    {
      public boolean hasComparisonKeys();
      public ComparisonKey getComparisonKey(Object o);
    }

    public interface ComparisonKey
    {
      public int compareTo(ComparisonKey target);
      public Object getSource();
    }
```

Now you need to support this addition to the framework in each sorter object. Since you don't want to change all your sorter-object implementations again and again, it's better to find any further optimizations now. One optimization is a sort that avoids a call to any method comparison. You can support that with a specific ComparisonKey class:

```
public class IntegerComparisonKey
  implements ComparisonKey
{
  public Object source;
  public int order;
  public IntegerComparisonKey(Object source, int order) {
     this.source = source;
     this.order = order;
  }
  public int compareTo(ComparisonKey target){
    return order - ((IntegerComparisonKey) target).order;
  }
  public Object getSource() {return source;}
}
```

Now you can reimplement your sorter class to handle these special optimized cases. Only the method that actually implemented the sort needs to change:

```
public class ArrayQuickSorter
  implements ArraySorter
{
  //everything else as previously
  ...

  public void sort(Comparator comparator, Object[] arr,
                   int startIndex, int length)
  {
    //If the comparator is part of the extended framework, handle
    //the special case where it recommends using comparison keys
    if (comparator instanceof KeyedComparator &&
        ((KeyedComparator) comparator).hasComparisonKeys())
    {
      //wrap the objects in the ComparisonKeys
      //but if the ComparisonKey is the special case of
      //IntegerComparisonKey, handle that specially
      KeyedComparator comparer = (KeyedComparator) comparator;
      ComparisonKey first = comparer.getComparisonKey(arr[startIndex]);
      if (first instanceof IntegerComparisonKey)
      {
        //wrap in IntegerComparisonKeys
        IntegerComparisonKey[] iarr = new IntegerComparisonKey[length];
        iarr[startIndex] = (IntegerComparisonKey) first;
        for(int j = length-1, i = startIndex+length-1; j > 0; i--, j--)
          iarr[j] = comparer.getComparisonKey(arr[i]);
```

```
        //sort using the optimized sort for IntegerComparisonKeys
        sort_intkeys(iarr, 0, length);

        //and unwrap
        for(int j = length-1, i = startIndex+length-1; j >= 0; i--, j--)
          arr[i] = iarr[j].source;
      }
      else
      {
        //wrap in IntegerComparisonKeys
        ComparisonKey[] karr = new ComparisonKey[length];
        karr[startIndex] = first;
        for(int j = length-1, i = startIndex+length-1; j > 0; i--, j--)
          karr[i] = comparer.getComparisonKey(arr[i]);

        //sort using the optimized sort for ComparisonKeys
        sort_keys(karr, 0, length);

        //and unwrap
        for(int j = length-1, i = startIndex+length-1; j >= 0; i--, j--)
          arr[i] = karr[i].getSource();
      }
    }
    else
      //just use the original algorithm
      sort_comparator(comparator, arr, startIndex, length);
}
public void sort_comparator(Comparator comparator, Object[] arr,
        int startIndex, int length)
{
  //quicksort algorithm implementation using Comparator.compare(Object, Object)
  ...
}
public void sort_keys(ComparisonKey[] arr, int startIndex, int length)
{
  //quicksort algorithm implementation using
  //ComparisonKey.compare(ComparisonKey)
  ...
}
public void sort_intkeys(IntegerComparisonKey[] arr,
        int startIndex, int length)
{
  //quicksort algorithm implementation comparing key order directly
  //using access to the IntegerComparisonKey.order field
  //i.e if (arr[i].order > arr[j].order)
  ...
}
}
```

Although the special cases mean that you have to implement the same algorithm three times (with slight changes to data type and comparison method), this is the kind of tradeoff you often have to make for performance optimizations. The maintenance impact is limited by having all implementations in one class, and once you've debugged the sort algorithm, you are unlikely to need to change it.

This framework now supports:

- An easy way to change the sorting algorithm being used at any specific point of the application.

- An easy way to change the pair-wise comparison method, by changing the `Comparator` object.

- Automatic support for comparison key objects. Comparison keys are optimal to use in sorts where the comparison method requires a calculation for each object being compared, and that calculation could be cached.

- An optimized integer key comparison class, which doesn't require method calls when used for sorting.

This outline should provide a good start to building an efficient sorting framework. Many further generic optimizations are possible, such as supporting a `LongComparisonKey` class and other special classes appropriate to your application. The point is that the framework should handle optimizations automatically. The most the application builder should do is decide on the appropriate `Comparator` or `ComparisonKey` class to build for the object to be sorted.

The last version of our framework supports the fastest sorting implementation from the previous section (the last implementation with no casts and direct access to the ordering field). Unfortunately, the cost of creating an `Integer-ComparisonKey` object for each object being sorted is significant enough to eliminate the speedup from getting rid of the casts. It's worth looking at ways to reduce the cost of object creations for comparison keys. This cost can be reduced using the object-to-array mapping technique from Chapter 4, *Object Creation*: the array of `IntegerComparisonKeys` is changed to a pair of `Object` and `int` arrays. By adding another interface you can support the needed mapping:

```
interface RawIntComparator
  //extends not actually necessary, but logically applies
  extends KeyedComparator
{
  public void getComparisonKey(Object o, int[] orders, int idx);
}
```

For the example `Sortable` class that was defined earlier, you can implement a `Comparator` class:

```
public class SortableComparator
  implements RawIntComparator
```

```
{
  //Required for Comparator interface
  public int compare(Object o1, Object o2){
    return ((Sortable) o1).order -((Sortable) o2).order;}
  //Required for Comparator interface
  public boolean hasComparisonKeys(){return true;}
  public ComparisonKey getComparisonKey(Object o){
    return new IntegerComparisonKey(o, ((Sortable) o).order);}
  //Required for RawIntComparator interface
  public void getComparisonKey(Object s, int[] orders, int index){
    orders[index] = ((Sortable) s).order;}
}
```

Then the logic to support the **RawIntComparator** in the sorting class is:

```
public class ArrayQuickSorter
  implements ArraySorter
{
  //everything else as previously except rename the
  //previously defined sort(Comparator, Object[], int, int)
  //method as previous_sort
  ...

  public void sort(Comparator comparator, Object[] arr,
                   int startIndex, int length)
  {
    //support RawIntComparator types
    if (comparator instanceof RawIntComparator)
    {
      RawIntComparator comparer = (RawIntComparator) comparator;
      Object[] sources = new Object[length];
      int[] orders = new int[length];

      for(int j = length-1, i = startIndex+length-1; j >= 0; i--, j--)
      {
          comparer.getComparisonKey(arr[i], orders, j);
          sources[j] = arr[i];
      }

      //sort using the optimized sort with no casts
      sort_intkeys(sources, orders, 0, length);

      //and unwrap
      for(int j = length-1, i = startIndex+length-1; j >= 0; i--, j--)
        arr[i] = sources[j];
    }
    else
      previous_ sort(comparator, arr, startIndex, length);
  }
```

```
public void sort_intkeys(Object[] sources, int[] orders,
        int startIndex, int length)
{
  quicksort(sources, orders, startIndex, startIndex+length-1);
}

public static void quicksort(Object[] sources, int[] orders, int lo, int hi)
{
  //quicksort algorithm implementation with a pair of
  //synchronized arrays. 'orders' is the array used to
  //compare ordering. 'sources' is the array holding the
  //source objects whicn needs to be altered in synchrony
  //with 'orders'
  if( lo >= hi )
    return;

  int mid = ( lo + hi ) / 2;
  Object tmp_o;
  int tmp_i;
  int middle = orders[ mid ];

  if( orders[ lo ] > middle )
  {
    orders[ mid ] = orders[ lo ];
    orders[ lo ] = middle;
    middle = orders[ mid ];
    tmp_o = sources[mid];
    sources[ mid ] = sources[ lo ];
    sources[ lo ] = tmp_o;
  }

  if( middle > orders[ hi ])
  {
    orders[ mid ] = orders[ hi ];
    orders[ hi ] = middle;
    middle = orders[ mid ];
    tmp_o = sources[mid];
    sources[ mid ] = sources[ hi ];
    sources[ hi ] = tmp_o;

    if( orders[ lo ] > middle)
    {
      orders[ mid ] = orders[ lo ];
      orders[ lo ] = middle;
      middle = orders[ mid ];
      tmp_o = sources[mid];
```

```
        sources[ mid ] = sources[ lo ];
        sources[ lo ] = tmp_o;
      }
    }

  int left = lo + 1;
  int right = hi - 1;

  if( left >= right )
    return;

  for( ;; )
  {
    while( orders[ right ] > middle)
    {
      right--;
    }

    while( left < right && orders[ left ] <= middle )
    {
      left++;
    }

    if( left < right )
    {
      tmp_i = orders[ left ];
      orders[ left ] = orders[ right ];
      orders[ right ] = tmp_i;
      tmp_o = sources[ left ];
      sources[ left ] = sources[ right ];
      sources[ right ] = tmp_o;
      right--;
    }
    else
    {
      break;
    }
  }

  quicksort(sources, orders, lo, left);
  quicksort(sources, orders, left + 1, hi);
  }
}
```

With this optimization, the framework quicksort is now as fast as the fastest hand-crafted quicksort from the previous section (see Table 9-2).

Table 9-2. Timings of the Various Sorting Tests Normalized to the Initial JDK 1.2 Test of Table 9-1

	1.2	1.2 no JIT	1.3	HotSpot 1.0	HotSpot 2nd Run
`Quicksort(Object[])` from Table 9-1	100%	322%	47%	56%	42%
`Quicksort(Sortable[])` using field access from Table 9-1	40%	115%	30%	28%	28%
`ArrayQuickSorter` using `Sortable.field`	36%	109%	49%[a]	60%	31%
`Arrays.sort()` from Table 9-1	109%	313%	57%	87%	57%

[a] The HotSpot server version manages to optimize the framework sort to be almost as fast as the direct field access sort. This indicates that the 1.3 VM, which uses HotSpot technology, is theoretically capable of similarly optimizing the framework sort. That it hasn't managed to in JDK 1.3 indicates that the VM can be improved further.

Better Than O(nlogn) Sorting

Computer-science analysis of sorting algorithms show that, on average, no generic sorting algorithm can scale faster than O(nlogn) (see the sidebar "Orders of Magnitude"). However, many applications don't require a "general" sort. You often have additional information that can help you to improve the speed of a particular sort.

For example, if you have 1000 items to sort, and each item can be given a unique ordering value that corresponds to a unique integer between 1 and 1000, the best sort is simply to slot the items directly into their correct locations in an array. No comparisons between the items are necessary.

Of course, typically you can't map your elements so neatly. But if you can map items to integer keys that are more or less evenly distributed, you can still take advantage of improved sorting characteristics. Bear in mind that an array of partially sorted items can be sorted faster than a typical unsorted array.

When you can guess the approximate final position of the items in the collection to be sorted, you can use this knowledge to improve sorting speed. You should specifically look out for sorts where:

- Items can be given an ordering value that can be mapped to integer keys.
- The distribution of the keys is regular, or any one of the following is true:
  - The distribution of the keys is fairly even, so that when mapped into array indexes, ordering is approximately kept.
  - The keys have evenly distributed clusters.
  - The distribution of the keys has a mapping into one of these other distributions.

Orders of Magnitude

When discussing the time taken for particular algorithms to execute, it is important to know not just how long the algorithm takes for a particular dataset, but also how long it takes for different-sized datasets, i.e., how it scales. For applications, the problems of handling 10 objects and handling 10 million objects are often completely different problems, not just different-sized versions of the same problem.

One common way to indicate the behavior of algorithms across different scales of datasets is to describe the algorithm's scaling characteristics by the dominant numerical function relating to the scaling behavior. The notation used is "O(*function*)," where *function* is replaced by the dominant numerical scaling function. It is common to use the letter "n" to indicate the number of data items being considered in the function. For example, O(n) indicates that the algorithm under consideration increases in time linearly with the size of the dataset. $O(n^2)$ indicates that the time taken increases according to the square of the size of the dataset.

These orders of magnitude do not indicate absolute times taken by the algorithm. Instead, they indicate how much longer the algorithm takes when the dataset increases in size. If an O(n) algorithm takes 200 seconds for n=10, it will take about 2000 seconds for n=100, i.e., a tenfold increase in the dataset size implies a tenfold increase in the amount of time taken by the algorithm. An $O(n^2)$ algorithm might take 5 seconds for n=10, and about 500 seconds for n=100, i.e., a tenfold increase in the dataset size implies a hundredfold increase in the time taken by the algorithm. Note that the scaled times are approximate, as the order-of-magnitude statistics include only the dominant scaling function, and there may be other smaller terms that adjust the actual time taken.

The order of magnitude does not indicate the relative speeds of two different algorithms for any specific dataset size. Instead, the order-of-magnitude statistics indicate how expensive one particular algorithm may be as your dataset grows. In the examples of the last paragraph, the time taken for the second $O(n^2)$ algorithm increases much faster than the first O(n) algorithm, but the $O(n^2)$ algorithm is still faster at n=100. However, by n=1000, it would be the slower of the two algorithms (50,000 seconds compared to 20,000 seconds for the O(n) algorithm).

To take a concrete example, hash tables have an O(1) order of magnitude for accessing elements. This means that the time taken to access elements in a hash table is independent of the size of the hash table. Accessing elements in an array by linearly searching through that array takes O(n). In absolute times, it might be quicker to execute the linear array search on a small array than to access from a hash table. But as the number of elements became larger, at some point the hash table will always become quicker.

The distribution of the keys is fairly critical. A regular distribution allows them to be mapped straightforwardly into array indexes. An uneven distribution is difficult to map. But if you have an uneven distribution and can specify a mapping that allows you to flatten out the keys in some way, it may still be possible to apply this methodology. For example, if you know that your keys will have a normal (bell-curve) distribution, you can apply an inverse bell-curve function to the keys to flatten them out to array indexes.

For this technique to work, the mapped keys do not need to be unique. Several keys or groups of keys can map to the same value or values. Indeed, it is quite difficult to make the index mapping unique. You need to be aware of this and handle the resulting collisions. Normally, you can map clusters of keys into subsections of the sorted array. These subsections are probably not internally sorted, but they may be correctly sorted against each other (i.e., all elements in subsection 1 are ordered below all elements in subsection 2, all elements in subsection 2 are ordered below all elements in subsection 3, etc.). This way, the problem has been modified to sort multiple smaller subsections (which is faster than sorting the whole array), and hence the array is sorted more quickly.

Note that `Object.hashCode()` provides a mechanism for generating an integer for any object. However, the resulting hash code is not guaranteed to be evenly distributed or even unique, nor is it at all guaranteed to be consistent across different VMs or even over multiple runs of one VM. Consequently, the hash code is of little use for any kind of mapping.

Karl-Dietrich Neubert* gives a detailed implementation of this approach, where the algorithm provides O(n) sorting behavior and also minimizes the extra memory needed to manage the sort.

NOTE   I also implemented Neubert's sort for a plain `int` array rather than for an array of objects. The results were the same as for the object array when the JIT was turned off. But with any type of JIT turned on, the two simpler reference-sort algorithms were optimized much better by the native code compiler, and were faster for all sizes of arrays I tested (up to several million elements). Their absolute sort times were sufficiently fast that their worse scaling behavior didn't matter. This curious difference in relative speeds applied only to sorting `int[]` arrays, not arrays of objects. For arrays of objects, Neubert's sort seems to be faster both with and without a JIT.

I include here a Java implementation of Neubert's algorithm with comments in the code. I have applied the implementation to an array of objects that have an

---

* Algorithm Alley, *Dr. Dobb's Journal*, February 1998.

integer field to specify the sort order, but of course the algorithm can be easily generalized to other cases where object ordering can be mapped to numbers. For a more detailed discussion of the algorithm, refer to Neubert's article. The implementation given here performs sorting significantly faster than either the sort in java.util.Arrays (in Java 2) or a handcrafted quicksort (the most optimized final version with no casts from the first section of this chapter); see Table 9-3. Note also that this sort is O(n), and thus increases linearly in time, whereas the other sorts are O(nlogn) and so have a superlinear speedup.

Table 9-3. Timings of the Various Sorting Tests Normalized to the Initial JDK 1.2 Test

	1.2	1.2 no JIT	1.3	HotSpot
Neubert's Flashsort	100%	258%	99%	174%
Handcrafted quicksort	282%	831%	188%	180%
Arrays.sort()	409%	990%	203%	304%

Note that the sort at the end of the Neubert algorithm is an insertion sort running over the entire array. Insertion sorts provide better performance than quicksorts for partially ordered arrays. This final insertion sort ensures that keys incorrectly classified by the group distribution end up in the right location:

```java
public interface FlashSortable{
   public int sortOrder();
}

public static void flashsort(FlashSortable[] arr)
{
   //Number of groups into which the elements are classified
   //Neubert suggests 0.2 to 0.5 times the number of elements in the array.
   int num_groups = (int) (0.4 * arr.length);

   //Count the number of elements in each group
   int[] groups = new int[num_groups];

   flashsort(arr, num_groups, groups);
}

public static void flashsort(FlashSortable[] arr, int num_groups, int[] groups)
{
   //First get the minimum and maximum values
   int min = arr[0].sortOrder();
   int max_idx = 0;
   int i;
   for (i = arr.length-1; i > 0; i--)
   {
      if (arr[i].sortOrder() < min)
         min = arr[i].sortOrder();
```

```
      if (arr[i].sortOrder() > arr[max_idx].sortOrder())
        max_idx = i;
}
//If they are the same, all elements are identical
//so the array is already sorted.
if (min == arr[max_idx].sortOrder())
  return;

//Count the number of elements in each group.
//Take care to handle possible integer overflow by
//casting to larger datatypes where this might occur.
double scaling_constant = (num_groups - 1) /
        ( ((double) arr[max_idx].sortOrder()) - min);
int group;
for (i = arr.length-1; i >= 0; i--)
{
  group = (int) (scaling_constant * (((long) arr[i].sortOrder()) - min));
  groups[group]++;
}

//Set the groups to point to the indexes in the array
//that are the last index for each group.
groups[0]--;
for (i = 1; i < groups.length; i++)
{
  groups[i] += groups[i-1];
}

//Put the biggest element at index 0 so that the swapping
//algorithm below starts on the largest element & max group.
FlashSortable old_value = arr[max_idx];
arr[max_idx] = arr[0];
arr[0] = old_value;

//start with element at index 0
int idx = 0;
//and the maximum group
group = num_groups - 1;

//Start moving elements into their groups.
//We need to make 'arr.length' moves at most,
//but if we have one move left in the outer loop
//then the remaining element is already in the right place,
//so we need test for only 'arr.length-1' moves.
int number_of_moves_left = arr.length - 1;

FlashSortable new_value;
while(number_of_moves_left > 0)
{
```

```
//When the first group fills up, we start scanning
//for elements left in the wrong groups, and move them.

//Note that we scan through the whole object array only once.
while(idx > groups[group])
{
  idx++;
  group = (int) (scaling_constant * (((long) arr[idx].sortOrder()) - min));
}


new_value = arr[idx];
//We run this loop until the first group fills up.
//Then we run the previous scan loop to get back into this loop.
while( idx != (groups[group]+1) )
{
  group = (int) (scaling_constant * (((long) new_value.sortOrder()) - min));
  old_value = arr[groups[group]];
  arr[groups[group]] = new_value;
  new_value = old_value;
  groups[group]--; //decrement the pointer to the next index
  number_of_moves_left--;
}
}


//Now we have our partially ordered array,
//we do an insertion sort to order the remainder.
for (i = arr.length - 3; i >= 0; i--)
{
  if (arr[i+1].sortOrder() < arr[i].sortOrder())
  {
    old_value = arr[i];
    idx = i;
    while(arr[idx+1].sortOrder() < old_value.sortOrder())
    {
      arr[idx] = arr[idx+1];
      idx++;
    }
    arr[idx] = old_value;
  }
}
}
```

Performance Checklist

Most of these suggestions apply only after a bottleneck has been identified:

- Eliminate casts in the sorting method.

- Reimplement a standard sort (such as quicksort) directly in the class being sorted.

- Make the comparison method faster.

- Directly access fields rather than calling methods.

- Sort linked lists with a merge sort.

- Use comparison keys to replace objects where the comparison method requires a calculation for each object being compared, and that calculation could be cached.

- Partially presort the array with a faster partial sort; then re-sort using the full comparison method.

- Use sorting interfaces to support different sorting algorithms.

- Support generic optimizations within a sorting framework. These optimizations include:

  — Comparison key objects that cache calculations that would otherwise need to be repeatedly executed

  — Comparison key objects that hold the ordering value in a directly accessible public field

  — Improved object creation by mapping arrays of comparison key objects into multiple arrays

- Use specialized sorting algorithms for faster times and better scaling behavior.

- Use specialized sorting algorithms when the sorting order of objects can be mapped directly to integer keys.

10

Threading

Major Premise: Sixty men can do a piece of work sixty times as quickly as one man.
Minor Premise: One man can dig a posthole in sixty seconds.
Conclusion: Sixty men can dig a posthole in one second.

—Ambrose Bierce
The Devil's Dictionary

Multithreading allows an application to do multiple things at the same time. While it is often possible to get the same effect with clever programming in a single thread, Java's extensive support of threads makes it easier to use multiple threads. In addition, single-threaded applications cannot take advantage of multi-processor machines.

However, multithreading can be difficult to implement effectively. Multithreading improves performance in many cases, but it also has drawbacks if the default mechanisms for cooperation between threads are used simplistically. In this chapter, we look at the benefits and the disadvantages threads offer to performance. We examine the likely problems that may be encountered and discuss how to minimize the performance downside while still gaining the benefits of multiple threads.

Multithreading needs more care in coding than single threading. When tuning threads, it is easy to make a little change here, and a little change there, and end up with total confusion, race conditions, and deadlock. Before you start tuning

Synchronization and Monitors

Synchronization can be confusing, so I felt it was worth including a short reminder of its subtleties here.

Two or more threads accessing and updating the same data variables have no way of knowing when a particular access or update will occur relative to any other thread accesses. Synchronization ensures that a group of statements (a synchronized block) will execute atomically as far as all synchronized threads are concerned. Synchronization does not address the problem of which thread executes the statements first: it is first come, first served.

Synchronization is achieved using monitors. Every object can have a monitor associated with it, so any object can synchronize blocks. Before a synchronized block can be entered, a thread needs to gain ownership of the monitor for that block. Once the thread has gained ownership of the monitor, no other thread synchronized on the same monitor can gain entry to that block (or any other block or method synchronized on the same monitor). The thread owning the monitor gets to execute all the statements in the block, and then automatically releases ownership of the monitor on exiting the block. At that point, another thread waiting to enter the block can acquire ownership of the monitor.

Note, however, that threads synchronized on different monitors can gain entry to the same block at any time. For example, a block defined with a synchron-ized(this) expression is synchronized on the monitor of the this object. If this is an object that is different for two different threads, both threads can gain ownership of their own monitor for that block, and both can execute the block at the same time. This won't matter if the block affects only variables specific to its thread (such as instance variables of this), but can lead to corrupt states if the block alters variables that are shared between the threads.

threads, it is important to have a good understanding of how they interact and how to make them cooperate and control each other. This book is not a tutorial on threads, so I don't intend to cover the subject from a non-performance-tuning standpoint in any great detail. Two excellent books on Java threads are *Java Threads* by Scott Oaks and Henry Wong (O'Reilly) and *Concurrent Programming in Java* by Doug Lea (Addison Wesley).

If you are not comfortable with Java synchronization and how it works, I strongly advise you to spend some time studying how to use threads and synchronization. Be sure you understand how race conditions and deadlocks occur (many articles and books on Java go into this in detail, and there are brief examples in the later sections of this chapter). Be sure you know how to correctly use the various `wait()` and `notify()` methods in the `Object` class as well as the `synchronized` keyword, and understand which monitor objects are used and how they are used when execution reaches a synchronized block or method.

User-Interface Thread and Other Threads

The user's impression of the performance of an application is greatly affected by its responsiveness. Putting the user interface into a separate thread from any other work makes the application feel far more responsive to the user and ensures that an unexpectedly long operation doesn't freeze the application's screen.

This user-interface thread is quite important in applets, where it is simple to use the screen-update thread to execute other tasks since you can easily call code from the `paint()` method. Although more effort is required to spawn a thread to execute other tasks, it is much better to do so, as otherwise you can easily block repainting the screen or other GUI responses. In Figure 10-1, the clock on the left has been resized to a quarter of its original size, but the `paint()` method has been unable to resize the clock drawing, as the `paint()` method is busy keeping the correct time. The clock on the right has been resized to a wide rectangular shape, and it keeps perfect time while also responding to the resize request, because its `paint()` method always completes quickly.

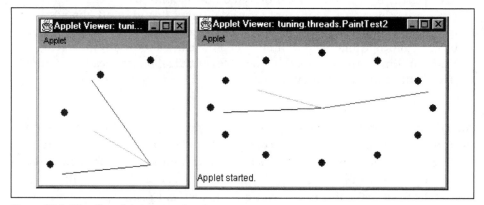

Figure 10-1. The effect of timing on redrawing

If you are able to separate operations that slow processing (such as I/O) into specialized threads, your application will run more smoothly. It can carry on its main work while another thread anticipates the need for data, saves data to disk, etc.

However, you should not pass work to another thread while your main thread just sits and waits until that other thread completes. In fact, doing this is likely to hurt performance rather than improve it. You should not use extra threads unless you have good design or performance reasons for doing so.

One useful technique is to use a separate thread to monitor the rest of the application and, when necessary, interrupt threads that are running beyond their expected execution time. This is more often a technique that ensures robustness, but it can apply to performance too, when a calculation provides successively better approximations to the required result. It may be reasonable to interrupt the calculation after a certain length of time, assuming you have a good approximation calculated. This technique does not specifically require a supervising thread, as the timeout checking could be done within the calculation. It is often used in animation; the frame-display rate can be adjusted according to the time taken to display the frames, which in turn depends on picture resolution and the system environment.

All in all, using multiple threads needs careful consideration, and should be planned for in the design stage. Retrofitting an application to use threads at an intermediate or advanced stage can sometimes be done quite simply in some sections of the application, but is not usually possible throughout the application. In any case, care should be taken when changing the design to use more threads, so that the problems illustrated in the next sections are avoided.

Race Conditions

A race condition occurs when two threads attempt to use the same resource at the same time. The following class demonstrates a simple race condition. Two threads simultaneously try to increment a counter. If each thread can complete the increment() method in its entirety without the other thread executing, then all is fine, and the counter monotonically increases. Otherwise, the thread context switcher has the opportunity to interrupt one thread in the middle of executing the increment() method, and let the other thread run through this method. Note that the thread can actually be interrupted anywhere, not necessarily in the middle of the increment() method, but I've greatly increased the likelihood of an interruption in the increment() method by including a print statement there:

```
package tuning.threads;

public class ThreadRace
  implements Runnable
{
  //global counter
  static int num=0;
```

```
    public static void increment()
    {
      int n = num;
      //This next line gives the context switcher an ideal
      //place to switch context.
      System.out.print(num+" ");
      //And when it switches back, n will still be the old
      //value from the old thread.
      num = n + 1;
    }

    public static void main(String args[])
    {
      ThreadRace d1 = new ThreadRace();
      ThreadRace d2 = new ThreadRace();

      Thread d1Thread = new Thread(d1);
      Thread d2Thread = new Thread(d2);

      d1Thread.start();
      d2Thread.start();
    }

    public void run()
    {
      for (int i = 200; i >= 0 ; i--)
      {
        increment();
      }
    }
}
```

The output from executing this class on a single-CPU test machine is:

```
0 1 2 3 4 5 6 7 8 9 10 11 12 13 14 15 16 16 17 18 19 20 21 22 23 24 25 26 27 28 29
30 31 32 17 18 19 20 21 22 23 24 25 26 27 28 29 30 31 32 33 33 34 35 36 37 38 39
40 41 42 43 44 45 46 47 48 49 34 35 36 37 38 39 40 41 42 43 44 45 46 47 48 49
```

You see that after 16, the next number is 16 again, and after the first 32, the next number is 17, as the threads switch back and forth in the middle of the increment() method. On a multiple-CPU machine, the situation is even more confused.

Synchronizing the increment() method ensures the correct behavior of a monotonically increasing counter, as this gives exactly the desired behavior: the method is forced to complete before another call to it from any thread can be started.

WARNING   In this test, because the counter is static, the increment() method needs to be a static method for synchronization to work correctly. If the increment() method is not static, synchronizing it locks the monitor for each this object rather than for the class. In the example I used a different object in each thread. A non-static increment() method is synchronized separately on each this object, so the updates remain unsynchronized across the two threads.

It is not simply that the num variable is static (though it needs to be for this particular example to work). The critical point is that the monitor that locks the method must be the same monitor for the two threads; otherwise, each thread gains its own separate lock with no synchronization occurring. Generally, deciding what to synchronize can be quite subtle, and you need to keep in mind which monitor is going to be locked by any particular thread.

Deadlocks

Ensuring that resources are used correctly between threads is easy in Java. Usually, it just takes the use of the synchronized keyword before a method. Because Java makes it seem so easy and painless to coordinate thread access to resources, the synchronized keyword tends to get used liberally. Up to and including Java 1.1, this was the attitude even from Sun. You can still see in the earlier defined classes (e.g., java.util.Vector) that all methods that update instance variables are synchronized. From JDK 1.2, the engineers at Sun became more aware of performance, and are now more careful to avoid synchronizing willy-nilly. Instead, many classes are built unsynchronized but are provided with synchronized wrappers (see the later section "Desynchronization and Synchronized Wrappers").

Synchronizing methods liberally may seem like good safe programming, but it is a sure recipe for reducing performance at best, and creating deadlocks at worst. The following Deadlock class illustrates the simplest form of race condition leading to deadlock. Here, the class Deadlock is Runnable. The run() method just has a short half-second delay and then calls hello() on another Deadlock object. The problem comes from the combination of the following three factors:

- Both run() and hello() are synchronized

- There is more than one thread

- The sequence of execution does not guarantee that monitors are locked and unlocked in correct order

The main() method accepts one optional parameter to set the delay in milliseconds between starting the two threads. With a parameter of 1000 (one second), there should be no deadlock. Table 10-1 summarizes what happens when the program runs without deadlock.

Table 10-1. Example Not Deadlocked

d1 Thread Activity	d1 Monitor Owned by	d2 Monitor Owned by	d2 Thread Activity
Acquire d1 monitor and execute d1.run()	d1Thread [in d1.run()]	None	
Sleeping in d1.run() for 500 milliseconds	d1Thread [in d1.run()]	None	
Acquire d2 monitor and execute d2.hello()	d1Thread [in d1.run()]	d1Thread [in d2.hello()]	
Sleeping in d2.hello() for 1000 milliseconds	d1Thread [in d1.run()]	d1Thread [in d2.hello()]	
Sleeping in d2.hello() for 1000 milliseconds	d1Thread [in d1.run()]	d1Thread [in d2.hello()]	Try to aquire d2 monitor to execute d2.run(), but block as d2 monitor is owned by d1Thread
Exit d2.hello() and release d2 monitor	d1Thread [in d1.run()]	None	Blocked until d2 monitor is released
Running final statements in d1.run()	d1Thread [in d1.run()]	d2Thread [in d2.run()]	Finally acquire d2 monitor and execute d2.run()
Exit d1.run() and release d1 monitor	None	d2Thread [in d2.run()]	Sleeping in d2.run() for 500 milliseconds
	d2Thread [in d1.hello()]	d2Thread [in d2.run()]	Acquire d1 monitor and execute d1.hello()
	d2Thread [in d1.hello()]	d2Thread [in d2.run()]	Sleeping in d1.hello() for 1000 milliseconds
	None	d2Thread [in d2.run()]	Exit d1.hello() and release d1 monitor
	None	None	Exit d2.run() and release d2 monitor

With a parameter of 0 (no delay between starting threads), there should be deadlock on all but the most heavily loaded systems. The calling sequence is shown in Table 10-2; Figure 10-2 summarizes the difference between the two cases. The critical difference between the deadlocked and nondeadlocked case is whether d1Thread can acquire a lock on the d2 monitor before d2Thread manages to acquire a lock on d2 monitor.

Table 10-2. Example Deadlocked

d1 Thread Activity	d1 Monitor Owned by	d2 Monitor Owned by	d2 Thread Activity
Acquire d1 monitor and execute d1.run()	d1Thread [in d1.run()]	None	
Sleeping in d1.run() for 500 milliseconds	d1Thread [in d1.run()]	d2Thread [in d2.run()]	Acquire d2 monitor and execute d2.run()
Blocked trying to acquire d2 monitor while starting d2.hello(), as d2Thread owns d2 monitor	d1Thread [in d1.run()]	d2Thread [in d2.run()]	Sleeping in d2.run() for 500 milliseconds
Blocked until d2 monitor is released	d1Thread [in d1.run()]	d2Thread [in d2.run()]	Blocked trying to acquire d1 monitor while starting d1.hello() as d1Thread owns d1 monitor
Blocked until d2 monitor is released	d1Thread [in d1.run()]	d2Thread [in d2.run()]	Blocked until d1 monitor is released

A heavily loaded system can delay the startup of d2Thread enough that the behavior executes in the same way as the first sequence. This illustrates an important issue when dealing with threads: different system loads can expose problems in the application and also provide different performance profiles. The situation is typically the reverse of this example, with a race condition not showing deadlocks on lightly loaded systems, while a heavily loaded system alters the application behavior sufficiently to change thread interaction to cause deadlock. Bugs like this are extremely difficult to track down.

The Deadlock class is defined as follows:

```
package tuning.threads;

public class Deadlock implements Runnable
{
    String me;
    Deadlock other;

    public synchronized void hello()
    {
        //print out hello from this thread then sleep one second.
        System.out.println(me + " says hello");
        try {Thread.sleep(1000);}
```

```
    catch (InterruptedException e) {}
  }

  public void init(String name, Deadlock friend)
  {
    //We have a name, and a reference to the other Deadlock object
    //so that we can call each other
    me = name;
    other = friend;
  }

  public static void main(String args[])
  {
    //wait as long as the argument suggests (or use 20 ms as default)
    int wait = args.length == 0 ? 20 : Integer.parseInt(args[0]);

    Deadlock d1 = new Deadlock();
    Deadlock d2 = new Deadlock();

    //make sure the Deadlock objects know each other
    d1.init("d1", d2);
    d2.init("d2", d1);

    Thread d1Thread = new Thread(d1);
    Thread d2Thread = new Thread(d2);

    //Start the first thread, then wait as long as
    //instructed before starting the other
    d1Thread.start();
    try {Thread.sleep(wait);}
    catch (InterruptedException e) {}
    d2Thread.start();
  }

  public synchronized void run()
  {
    //We say we're starting, then sleep half a second.
    System.out.println("Starting thread " + me);
    try {Thread.sleep(500);}
    catch (InterruptedException e) {}

    //Then we say we're calling the other guy's hello(), and do so
    System.out.println("Calling hello from " + me + " to " + other.me);
    other.hello();
    System.out.println("Ending thread " + me);
  }
}
```

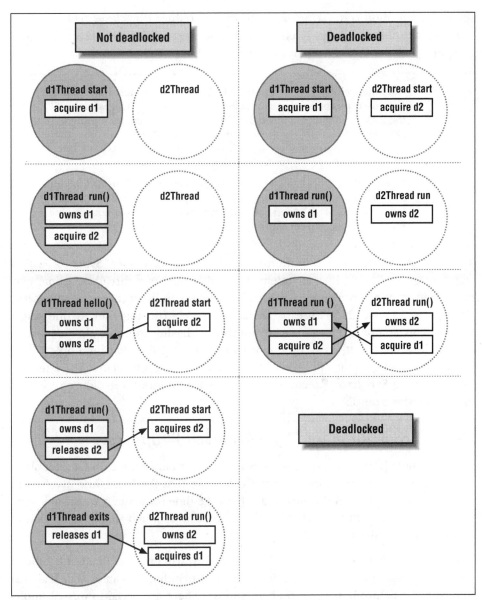

Figure 10-2. The difference between nondeadlocked and deadlocked execution

Synchronization Overheads

There are two separate costs of synchronization. Firstly, there is the operational cost of managing the monitors. This overhead can be significant: acquiring and testing for locks on the monitor for every synchronized method and block can impose a lot of overhead. Attempting to acquire a lock must itself be a synchronized activity within the VM; otherwise, two threads can simultaneously execute the lock-acquisition code. This overhead can be reduced by clever techniques in the VM, but never completely eliminated. The next section addresses this overhead and looks at ways to avoid it whenever possible.

TIP   Attempts to lock on different objects in two threads must still be synchronized to ensure that the object identity check and granting of the lock are handled atomically. This means that even attempting to get a lock on any object by two or more threads at the same time can still cause a performance degradation, as the VM grants only one thread at a time access to the lock-acquisition routine.

In some VMs, synchronizing static methods takes significantly longer than synchronizing nonstatic methods, suggesting that code is global in these VMs for the static synchronizations. (This is not strictly speaking a bug, but certainly not optimal for performance.)

The second cost of synchronization is in what it actually does. Synchronization serializes execution of a set of statements so that only one thread at a time executes that set. Whenever multiple threads simultaneously try to execute the same synchronized block, those threads are all effectively run together as one single thread. This completely negates the purpose of having multiple threads and is potentially a huge bottleneck in any program. On machines with multiple CPUs, you can leave all but one CPU idle when serialized execution occurs. The later section "Avoiding Serialized Execution" addresses techniques for avoiding serialized execution where possible.

Desynchronization and Synchronized Wrappers

As we just noted, synchronized methods have performance costs. In fact, for short methods, using a synchronized method can mean that the basic time involved in calling the method is significantly larger than the time for actually running it. The overhead of calling an unsynchronized method can be much smaller than that of calling a synchronized method.

You should be aware of when you do not need to synchronize. Read-only objects never need synchronization. Stateless objects (including no-static state) almost never need synchronization on their methods. (There are certain unusual implementations when methods may be altering state directly in another shared object, where synchronization would be required.) Some objects with state may have no need for synchronization because access to the object is highly restricted, and the synchronization is handled by other objects. Some objects can implement a copy-on-write mechanism (`StringBuffer` uses this; see Chapter 5, *Strings*). You can define copy-on-write in such a way to allow multithreaded updates of that object.

Many multithreaded applications actually use most of their objects in a single-threaded manner. Each individual thread maintains its own references to most objects, with just a few data or utility objects actually being used by multiple threads. From a performance standpoint, it seems a shame to have the overhead of synchronized objects on many classes where synchronization is not needed or used. On the other hand, when you design and build a particular class, it is seldom possible to anticipate that it will never be shared among several threads, so to be on the safe side, typically the class is built with synchronization.

When you have identified a bottleneck that uses synchronized objects, you can sometimes remove synchronization on those objects by giving different threads their own unsynchronized copies of those objects. This is especially easy to achieve when you use objects that have an unsynchronized implementation held in a *synchronized wrapper.*

The idea behind synchronized wrappers is that you build your class completely unsynchronized, as if it is to be used single-threaded. But you also provide a wrapper class with exactly the same interface. The difference in the wrapper class is that all methods that require synchronization are defined with the `synchronized` modifier. The wrapper could be a subclass with methods reimplemented, but more typically, it is a separate class that holds an internal reference to an instance of the unsynchronized class and wraps all the methods to call that internal object. Using synchronized wrappers allows you the benefits of thread-safe objects by default, while still retaining the capability to selectively use unsynchronized versions of those classes in bottlenecks.

From Java 2, the framework of using synchronized wrappers has become standard. All the new collection classes in `java.util` are now defined unsynchronized, with synchronized wrappers available for them. Old collection classes (e.g., `Hashtable`, `Vector`) that are already synchronized remain so for backward compatibility. The wrappers are usually generic, so you can actually create wrapped synchronized objects from any object of the right type.

I include a short example of the synchronized-wrapper framework here for clarity. If class `UnsyncedAdder` is defined as follows:

```
public interface Adder {
  public void add(int aNumber);
}

public class UnsyncedAdder
  implements Adder
{
  int total;
  int numAdditions;
  public void add(int aNumber) {total += aNumber; numAdditions++;}
}
```

Then the synchronized wrapper for this class can be:

```
public class SyncedAdder
  implements Adder
{
  Adder adder;
  public SyncedAdder(Adder a) {adder = a;}
  public synchronized void add(int aNumber) { adder.add(aNumber);}
}
```

Obviously, you refer to `Adder` objects in your code; don't refer explicitly to concrete implementations of `Adder` classes (such as `UnsyncedAdder` and `SyncedAdder`) except in the constructor or factory classes. Note that the synchronized wrapper is completely generic. It wraps any implementation of `Adder`, providing synchronization on the `add()` method irrespective of the underlying concrete implementation of the `Adder` class.

Using unsynchronized classes gives a performance advantage, but it is a maintenance drawback. There is every likelihood that initial implementation of any application will use the unsynchronized classes by default, leading to many subtle threading bugs that can be a debugging and maintenance nightmare. Typical development scenarios then try to identify which objects need to be synchronized for the application, and then wrap those objects in their synchronized wrappers.

Under the stress of project milestones, I know of one project where the developers went through all their code with a recursive routine, chopping out every `synchronized` keyword in method declarations. This seemed quicker than carefully tuning the code, and did in fact give a performance improvement. They put a few `synchronized` keywords back in after the regression tests. This type of tuning is exactly the opposite of what I recommend.

Instead, you should use synchronized wrapped objects throughout the application by default, but ensure that you have the capability to easily replace these with the unsynchronized underlying objects. (Remember, tuning is better done after the application works correctly, not at the beginning.) When you come to tune the application, identify the bottlenecks. Then, when you find that a particular class needs to be speeded up, determine whether that class can be used unsynchronized. If so, replace it with its unsynchronized underlying object, and document this thoroughly. Any changes in the application must reexamine these particular tuning changes to ensure that these objects do not subsequently need to become synchronized.*

---

* When the design indicates that a class or a set of methods should definitely be synchronized or definitely does not need synchronization, then of course you should apply that design decision. For example, stateless objects can often be specified with no synchronization. However, there are many classes and methods where this decision is uncertain, and this is where my recommendation applies.

Be aware, though, that there is no win-win situation here. If you tend towards unsynchronized classes by default, you leave your application open to corruption. If you prefer my recommended "synchronized by default" approach, your application has an increased chance of encountering deadlocks. On the basis that deadlocks are both more obvious and easier to fix than corrupt objects, I prefer the "synchronized by default" option. Implementing with interfaces and synchronized wrappers gives you an easy way to selectively back out of synchronization problems.

The next test gives you an idea of the relative performance of synchronized and unsynchronized methods, and of synchronized wrappers. The test compares synchronized (`Vector`), unsynchronized (`ArrayList`), and synchronized wrapper (`ArrayList` wrapped) classes:

```
package tuning.threads;

import java.util.*;

public class ListTesting
{
  public static final int CAPACITY = 100000;
  public static void main(String args[])
  {
    //In order to isolate the effects of synchronization, we make sure
    //that the garbage collector doesn't interfere with the test. So
    //we use a bunch of pre-allocated, pre-sized collections, and
    //populate those collections with pre-existing objects. No objects
    //will be created or released during the timing phase of the tests.
    List[] l = {new Vector(CAPACITY), new Vector(CAPACITY),
      new Vector(CAPACITY), new ArrayList(CAPACITY),
      new ArrayList(CAPACITY), new ArrayList(CAPACITY),
      Collections.synchronizedList(new ArrayList(CAPACITY)),
      Collections.synchronizedList(new ArrayList(CAPACITY)),
      Collections.synchronizedList(new ArrayList(CAPACITY))};
    int REPEAT = (args.length > 0) ? Integer.parseInt(args[0]) : 100;

    //Vary the order.
    test(l[0], REPEAT, "Vector");
    test(l[6], REPEAT, "sync ArrayList" );
    test(l[3], REPEAT, "ArrayList");
    test(l[1], REPEAT, "Vector");
    test(l[4], REPEAT, "ArrayList");
    test(l[7], REPEAT, "sync ArrayList" );
    test(l[2], REPEAT, "Vector");
    test(l[5], REPEAT, "ArrayList");
    test(l[8], REPEAT, "sync ArrayList" );
  }

  public static void test(List l, int REPEAT, String ltype)
  {
```

```
        //need to initialize for set() to work. Don't measure this time
        for (int j = 0; j < CAPACITY; j++)
          l.add(Boolean.FALSE);

        long time = System.currentTimeMillis();
        //The test sets elements repeatedly. The set methods are
        //very similar. Apart from synchronization, the Vector.set()
        //is slightly more efficient than the ArrayList.set(), which
        //is in turn more efficient than the wrapped ArrayList because
        //there is one extra layer of method calls for the wrapped object.
        for (int i = REPEAT; i > 0; i--)
          for (int j = 0; j < CAPACITY; j++)
            l.set(j, Boolean.TRUE);
        System.out.println(ltype + " took " +
            (System.currentTimeMillis()-time));
    }
  }
```

The normalized results from running this test are shown in Table 10-3.

Table 10-3. Timings of the Various Array-Manipulation Tests, Normalized to the JDK 1.2 Vector Test

	1.2	1.2 no JIT	1.3	HotSpot 1.0	HotSpot 2nd Run
Vector	100%	179%	25%[a]	64%	32%
ArrayList	23%	382%[b]	22%	17%	24%
Wrapped ArrayList	170%	797%	36%	72%	39%

[a] The 1.3 VM manages to execute the initial Vector test slightly faster than the ArrayList. But unfortunately, the VM then appears to unoptimize the Vector test, making all subsequent test runs slower.
[b] I have no idea why the non-JIT VM runs the ArrayList slower. The ArrayList methods are defined with slightly more testing, but I wouldn't have thought there was enough to make such a difference.

There are some reports that the latest VMs have negligible overheads for synchronized methods; however, my own tests show that synchronized methods continue to incur significant overheads (VMs up to and including JDK 1.2). HotSpot has at times shown different behavior. My tests using HotSpot show that synchronized methods can sometimes be optimized to run faster than unsynchronized versions. However, by varying the order and type of tests, it becomes clear that HotSpot is very inconsistent in its optimizations. This variation can exist for a number of different reasons: profiler overheads, aggressive compiler cutting in, deoptimizations occasionally necessary, etc. The variability in this particular test probably comes from speculatively inlining methods and sometimes having to undo the speculative inline. This can result in tests where a synchronized method apparently gets optimized more effectively than a nonsynchronized method.

The results from running the ListTesting class just defined in a HotSpot VM show how difficult it can be to get consistent results from HotSpot. For my test results, I take the first three and next three results, but I also find that altering the order of the tests can make a big difference to the times:

```
Vector took 5548
sync ArrayList took 6239
ArrayList took 1472
Vector took 2734
ArrayList took 2103
sync ArrayList took 3385
Vector took 7811
ArrayList took 6469
sync ArrayList took 3696
```

Avoiding Serialized Execution

One way of completely avoiding the requirement to synchronize methods is to use separate objects and storage structures for different threads. Care must be taken to avoid calling `synchronized` methods from your own methods, or you will lose all your carefully built benefits. For example, `Hashtable` access and update methods are `synchronized`, so using one in your storage structure can eliminate any desired benefit. Prior to JDK 1.2, there is no unsynchronized hash table in the JDK, and you have to build or buy your own unsynchronized version. From JDK 1.2, unsynchronized collection classes are available, including `Map` classes.

As an example of implementing this framework, I look at a simple set of global counters, keyed on a numeric identifier. Basically, the concept is a global counter to which any thread can add a number. This concept is extended slightly to allow for multiple counters, each counter having a different key. `String` keys are more useful, but for simplicity I use integer keys in this example. To use `String` keys, an unsynchronized `Map` replaces the arrays.

The simple, straightforward version of the class looks like this:

```java
package tuning.threads;

public class Counter1
{
  //For simplicity make just 10 counters
  static long[] vec = new long[10];

  public static void initialize(int key)
  {
    vec[key] = 0;
  }

  //And also just make key the index into the array
  public static void addAmount(int key, long amount)
  {
```

```
    //This is not atomically synchronized since we do an array
    //access together with an update, which are two operations.
    vec[key] += amount;
  }

  public static long getAmount(int key)
  {
    return vec[key];
  }
}
```

This class is basic and easy to understand. Unfortunately, it is not thread-safe, and leads to corrupt counter values when used. A test run on a particular single-CPU configuration with four threads running simultaneously, each adding the number 1 to the same key 10 million times, gives a final counter value of around 26 million instead of the correct 40 million.* On the positive side, the test is blazingly fast, taking very little time to complete and get the wrong answer.

To get the correct behavior, you need to synchronize the update methods in the class. Here is Counter2, which is just Counter1 with the methods synchronized:

```
package tuning.threads;

public class Counter2
{
  //For simplicity make just 10 counters
  static long[] vec = new long[10];

  public static synchronized void initialize(int key)
  {
    vec[key] = 0;
  }

  //And also make the just make key the index into the array
  public static synchronized void addAmount(int key, long amount)
  {
    //Now the method is synchronized, so we will always
    //complete any particular update
    vec[key] += amount;
  }
  public static synchronized long getAmount(int key)
  {
    return vec[key];
  }
}
```

---

* The results discussed are for one particular test run. On other test runs, the final value is different, but it is almost never the correct 40 million value. If I use a faster CPU or a lower total count, the threads can get serialized by the operating system (by finishing quickly enough), leading to consistently correct results for the total count. But those correct results are an artifact of the environment, and are not guaranteed to be produced. Other system loads and environments generate corrupt values.

Now you get the correct answer of 40 million for the same test as before. Unfortunately, the test takes 20 times longer to execute (see Table 10-4). Avoiding the synchronization is going to be more work. To do this, create a set of counters, one for each thread, and update each thread's counter separately.* When you want to see the global total, you need to sum the counters across the threads. The class definition follows:

```
package tuning.threads;

public class Counter3
{
  //support up to 10 threads of 10 counters
  static long vec[][] = new long[10][];

  public static synchronized void initialize(CounterTest t)
  {
    //For simplicity make just 10 counters per thread
    vec[t.num] = new long[10];
  }

  public static void addAmount(int key, long amount)
  {
    //Use our own threads to make the mapping easier,
    //and to illustrate the technique of customizing threads.
    //For generic Thread objects, could use an unsynchronized
    //HashMap or other Map,
    //Or use ThreadLocal if JDK 1.2 is available

    //We use the num instance variable of the CounterTest
    //object to determine which array we are going to increment.
    //Since each thread is different, here is no conflict.
    //Each thread updates its own counter.
    long[] arr = vec[((CounterTest) Thread.currentThread()).num];
    arr[key] += amount;
  }
  public static synchronized long getAmount(int key)
  {
    //The current amount must be aggregated across the thread
    //storage arrays. This needs to be synchronized, but
    //does not matter here as I just call it at the end.
    long amount = 0;
    for (int threadnum = vec.length-1; threadnum >= 0 ; threadnum--)
    {
      long[] arr = vec[threadnum];
```

---

* Although ThreadLocal variables might seem ideal to ensure the allocation of different counters for different threads, they are of no use here. The underlying implementation for ThreadLocal objects uses a synchronized map to allocate per-thread objects, and that defeats the intention to avoid synchronization completely.

```
        if (arr != null)
            amount += arr[key];
    }
    return amount;
  }
}
```

Using Counter3, you get the correct answer for the global counter, and the test is quicker than Counter2. The relative timings for a range of VMs are listed in Table 10-4.

Table 10-4. Timings of the Various Counter Tests, Normalized to the JDK 1.2 Counter2 Test

	1.2	1.2 no JIT	1.3	HotSpot 1.0	HotSpot 2nd Run	1.1.6
Counter2	100%	397%	383%	191%	755%	180%
Counter3	70%	384%	175%	156%	190%	95%
Counter1 *(incorrect result)*	5%	116%	10%	78%	17%	5%

The serialized execution avoidance class is a significant improvement on the synchronized case. The Counter2 timings can be extremely variable. This variation is generated from the nature of multithreaded context switching, together with the fact that the activity taking much of the time in this test is lock management. Switching is essentially unpredictable, and the amount of switching and where it occurs affects how often the VM has to release and reacquire locks in different threads. Nevertheless, across a number of measurements, Counter3 was always faster than Counter2, often several times faster.

The listed times were measured on a single-processor machine. Consider what happens on a multiprocessor machine where the threads can run on different CPUs (i.e., where the Java runtime and operating system support preemptive thread scheduling on separate CPUs). Counter3 (the serialized execution avoidance class) is parallelized automatically and scales very nicely. This same test with Counter3, running on a four-CPU machine, tends towards one-quarter of the single-CPU time, assuming that the four CPUs have the same power as the single CPU we tested earlier. On the other hand, the synchronized version of the counter, Counter2, always has serialized execution (that's what synchronized does). Consequently, it does not scale and generally performs no better than in the single-CPU test (except for the advantage of running the OS on another CPU).

Timing Multithreaded Tests

I measured timings of the three Counter classes in the previous section using another class, CounterTest. This timing class illustrates some pitfalls you need to avoid when timing multithreaded applications, so I'll go into a little detail about the CounterTest definition.

The first naive implementation of CounterTest is quite simple. Just create a Thread subclass with the run() method running timed tests of the classes you are measuring. You need an extra instance variable for the Counter3 class, so the class can be defined as:

```
package tuning.threads;

public class CounterTest
  extends Thread
{
  //instance variable to specify which thread we are.
  int num;

  public CounterTest(int threadnum)
  {
    super();
    num = threadnum;
  }

  // main forks four threads
  public static void main(String[] args)
  {
    int REPEAT = (args.length > 0) ? Integer.parseInt(args[0]) : 10000000;
    for (int i = 0; i < 4; i++)
      (new CounterTest(i)).start();
  }

  public void run()
  {
    Counter1.initialize(0);
    long time = System.currentTimeMillis();
    for (int i = REPEAT; i > 0; i--)
      Counter1.addAmount(0, 1);
    System.out.println("Counter1 count: " + Counter1.getAmount(0)
      + " time: " + (System.currentTimeMillis()-time));

    Counter2.initialize(0);
    time = System.currentTimeMillis();
    for (int i = REPEAT; i > 0; i--)
      Counter2.addAmount(0, 1);
    System.out.println("Counter2 count: " + Counter2.getAmount(0)
      + " time: " + (System.currentTimeMillis()-time));

    Counter3.initialize(this);
    time = System.currentTimeMillis();
    for (int i = REPEAT; i > 0; i--)
```

```
        Counter3.addAmount(0, 1);
      System.out.println("Counter3 count: " + Counter3.getAmount(0)
        + " time: " + (System.currentTimeMillis()-time));
    }
  }
```

Unfortunately, this class has two big problems. First, there is no way of knowing that the four threads are running the same test at the same time. With this implementation, it is perfectly possible that one thread is running the `Counter1` test, while another has already finished that test and is now running the `Counter2` test concurrently. This gives incorrect times for both tests, since the CPU is being used by another test while you measure the first test. And the synchronization costs are not measured properly, since the intention is to test the synchronization costs of running four threads using the same methods at the same time.

The second problem is with the times you are measuring. The timings are for each thread running its own threaded update to the `Counter` class. But you should be measuring the time from the first update in any thread to the last update in any thread.

One way to avoid the first pitfall is to synchronize the tests so that they are not started until all the threads are ready. Then all threads can be started at the same time. The second pitfall can be avoided by setting a global time at the start of the first update, then printing the time difference when the last thread finishes.

The full `tuning.threads.CounterTest` implementation with the correct handling for measurements can be found along with all the other classes from this book by clicking on the "Examples" link from the book's catalog page, *http://www. oreilly.com/catalog/javapt/*.

Atomic Access and Assignment

Variables shared between multiple threads (e.g., instance variables of objects) have atomic assignment guaranteed by the Java language specification for all data types except for `longs` and `doubles`. Actually, the storing of a value into a variable takes two primitive operations, a *store* and a *write*. However, the language specification also states that once a store operation occurs on a particular variable, no other store operation is allowed on that variable until the write operation has occurred. The specification allows `longs` and `doubles` to be stored in two separate sets of store+write operations, hence their exception to atomicity. A similar atomic specification applies for reading variables.

This means that access and update of variables are automatically synchronized (as long as they are not `longs` or `doubles`). If a method consists solely of a variable access or assignment, there is no need to make it `synchronized` for thread safety, and every reason not to do so for performance. Thread safety extends further to any set of statements that are accessing or assigning to a variable independently of any other variable values. The exclusion here precludes setting a variable that depends on the value of another variable as being thread-safe; this would be two separate operations, which is inherently not thread-safe. For example:

```
public void setMe(Object o) {me = o;}
public Object getMe() {return me;}
```

are thread-safe methods, with no need for **synchronized** modifiers to be added to the method declaration. On the other hand:

```
public void setMe(Object o) {if(overwrite) me = o;}
```

is not thread-safe: **overwrite** may be true at the time of checking in the **if** statement, but false by the time of the subsequent assignment statement. Anything more complex than simple assignments and accesses is probably not thread-safe: it depends on whether any particular intermediate state that can be accessed is considered corrupt by the application. Consider the code being halted before or after any particular atomic statement, and decide whether or not another thread could now access a corrupt application state.

Combining several calls to methods that atomically assign variables is the same problem as combining several calls to synchronized methods. The individual calls are executed atomically, but the combination is not necessarily atomic:

```
public void setMe1(Object o) {me = o;}
public void setMe2(Object o) {me = o;}
public void setBoth(Object o1, Object o2) {setMe1(o1);setMe2(o2);}
```

For these three methods, it does not matter whether **setMe1()** and **setMe2()** are synchronized or not. **setBoth()** is not synchronized, so it can be interrupted between the calls to **setMe1()** and **setMe2()**, allowing another thread to update one of the instance variables. This can leave the object in a potentially corrupt application state if both instance variables are always supposed to be updated together. Specifically, if two threads call the **setBoth()** method simultaneously, the outcome is not predictable unless **setBoth()** is synchronized.

A longer discussion about Java's atomicity can be found in an article by Art Jolin,[*] where he discusses unsynchronized thread-safe data structures, including why a binary tree (specifically the **AWTEventMulticaster** class) can be thread-safe without any **synchronized** methods.

---

[*] "Java's Atomic Assignment," *Java Report*, August 1998.

Synchronization Ordering

It is easy to confuse exactly what synchronization does. Synchronization ensures that a set of statements executes exclusively for a particular monitor. Synchronization does not guarantee the order of execution of synchronized blocks. If two threads try to execute a synchronized block simultaneously, one succeeds first, but there is no guarantee as to which one that is.

Atomic assignment is the case where the set of synchronized statements is one statement, and the synchronization is set by the VM. When considering atomic assignment, you might ask the question, "What if a context switch occurs during the method call setup or tear down? When does the synchronization happen, and what happens with the context switch?" The actual moment when the synchronization occurs does not matter. It does not matter if a context switch happens at any time before or after a set of synchronized statements. Either the synchronized set has not been entered, or it has been completed. Only the actual granting of the lock matters, and that is atomic with respect to all interested threads.

Until you reach an atomic assignment statement, it makes no difference whether another atomic assignment on the same variable occurs. This is purely the ordering of assignments, which is not guaranteed with synchronization anyway. After the atomic assignment is finished, it is complete. A context switch hitting the method tear down does not matter. The only reason to synchronize a simple updator is to avoid a corrupt assignment, i.e., two threads simultaneously updating the same variable, and the resulting value being neither of the updated values. This can indeed occur for `doubles` and `longs`, but not for other data types.

For serious number crunching involving `doubles` and `longs`, I recommend using separate data structures for each thread or using a VM that guarantees atomic assignment for `doubles` and `longs`.

Thread Pools

The VM is optimized for creating threads, so you can usually create a new thread when you need to without having to worry about performance. But in some circumstances, maintaining a pool of threads can improve performance. For example, in a case where you would otherwise create and destroy many short-lived threads, you are far better off holding on to a (variable-sized) pool of threads. Here, the tasks are assigned to an already created thread, and when a thread completes its task, it is returned to the pool, ready for the next task. This improves performance because thread creation (and, to some extent, destruction) does have a significant overhead that is better avoided for short-lived threads.

A second situation is where you want to limit the number of threads in your application. In this case, your application needs to make all thread requests through a centralized pool manager. Although a pool manager does not prevent other threads from being started, it is a big step towards that goal. (Strictly speaking, limiting threads does not require a pool of threads, just a centralized pool manager, but the two usually come together.) Every system has a response curve with diminishing returns after a certain number of threads are running on it. This response curve is different for different systems, and you need to identify values for your particular setup. A heavy-duty server needs to show good behavior across a spectrum of loads, and at the high end, you don't want your server crashing when 10,000 requests try to spawn 10,000 threads; instead, you want the server response to degrade (e.g., by queuing requests) and maintain whatever maximum number of threads is optimal for the server system.

When deciding which thread to run next, there may be a slight gain by choosing the available thread that ran most recently. This thread is most likely to have its working set still fully in memory: the longer it has been since a thread was last used, the more likely it is that the thread has been paged or swapped out. Also, any caches (at any level of the system and application) that may apply are more likely to contain elements from the most recently used thread. By choosing the most recently used thread, paging and cache overhead may be minimized.

Thread pools can be completely generic if necessary. By using the `java.lang.reflect` package, you can execute any (public) methods from your threads, thus allowing you to implement a thread pool that can handle general requests that have not been anticipated or specified at implementation time.

Load Balancing

Load balancing is a technique for improving performance when many activities are processed concurrently. These activities could be in separate processes on different machines, in separate processes on the same machine, or in separate threads within the same process. The architecture makes no difference to the basic guidelines.

To support load balancing, a standard design is to have:

- One point of entry for all requests (the request queue)
- One or more request-processor objects behind the queue
- A mechanism for the queue to decide which request processor to hand a particular request to

You also need communication lines between the queue and processors and a way to internally identify requests, but this is an obvious part of the infrastructure. The decision mechanism is typically a simple load-balancing system that distributes requests to those available processors. The request processors specify when they are available or busy. When the queue has a request to process, it chooses the first available request processor. Some applications need more complex decision-making, and use a decision mechanism that allocates requests depending on the type of request.

Our main concern with this architecture is that the queue is a potential bottleneck, so it must pass on requests quickly and be fairly continually ready.* The pool of request processors behind the queue can be running in one or more threads or processes, usually one request processor per thread. The pool of threaded request processors can be prestarted or started on demand, or you can have a combination of these. Typically for this kind of setup, there are configuration options that specify how many prestarted request processors there should be, the maximum number of request processors to have running simultaneously, and how long to wait before terminating a request processor since it last processed a request.

Note that there is always a point of diminishing returns on response time versus the number of threads in a system. If you have too many threads running concurrently, the system's overall response time gets worse. The operating-system thread scheduler (or Java-system thread scheduler, if you're not using OS threads) spends more and more time managing threads, and this overhead takes up the CPU time rather than allowing the threads to run.

You also need to consider whether the queue object handles the responses (collecting them from the request processes and handing them back to the clients) or whether the request-processor objects can hand the responses back directly. The former design has the advantage that the client cannot get any direct access to the request-processor objects, but the disadvantage that you are introducing an unnecessary bottleneck in processing terms. The latter option (handing responses back directly), of course, has the opposite characteristics: no extra bottleneck, but access to client objects is enabled.

Free Load Balancing from TCP/IP

If you use sockets to handle incoming requests within one process, the operating system provides some load-balancing support. If you want, the operating system will provide the queue for free. TCP sockets can have multiple threads reading or

---

* The queue is also a single point of failure. For this reason, an advanced load-balancing design does not rely on a single queue. Instead, any queues in the application are distributed, redundantly copied, and monitored so that any queue failure results in only a small performance degradation at worst. Some designs use persistent queue elements so that a critical failure does not lose queued elements. The Java Messaging Service supports persistent queue elements.

accepting on them. A connectionless TCP server (such as a web server) performs the following process:

1. Opens a server socket.

2. Starts however many threads you want.

3. Each thread sits on an `ServerSocket.accept()` call, waiting for the call to return (all threads call `accept()` on the identical `ServerSocket` object).

4. Whenever a client connects to the server socket, the operating-system TCP stack hands the connection off to only one thread that is blocked on the `accept()` call. This is guaranteed behavior for TCP.

5. The thread that returns from the `accept()` call gets the client connection (`Socket` object), reads the request, processes it, and writes the request back (directly to the client).

6. The thread goes back into the `accept()` call, waiting for the next connection.

At any time, you can start further threads to scale up the server as long as each thread has access to the previously created `ServerSocket` object. TCP does not allow more than one `ServerSocket` object to be bound to the same port on any machine (actually, any one network interface). It is therefore not possible to have multiple separate processes (i.e., independent operating-system processes, rather than threads within one operating-system process) serving on the same server socket. (Strictly speaking, it is possible to fork a process into multiple system processes after the socket has been opened. This is a standard practice on Unix servers. Multiprocess TCP servers have some small disadvantages over multithreaded TCP servers, mainly when they need to communicate between themselves or use other expensive resources. However, multiprocess TCP servers do have one big advantage over multithreaded servers, which is that if one server process crashes, the others can continue running independently, unaffected by the crash. Win32 does not support a fork procedure.)

With UDP sockets, the architecture can be slightly different, as you can open a UDP server socket on a port that already has a server socket bound to it. A UDP socket is not connection-oriented but packet-oriented, so there is no `accept()` call to wait on. Instead, all the threads (from potentially multiple system processes) sit on a `read()` call on the UDP socket, and the UDP stack hands off each incoming packet to just one of the threads that is waiting on the `read()`. The server then has to use the information from the packet (either at the application level or the protocol level) to determine the return address to send the result of the processed request (again, directly back to the client).

Load-Balancing Classes

If you need to implement your own queuing system, you have to consider whether the queue controls the request processors, or whether the processors access the queue. The latter model is how the socket model works: each request processor sits on the queue and waits for it to pass a request. This looks rather like the following class:

```
public class PassiveRequestQueue
{
  //The queue of requests
  FIFO_Queue queue = new FIFO_Queue();

  public synchronized void acceptRequest(Request r)
  {
    //Add to the queue, then notify all processors waiting
    //on the releaseRequest() method
    queue.add(r);
    notify();
  }

  public synchronized Request releaseRequest()
  {
    for(;;)
    {
      //if the queue is empty, just go back into the wait call
      if (queue.isEmpty())
        try {wait();} catch (InterruptedException e){}
      //Need to check again if the queue is empty, in case
      //we were interrupted
      if (!queue.isEmpty())
        return (Request) queue.pop();
    }
  }
}
```

The former model, in which the request processors are passive and the queue actively manages them, looks more like the following class:

```
public class ActiveRequestQueue
  //subclass the passive queue which holds the behavior
  //needed for managing the queue of requests
  extends PassiveRequestQueue
  //and make us able to run in our own thread
  implements Runnable
{
  int MAXIMUM_NUM_SERVERS=3;

  //Data for the public queue - a list of private servers
  ActiveRequestQueue[] servers;
```

```
//Data for the private (internal) queues
//the RequestProcessor
RequestProcessor requestProcessor;
//Retain a handle on my thread so that we can easily access
//it if we need control
Thread myThread;
//Keep a handle on the 'public' queue - the one which
//actually holds the objects
ActiveRequestQueue queueServer;
//Availability
boolean isAvailable = true;


//Internal queue object - processes requests
private ActiveRequestQueue(ActiveRequestQueue q)
{
  queueServer = q;
  requestProcessor=new RequestProcessor();
}


//External queue object - accepts requests and manages a queue of them
public ActiveRequestQueue(int num_servers)
{
  //Create a pool of queue servers and start them in their own threads
  servers = new ActiveRequestQueue[num_servers];
  Thread t;
  for (int i = servers.length-1; i>=0 ; i--)
  {
    servers[i] = new ActiveRequestQueue(this);
    (t = new Thread(servers[i])).start();
    servers[i].myThread = t;
  }
}

public synchronized void acceptRequest(Request r)
{
  //Override the super class accept to increase the number
  //of servers if they are all busy

  //If we already have the maximum number of threads,
  //just queue the request
  if (servers.length >= MAXIMUM_NUM_SERVERS)
  {
      super.acceptRequest(r);
      return;
  }

  //otherwise, if one of the servers is available, just queue
  //the request
  for (int i = servers.length-1; i>=0 ; i--)
  {
```

```
      if (servers[i].isAvailable())
      {
        super.acceptRequest(r);
        return;
      }
    }

    //otherwise, increase the server pool by one, then queue the request
    Thread t;
    ActiveRequestQueue[] tmp_servers = servers;
    servers = new ActiveRequestQueue[tmp_servers.length+1];
    System.arraycopy(tmp_servers, 0, servers, 0, tmp_servers.length);
    servers[tmp_servers.length] = new ActiveRequestQueue(this);
    (t = new Thread(servers[tmp_servers.length])).start();
    servers[tmp_servers.length].myThread = t;
    super.acceptRequest(r);
  }

  public void run()
  {
    Request request;
    RequestResult result;

    //Private queues use this method.

    //Basically, we just ask the public server for a request.
    //The releaseRequest() method blocks until one is available.
    //Then we process it and start again.
    for(;;)
    {
      request = queueServer.releaseRequest();
      isAvailable = false;
      result = requestProcessor.processRequest(request);
      returnResult(result);
      isAvailable = true;
    }
  }

  public boolean isAvailable() { return isAvailable;}
  public void returnResult(RequestResult r) {}
}
```

Note that the server classes as they stand can be tested with the following minimal implementations for support classes:

```
class FIFO_Queue {
  java.util.Stack v = new java.util.Stack();
  public void add(Object o){v.push(o);}
  public Object pop(){return v.pop();}
  public boolean isEmpty(){return v.isEmpty();}
}
```

```
class RequestProcessor {
  public RequestResult processRequest(Request r)
  {
    System.out.println("Processing request: " + r);
    try{Thread.sleep(2000);}catch(InterruptedException e){}
    return new RequestResult();
  }
}


class RequestResult {}

class Request {}
```

A Load-Balancing Example

It may help to look at a concrete implementation of load balancing. I'll consider the task of downloading many pages from a web server as quickly as possible.

WARNING   It is impolite to batch download at high speeds from a single web server. Automated programs that download multiple pages from web servers have a voluntary protocol they should adhere to. More information can be found at *http://info.webcrawler.com/mak/projects/robots/ robots.html* and *http://web.nexor.co.uk/mak/doc/robots/guidelines.html*. One item of the protocol is to avoid overloading web servers by downloading many pages at a high access rate. Automated download programs that are polite specifically stagger downloads over a long period in order to minimize the load on the web server.

The individual page download code is quite simple. Open a URL, read the data, and dump it into a local file:

```
/* Two args, the local file to put the downloaded page into,
 * and the URL where the page to download is.
 */
public static void dowload(String file, String url)
  throws IOException
{
  URL u = new URL(url);
  InputStream in = null;
  //Try repeatedly to get the page opened. Note that catching
  //all exceptions is not such a good idea here. It would be
  //much better to catch individual execption types and handle
  //them separately. Some exceptions should not lead to a repeated
  //attempt to access the page. But this definition is okay for testing.
  while(in == null)
    try{in = u.openStream();}
    catch(Exception e){try {Thread.sleep(500);}catch(Exception e2){}}
  FileOutputStream out = new FileOutputStream(file);
  byte[] buffer = new byte[8192];
```

```
    //read until the connection terminates (this is not a
    //keep-alive connection), and write to the file.
    int len = in.read(buffer);
    while(len != -1)
    {
      out.write(buffer, 0, len);
      len = in.read(buffer);
    }
    out.close();
    in.close();
}
```

All our tests use this same `download()` method. The most straightforward test implementation is extremely simple. Simply take a list of URLs and corresponding data files, and loop calling `download()` for each URL/file pair:

```
//Use one array to hold alternate file and URL elements
public static void iterativeTest(String[] files)
  throws IOException
{
  for (int i = 0; i < files.length; i+=2)
    download(files[i], files[i+1]);
}
```

The opposite to downloading pages one by one is to try to download everything at the same time. Once again, the code is quite straightforward (apart from timing issues: see the earlier section "Timing Multithreaded Tests"). You simply define a `Runnable` class, and loop starting a thread for every download:

```
public class LoadBalancing
  implements Runnable
{
  String url;
  String localfilename;

  public static void massivelyParallelTest(String[] files)
    throws IOException
  {
    for (int i = 0; i < files.length; i+=2)
      (new Thread(new LoadBalancing(files[i], files[i+1]))).start();
  }

  public LoadBalancing(String f, String u)
  {
    localfilename = f;
    url = s;
  }

  public void run()
  {
```

```
    try
    {
      download(localfilename, filename);
    }
    catch(Exception e) {e.printStackTrace();}
  }
```

The earlier iterative test takes seven times longer than the latter multithreaded test.* However, the latter test suffers from significant resource problems. Creating so many threads simultaneously can seriously strain a system. In fact, every system has a limit to the number of threads it can create. If the download requires more threads than the system is capable of supporting, this multithreaded test fails to download many pages. In addition, with so many threads running simultaneously, you are using more of the system's resources than is optimal.

Let's look at a more balanced approach. In fact, you can create a very simple load-balanced test with one small variation to the last test. Simply add a delay between each thread creation to stagger the system load from threads and downloading. This new version of the `massivelyParallelTest()` method is simple:

```
public static void roughlyParallelTest(String[] files, int delay)
  throws IOException
{
  for (int i = 0; i < files.length; i+=2)
  {
    (new Thread(new LoadBalancing(files[i], files[i+1]))).start();
    try{Thread.sleep(delay);}catch(InterruptedException e){}
  }
}
```

Now you have a tuning parameter that needs to be optimized. Obviously, a delay of zero is the same test as the previous test, and a very large delay means that the test is spending most of its time simply waiting to create the next thread. Somewhere in between is an optimal range that creates threads fast enough to fully use the system resources, but not so fast that the system is overloaded.

This range is different depending on the full environment, and probably needs to be experimentally determined. But you can make a decent first guess by considering the bottlenecks of the system. In this case, the bottlenecks are CPU, system memory, disk throughput, network-connection latency, server-download rates, and network throughput. In my tests, system memory and CPU limit the number of threads and download speed for the massively parallel case, but you are using a delay specifically to reduce the load on those resources. System memory constrains

---

* For my tests, I downloaded a large number of pages. I validated the tests over the Internet, but not surprisingly, Internet access times are extremely variable. For detailed repeatable tests, I used a small local HTTP server that allowed me to control all the parameters to the tests very precisely. The full test class, tuning.threads.LoadBalancing, is available with the other classes from this book.

the number of threads you can use, but again, the delay avoids overloading this resource (provided that the delay is not too short). Disk throughput can be significant, but network and server throughput are far more likely to limit data-transfer rates. So we are left with network-transfer rates and network-connection latency to consider.

Now you can make a good guess as to a starting point for the delay. You can evaluate the average number of bytes to transfer for each download, and work out the amount of time this takes based on the available network throughput. You can also estimate the average time taken to make a connection (by measuring some real connections). A straightforward guess is to set the delay at a value below the higher of these two averages. In my tests, the files being downloaded are not large, and the average connection time is the larger time. I started with a delay of about half the average connection time and ran tests increasing and decreasing the delay in steps of about 10% at a time. Figure 10-3 shows the results of varying the delay times. An optimum choice for the delay in this particular test environment is approximately 70% of the average connection time. The flat line in the middle of the graph shows the relative time taken for the massively parallel test.

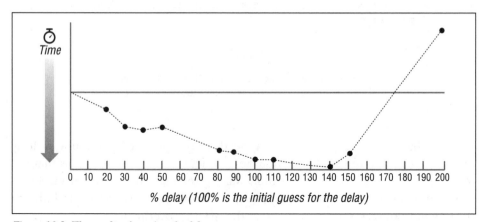

Figure 10-3. The results of varying the delay

The results show that for this environment there are several advantages to running with a delay. A decisive advantage is that you never run out of system resources. There are never so many threads running simultaneously that you run out of memory and completely lose URLs, as occurred with the massively parallel test. In fact, the system doesn't even need to run to full capacity for most of the test.

Another significant advantage is that by tuning the delay, you can run the test faster. The optimum value for the delay, at 70% of the average connection time, executes the full test in 90% of the massively parallel time.

What about our nice load-balancing architecture classes? Let's test these to see how they compare to the last simple optimization you made. You need to add a few support classes so that your load-balancing architecture is running the same download test. Basically, there are three classes to define: Request, RequestProcessor, and RequestResult. They are fairly simple to implement. Request needs to hold only a URL and a local file for storing the downloaded page. RequestProcessor simply needs to call the download() method. RequestResult does not need any extra behavior for the test.* The classes are as follows:

```
class RequestProcessor {
  public RequestResult processRequest(Request r)
  {
    try
    {
      LoadBalancing.dowload(r.localfilename, r.url);
    }
    catch(Exception e) {e.printStackTrace();}
    return new RequestResult();
  }
}

class Request
{
  String localfilename;
  String url;
  public Request(String f, String u)
  {
    localfilename = f;
    url = u;
  }
}

class RequestResult {}
```

In addition, of course, you need to define the method that kicks off the test itself:

```
public static void loadBalancedTest(String[] files, int numThreads)
  throws IOException
{
ActiveRequestQueue server = new ActiveRequestQueue(numThreads);
for (int i = 0; i < files.length; i+=2)
  server.acceptRequest(new Request(files[i], files[i+1]));
}
```

I have included a variable to determine the optimum number of threads. As with the earlier test that used a variable delay, the optimum number of threads for this test needs to be experimentally determined. For my test environment, the bottleneck is likely to be my small network throughput. This is easy to see: each thread

---

* RequestResult does need extra state and behavior in order to make timing measurments, and RequestProcessor is similarly a bit more complicated for timing purposes. For full details, see the test class, tuning.threads.LoadBalancing, which is available with the other classes from this book.

corresponds to one download. So for *n* threads to be working at full capacity, they need to be downloading *n* files, which amounts to a throughput of *n* times the average file size. This means that for my test environment, about 10 threads reach capacity. In fact, since files are not all the same size and there are some overheads in the architecture, I would expect the optimum number of threads to be slightly larger than 10.

Running the test with different numbers of threads shows that for 12 or more threads, the time taken is essentially the same (see Figure 10-4). This time is also the same as that achieved with the previous most optimal test. This is not surprising. Both tests optimized the downloads enough that they have reached the same network-throughput bottleneck. This bottleneck cannot be optimized any further by either test.

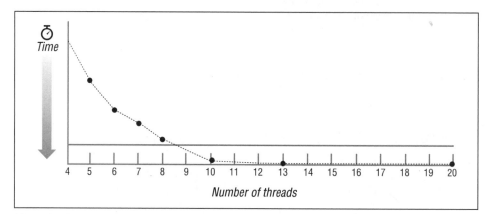

Figure 10-4. Time taken for the load-balanced download versus number of threads

The load-balancing architecture is more complex than adding a delay between threads, but it is much more flexible and far more controlled. If you want to vary your download in a number of ways, such as prioritizing URLs or repeating certain failed ones, it is much easier to do so with the load-balancing architecture. By looking at the CPU utilization graphs for the load-balancing architecture compared to the other tests in Figure 10-5, you can easily see how much more controlled it is and how it uses resources in a far more consistent manner.

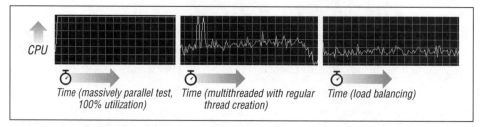

Figure 10-5. CPU utilization for various download tests

Threaded Problem-Solving Strategies

There are many techniques that reduce the time taken to solve intensive problems by using multiple threads to farm out parts of the problem. Here are a few of the strategies:

- Start multiple threads running to solve the whole of a particular problem, each starting from a different point in the solution space. The first to finish is the winner. This technique has, for instance, been used to speed up a graph-coloring problem. The specific strategy followed* was to run several problem solvers at the same time, one at a higher priority than the others (the main thread). Normally the main thread would win, but on occasion, one of the background threads was lucky due to its starting point and finished quickly. By stopping the main thread if it looked to be far behind in the solution, the problem was solved in one-tenth of the time, on average, compared to the time taken when the main thread was not terminated. This improvement was in spite of the fact that this was a single-processor machine. The improvement comes about because the problem can be solved much quicker from some starting points than from others. There would be similar improvements if you also used several different problem-solving strategies in the various threads, where some of the strategies are sometimes quicker than others.

- In the same article, a variation of this strategy was applied to network connections for bypassing congestion. By opening multiple connections to download the same large data source on a highly congested network (the Internet), some connections were less likely than others to be slowed significantly or broken. This resulted in the data being downloaded faster. Of course, if everyone on the network used this technique, downloads would be slower for everyone.

- Break up the search space into logically parallelized search spaces. This does not work too well if the problem is entirely CPU-bound, but if there is any significant I/O or if multiple processors are available, this technique works nicely. An example would be searching a disk-based database for items. If the database is partitioned into multiple segments, then having one thread searching per segment makes the search faster (both on average and in the worst case).

- The classic blackboard architecture approach, in which multiple different solvers work on the parts of a problem in which they have expertise, independently of other solver threads. The threads use a "blackboard" (a sort of globally accessible hash table with published keys) to communicate. The blackboard posts both intermediate and full results. This allows a thread to pick up

---

* Charles Seife, "A Snail's Pace," *New Scientist*, 21 February 1998. This article reports on the technique used by Bernardo Huberman of Xerox Parc.

any (intermediate or full) results other threads may publish that help that particular thread with its own problem-solving routines. JavaSpaces is an implementation of blackboards.

Performance Checklist

Many of these suggestions apply only after a bottleneck has been identified:

- Include multithreading at the design stage.
  - Parallelize tasks with threads to speed up calculations.
  - Run slow operations in their own threads to avoid slowing down the main thread.
  - Keep the interface in a separate thread from other work so that the application feels more responsive.
  - Avoid designs and implementations that force points of serialized execution.
  - Use multiple resolution strategies racing in different threads to get quicker answers.
- Avoid locking more resources than necessary.
  - Avoid synchronizing methods of stateless objects.
  - Build classes with synchronized wrappers, and use synchronized versions except when unsynchronized versions are definitely sufficient.
  - Selectively unwrap synchronized wrapped classes to eliminate identified bottlenecks.
  - Avoid synchronized blocks by using thread-specific data structures, combining data only when necessary.
  - Use atomic assignment where applicable.
- Load-balance the application by distributing tasks among multiple threads, using a queue and thread-balancing mechanism for distributing tasks amongst task-processing threads.
  - Use thread pools to reuse threads if many threads are needed or if threads are needed for very short tasks.
  - Use a thread pool manager to limit the number of concurrent threads used.

11

Appropriate Data Structures and Algorithms

> *And this is a table ma'am. What in essence it consists of is a horizontal rectilinear plane surface maintained by four vertical columnar supports, which we call legs. The tables in this laboratory, ma'am, are as advanced in design as one will find anywhere in the world.*
>
> —Michael Frayn
> *The Tin Men*

In this chapter, we look at the performance problems that can stem from using an inappropriate or nonoptimal data structure. Of course, I cannot cover every possible structure. Instead, my focus is on how to performance-tune structures and associated algorithms. Those structures I do cover are provided as examples to give you an idea of how the tuning procedure looks.

For performance-tuning purposes, be aware of alternative structures and algorithms, and always consider the possibility of switching to one of these alternatives rather than tuning the structure and algorithm that is already being used. Being aware of alternative data structures requires extensive reading of computer literature.* One place to start is with the JDK code. Look at the structures that are provided and make sure that you know all about the available classes. There are already several good books on data structures and algorithms in Java, as well as many packages available from the Web with extensive documentation and often source code too. Some popular computer magazines include articles about structures and algorithms (see Chapter 15, *Further Resources*).†

---

* An interesting analysis of performance-tuning a "traveling salesman" problem is made by Jon Bentley in his article "Analysis of Algorithms," *Dr. Dobb's Journal*, April 1999.

† The classic reference is *The Art of Computer Programming* by Donald Knuth (Addison Wesley). A more Java-specific book is *Data Structures and Algorithm Analysis in Java* by Mark Weiss (Peachpit Press).

When tuning, you often need to switch one implementation of a class for another, more optimal implementation. Switching data structures is easier because you are in an object-oriented environment, so you can usually replace one or a few classes with different implementations while keeping all the interfaces and signatures the same.

When tuning algorithms, one factor that should pop to the front of your mind concerns the scaling characteristics of the algorithms you use. For example, bubblesort is an $O(n^2)$ algorithm, while quicksort is $O(nlogn)$. (The concept of "order of magnitude" statistics is described in "Better Than $O(nlogn)$ Sorting" in Chapter 9, *Sorting.*) This tells you nothing about absolute times for using either of these algorithms for sorting elements, but it does clearly tell you that quicksort has the better scaling characteristics, and so is likely to be the better candidate as your collections increase in size. Similarly, hash tables have an $O(1)$ searching algorithm where an array requires $O(n)$ searching.

Collections

Collections are the data structures that are most easily altered for performance-tuning purposes. Using the correct or most appropriate collection class can improve performance with little change to code. For example, if a large ordered collection has elements frequently deleted or inserted throughout it, it usually can provide better performance if based on a linked list rather than an array. On the other hand, a static (unchanging) collection that needs to be accessed by index performs better with an underlying implementation that is an array.

If the data is large and insertions are allowed (for example, a text buffer), then a common halfway measure is to use a *linked list of arrays.* This structure copies data within a single array when data is inserted or deleted. When an array gets filled, the collection inserts a new empty array immediately after the full array, and moves some data from the full to the empty array so that both old and new arrays have space. A converse structure provides optimized indexed access to a linked-list structure by holding an array of a subset of the link nodes (e.g., every 20th node). This structure allows for quick navigation to the indexed nodes, and then slower nodal access to nodes in between.* The result is a linked-list implementation that is much faster at index access, though it occupies more space.

It is sometimes useful to provide two collections holding the same data, so that the data can be accessed using the most appropriate (and fastest) procedure. This is common for indexed data (database-type indexes as opposed to array indexes),

---

* Skip lists are an implementation of this concept. See "The Elegant (and Fast) Skip List" by T. Wenger, *Java Pro,* April-May 1998.

but entails extra overhead at the build stage. In a similar way, it may be that a particular data set is best held in two (or more) different collections over its lifetime, but with only one collection being used at any one time. For example, you may use a linked-list implementation of a vector type collection while building the collection because your collection requires many insertions while it is being built. However, this provides suboptimal random access. After the build is completed, the collection can be converted into one based on an array, thus speeding up access.

It can be difficult to identify optimal algorithms for particular data structures. For example, in the Java 2 `java.util.Collections.sort()` method, a linked list is first converted to an array in order to sort it. This is detrimental to performance, and it would be significantly faster to sort a linked list directly using a merge sort.[*] In any case, frequently converting between collections and arrays is likely to cause performance problems.

The fastest ordered collections available in Java are plain arrays (e.g., `int[]`, `Object[]`, etc.). The drawback to using these directly is the lack of object-oriented methodology you can apply. Arrays are not proper classes that can be extended. However, I occasionally find that there are situations when I want to pass these raw arrays directly between several classes, rather than wrap the arrays in a class with the behavior required. This is unfortunate in design terms, but does provide speed. An example would be in some communications layers. Here, there are several layers of protocols you need to pass your message through before it is transmitted, for example, a compression layer and an encryption layer. If you use an object as a message being passed through these layers, each layer has to request the message contents (copying it), change the contents, and then assign back the new contents (copying again). An alternative is to implement the content-manipulation methods in the message object itself, which is not a very extensible architecture. Assuming that you use an array to hold the contents, you can allow the message-contents array itself to be passed directly to the other compression and encryption layer objects. This provides a big speedup, avoiding several copies. `String` objects also illustrate the point. If you want to iterate over the characters in a `String`, you must either repeatedly call `String.charAt()` or copy the characters into your own array using `String.getChars()`, and then iterate over them. Depending on the size of the `String` and how many times you iterate through the characters, one or the other of these methods is quicker, but if you could iterate directly on the underlying `char` array, you would avoid the repeated method calls and the copy (see Chapter 5, *Strings*).

A final point is that the collections that come with Java and other packages are usually not type-specific. This generality comes at the cost of performance. For

---

[*] See "Sorting and Searching Linked Lists in Java" by John Boyer, *Dr. Dobb's Journal*, May 1998.

example, if you are using `java.util.Vector` to hold only `String` objects, then you have to keep casting to `String` each time you access elements. If you reimplement the `Vector` class yourself using an underlying `String[]` array, and then change signature parameters and return types of methods from `Object` to `String`, the re-implemented class is faster. It is also clearer to use: you get rid of all those casts from your code. The cost is that you lose the general collection interface (see "Replacing JDK Classes" in Chapter 3, *Underlying JDK Improvements*, for an example).

It is straightforward to test the performance costs of generalized collections compared to specialized collections. Access that does not involve a cast takes place at essentially the same speed, i.e., all the following accesses take the same time:

```
int i =  integerArrayList.get(someIndex);
String s = stringArrayList.get(someIndex);
Object o = objectArrayList.get(someIndex);
```

But the cost of a cast can make the access take 50% longer:

```
//It can take 50% longer to access the string because of the cast
String s = (String) objectArrayList.get(someIndex);
```

Update time can also be significantly faster. Updates to underlying arrays of primitive data types can be 40% faster than to object arrays.* The biggest difference is when a primitive data type needs to be wrapped and unwrapped in order to store into an array:

```
//Simpler and much faster using a specialized IntArrayList
integerArrayList.set(someIndex, someNum);
int num = integerArrayList.get(someIndex);

//Using a generalized ArrayList requires wrapping, casting & unwrapping
integerArrayList.set(someIndex, new Integer(someNum));
int num = ((Integer) integerArrayList.get(someIndex, someNum)).intValue();
```

For this example, the cost of creating a new `Integer` object to wrap the `int` makes setting values take more than ten times longer when using the generalized array. Accessing is not as bad, taking only twice as long after including the extra cast and method access to get to the `int`.

Java 2 Collections

The collections framework introduced with Java 2 comes with a set of collection classes in the JDK. Each class has its own performance strengths and weaknesses,

---

* Even updating a typed object array with objects of the given type (e.g., `String`s into an underlying `String[]` array of an array list) seems to be faster by about 10%. The only reason I can think of for this is that the JIT compiler manages to optimize the update to the specialized array.

which I cover here. The collection implementations use the synchronized-wrapper framework to provide synchronized classes; otherwise, the implementations are unsynchronized (except for two exceptions noted shortly). Collection classes wrapped in synchronized wrappers are always slower than unwrapped, unsynchronized classes. Nevertheless, my recommendation is generally to use objects within synchronized wrappers. You can selectively "unwrap" objects when they have been identified as part of a bottleneck and when the synchronization is not necessary. (The performance aspects of thread-safe collections are discussed in detail in Chapter 10, *Threading*. Synchronized wrappers are also discussed in that chapter, in the "Desynchronization and Synchronized Wrappers" section.)

Table 11-1 summarizes the performance attributes of the collection classes.

Table 11-1. Performance Attributes of Java 2 Collection Classes

Interface	Class	Synchronized?	
Set	HashSet	No	Fastest Set; slower than HashMap but implements the Set interface (HashMap does not)
	TreeSet	No	Slower than HashSet; provides iteration of keys in order
Map	HashMap	No	Fastest Map
	Hashtable	Yes	Slower than HashMap, but faster than synchronized HashMap
	TreeMap	No	Slower than Hashtable and HashMap; provides iteration of keys in order
List	ArrayList	No	Fastest List
	Vector	Yes	Slower than ArrayList, but faster than synchronized ArrayList
	Stack	Yes	Same speed as Vector; provides LIFO queue functionality
	LinkedList	No	Slower than other Lists, but may be faster for some types of queue

Implementations of Set are slower to update than most other collection objects and should be avoided unless you need Set functionality. Of the two available Set implementations, HashSet is definitely faster than TreeSet. HashSet uses an underlying HashMap, so the way HashSet maintains uniqueness is extremely straightforward. Objects are added to the set as the keys to the HashMap, so there is no need to search the set for the elements. This optimizes unique element addition. If you need Set functionality but not specifically a Set implementation, it is faster to use a HashMap directly.

Map has three general-purpose implementations, Hashtable, HashMap, and TreeMap. In addition, there are several specialized implementations that do not provide any performance improvements.* TreeMap is significantly slower than the other two Maps, and should not be used unless you need the extra functionality of iterating ordered keys. Hashtable is a synchronized Map, and HashMap is an unsynchronized Map. Hashtable is present for backward compatibility with earlier versions of the JDK. Nevertheless, if you need to use a synchronized Map, a Hashtable is faster than using a HashMap in a synchronized wrapper.

Hashtable, HashMap, and HashSet are all O(1) for access and update, so they should scale nicely if you have the available memory space.

List has four general-purpose implementations, Vector, Stack, ArrayList, and LinkedList. Vector, Stack, and ArrayList have underlying implementations based on arrays. LinkedList has an underlying implementation consisting of doubly linked list. As such, LinkedList's performance is worse than any of the other three Lists for most operations. For very large collections that you cannot presize to be large enough, LinkedLists provides better performance when adding or deleting elements towards the middle of the list, if the array-copying overhead of the other Lists is higher than the linear access time of the LinkedList. Otherwise, LinkedList's only likely performance advantage is as a first-in-first-out queue or double-ended queue. (A circular array-list implementation provides better performance for a FIFO queue.) Vector is a synchronized List, and ArrayList is an unsynchronized List. Vector is present for backward compatibility with earlier versions of the JDK. Nevertheless, if you need to use a synchronized List, a Vector is faster than using an ArrayList in a synchronized wrapper. (See the comparison test at the end of "Desynchronization and Synchronized Wrappers" in Chapter 10.) Stack is a subclass of Vector with the same performance characteristics, but with additional functionality as a last-in-first-out queue.

Hashtables and HashMaps

Because Hashtables and HashMaps are the most commonly used nonlist structures, I will spend a little extra time discussing them. Hashtables and HashMaps are pretty fast and provide adequate performance for most purposes. I rarely find that I have a performance problem using Hashtables or HashMaps, but here are some points that will help you tune them, or, if necessary, replace them:

- Hashtable is synchronized. That's fine if you are using it to share data across threads, but if you are using it single-threaded, you can replace it with

---

* Attributes simply wraps a HashMap, and restricts the keys to be ASCII-character alphanumeric Strings, and values to be Strings. WeakHashMap can maintain a cache of elements that are automatically garbage-collected when memory gets low. RenderingHints is specialized for use within the AWT packages. Properties is a Hashtable subclass specialized for maintaining key value string pairs in files. UIDefaults is specialized for use within the Swing packages

an unsynchronized version to get a small boost in performance. `HashMap` is an unsynchronized version available from JDK 1.2.

- `Hashtables` and `HashMaps` are resized whenever the number of elements reaches the [capacity * `loadFactor`]. This requires reassigning every element to a new array using the rehashed values. This is not simply an array copy; every element needs to have its internal table position recalculated using the new table size for the hash function. You are usually better off setting an initial capacity that handles all the elements you want to add. This initial capacity should be the number of elements divided by the `loadFactor` (the default load factor is 0.75).

- `Hashtables` and `HashMaps` are faster with a smaller `loadFactor`, but take up more space. You have to decide how this tradeoff works best for you.

- The hashing function should work better with a capacity that is a prime number. Failing this, always use an odd number, never an even number (add one if you have an even number). The rehashing mechanism creates a new capacity of twice the old capacity, plus one. A useful prime number to remember is 89. The sequence of numbers generated by successively multiplying by two and adding one includes several primes when the sequence starts with 89. (The default size for `Hashtables` is 101. However, in my tests using a size of 89, I gained a statistically significant speedup of only 2 or 3%. The variation in test runs was actually larger than this speedup.)

- Access to the `Map` requires asking the key for its `hashCode()` and also testing that the key `equals()` the key you are retrieving. You can create a specialized `Map` class that bypasses these calls if appropriate. Alternatively, you can use specialized key classes that have very fast method calls for these two methods. Note, for example, that Java `String` objects have `hashCode()` methods that iterate and execute arithmetic over a number of characters to determine the value, and the `String.equals()` method checks that every character is identical for the two strings being compared. Considering that strings are used as the most common keys in `Hashtables`, I'm often surprised to find that I *don't* have a performance problem with them, even for largish tables. From JDK 1.3, `Strings` cache their hash code in an instance variable, making them faster and more suited as `Map` keys.

- If you are building a specialized `Hashtable`, you can map objects to array elements to preallocate `HashtableEntry` objects and speed up access as well. The technique is illustrated in the "Search Trees" section later in this chapter.

Here is a specialized class to use for keys in a `Hashtable`. This example assumes that I am using `String` keys, but all my `String` objects are nonequal, and I can reference keys by identity. I use a utility class, `tuning.dict.Dict`, which holds a large array of nonequal words taken from an English dictionary. I compare the access times against all the keys using two different Hashtables, one using the plain String objects as keys, the other using my own StringWrapper objects as keys. The StringWrapper objects cache the hash value of the string and assume that equality comparison is the same as identity comparison. These are the fastest possible equals() and hashCode() methods. The access speedups are illustrated in the following table of measurements (times normalized to the JDK 1.2 case):

	JDK 1.2	JDK 1.3[a]	JDK 1.1.6	JDK 1.2 no JIT	HotSpot 1.0
String keys	100%	45%	91%	478%	165%
String-wrapped keys	53%	40%	64%	282%	65%

[a] The limited speedup in JDK 1.3 reflects the improved performance of Strings having their hash code cached in the String instance.

If you create a hash-table implementation specialized for the StringWrapper class, you avoid calling the hashCode() and equals() methods completely. Instead, the specialized hash table can access the hash-instance variable directly and use identity comparison of the elements. The speedup is considerably larger, and for specialized purposes, this is the route to follow:

```
package tuning.hash;

import java.util.Hashtable;
import tuning.dict.Dict;

public class SpecialKeyClass
{

  public static void main(String[] args)
  {
    //Initialize the dictionary
    try{Dict.initialize(true);}catch(Exception e){}
    System.out.println("Started Test");

    //Build the two hashtables. Keep references to the
    //StringWrapper objects for later use as accessors.
    Hashtable h1 = new Hashtable();
    Hashtable h2 = new Hashtable();
    StringWrapper[] dict = new StringWrapper[Dict.DICT.length];
    for (int i = 0; i < Dict.DICT.length; i++)
    {
      h1.put(Dict.DICT[i], Boolean.TRUE);
      h2.put(dict[i] = new StringWrapper(Dict.DICT[i]), Boolean.TRUE);
    }
    System.out.println("Finished building");

    Object o;
```

```
      //Time the access for normal String keys
      long time1 = System.currentTimeMillis();
      for (int i = 0; i < Dict.DICT.length; i++)
        o = h1.get(Dict.DICT[i]);
      time1 = System.currentTimeMillis() - time1;
      System.out.println("Time1 = " + time1);

      //Time the access for StringWrapper keys
      long time2 = System.currentTimeMillis();
      for (int i = 0; i < Dict.DICT.length; i++)
        o = h2.get(dict[i]);
      time2 = System.currentTimeMillis() - time2;
      System.out.println("Time2 = " + time2);

  }
}

final class StringWrapper
{
  //cached hash code
  private int hash;
  private String string;
  public StringWrapper(String str)
  {
    string = str;
    hash = str.hashCode();
  }
  public final int hashCode()
  {
    return hash;
  }
  public final boolean equals(Object o)
  {
    //The fastest possible equality check
    return o == this;

/*
    //This would be the more generic equality check if we allowed
    //access of the same String value from different StringWrapper objects.
    //This is still faster than the plain Strings as keys.
    if(o instanceof StringWrapper)
    {
      StringWrapper s = (StringWrapper) o;
      return s.hash == hash && string.equals(s.string);
    }
    else
      return false;
*/
  }
}
```

Cached Access

Caches use local data when present, and thus don't need to access nonlocal data. If the data is not present locally, the nonlocal data must be accessed or calculated; this is then stored locally as well as being returned. So after the first access, the data is then available locally, and access is quicker. How much quicker depends on the type of cache.

Most caches have to maintain the consistency of the data held in the cache: it is usually important for the data in the cache to be up to date. When considering the use of a cache, bear in mind the expected lifetime of the data and any refresh rate or time-to-live values associated with the data. Similarly, for output data, consider how long to keep data in the cache before it must be written out. You may have differing levels of priority for writing out different types of data. For example, some filesystems keep general written data in a write cache, but immediately write critical system data that ensures system consistency in case of crashes. Also, as caches cannot usually hold all the data you would like, a strategy for swapping data out of the cache to overcome cache space limitations is usually necessary. The memory used by the cache is often significant, and it is always better to release the resources used by it explicitly when it is no longer needed, or reduce resources being used by the cache when possible, even if the cache itself is still required.

Caching can apply to data held in single objects or groups of objects. For single objects, it is usual to maintain a structure or instance variable that holds cached values. For groups of objects, there is usually a structure maintained at the point of access to the elements of the group. In addition, caching applies generally to two types of locality of access, usually referred to as *spatial* and *temporal*. Spatial locality refers to the idea that if something is accessed, it is likely that something else nearby will be accessed soon. This is one of the reasons buffering I/O streams works so well. If every subsequent byte read from disk was in a completely different part of the disk, I/O buffering would provide no help at all. Temporal locality refers to the idea that if you access something, you are likely to access it again in the near future. This is the principle behind browsers holding files locally, once downloaded.

There is a lot of research into the use of caches, but most of it is related to CPU or disk hardware caches. Nevertheless, any good article or book chapter on caches should cover the basics and the pitfalls, and these are normally applicable (with some extra thinking effort) to caches in applications. One thing you should do is monitor cache-hit rates, i.e., the number of times that accessing data retrieves data from the cache, compared to the total number of data accesses. This is important because if the cache-hit rate is too low, the overhead of having a cache may be more than any actual gain in performance. In this case, you want to tune or disable the cache. It is frequently useful to build in the option of disabling and emptying the cache. This can be very helpful for two reasons. First, you can make direct comparisons of operations with and without the cache, and second, there are times when you want to measure the overhead in filling an empty cache. In this case, you may need to repeatedly fill an empty cache to get a good measurement.

Caching Example I

When accessing elements from sets of data, it is often the case that some elements are accessed much more frequently than others. In these cases, it is possible to apply caching techniques to speed up access to these frequently accessed elements. This is best demonstrated with the following example.

Consider a CacheTest class that consists mainly of a Map populated with Integer objects. I use Integer objects for convenience to populate the Map with many elements, but the actual object type is of no significance since you use only the hashCode() and equals() methods, just as the Map does.

Basically, you provide two ways to access the elements of the Map. The first, plain_access(), just calls the Map.get() method as normal. The second method, cached_access(), uses the lower bits of the hash code of the object to obtain an index value into an array. This index is then checked to see whether the object is there. If it is, the corresponding value in a parallel value array is returned. If it's not, the object is placed there with the value in the corresponding value array.

This is about the simplest example of general cached access. It demonstrates the advantages and pitfalls of cached access. I have selected 10 integers that do not map to the same indexes for the example. Running the class gives a straightforward comparison between the two access methods, and I get the result that the cached access varies significantly depending on the VM used. The access speedups are illustrated in the following table of measurements. Times have been normalized to the JDK 1.2 case for using a HashMap. The first time of each entry is the measurement using a HashMap (not available in JDK 1.1.6), and the second is the measurement using a Hashtable. For any one VM, the cached access is significantly faster.

	JDK 1.2	JDK 1.3	JDK 1.1.6	JDK 1.2 no JIT	HotSpot 1.0
Plain access (HashMap/ Hashtable)	100%/ 317%	198%/ 203%	-/ 444%	1646%/ 2730%	329%/ 238%
Cached access (HashMap/ Hashtable)	35%/ 32%	73%/ 73%	-/ 32%	1188%/ 1120%	120%/ 101%

This test is artificial in that I chose integers where no two map to the same index. If there is more than one integer that maps to the same cache array index, this is called a *collision*. Clearly, with collisions, performance is not as good because you are constantly entering the code that puts the objects into the cache. Collisions are a general problem with cached data, and you need to minimize them for optimal performance. This can be done by choosing an appropriate mapping function to generate indexes that minimize your collisions:

```
package tuning.cache;

import java.util.HashMap;
import java.util.Hashtable;
import java.lang.Math;

public class CacheTest
{
  //The cache array for the keys
  static Object[] cache_keys = new Object[128];
  //The array for the values corresponding to cached keys
  static Object[] cache_values = new Object[128];
  //static Hashtable hash = new Hashtable();
  static HashMap hash = new HashMap();

  public static void main(String[] args)
  {
    try
    {
      System.out.println("started populating");
      populate();
      System.out.println("started accessing");
      access_test();
    }
    catch(Exception e){e.printStackTrace();}
  }

  public static void populate()
  {
    for (int i = 0; i < 100000; i++)
      hash.put(new Integer(i), new Integer(i+5));
  }

  public static Object plain_access(Integer i)
  {
    //simple get() call to the hash table
    return hash.get(i);
  }
```

```java
public static Object cached_access(Integer i)
{
  //First get access index
  int access = Math.abs(i.hashCode()) & 127;
  Object o;
  //if the access index has an object, and that object is equal to key
  //then return the corresponding value in the parallel values array.
  if ( (o = cache_keys[access]) == null || !o.equals(i))
  {
    //otherwise, we got a collision. We need to replace the
    //object at that access index with the new one that we
    //get from the hashtable using normal Hashtable.get(),
    //and then return the value retrieved this way
    if (o != null)
      System.out.println("Collsion between " + o + " and " + i);
    o = hash.get(i);
    cache_keys[access] = i;
    cache_values[access] = o;
    return o;
  }
  else
  {
    return cache_values[access];
  }
}

public static void access_test()
{
  //Ten integers that do not collide under the mapping scheme
  //This gives best performance behavior for illustration purposes
  Integer a0 = new Integer(6767676);
  Integer a1 = new Integer(33);
  Integer a2 = new Integer(998);
  Integer a3 = new Integer(3333);
  Integer a4 = new Integer(12348765);
  Integer a5 = new Integer(9999);
  Integer a6 = new Integer(66665);
  Integer a7 = new Integer(1234);
  Integer a8 = new Integer(987654);
  Integer a9 = new Integer(3121219);
  Object o1,o2,o3,o4,o5,o6,o7,o8,o9,o0;
  long time = System.currentTimeMillis();
  for (int i = 0; i < 1000000; i++)
  {
    o1 = plain_access(a0);
    o2 = plain_access(a1);
    o3 = plain_access(a2);
    o4 = plain_access(a3);
    o5 = plain_access(a4);
```

```java
            o6 = plain_access(a5);
            o7 = plain_access(a6);
            o8 = plain_access(a7);
            o9 = plain_access(a8);
            o0 = plain_access(a9);
        }
        System.out.println("plain access took " +
            (System.currentTimeMillis()-time));

        time = System.currentTimeMillis();
        for (int i = 0; i < 1000000; i++)
        {
            o1 = cached_access(a0);
            o2 = cached_access(a1);
            o3 = cached_access(a2);
            o4 = cached_access(a3);
            o5 = cached_access(a4);
            o6 = cached_access(a5);
            o7 = cached_access(a6);
            o8 = cached_access(a7);
            o9 = cached_access(a8);
            o0 = cached_access(a9);
        }
        System.out.println("cached access took " +
            (System.currentTimeMillis()-time));

    }
}
```

Caching Example II

In a second example, we add an instance variable to the keys to provide the mapping into the cache. This example uses a circular cache that holds just the last (most recent) 128 keys accessed. This has an even larger speedup than the previous example, due to more optimal cache access:

```java
package tuning.cache;

import java.util.Hashtable;
import java.lang.Math;

public class Test2
{
    //The cache array for the keys
    static Test2[] cache_keys = new Test2[128];
    //The array for the values corresponding to cached keys
    static Object[] cache_values = new Object[128];
    static Hashtable hash = new Hashtable();
```

```java
//The index to use for the next object added to the cache
static int freeIndex = 0;

//The current index in the cache referenced by this object
int cacheRef = -1;
//Unique integer for each object, can be used as hash code
int value;

public static void main(String[] args)
{
  try
  {
    System.out.println("started populating");
    populate();
    System.out.println("started accessing");
    access_test();
  }
  catch(Exception e){e.printStackTrace();}
}


public Test2(int i)
{
  value = i;
}


public int hashCode()
{
  return value;
}
public boolean equals(Object obj)
{
  //Equality test requires null check, type check, and value check
  if ((obj != null) && (obj instanceof Test2))
    return value == ((Test2) obj).value;
  else
    return false;
}

public static void populate()
{
  for (int i = 0; i < 100000; i++)
    hash.put(new Test2(i), new Integer(i+5));
}

public static Object plain_access(Test2 i)
{
  return hash.get(i);
}
```

```java
public static Object cached_access(Test2 i)
{
  //Access index into the cache is quick and easy to get
  int access = i.cacheRef;
  Object o;

  //If it is -1 then it is not in the cache
  if (access == -1)
  {
    //get the object using the hash table
    o = hash.get(i);
    //Get the next available index in the cache.
    //Wind round to the start of the cache if it is off the end
    if (freeIndex >= cache_keys.length)
      freeIndex = 0;
    //set the cache index; increment the next cache index too
    access = i.cacheRef = freeIndex++;
    //If there was already something in the cache at that location,
    //uncache it
    if (cache_keys[access] != null)
    {
      System.out.println("Collsion between " + cache_keys[access] +
              " and " + i);
      cache_keys[access].cacheRef = -1;
    }
    //And cache our new value.
    cache_keys[access] = i;
    cache_values[access] = o;
    return o;
  }
  else
  {
    return cache_values[access];
  }
}

public static void access_test()
{
  Test2 a0 = new Test2(6767676);
  Test2 a1 = new Test2(33);
  Test2 a2 = new Test2(998);
  Test2 a3 = new Test2(3333);
  Test2 a4 = new Test2(12348765);
  Test2 a5 = new Test2(9999);
  Test2 a6 = new Test2(66665);
  Test2 a7 = new Test2(1234);
  Test2 a8 = new Test2(987654);
  Test2 a9 = new Test2(3121219);
  Object o1,o2,o3,o4,o5,o6,o7,o8,o9,o0;
  long time = System.currentTimeMillis();
```

```
        for (int i = 0; i < 1000000; i++)
        {
            o1 = plain_access(a0);
            o2 = plain_access(a1);
            o3 = plain_access(a2);
            o4 = plain_access(a3);
            o5 = plain_access(a4);
            o6 = plain_access(a5);
            o7 = plain_access(a6);
            o8 = plain_access(a7);
            o9 = plain_access(a8);
            o0 = plain_access(a9);
        }
        System.out.println("plain access took " +
            (System.currentTimeMillis()-time));

        time = System.currentTimeMillis();
        for (int i = 0; i < 1000000; i++)
        {
            o1 = cached_access(a0);
            o2 = cached_access(a1);
            o3 = cached_access(a2);
            o4 = cached_access(a3);
            o5 = cached_access(a4);
            o6 = cached_access(a5);
            o7 = cached_access(a6);
            o8 = cached_access(a7);
            o9 = cached_access(a8);
            o0 = cached_access(a9);
        }
        System.out.println("cached access took " +
            (System.currentTimeMillis()-time));

    }

}
```

These are examples of general data caching. Sometimes you will know beforehand exactly which objects will be frequently accessed. In this case, you can create a specialized class that provides an accessor that optimizes access for just these objects. This can be as simple as a switch statement or multiple if statements. For example:

```
public Object get(Object key)
{
    if (key == FAST_KEY1)
        return value1;
    else if (key.equals(FASTISH_KEY2))
        return value2;
```

```
    else if (key.equals(possibly_fast_key_assigned_at_runtime))
      return value3;
    else
      return hash.get(key);
}
```

Finding the Index for Partially Matched Strings

The problem considered here concerns a large number of string keys that need to be accessed by full or partial match. Each string is unique, so the full-match access can easily be handled by a standard hash-table structure (e.g., `java.util.HashMap`). But the partial-match access needs to collect all objects that have string keys starting with a particular substring.

So, for example, if you had the hash consisting of keys and values:

```
    "hello"        1
    "bye"          2
    "hi"           3
```

Then the full match for key `"hi"` retrieves 3, and the partial match against strings starting with `"h"` retrieves the collection {1,3}. Using a hash-table structure for the partial-match access is expensive because it requires that all keys be iterated over, and then each key matching the corresponding object needs to be collated.

Of course, I am considering here a large collection of strings. Alternatives are not usually necessary for a few (or even a few thousand) strings. But for large collections, performance-tuning techniques become necessary.

The tuning procedure here should be to look for data structures that quickly match any partial string. The task is somewhat simpler than the most generic version of this type of problem, because you need to match only the first few consecutive characters. This means that some sort of tree structure is probably ideal. Of the structures available from the JDK, `TreeMap` looks like it can provide exactly the required functionality; it gives a minimal baseline and, if the performance is adequate, there is no more tuning to do. But `TreeMap` is 5 to 10 times slower than `HashMap` for access and update. The target is to obtain `HashMap` access speed for single-key access.

Don't get carried away searching for the perfect data structure. Thinking laterally, you can consider other possibilities. If you have the strings in a sorted collection, you can apply a binary search to find the index of the string that is greater than or less than the partial string, and then obtain all the strings (and hence corresponding objects) in between.

More specifically, from the hash table you can construct a sorted array of all the keys. Then, if you want to find all strings starting with "h", you can run a binary search for the strings "h" and "h\uFFFF". This gives all the indexes of the band for all the keys that start with "h". Note that a binary search can return the index where the string would be even if it is not actually in the array. (The correct solution actually goes from "h" inclusive to "i" exclusive, but this solution will do for strings that don't include character \uFFFF.)

Having parallel collections can lead to all sorts of problems in making sure both collections contain the same elements. Solutions that involve parallel collections should hide all accesses and updates to the parallel collections through a separate object to ensure that all accesses and updates are consistent. The solution here is suitable mainly when the collections are updated infrequently, e.g., they are built once or periodically, and read from quite often. Here is a class implementing this solution:

```java
package tuning.struct;

import java.util.Hashtable;
import java.util.Enumeration;

public class PartialSearcher
{
    Hashtable hash;
    String[] sortedArray;

    public static void main(String args[])
    {
        //Populate a Hashtable with ten strings
        Hashtable h = new Hashtable();
        h.put("hello", new Integer(1));
        h.put("hell", new Integer(2));
        h.put("alpha", new Integer(3));
        h.put("bye", new Integer(4));
        h.put("hello2", new Integer(5));
        h.put("solly", new Integer(6));
        h.put("sally", new Integer(7));
        h.put("silly", new Integer(8));
        h.put("zorro", new Integer(9));
        h.put("hi", new Integer(10));

        //Create the searching object
        PartialSearcher p = new PartialSearcher(h);
        //Match against all string keys given by
        //the first command line argument
        Object[] objs = p.match(args[0]);
        //And print the matches out
        for(int i = 0; i<objs.length; i++)
```

```java
      System.out.println(objs[i]);

}

public PartialSearcher(Hashtable h)
{
  hash = h;
  createSortedArray();
}

public Object[] match(String s)
{
  //find the start and end positions of strings that match the key
  int startIdx = binarySearch(sortedArray, s,
                              0, sortedArray.length-1);
  int endIdx = binarySearch(sortedArray, s+ '\uFFFF',
                            0, sortedArray.length-1);

  //and return an array of the matched keys
  Object[] objs = new Object[endIdx-startIdx];
  for (int i = startIdx ; i < endIdx; i++)
    objs[i-startIdx] = sortedArray[i];
  return objs;
}

public void createSortedArray()
{
  //Create a sorted array of the keys of the hash table
  sortedArray = new String[hash.size()];
  Enumeration e = hash.keys();
  for (int i = 0; e.hasMoreElements(); i++)
    sortedArray[i] = (String) e.nextElement();
  quicksort(sortedArray, 0, sortedArray.length-1);
}

/**
 * Semi-standard binary search returning index of match location or
 * where the location would match if it is not present.
 */
public static int binarySearch(String[] arr, String elem,
                               int fromIndex, int toIndex)
{
  int mid,cmp;
  while (fromIndex <= toIndex)
  {
    mid =(fromIndex + toIndex)/2;
    if ( (cmp = arr[mid].compareTo(elem)) < 0)
      fromIndex = mid + 1;
    else if (cmp > 0)
```

```
      toIndex = mid - 1;
    else
      return mid;
  }
  return fromIndex;
}


/**
 * Standard quicksort
 */
public void quicksort(String[] arr, int lo, int hi)
{
  if( lo >= hi )
    return;

  int mid = ( lo + hi ) / 2;
  String tmp;
  String middle = arr[ mid ];

  if( arr[ lo ].compareTo(middle) > 0 )
  {
    arr[ mid ] = arr[ lo ];
    arr[ lo ] = middle;
    middle = arr[ mid ];
  }

  if( middle.compareTo(arr[ hi ]) > 0)
  {
    arr[ mid ] = arr[ hi ];
    arr[ hi ] = middle;
    middle = arr[ mid ];

    if( arr[ lo ].compareTo(middle) > 0)
    {
      arr[ mid ] = arr[ lo ];
      arr[ lo ] = middle;
      middle = arr[ mid ];
    }
  }

  int left = lo + 1;
  int right = hi - 1;

  if( left >= right )
    return;

  for( ;; )
  {
    while( arr[ right ].compareTo(middle ) > 0)
```

```
      {
        right--;
      }

      while( left < right && arr[ left ].compareTo(middle ) <= 0)
      {
        left++;
      }

      if( left < right )
      {
        tmp = arr[ left ];
        arr[ left ] = arr[ right ];
        arr[ right ] = tmp;
        right--;
      }
      else
      {
        break;
      }
    }

    quicksort(arr, lo, left);
    quicksort(arr, left + 1, hi);
  }
}
```

Note that this solution is more generic than for only string keys. Any type of object can be used as a key as long as you can create a methodology to compare the order of the keys. This is therefore a reasonable solution for several types of indexing.

Search Trees

Here's an alternate solution to the problem presented in the last section. I looked for a more obvious solution, another tree structure that would handle the search, provide full keyed access, and give plenty of scope for tuning. Jon Bentley and Bob Sedgewick* detail a potential solution that offers an interesting structure and provides a good tuning exercise, so I will use it here.

A ternary tree is a three-way branching tree, i.e., each node has three branches. The structure is a halfway point between binary trees of strings (one string per node) and digital tries. A *digital trie* stores strings character by character, and has an *n*-way branching where *n* is the number of possible characters in the string (e.g., 26, if all strings have only lowercase alphabetic characters; 256, if strings can

---

* "Ternary Search Trees," Jon Bentley and Bob Sedgewick, *Dr. Dobb's Journal*, April 1998.

contain any 8-byte character; 34,000-way branching, if each node can be any Unicode character). Digitial tries are lightning-fast to search, but have exorbitant space costs that typically rule them out as a solution.

The ternary tree node searches by comparing the current character with the current node's character. If equal, the next character in the string becomes the current character, and the node at the "equal" pointer becomes the current node. Otherwise, the current character in the string remains the current character, and the node at the "higher" or "lower" pointer becomes the current node. A TernarySearchTreeNode class has the Java class structure given as follows (the extra "value" instance variable is to allow any object to be stored as the value for a particular key):

```
class TernarySearchTreeNode
{
  char splitchar;
  TernarySearchTreeNode low;
  TernarySearchTreeNode high;
  TernarySearchTreeNode equal;
  Object value;
}
```

Bentley and Sedgewick provide code (in C, but easily ported) to search and insert into the tree. The recursive versions are:

```
public static Object search(TernarySearchTreeNode p, String str, int strIdx)
{
  //Start from a node
  char c;
  //if the node is null, return null.
  //This means there was no match to the string.
  if (p == null)
    return null;
  //otherwise if the current character is less than
  //the splitchar value, replace the current node with
  //the low node, and carry on searching at this character
  else if ( (c=str.charAt(strIdx)) < p.splitchar)
    return search(p.low, str, strIdx);
  //or if the current character is larger than the
  //splitchar value, replace the current node with the
  //high node, and carry on searching at this character
  else if (c > p.splitchar)
    return search(p.high, str, strIdx);
  else
  {
    //otherwise, we match the current string character with
    //the character at this node. If we have finished the
    //string, then this is the searched for node, and
    //we can return the value stored at this node.
```

```java
      if (strIdx == (str.length()-1))
        return p.value;
      else
        //or this is not the end of the string, so replace
        //the current node with the equal node, and carry on
        //searching at the next string character
        return search(p.equal, str, strIdx+1);
  }
}


public static TernarySearchTreeNode insert(TernarySearchTreeNode p, String str,
      int strIdx, Object o)
{
  //Start from a node. If there is no node, then we create a new node
  //to insert into the tree. This could even be the root node.
  char c;
  if (p == null)
  {
    p = new TernarySearchTreeNode(str.charAt(strIdx));
  }

  //Now navigate the tree just as for the search method, inserting
  //nodes as required. For each recursive insert() call, the
  //returned node is the one we assign to the current nodes low,
  //high or equal node, depending on the comparison of the
  //current string character and the current node character.
  if ( (c = str.charAt(strIdx)) < p.splitchar)
    p.low = insert(p.low, str, strIdx, o);
  else if (c == p.splitchar)
  {
    //When we finally get to the last node (matched or inserted,
    //doesn't matter), we insert the value, given by Object o
    if (strIdx == (str.length()-1))
      p.value = o;
    else
      p.equal = insert(p.equal, str, strIdx+1, o);
  }
  else
    p.high = insert(p.high , str, strIdx, o);

  return p;
}


//Simple constructor, just assigns the character.
public TernarySearchTreeNode(char c)
{
  splitchar = c;
}
```

A class to use these methods, with get() and put() methods such as Map, looks like this:

```
public class TernarySearchTree
{
    TernarySearchTreeNode root;

    public Object get(String key)
    {
        return TernarySearchTreeNode.search(root, key, 0);
    }

    public Object put(String key, Object value)
    {
        //Note there is no need to initialize root. The recursive insert()
        //call creates a root object the first time through.
        root = TernarySearchTreeNode.insert(root, key, 0, value);
        return null; //fake old value for now
    }
}
```

This is fairly straightforward. (Note that the Map.put() should return the old value, if any, at the key being set, but we have not implemented that functionality just yet.) The accessor and updator just follow the described algorithm, comparing the current character to the character at the current node and taking the appropriate next branch unless you have reached the end of the string. In that case, the value is returned or updated according to whether this is a search or insert.

If you compare update and access times against HashMap, you'll find the TernarySearchTree is much slower. We are expecting this slowdown, because the referred article does the same comparison and indicates that many optimizations are necessary to achieve similar times to the HashMap. Since they do achieve similar times after optimizing, assume that you can too, and run through a tuning phase to see what improvements you can make.

The target is always the HashMap times, since you already have TreeMap if you need the partial-matching functionality without HashMap access speed. If TreeMap does not exist, or you tune another structure with no counterpart, you still need a goal for the performance. This goal should be based on the application requirements. In the absence of application requirements, you should aim for the performance of some other existing class that provides similar or partial functionality. For this example, it is still sensible to use HashMap to provide the performance target because the full key-match access time for the structure will probably be compared to HashMap access times by most developers.

The baseline is a large dictionary of words. Knowing that tree access and update are susceptible to the order of keys added, you are testing both for randomized order of insertion and mostly sorted order, so that you know the near worst case and (probable) average case. Take a `HashMap` that is presized (i.e., large enough to avoid rehashing after addition of all keys), using the case where the keys are mostly sorted as a baseline. Assign the time taken to build the collection as 100%, and also assign the time taken to access every key in it as 100% (i.e., each of the access and update values, which are different, are separately assigned 100%). If the `HashMap` is not presized, there is a cost of approximately another 30% to 60% on the `HashMap` inserts (i.e., 30% to 60% longer in time). The following chart shows the times using Sun VM Version 1.2 with JIT (the ratios vary under other VMs):

	Sorted Insert	Random Insert	Sorted Access	Random Access
HashMap	100%	113%	100%	140%
TernarySearchTree	823%	577%	921%	410%

You can see that you need to gain an order of magnitude to catch up to the `HashMap` performance.

Profiling is not a huge help; it says only that you need to improve the times on these few methods you have. So you need to target basics. First, by using a `char` array at the beginning, get rid of the overhead of accessing the characters from the string key one at a time through the string accessor. Also, by passing the length as a parameter, remove the overhead of repeatedly accessing the string size through its `length()` method. At the same time, rather than create a new `char` array for each string every time you insert or search the tree, repeatedly use the same `char` buffer. The new classes look like:

```
public class TernarySearchTree
{
  TernarySearchTreeNode root;
  char[] buff = new char[5000];

  public Object get(String key)
  {
    key.getChars(0, key.length(), buff, 0);
    return TernarySearchTreeNode1.search(root, buff, 0, key.length()-1);
  }

  public Object put(String key, Object value)
  {
    key.getChars(0, key.length(), buff, 0);
    root = TernarySearchTreeNode.insert(root, buff, 0, key.length()-1, value);
    return null; //fake it for now
  }
}
```

```
class TernarySearchTreeNode
{
  char splitchar;
  TernarySearchTreeNode low;
  TernarySearchTreeNode high;
  TernarySearchTreeNode equal;
  Object value;

  public static Object search(TernarySearchTreeNode p, char[] str,
                              int strIdx, int strMaxIdx)
  {
    char c;
    if (p == null)
      return null;
    else if ( (c=str[strIdx]) < p.splitchar)
      return search(p.low, str, strIdx, strMaxIdx);
    else if (c > p.splitchar)
      return search(p.high, str, strIdx, strMaxIdx);
    else
    {
      if (strIdx == strMaxIdx)
        return p.value;
      else
        return search(p.equal, str, strIdx+1, strMaxIdx);
    }
  }

  public static TernarySearchTreeNode insert(TernarySearchTreeNode p, char[] str,
                                             int strIdx, int strMaxIdx, Object o)
  {
    char c;
    if (p == null)
    {
      p = new TernarySearchTreeNode(str[strIdx]);
    }
    if ( (c = str[strIdx]) < p.splitchar)
      p.low = insert(p.low, str, strIdx, strMaxIdx, o);
    else if (c == p.splitchar)
    {
      if (strIdx == strMaxIdx)
        p.value = o;
      else
        p.equal = insert(p.equal, str, strIdx+1, strMaxIdx, o);
    }
    else
      p.high = insert(p.high , str, strIdx, strMaxIdx, o);
    return p;
  }
```

```
public TernarySearchTreeNode(char c)
{
  splitchar = c;
}
}
```

The algorithms all stay the same; we have applied only the most basic tuning. The following table illustrates the measured values:

	Sorted Insert	Random Insert	Sorted Access	Random Access
HashMap	100%	113%	100%	140%
TernarySearchTree	660%	464%	841%	391%
Original implementation	*823%*	*577%*	*921%*	*410%*

Well, it's a little better, but it should be quite a lot better. Bentley and Sedgewick suggest one obvious improvement: changing the recursive algorithms to iterative ones. This is a standard tuning technique, but it can be difficult to achieve. You can use the implementations here as a sort of template: look at how the recursion has been converted into iteration by having a "current" node, p, which is changed on each pass. This is the normal way of moving from recursion to iteration (see also the sections "Recursion" and "Recursion and Stacks" in Chapter 7, *Loops and Switches*). The classes now look like:

```
public class TernarySearchTree
{
  TernarySearchTreeNode root;
  char buff[] = new char[5000];

  public Object get(String key)
  {
    if(root == null)
      return null;
    else
    {
      key.getChars(0, key.length(), buff, 0);
      return root.search(buff, 0, key.length() - 1);
    }
  }

  public Object put(String key, Object obj)
  {
    key.getChars(0, key.length(), buff, 0);
    if(root == null)
      root = new TernarySearchTreeNode(buff[0]);
    return root.insert(buff, 0, key.length() - 1, obj);
  }
}
```

```
class TernarySearchTreeNode
{
  char splitchar;
  TernarySearchTreeNode low;
  TernarySearchTreeNode high;
  TernarySearchTreeNode equal;
  Object value;

  public Object search(char str[], int strIdx, int strMaxIdx)
  {
    char c;
    for(TernarySearchTreeNode p = this; p != null;)
    {
      if((c = str[strIdx]) < p.splitchar)
        p = p.low;
      else if(c == p.splitchar)
      {
        if(strIdx == strMaxIdx)
          return p.value;
        strIdx++;
        p = p.equal;
      }
      else
        p = p.high;
    }
    return null;
  }

  public Object insert(char str[], int strIdx, int strMaxIdx, Object o)
  {
    TernarySearchTreeNode p = this;
    char c;
    while(true)
    {
      if ( (c = str[strIdx]) < p.splitchar)
      {
        if(p.low == null)
          p.low = new TernarySearchTreeNode(c);
        p = p.low;
      }
      else if(c == p.splitchar)
      {
        if(strIdx == strMaxIdx)
        {
          Object old = p.value;
          p.value = o;
          return old;
        }
        strIdx++;
```

```
      c = str[strIdx];
      if(p.equal == null)
        p.equal = new TernarySearchTreeNode(c);
      p = p.equal;
    }
    else
    {
      if(p.high == null)
        p.high = new TernarySearchTreeNode(c);
      p = p.high;
    }
  }
}

public TernarySearchTreeNode(char c)
{
  splitchar = c;
}
}
```

The iterative implementation of insert() allows you to return the old object easily, thus making the implementation of put() have correct functionality for a Map. The following table illustrates the resulting measurements (the previous measurements are in parentheses):

	Sorted Insert	Random Insert	Sorted Access	Random Access
HashMap	100%	113%	100%	140%
TernarySearchTree	558% (660%)	373% (464%)	714% (841%)	353% (391%)
Original implementation	*823%*	*577%*	*921%*	*410%*

The performance has improved, but it's still a long way from the HashMap performance. It is worth noting that these simple optimizations have already cut the times by over a third. To get a big boost, you need to target something large. Object creation can be a serious performance problem, as we saw in Chapter 4, *Object Creation*. Bentley and Sedgewick state that their major performance optimization is to preallocate memory for the tree. So let's change the node creation in the insert call to assign nodes from a precreated pool of nodes, i.e., create a large pool of nodes at the initial creation of TernarySearchTree, and assign these as required in the tree insert() method. The code is straightforward, replacing the new TernarySearchTreeNode() call with a newNode() call, and the pool management is simple:

```
public static TernarySearchTreeNode newNode(char c,
                            TernarySearchTreeNode pool)
```

```
  {
    TernarySearchTreeNode p = pool;
    pool = pool.equal;
    p.splitchar = c;
    p.low = p.equal = p.high = null;
    return p;
  }

  TernarySearchTreeNode static createPool(int size)
  {
    TernarySearchTreeNode last;
    TernarySearchTreeNode pool;
    for (int i = size; i > 0; i--)
    {
      last = pool;
      pool = new TernarySearchTreeNode();
      pool.equal=last;
    }
    return pool;
  }
```

The following chart shows the new measurements (previous measurements in parentheses):

	Sorted Insert	**Random Insert**	**Sorted Access**	**Random Access**
HashMap	100%	113%	100%	140%
TernarySearchTree	368% (558%)	234% (373%)	654% (714%)	315% (353%)
Original implementation	*823%*	*577%*	*921%*	*410%*

We are getting closer for the average (random) case. But why is there such a discrepancy between the average and worst (mostly sorted) case now, and why is there an improvement in the access times when the change should have altered only the insertion times? The discrepancy between the average and worst cases may indicate that the worst times are a result of the time spent in the stack due to the depth of the insert/search loops, rather than node creation. The improvement in the access times may be due to internal memory management of the VM: all the nodes being created one after the other may be the reason for the improved access. (Although since everything is in memory, I'm not quite sure why this would be so. Possibly, the heap space is segmented according to requisition from the OS, and you may have paged slightly to disk, which could explain the discrepancy. But I have discarded any timings that had any significant paging, so the discrepancy is not entirely clear.) There is an extra issue now, since you have not been measuring the time taken in creating the tree. The last optimization has increased this time, as the nodes were previously created during the insert, but are now all created at tree creation. Consequently, you might now need to consider this creation time, depending on how the data structure is used.

The creation time is actually rather large. It would be nice if there was a way to create all nodes required in one VM call, but there is none provided in Java (at least up to JDK 1.3). You can finesse this shortcoming by implementing your own memory management using arrays, and it is certainly worth doing so as an exercise to see if the technique gives any advantages. Another possibility is to create objects at initialization in a separate thread, but this requires previous knowledge of many things, so I will not consider that option here.

Fortunately, the node structure is simple, so you can map it into an array of ints. Each node takes five indexes: the first to hold the character, the next three to hold index values for other nodes, and the last to hold an index value into an `Object` array (which can hold the `Object` values).

Now you no longer have the separate node class; all management is in the `TernarySearchTree` class:

```java
public class TernarySearchTree
{
  //offsets into the array for each node
  final static int INITIAL_NODE = 1;
  final static int LOW_OFFSET = 1;
  final static int HIGH_OFFSET = 2;
  final static int EQUAL_OFFSET = 3;
  final static int VALUE_OFFSET = 4;
  final static int NODE_SIZE = 5;

  //A buffer for the string
  char[] buff = new char[5000];
  //the array of node 'object's
  int[] nodes;
  //the array of Object values, one for each node
  Object[] objects;
  //The index to the next available unused node.
  //Note that it is at index 1,
  //not zero
  int nextNode = INITIAL_NODE;
  //The index to the next object
  int nextObject = 0;

  //default constructor
  public TernarySearchTree()
  {
    this(500000);
  }
```

```java
//Constructor to create a pre-sized Ternary tree
public TernarySearchTree(int size)
{
  //create all the nodes.
  //Each node is five int indexes and one Object index
  nodes = new int[NODE_SIZE*size];
  objects = new Object[size];
}

public Object get(String key)
{
  key.getChars(0, key.length(), buff, 0);
  return search(buff, 0, key.length()-1);
}

public Object put(String key, Object value)
{
  key.getChars(0, key.length(), buff, 0);
  if (nextNode == INITIAL_NODE)
  {
    nodes[INITIAL_NODE] = buff[0];
    nextNode+=NODE_SIZE;
  }
  return insert(buff, 0, key.length()-1, value);
}

/**
 * The node search and insert methods just map from the previous
 * implementations using the mappings
 *    p.splitchar -> nodes[p]
 *    p.low -> nodes[p+LOW_OFFSET]
 *    p.high -> nodes[p+HIGH_OFFSET]
 *    p.equal -> nodes[p+EQUAL_OFFSET]
 *    p.value -> objects[nodes[p+VALUE_OFFSET]]
 */
public Object search(char[] str, int strIdx, int strMaxIdx)
{
  int p = INITIAL_NODE;
  int c;
  while (p != 0)
  {
    if ( (c = str[strIdx]) < nodes[p])
      p = nodes[p+LOW_OFFSET];
    else if (c == nodes[p])
    {
      if (strIdx == strMaxIdx)
        return objects[nodes[p+VALUE_OFFSET]];
      else
      {
```

```
          strIdx++;
          p = nodes[p+EQUAL_OFFSET];
        }
      }
      else
        p = nodes[p+HIGH_OFFSET];
  }
  return null;
}

public Object insert(char[] str, int strIdx, int strMaxIdx, Object o)
{
  int p = INITIAL_NODE;
  int c = str[strIdx];
  Object old;
  for(;;)
  {
    if ( c < nodes[p])
    {
      if (nodes[p+LOW_OFFSET] == 0)
      {
        nodes[p+LOW_OFFSET] = nextNode;
        nodes[nextNode] = c;
        nextNode+=NODE_SIZE;
      }
      p = nodes[p+LOW_OFFSET];
    }
    else if (c == nodes[p])
    {
      if (strIdx == strMaxIdx)
      {
        if (nodes[p+VALUE_OFFSET] == 0)
        {
          nodes[p+VALUE_OFFSET] = nextObject;
          nextObject++;
        }
        old = objects[nodes[p+VALUE_OFFSET]];
        objects[nodes[p+VALUE_OFFSET]] = o;
        return old;
      }
      else
      {
        strIdx++;
        c=str[strIdx];
        if (nodes[p+EQUAL_OFFSET] == 0)
        {
          nodes[p+EQUAL_OFFSET] = nextNode;
          nodes[nextNode] = c;
          nextNode+=NODE_SIZE;
        }
```

```
            p = nodes[p+EQUAL_OFFSET];
        }
    }
    else
    {
      if (nodes[p+HIGH_OFFSET] == 0)
      {
        nodes[p+HIGH_OFFSET] = nextNode;
        nodes[nextNode] = c;
        nextNode+=NODE_SIZE;
      }
      p = nodes[p+HIGH_OFFSET];
    }
  }
 }
}
```

Although the class may look a little complex, it is pretty easy to see what is happening if you bear in mind that `nodes[p+HIGH_OFFSET]` is equivalent to the `p.high` in the previous version of the tree (i.e., the tree that had the separate node class). There are only two slightly more complex differences. First, the equivalent of `p.value` is now `objects[nodes[p+VALUE_OFFSET]]`, because the `nodes` array holds only `int`s, and the value can be any `Object` (hence requiring a separate `Object` array). Second, a new node is allocated by providing the index of the current high-water mark in the `nodes` array, held by variable `nextNode`. This index is then incremented by the size of the node, `NODE_SIZE` (which is five fields), for the next node allocation.

This alternative implementation does not affect the external interface to the class, and so the complexity remains hidden from any other class. This implementation is much closer to the C implementation provided by Bentley and Sedgewick, where nodes were allocated in a similar large chunk. Now the question is, have we improved performance? The next table shows the current measurements (previous measurements in parentheses):

	Sorted Insert	Random Insert	Sorted Access	Random Access
HashMap	100%	113%	100%	140%
TernarySearchTree	249% (368%)	200% (234%)	334% (654%)	200% (315%)
Original implementation	*823%*	*577%*	*921%*	*410%*

Overall, these are the best results so far, and the worst case is much closer to the average case. Also, the object-creation time is much better: it is essentially as fast as possible in a VM since you are creating just two new significant objects (which are very large arrays), and so the limitation is purely down to how quickly the VM can allocate the memory space.

You might be satisfied to stop at this point, even though your structure is slower than a `HashMap` by a factor of two. It does provide the extra required functionality of partial matching, as well as the full matching that `HashMaps` provide, and relative performance is acceptable.

But there is one more major change to consider. You know that digital search tries are extremely fast, but inefficient in space. If you are prepared to accept the extra space taken, you can still consider using digital tries to achieve improved performance. If you are using strings that contain mainly the ASCII character set, consider using a digital search trie for the first couple of characters. A two-node digital search trie has 256 nodes for a one-character string, and 256 nodes for the first character in multicharacter strings. For the multicharacter strings, the second node has 256 nodes for each node of the first character, giving $256 \times 257 = 65,792$ nodes. With each node using 4 bytes, you would use $65792 \times 4 = 263,168$ bytes. So you have a quarter of a megabyte before you even start to use this structure. However, if you use this structure for a large amount of string data, you may find this memory usage small compared to the final overall size. Assuming this is acceptable, let's look at how it is implemented and how it performs.

Basically, you implement a trie for the first two characters, but each two-character node then points to the root of a ternary tree. The two-digit trie needs a parallel `Object` structure to store the `Object` values that correspond to one- or two-digit strings. This is, of course, occupying a lot of space, and there are methods for reducing the space requirements (for example, you can optimize for just the alphanumeric characters, mapping them into smaller arrays), but for this exercise, let's keep it simple. The class now looks as follows:

```
public class TernarySearchTree
{
    final static int LOW_OFFSET = 1;
    final static int HIGH_OFFSET = 2;
    final static int EQUAL_OFFSET = 3;
    final static int VALUE_OFFSET = 4;
    final static int NODE_SIZE = 5;
    final static int INITIAL_TRIE_NODE = 1 + NODE_SIZE;
    final static int INITIAL_NODE = 1;

    char[] buff = new char[5000];
    int[] nodes;
    Object[] objects;
    int nextNode = INITIAL_TRIE_NODE;
    int nextObject = 0;
    int initial = -1;
```

```
    Object[] trie1Objects;
    int[][] trie2;
    Object[][] trie2Objects;

    public TernarySearchTree()
    {
      this(500000);
    }

    public TernarySearchTree(int size)
    {
      trie1Objects = new Object[256];
      trie2 = new int[256][256];
      trie2Objects = new Object[256][256];
      nodes = new int[NODE_SIZE*size+1];
      objects = new Object[size];
    }

    public Object get(String key)
    {
      int len = key.length();
      key.getChars(0, len, buff, 0);
      int first = buff[0];
      int second = buff[1];
      if (len == 1 && (first < 256))
      {
        return trie1Objects[first];
      }
      else if (len == 2 && (first < 256) && (second < 256))
      {
        return trie2Objects[first][second];
      }
      else if ((first < 256) && (second < 256))
      {
        int nodep = trie2[first][second];
        if (nodep == 0)
        {
          return null;
        }
        return search(buff, 2, len-1, nodep);
      }
      else
      {
        //Use node[0] as a flag to determine if entered here
        if (nodes[0] == 0)
        {
          return null;
        }
        return search(buff, 0, len-1, INITIAL_NODE);
```

```java
    }
  }

  public void release()
  {
    nodes = null;
    objects = null;
  }

  public Object search(char[] str, int strIdx, int strMaxIdx, int p)
  {
    int c;
    while (p != 0)
    {
      if ( (c = str[strIdx]) < nodes[p])
        p = nodes[p+LOW_OFFSET];
      else if (c == nodes[p])
      {
        if (strIdx == strMaxIdx)
          return objects[nodes[p+VALUE_OFFSET]];
        else
        {
          strIdx++;
          p = nodes[p+EQUAL_OFFSET];
        }
      }
      else
        p = nodes[p+HIGH_OFFSET];
    }
    return null;
  }

  public Object put(String key, Object value)
  {
    int len = key.length();
    key.getChars(0, len, buff, 0);
    int first = buff[0];
    int second = buff[1];
    if (len == 1 && (first < 256))
    {
      Object old = trie1Objects[first];
      trie1Objects[first] = value;
      return old;
    }
    else if (len == 2 && (first < 256) && (second < 256))
    {
      Object old = trie2Objects[first][second];
      trie2Objects[first][second] = value;
      return old;
    }
```

```
      else if ((first < 256) && (second < 256))
      {
        int nodep = trie2[first][second];
        if (nodep == 0)
        {
          nodep = trie2[first][second] = nextNode;
          nodes[nextNode] = buff[2];
          nextNode+=NODE_SIZE;
        }
        return insert(buff, 2, len-1, value, nodep);
      }
      else
      {
        //Use node[0] as a flag to determine if entered here
        if (nodes[0] == 0)
        {
          nodes[0] = 1;
          nodes[INITIAL_NODE] = first;
        }
        return insert(buff, 0, len-1, value, INITIAL_NODE);
      }
    }

    public Object insert(char[] str, int strIdx, int strMaxIdx,
                         Object value, int p)
    {
      int c = str[strIdx];
      int cdiff;
      Object old;
      for(;;)
      {
        if ( (cdiff = c - nodes[p]) < 0)
        {
          if (nodes[p+LOW_OFFSET] == 0)
          {
            nodes[p+LOW_OFFSET] = nextNode;
            nodes[nextNode] = c;
            nextNode+=NODE_SIZE;
          }
          p = nodes[p+LOW_OFFSET];
        }
        else if (cdiff == 0)
        {
          if (strIdx == strMaxIdx)
          {
            if (nodes[p+VALUE_OFFSET] == 0)
            {
              nodes[p+VALUE_OFFSET] = nextObject;
              nextObject++;
            }
```

```
        old = objects[nodes[p+VALUE_OFFSET]];
        objects[nodes[p+VALUE_OFFSET]] = value;
        return old;
      }
      else
      {
        strIdx++;
        c=str[strIdx];
        if (nodes[p+EQUAL_OFFSET] == 0)
        {
          nodes[p+EQUAL_OFFSET] = nextNode;
          nodes[nextNode] = c;
          nextNode+=NODE_SIZE;
        }
        p = nodes[p+EQUAL_OFFSET];
      }
    }
    else
    {
      if (nodes[p+HIGH_OFFSET] == 0)
      {
        nodes[p+HIGH_OFFSET] = nextNode;
        nodes[nextNode] = c;
        nextNode+=NODE_SIZE;
      }
      p = nodes[p+HIGH_OFFSET];
    }
  }
}
}
```

This table shows the measurements (previous measurements in parentheses):

	Sorted Insert	Random Insert	Sorted Access	Random Access
HashMap	100%	113%	100%	140%
TernarySearchTree	103% (249%)	158% (200%)	140% (334%)	205% (200%)
Original implementation	*823%*	*577%*	*921%*	*410%*

The results are the best yet for all values except the random access, which is roughly the same as before. Perhaps the most interesting aspect is that you now get better times on the mostly sorted input than on the randomized input (which is also the case for the HashMap). The result is still slower than a HashMap, but has the extra capability to identify partial matches efficiently. For more specialized versions, such as those needed for a particular application, you can make an implementation that is significantly faster (just as for the hash-table structures earlier in this chapter).

All in all, we've taken a particular structure in its initial form, optimized it using various techniques, and made it two to eight times faster accessing and updating elements.

Note that there are also costs beyond the extra space costs for this last hybrid structure. The implementation before this last one is still a pure ternary tree. That pure implementation has some elegant and simple recursive algorithms for iterating through the tree in order and for identifying partial matches. However, implementing the equivalent algorithms for the last hybrid structure is quite a bit more complicated, as you have to jump between the two structures it uses.

There is not much educational value in proceeding further with these classes here. We've covered the uses of different structures and how to reimplement classes to use different underlying structures for the purpose of improving performance. This book is not intended to provide finished components, so if you feel that this structure may be useful to you in some situation, you'll need to complete it yourself.

Just a few final performance notes about the optimized class. Obviously, you want to optimize its use of space. So note that its size is given by the high-water mark, which is easily determined. And if you want to make the class dynamically growable at large sizes, you may be better off catching the exception thrown when the high-water mark grows past the end of the nodes array and then copying to a larger array, rather than making a test on each insertion.

Performance Checklist

Most of these suggestions apply only after a bottleneck has been identified:

- Test using either the target size for collections or, if this is not definite, various sizes of collections.

- Test updating collections using the expected order of the data or, if this is not definite, various orders of data, including sorted data.

- Match the scaling characteristics of the structures against the volumes of data likely to be applied.

- Presize collections to their final sizes when possible.

- Consider switching to alternative data structures or algorithms.

  — Use the most appropriate collection class available.

  — Consider using two collections with different performance characteristics to hold the same data.

  — Consider using plain arrays, e.g., int[], Object[].

  — Consider using hybrid data structures.

— Use specialized collections that avoid casts or unnecessary method calls.

— Consider wrapping the elements of the collection in a specialized class that improves access times (e.g., `Hashtable` key class with faster `hashCode()` and `equals()` methods).

— Add caching or specialized accessors to collections where some elements are accessed more often than others.

- Access the underlying collection structure when iterating over the elements of a collection.

— Copy the elements into an array rather than access many elements one at a time through the collection element accessors.

- Preallocate memory for element storage rather than allocating at update time.

— Reuse element-storage objects when they are released.

— Map elements into one or more arrays of data variables to allocate the whole collection in as few calls as possible.

- Test if changing a recursive algorithm to an iterative one provides a useful speedup.

- Make recursive methods tail-recursive.

12

Distributed Computing

> *On a 56K modem, this report will take about half an hour to download (for a 30-second download of just the information contained in the report, click here).*
>
> —From a web site that shall remain unnamed

Distributed-application bottlenecks are of two general types. The first type occurs within application subcomponents. This type of bottleneck is essentially independent of the distributed nature of the application, and the other chapters in this book deal with how to tune this type of bottleneck. In this chapter, we deal with the second type of bottleneck, which occurs within the distribution infrastructure. This latter type of bottleneck is specific to the distributed nature of the application, and can be tuned using a number of techniques:

Caching

When an application repeatedly distributes the same data, a significant gain in performance can be obtained by caching the data, thus changing some distributed requests to local ones.

Compression

If the volume of data being transferred is large or causes multiple chunks to be transferred, then compressing the transferred data can improve performance by reducing transfer times.

Message reduction

Most distributed applications have their performance limited by the latency of the connections. Each distributed message incurs the connection-latency overhead, and so the greater the number of messages, the greater the cumulative performance delay due to latency. Reducing the number of messages transferred by a distributed application can produce a large improvement in the application performance.

Application partitioning

The performance of any distributed function in a distributed application normally has at least two factors involved. These two factors are the location for the function to execute and the location where the data for the function resides. Typically, the application developers are faced with the choice of moving the function to the location of the data, or moving the data to the location of the function. These decisions depend on the volume and nature of the data to be processed, the relative power and availability of the CPUs in the different locations, and how much of the data will be transferred after the function completes. If the function's result is to transfer a relatively small amount of data, it should be located on the machine where the data used by the function resides.

Batching

There are several ways that batching can improve the performance of a distributed application. First, the number of messages can be reduced by combining multiple messages into fewer batched messages. Second, data can be split up and transferred in shorter batches if waiting for all the data is the cause of the delay in response times. Third, data requirements can be anticipated, and extra data can be transferred in batches together with the data that is needed at that moment, in anticipation of the extra data that will be needed soon. Further batching variations can be used by extending these strategies.

Stubbing

When data needs to be transferred across a distributed application, the distribution infrastructure often uses general mechanisms for transfers. This results in transferring more data than is actually required. By selectively "stubbing out" data links, only the data that is needed is transferred. Instance variables of objects can be replaced with "stub" objects that respond to messages by transferring the required data (if the fields are defined using an interface). Java also supports the `transient` modifier, which can be used to eliminate unnecessary data transfers. Fields defined as `transient` are not transferred when serialization is used, but this is a rather blunt technique that leads to all-or-nothing transfers of fields.

Asynchronous activities

Distributed systems should make maximum use of asynchronous activities wherever possible. No part of the application should be blocked while waiting for other parts of the application to respond, unless the application logic absolutely requires such blocked activities.

In the following sections, we look at examples of applying some of these techniques to optimize performance.*

Tools

A number of tools for monitoring distributed applications are listed in the section "Client/Server Communications" in Chapter 2, *Profiling Tools*, as well as in "Network I/O" in Chapter 14, *Underlying Operating System and Network Improvements*. In addition, there is one other monitoring tool I often find useful when dealing with distributed applications: a *relay server*. This is a simple program that accepts incoming socket connections and simply relays all data on to another outgoing socket. Normally, I customize the server to identify aspects of the application being monitored, but having a generic relay server as a template is useful, so I present a simple one here:

```java
package tuning.distrib;

import java.io.*;
import java.net.*;


class RelayServer
  implements Runnable
{
  //Simple input and output sockets
  Socket in_s;
  Socket out_s;

  //A string message to printout for logging identification
  String message;

  //Simple constructor just assigns the three parameters
  public RelayServer(Socket in, Socket out, String msg)
  {
    in_s = in;
    out_s = out;
    message = msg;
  }

  //The required method for Runnable.
  //Simply repeatedly reads from socket input, logs the read data
  //to System.out, and then relays that data on to the socket output
```

---

* I will not be considering higher-level optimizations such as Enterprise bean optimizations. A very useful article by Jason Westra in the April 2000 edition of the *Java Developer's Journal* titled "What Do MTS and EJB Have in Common?" provides an insight into why developing with stateless beans gains a higher level of scalability than with stateful beans. The article is available from the *Java Developer's Journal* web site at *http://www.JavaDevelopersJournal.com*.

```java
public void run()
{
  try
  {
    InputStream in = in_s.getInputStream();
    OutputStream out = out_s.getOutputStream();
    byte[] buf = new byte[8192];
    int len;
    for(;;)
    {
      len = in.read(buf);
      System.out.print(message);
      System.out.println(new String(buf, 0, len));
      out.write(buf, 0, len);
    }
  }
  catch (Exception e)
  {
    System.out.print(message);
    System.out.println(" TERMINATED");
    System.out.flush();
    try{in_s.close();}catch(Exception e2){}
    try{out_s.close();}catch(Exception e2){}
  }
}

//Basic main() takes two arguments, a host and port. All incoming
//connections will be relayed to the given host and port.
public static void main(String[] args)
{
  ServerSocket srvr = null;
  try
  {
    //Start a server socket on the localhost at the given port
    srvr = new ServerSocket(Integer.parseInt(args[1]));
    for(;;)
    {
      //Block until a connection is made to us.
      Socket sclient = srvr.accept();
      System.out.println("Trying to connect to " + args[0]);
      //Connect to the 'real' server
      Socket ssrvr = new Socket(args[0], Integer.parseInt(args[1]));
      System.out.println("Connected to " + args[0]);
      //Start two threads, one to relay client to server comms,
      //and one to relay server to client communications.
      (new Thread(new RelayServer(sclient, ssrvr,
          "CLIENT->SERVER"))).start();
      (new Thread(new RelayServer(ssrvr, sclient,
          "SERVER->CLIENT"))).start();
    }
  }
```

```
      catch (Exception e)
      {
        System.out.println("SERVER TERMINATED: " + e.getMessage());
        try{srvr.close();}catch(Exception e2){}
      }
    }
  }
```

As listed here, the relay server simply accepts any incoming connections on the given port and relays all communication to the outgoing server, while at the same time printing all communication to System.out. To test the relay server using an HTTP connection, you could start it with the command line:

```
java someserver 80
```

Then you could try connecting to someserver using a web browser with the URL *http://localhost/some/path/*. This instructs the browser to connect to the relay server, and the relay server acts like a web server at someserver (i.e., as if the URL had been *http://someserver/some/path/*).

Message Reduction

Let's look at a simple example of reducing message calls. For later infrastructure comparison, we will use three different distributed-application infrastructures, CORBA, RMI, and a proprietary distribution mechanism using plain sockets and serialization (see the sidebar "Proprietary Communications Infrastructures"). In the example, I present a simple server object that supports only three instance variables and three methods to set those instance variables.

CORBA Example

The CORBA IDL definition is quite simple:

```
module tuning {
  module distrib {
    module corba {
      interface ServerObject {
        void setBoolean(in boolean flag);
        void setNumber(in long i);
        void setString(in string obj);
}; }; }; };
```

The server class implementation for this IDL definition is:

```
package tuning.distrib.corba;

public class ServerObjectImpl
  extends _ServerObjectImplBase
```

Proprietary Communications Infrastructures

You can easily create your own communication mechanisms by connecting two processes using standard sockets. Creating two-way connections with `Sockets` and `ServerSockets` is very straightforward. For basic communication, you decide on your own communication protocol, possibly using serialization to handle passing objects across the communication channel.

However, using proprietary communications is not a wise thing to do, and can be a severe maintenance overhead unless your communication and distribution requirements are simple. I occasionally use proprietary communications for testing purposes and for comparison against other communications infrastructures, as I have done in this chapter.

In this chapter, I use a simple generic communication infrastructure that automatically handles remotely invoking methods: basically, a stripped-down version of RMI. I generate a server skeleton and client proxy using reflection to identify all the public methods of the distributable class. Then I copy the RMI communication protocol (which consists of passing method identifiers and parameters from proxies to server objects identified by their own identifiers). The only other item required is a lookup mechanism, which again is quite simple to add as a remotely accessible table. The whole infrastructure is in one fairly simple class, `tuning.distrib.custom.Generate`, which is available from the "Examples" link on this book's catalog page, *http://www.oreilly.com/ catalog/javapt/*.

```
{
    boolean bool;
    int num;
    String string;
    public void setBoolean(boolean b) {bool = b;}
    public void setNumber(int i) {num = i;}
    public void setString(String s) {string = s;}
}
```

All the support classes are generated using the *idlj* utility. For JDK 1.3, this generates interfaces `ServerObject` and `ServerObjectOperations`; skeleton classes `_ServerObjectImplBase` and `_ServerObjectStub`; and server object assistant classes `ServerObjectHelper` and `ServerObjectHolder`. In addition, I define a `main()` method that installs an instantiation of the server object in the name service and then remains alive to serve client requests. All classes are defined in the `tuning.distrib.corba` package.

My client simply resolves the server object from the name service, obtaining a proxy for the server, and then calls the three methods and sets the three instance variables. For the test, I repeat the method calls a number of times to obtain average measurements.

The optimization to reduce the number of method calls is extremely simple. Just add one method, which sets all three instance variables in one call, i.e., adding the following IDL definition:

```
void setAll(in boolean flag, in long i, in string obj);
```

The corresponding method is added to the server class:

```
public void setAll(boolean b, int i, String s)
{
  bool = b; num = i; string = s;
}
```

The result is that the single method call requires one-third of the network transfers and takes one-third of the time, compared to the triple method calls (see the later section "Comparing Communication Layers").

RMI Example

The RMI implementation is essentially the same. The server-object interface (with optimized method) is defined as:

```
package tuning.distrib.rmi;

import java.rmi.Remote;
import java.rmi.RemoteException;

public interface ServerObject
    extends Remote
{
  public abstract void setBoolean(boolean flag)
    throws RemoteException;
  public abstract void setNumber(int i)
    throws RemoteException;
  public abstract void setString(String obj)
    throws RemoteException;
  public abstract void setAll(boolean flag, int i, String obj)
    throws RemoteException;
}
```

The RMI server-object implementation is the same as the CORBA version, except that it extends UnicastRemoteObject, implements ServerObject, and defines the methods as throwing RemoteException. All the support classes are generated using the *rmic* utility. For JDK 1.3, this generates skeleton classes ServerObjectImpl_Skel and ServerObjectImpl_Stub. In addition, I define a main() method that sets a security manager and installs an instantiation of the server object in the name service. All classes are defined in the tuning.distrib.rmi package.

Once again, the result is that the single method call requires one-third of the network transfers and takes one-third of the time, compared to the triple method calls (see "Comparing Communication Layers").

Proprietary Communications Layer

A distributed system can be defined with sockets and serialization. I have implemented a simple generator that provides all the basic stub and skeleton behavior for a distributed application (`tuning.distrib.custom.Generate` class; see the sidebar "Proprietary Communications Infrastructures"). The server object is defined as before, with the interface:

```
package tuning.distrib.custom;

public interface ServerObject
{
  public abstract void setBoolean(boolean flag);
  public abstract void setNumber(int i);
  public abstract void setString(String obj);
  public abstract void setAll(boolean flag, int i, String obj);
}
```

This server-object implementation is the same as the CORBA version, though without the need to extend any class: it implements only `ServerObject`.

Yet again, the result is that the single method call requires one-third of the network transfers and takes one-third of the time, compared to the triple method calls (see the next section).

Comparing Communication Layers

In the previous sections, we saw how reducing the number of messages led to a proportional reduction in the time taken by the application to process those messages. Table 12-1 compares the performance between the different communication layers used in those sections.

Table 12-1. Comparison of Different Communication Layers

	Executing Three Separate Methods			Executing One Combined Method		
	Time Taken	Bytes Written	Overhead Time	Time Taken	Bytes Written	Overhead Time
CORBA	512%	291	194%	175%	106	66%
RMI	356%	136	181%	113%	54	56%
Proprietary	293%	40	80%	100%	20	31%

Here, I detail the measurements made for the three communication layers using the tests defined in the previous "Message Reduction" section. The first three columns list measurements taken while executing the three updating methods together. The second three columns list the measurements taken when the single updating method updates the server object. Within each set of three columns, the first column lists the round trip time taken for executing the methods, with all times normalized to the proprietary communications layer time in the combined method case. (The network round trip overhead is a 10-millisecond ping time in these tests.) The second column lists the number of bytes written from the client to the server to execute one set of methods, and the third column lists the time taken to run the test with no latency (i.e., client and server on the same machine), using the same time scale as the first column.

As you can see, CORBA has more overhead than RMI, which in turn has more overhead than the proprietary system. For simple distributed applications such as those used in the examples, using a proprietary-distribution mechanism is a big win. If you include optimized serialization, which can be easily done only for the proprietary layer, the advantages would be even greater. (See "Serialization" in Chapter 8, *I/O, Logging, and Console Output*, for examples of optimizing serialization.) However, the proprietary layer requires more work to support the distribution mechanisms, and the more complicated the application becomes, the more onerous the support is.

There is some evidence that CORBA scales significantly better than RMI as applications grow in any dimension (number of clients, number of servers, number of objects, sizes of objects, etc.). RMI was designed as a relatively simple distributed-application communications layer for Java, whereas CORBA has a much more complex architecture, aimed specifically at supporting large enterprise systems. Given this difference, it is probably not surprising that CORBA has the better scaling characteristics. RMI uses significantly more resources to support certain features such as distributed garbage collection, which can impose heavy overhead at large scales. CORBA directly supports asynchronous communications at the method-definition level by allowing methods to be defined as one-way message transfers.

It appears that for simple distributed applications, a proprietary communications layer is most efficient and can be supported fairly easily. For distributed applications of moderate complexity and scale, RMI and CORBA are similar in cost, though it is easier to develop with RMI. For large-scale or very complex distributed applications, CORBA appears to win out in performance.

Caching

To illustrate caching, I extend the server object used in the previous sections. I add three accessor methods to access the three server instance variables:

```
public boolean getBoolean();
public int getNumber();
public String getString ();
```

Now you can add a generic server-object proxy implementation that handles caching. The implementation is essentially the same for all three communication layers:

```
package tuning.distrib.custom;

public class ServerObjectCacher
  implements ServerObject
{
  ServerObject stub;
  boolean b;
  boolean bInit;
  int i;
  boolean iInit;
  String s;
  boolean sInit;

  public ServerObjectCacher(ServerObject stub)
  {
    super ();
    this.stub = stub;
  }

  public boolean getBoolean()
  {
    if (bInit)
      return b;
    else
    {
      b = stub.getBoolean();
      bInit = true;
      return b;
    }
  }

  public int getNumber()
  {
    if (iInit)
      return i;
    else
    {
      i = stub.getNumber();
```

```
      iInit = true;
      return i;
    }
  }

  public String getString ()
  {
    if (sInit)
      return s;
    else
    {
      s = stub.getString();
      sInit = true;
      return s;
    }
  }

  public void setBoolean(boolean flag)
  {
    bInit = false;
    stub.setBoolean(flag);
  }

  public void setNumber (int i)
  {
    iInit = false;
    stub.setNumber(i);
  }

  public void setString(String obj)
  {
    sInit = false;
    stub.setString(obj);
  }

  public void setAll(boolean flag, int i, String obj)
  {
    bInit = iInit = sInit = false;
    stub.setAll(flag, i, obj);
  }
}
```

As you can see, this is a simple proxy object. Each accessor is lazily initialized, and calling any updating method resets the accessors so that they need to be reinitialized from the server. This ensures that any logic executed on the server is not bypassed. If the server object can be changed by other client programs, you need to add callback support for this caching proxy so that whenever the server object is changed, the client proxy is reset.

Running access tests using this caching proxy is simple. The client code needs to be changed in only one place; once the server object is resolved, the resolved proxy is wrapped in this caching proxy. Then it is used exactly as previously:

```
ServerObject obj = (ServerObject) Naming.lookup("/ServerObj");
//now wrap the server object with the caching proxy
obj = new ServerObjectCacher(obj);
//All the rest of the code is the same
```

The timing results are dependent on how many iterations you test of the uncached versus cached access. After the first access, the cached proxy access is a simple local-variable access, whereas the uncached access requires remote messaging. The difference in timings between these two access mechanisms is more than a factor of 1000, so the more iterations of the tests you make, the bigger the overall relative difference in timings you measure. For example, with accesses repeated 500 times, the average cached access takes about 0.5% of the average uncached access time. Doubling the number of repeated accesses to 1000 times doubles the time taken for the uncached access, but the cached access time is essentially the same, so the time is now 0.25% of the average uncached access time.

Batching I

One form of batching optimization is to combine multiple messages into one message. For the examples we've examined so far, this is easily illustrated. Simply add a method to access all attributes of the server object in one access:*

```
class ServerObjectDataCopy
{
  public boolean bool;
  public int number;
  public String string;
}

public class ServerObjectImpl
{
  public ServerObjectDataCopy getAll();
  ...
```

Using this method to batch the three access methods into one access makes the combined (uncached) access of all the attributes three times faster.

---

* The various communication layers handle distributed classes differently. This book is not a tutorial on CORBA or RMI, so I have elected to show a standard Java representation of the required classes.

Application Partitioning

A simple but dramatic example of the benefits of application partitioning is to run two identical queries on a collection. One query runs on the server and returns only the result of the query; the second query runs on the client, requiring the collection to be copied to the client.*

It's pretty obvious that since the only difference between the two queries is the amount of data being copied across the network, the second query that copies much more data is slower. For the example, I use a large array of strings and create a query that returns that subset of strings that includes the query string, e.g., "el" is included in "hello" but not in "hi."

The query method is straightforward:

```
public static String[] getQuery(String obj, String[] array)
{
  Vector v = new Vector();
  for (int i = 0; i < array.length; i++)
    if (array[i].indexOf(obj) != -1)
      v.addElement(array[i]);
  String[] result = new String[v.size()];
  for (int i = 0; i < result.length; i++)
    result[i] = (String) v.elementAt(i);
  return result;
}
```

To run the query as a server method, I declare one server method in a server object (i.e., in the ServerObject interface):

```
public String[] getServerQuery(String obj);
```

This is also straightforward. The client calls getServerQuery() on the server proxy object and receives the results. To run the query on the client, I declare a method (again in the ServerObject interface) giving access to the String array containing the strings to be compared:

```
public String[] getQueryArray();
```

The server implementation of getServerQuery() is simple (declared in the class that implements the ServerObject interface):

```
public String[]getServerQuery(String obj)
{
  return getQuery(obj, getQueryArray());
}
```

---

* This example is based on a demonstration originally created by GemStone to show the benefits of application partitioning using their application server.

The client query implementation is also similarly straightforward (this could be declared in any client class that has access to the proxy object, including the stub class*):

```
public String[] getClientQuery(ServerObject serverProxy, String obj)
{
  return getQuery(obj, serverProxy.getQueryArray());
}
```

In fact, there isn't much difference between the two method definitions. But when a test is run to compare the two different queries, the results are startling. For my test, I used an array of 87,880 four-letter strings. The test query result produced five strings. Using RMI, the client query took 35 times longer than the server query, and required the transfer of over 600,000 bytes compared to under 100 bytes for the server query. In absolute times, the server query gave a reasonable response time of well under a second. The client query produced an unacceptable response time of over 15 seconds that would have users wondering what could possibly be taking so long.

Application partitioning similarly applies to moving some of the "intelligence" of the server to the client to reduce messaging to the server. A simple example is a client form where various fields need to be filled in. Often, some of the fields need to be validated according to data format or ranges. For example, a date field has a particular format, and the parts of the date field must fall in certain ranges (e.g., months from 1 to 12). Any such validation logic should be executed on the client; otherwise, you are generating a lot of unnecessary network transfers. The example of date-field validation is perhaps too obvious. Most applications have a widget customized to handle their date-field entries. But the general area of user-interface presentation logic is one in which the logic should reside mostly on the client.

Batching II

To illustrate a second type of batching, we make a slightly different test query to the example in the last section. The only difference is in the choice of string to pass into the query, so that the result of the query is a large set. In this test, the result set is over 25,000 strings. The client query is still significantly longer than the server query, but even the server query now takes several seconds in absolute time.

There is no reason to make the user wait for the whole result set to be transferred before displaying some of the results. Altering the application to send results in

---

* The client query method is logically defined in the client stub or the client proxy object defined for the application. But technically, it is not forced to be defined in these classes and can be defined in any client class that has access to the server proxy object.

batches is quite easy. You need to add an intermediate object to hold the results on the server, which can send the results in batches as required:

```
public class QueryResultHolderImpl
  implements QueryResultHolder
{
  String[] results;
  int sentSoFar;
  public QueryResultHolderImpl(String[] results)
  {
    this.results = results;
    sentSoFar = 0;
  }

  public resultSize(){return results.length;}
  public nextBatch(int batchSize)
  {
    String[] batch = new String[batchSize];
    System.arraycopy(results, sentSoFar, batch, 0, batchSize);
    sentSoFar += batchSize;
    return batch;
  }
}
```

You also need to add methods in the server object to support this batching object:

```
public QueryResultHolder getBatchedServerQuery(String obj)
{
  return new QueryResultHolderImpl(getQuery(obj, getQueryArray()));
}
```

Now the client has the flexibility to request batches of results. The initial call to the query returns as fast as possible, with minimal network-transfer overhead: only one small proxy object is sent back in reply to the query. Note that the assumption here is that the QueryResultHolder object is not serialized when returned; instead, a proxy to the real object is passed to the client. The actual QueryResultHolder object holding the result set remains on the server. By wrapping the QueryResultHolder proxy, the optimization can be made completely transparent.

Low-Level Communication Optimizations

There are number of optimizations you can make to the low-level communication infrastructure. These optimizations can be difficult to implement, and it is usually easier to buy these types of optimizations than to build them.

Compression

Where the distributed application is transferring large amounts of data over a network, the communications layer can be optimized to support compression of the data transfers. In order to minimize compression overhead for small data transfers, the compression mechanism should have a filter size below which compression is not used for data packets.

The JDK documentation includes an extended example of installing a compression layer in the RMI communications layer (the main documentation index page leads to RMI documentation under the "Enterprise Features" heading). The following code illustrates a simple example of adding compression into a communications layer. The bold type shows the extra code required:

```java
void writeTransfer(byte[] transferbuffer, int offset, int len)
{
  if (len <= 0)
    return;
  int newlen = compress(transferbuffer, offset, len);
  communicationSocket.write(len);
  communicationSocket.write(newlen);
  communicationSocket.write(transferbuffer, offset, newlen);
  communicationSocket.flush();
}

byte[] readTransfer()
  throws IOException
{
  int len = communicationSocket.read();
  if (len <= 0)
    throw new IOException("blah blah");
  int newlen = communicationSocket.read();
  if (newlen <= 0)
    throw new IOException("blah blah");
  int readlen = 0;
  byte[] transferbuffer = new byte[len];
  int n;
  while(readlen < newlen)
  {
    //n = communicationSocket.read(transferbuffer, readlen, len-readlen);
    n = communicationSocket.read(transferbuffer, readlen, newlen-readlen);
    if (n >= 0)
      readlen += n;
    else
      throw new IOException("blah blah again");
  }
  int decompresslen = decompress(transferbuffer, 0, newlen);
  if (decompresslen != len)
    throw new IOException("blah blah decompression");
  return transferbuffer;
}
```

Caching

Caching at the low-level communications layer is unusual and often a fallback position where the use of the communications layer is spread too widely within the application to retrofit low-level caching in the application itself. But caching is generally one of the best techniques for speeding up client/server applications and should be used whenever possible, so you could consider low-level caching when caching cannot be added directly to the application. Caching at the low-level communications layer cannot be achieved generically. The following code illustrates an example of adding the simplest low-level caching in the communications layer. The bold type shows the extra code required:

```
void writeTransfer(byte[] transferbuffer, int offset, int len)
{
  if (len <= 0)
    return;
  //check if we can cache this code
  CacheObject cacheObj = isCachable(transferbuffer, offset, len);
  if (cacheObj != null)
  {
    //Assume this is simple non-interleaved writes, so we can simply
    //set this cache obj as the cache to be read. The isCachable()
    //method must have filled in the cache, so it may include a
    //remote transfer if this is the first time we cached this object.
    LastCache = cacheObj;
    return;
  }
  else
  {
    cacheObj = null;
    realWriteTransfer(transferbuffer, offset, len);
  }
}

void realWriteTransfer(byte[] transferbuffer, int offset, int len)
{
  communicationSocket.write(len);
  communicationSocket.write(transferbuffer, offset, len);
  communicationSocket.flush();
}

byte[] readTransfer()
  throws IOException
{
  if (LastCache != null)
  {
    byte[] transferbuffer = LastCache.transferBuffer();
    LastCache = null;
    return transferbuffer;
  }
```

```
int len = communicationSocket.read();
if (len <= 0)
  throw new IOException("blah blah");
int readlen = 0;
byte[] transferbuffer = new byte[len];
int n;
while(readlen < newlen)
{
  n = communicationSocket.read(transferbuffer, readlen, len-readlen);
  if (n >= 0)
    readlen += n;
  else
    throw new IOException("blah blah again");
}
return transferbuffer;
}
```

Transfer Batching

Batching can be useful when your performance analysis indicates there are too many network transfers occurring. The standard batching technique uses two cut-off values: a timeout and a data limit. The technique is to catch and hold all data transfers at the batching level (just above the real communication-transfer level) and send all data transfers together in one transfer. The batched transfer is triggered either when the timeout is reached or when the data limit (which is normally the batch buffer size) is exceeded. Most message-queuing systems support this type of batching. The following code illustrates a simple example of adding batching to the communications layer. The bold type shows the extra code required:

```
//method synchronized since there will be another thread
//which sends the batched transfer if the timeout is reached
void synchronized writeTransfer(byte[] transferbuffer, int offset, int len)
{
  if (len <= 0)
    return;
  if (len >= batch.length - 4 - batchSize)
  {
    //batch is too full to take this chunk, so send off the last lot
    realWriteTransfer(batchbuffer, 0, batchSize);
    batchSize = 0;
    lastSend = System.currentTimeMillis();
  }
  addIntToBatch(len);
  System.arraycopy(transferbuffer, offset, batchBuffer, batchSize, len);
  batchSize += len;
}
```

```
void realWriteTransfer(byte[] transferbuffer, int offset, int len)
{
  communicationSocket.write(len);
  communicationSocket.write(transferbuffer, offset, len);
  communicationSocket.flush();
}


//batch timeout thread method
void run()
{
  int elapsedTime;
  for(;;)
  {
    synchronized(this)
    {
      elapsedTime = System.currentTimeMillis() - lastSend;
      if ((elapsedTime >= timeout) && (batchSize > 0))
      {
        realWriteTransfer(batchbuffer, 0, batchSize);
        batchSize = 0;
        lastSend = System.currentTimeMillis();
      }
    }
    try{Thread.sleep(timeout - elapsedTime);}catch(InterruptedException e){}
  }
}


realReadTransfer()
  throws IOException
{
  //Don't socket read until the buffer has been completely used
  if (readBatchBufferlen - readBatchBufferOffset > 0)
    return;

  //otherwise read in the next batched communication
  readBatchBufferOffset = 0;
  int readBatchBufferlen = communicationSocket.read();
  if (readBatchBufferlen <= 0)
    throw new IOException("blah blah");
  int readlen = 0;
  byte[] readBatchBuffer = new byte[readBatchBufferlen];
  int n;
  while(readlen < readBatchBufferlen)
  {
    n = communicationSocket.read(readBatchBuffer, readlen,
                                 readBatchBufferlen-readlen);
    if (n >= 0)
      readlen += n;
    else
      throw new IOException("blah blah again");
```

```
      }
   }

   byte[] readTransfer()
     throws IOException
   {
     realReadTransfer();
     int len = readIntFromBatch();
     if (len <= 0)
        throw new IOException("blah blah");
     byte[] transferbuffer = new byte[len];
     System.arraycopy(readBatchBuffer, readBatchBufferOffset,
                         transferBuffer, 0, len);
     readBatchBufferOffset += len;
     return transferbuffer;
   }
```

Multiplexing

Multiplexing is a technique where you combine multiple pseudo-connections into one real connection, intertwining the actual data transfers so that they use the same communications pipe. This reduces the cost of having many communications pipes (which can incur a heavy system load) and is especially useful when you would otherwise be opening and closing connections a lot: repeatedly opening connections can cause long delays in responses. Multiplexing can be managed in a similar way to the transfer-batching example in the previous section.

Distributed Garbage Collection

Distributed systems typically require distributed garbage collection. If a client holds a proxy to an object in the server, it is important that the server does not garbage-collect that object until the client releases the proxy (and it can be validly garbage-collected). Most third-party distributed systems, such as RMI, handle the distributed garbage collection, but that does not necessarily mean it will be done efficiently. The overhead of distributed garbage collection and remote reference maintenance in RMI can slow network communications by a significant amount when many objects are involved.

Of course, if you need distributed reference maintenance, you cannot eliminate it, but you can reduce its impact. You can do this by reducing the number of temporary objects that may have distributed references. The issue is considerably more complex in a multiuser distributed environment, and here you typically need to apply special optimizations related to the products you use in order to establish your multiuser environment. However, in all environments, reducing the number and size of the objects being used is typically the most effective optimization.

The techniques described in Chapter 4, *Object Creation*, are relevant to reducing the number of objects in a distributed system, and should be applied where possible.

Databases

Databases all have particular features that allow performance optimizations. Usually, the database documentation includes a section on optimizing performance, and that is the place to start.

Here are some hints applicable to many databases:

- Object databases are usually faster than relational databases for applications with strongly object-oriented designs, especially when navigating object networks* is a significant part of the application.

- Relational databases are generally faster than object databases when dealing with large amounts of basic data types, e.g., for objects whose object types are easily mapped into relational tables.

- Application partitioning is important for database access. Reducing the amount of data being transferred over the network is often the key to good performance with databases.

- Application partitioning applies to accessing relational databases. Most relational-database products have the ability to execute server-side code in the form of stored procedures. Stored procedures are precompiled SQL code that can be executed by the database server. Some relational-database products can now run Java on the server too (e.g., Oracle).

- Database queries are often faster if they are statically defined queries, i.e., queries that are defined and precompiled. For relational databases, these take the form of prepared statements that can usually accept parameters. Many object databases also support statically defined queries that can navigate object networks more quickly using internal nodal access rather than executing methods.

- Many databases support batching queries to reduce the number of network round trips, and these batching features should be used to improve performance.

- Transactional access to databases is slower than nontransactional access, so use the nontransactional form whenever possible.

- JDBC optimizations mostly condense down to:
  - Using prepared statements
  - Making SQL requests specific (e.g., avoiding *)

---

* By "navigating object networks," I mean the activity of repeatedly accessing objects from one object's instance variables to another's. The structure formed by the graph of objects reachable through nested instance variable access is a network.

— Keeping transactions short

— Reusing connections (e.g., using connection pools)

— Ensuring that you deallocate resources when finished with them

— Reducing round trips by batching requests

Several articles cover JDBC optimizations in more detail:

- "Best Practices for JDBC Programming," by Derek C. Ashmore, *Java Developer's Journal*, April 2000, available at *http://www. JavaDevelopersJournal.com.*

- "Optimizing Database Transactions with the JDBC," by Chad Darby, *Java Report*, May 1998.

- "Object Persistence Beyond Serialization," by a group of software engineers from IBM's VisualAge Group, *Dr. Dobb's Journal*, May 1999. This is a higher-level, non-Java-specific view.

Performance Checklist

- Use a relay server to examine data transfers.

- Reduce the number of messages transferred.

  — Cache data and objects to change distributed requests to local ones.

  — Batch messages to reduce the number of messages transferred.

  — Compress large transfers.

  — Partition the application so that methods execute where their data is held.

  — Multiplex communications to reduce connection overhead.

  — Stub out data links to reduce the amount of data required to be transferred.

- Design the various components so that they can execute asynchronously from each other.

  — Anticipate data requirements so that data is transferred earlier.

  — Split up data so that partial results can be displayed.

  — Avoid creating distributed garbage.

- Optimize database communications. Application partitioning is especially important with databases.

  — Use statically defined database queries.

  — Avoid database transactional modes if possible.

  — Use JDBC optimizations such as prepared statements, specific SQL requests, etc.

13

When to Optimize

Faster, better, cheaper—choose two of the above.
—Old engineering proverb

When developing an application, it is important to consider performance optimizations and apply these where appropriate in the development cycle. Forgetting these optimizations (or getting them wrong) can be expensive to correct later in development.* In this chapter, we follow the various stages of the full product life cycle and consider when and why you might need to include some performance optimizations.

Performance tuning is frequently a matter of tradeoffs. Occasionally, you have the wonderful situation that a change to the application is better in every way: it provides better performance, cleaner code, and a more maintainable product. But more often, the performance of parts of an application are interrelated. Tuning one part of the application affects other parts, and not necessarily for the better. The more complicated the application, the more often this is true. You should always consider how a particular performance change will affect other parts of the application. This means that tuning can be a lengthy process simply because it must be iterative. The full performance-tuning sequence (identifying the bottleneck, tuning, and then benchmarking) is necessary to make sure that tuning one part of the application is not too detrimental to another part.

Performance tuning at the analysis and design phases differs from performance tuning at the implementation phase. Designing-in a performance problem usually results in a lot of trouble later on, requiring a large effort to correct. On the other

---

* When I talk about expense, I mean cost in both time and money.

hand, coding that results in poor performance simply requires a tuning phase to eliminate bottlenecks, and is much simpler (and cheaper) to correct. As a rule of thumb, a performance problem created (or left uncorrected) in one phase requires roughly five times as much effort to correct in the following development phase. Leaving the problem uncorrected means that the effort required to correct it snowballs, growing fivefold through each development phase (planning, analysis, schematic design, technical design, construction, deployment, production).*

Now on to the specifics. Before discussing when to optimize, I'll start with when you should not optimize.

When Not to Optimize

At the code-writing stage, your emphasis should not be on optimizing: it should be entirely on functionality and producing correct bug-free code. Apart from optimizations (such as canonicalizing objects) that are good design, you should normally ignore performance while writing code. Performance tuning should be done after the code is functionally correct. Alan Knight† wrote:

> If testing and documentation are inadequate, most people won't notice or care how fast a particular list box updates. They'll have given up on the program before they ever got to that window.

This is definitely a view to which I subscribe. Many implementation-level optimizations can make code more complicated and difficult to read. Delay optimizing until the program is mostly functionally correct. But make sure you have planned for a tuning phase.

I am not saying that you should create the whole application without considering performance until just before deployment. That would be foolhardy. Performance should be considered and planned for at all phases of the development process (especially design and architecture). You need to rule out designs that lead to a badly performing application. Optimizations that are good design should be applied as early as possible. When parts of the application are complete, they should be tuned. And benchmarks should be run as soon as possible: they give a good idea of where you are and how much effort will be needed for the tuning phase after code writing is mostly complete.

---

* The fivefold increase is an average across the phases. Studies of the costs of fixing uncorrected problems have found that some phases have a higher cost than others.

† *Smalltalk Report*, March-April 1996. This is a nice article about when and why to performance-tune.

Tuning Class Libraries and Beans

Most code can be categorized into one of two general types:

- *Application-specific code*, normally used for one particular application. If this code is reused, it usually provides only a skeleton that needs reimplementing. Occasionally, application-specific code is generic enough to reuse in another application, but even then it usually needs some rewriting to make it more generic.

- Classes written specifically with reusability in mind. This type of code is usually referred to as class libraries, frameworks, components, and beans. I refer to all of these together as *reusable code*.

The first type of code, application-specific code, is considerably easier to tune. You can run the application as it is intended to be used, determine any bottlenecks, and successively tune away those bottlenecks. Typically, 80% of the application time is spent in less than 20% of the code, and only 5% of the application code actually needs to be changed during the tuning process.

The second type of code, reusable code, is much more difficult to tune. This code may be used in many situations that could never be foreseen by the developers. Without knowing how the code will be used, it is very difficult to create tests that appropriately determine the performance of reusable code. There is no truly valid technique that can be applied. Even exhaustively testing every method is of little use (not to mention generally impractical), since you almost certainly cannot identify useful performance targets for every method. Well-tuned reusable code can have 95% of the code altered in some way by the tuning process.*

The standard way to tune reusable code is to tune in response to identified problems. Usually the development team releases alpha and beta versions to successively larger groups of testers: other team developers, demo application developers, the quality-assurance team, identified beta testers, general beta testers, customers of the first released version (some of these groups may overlap). Each of these groups provides feedback in identifying both bugs and performance problems. In fact, as we all know, this feedback process continues throughout the lifetime of any reusable code. But the majority of bugs and performance problems are identified by this initial list of users. This reactive process is hardly ideal, but any alternative

---

* I have not seen any studies that show this cost. Instead, I base it on my own impression from examining early versions of various class libraries and comparing these classes with later versions. I find that most methods in a random selection of classes are altered in some way that I can identify as giving performance improvements.

makes tuning reusable code very expensive. This is unlike bug testing, in which the quality of the test suite and quality-assessment process makes a big difference to the reliability of the released version, and is fully cost-effective.

There are several consequences to this reactive process. First, from the viewpoint of the developer using reusable components, you need to be aware that first versions frequently have suboptimal performance. Note that this does not imply anything about the quality of the software: it may have wonderfully comprehensive features and be delightfully bug-free. But even in a large beta testing program with plenty of feedback, there is unlikely to be sufficient time to tune the software and repeat the test and release procedures. Getting rid of identified bugs rightfully takes precedence, and developers normally focus on the (next) released version being as bug-free as possible.

Second, for developers *creating* reusable code, the variety of applications testing the reusable code is more important than the absolute number of those applications. Ten people telling you that method X is slow is not as useful as two telling you that method X is slow and two telling you that method Y is slow.

A further consequence when developing reusable code is that to provide greater performance flexibility for the users of those classes, you need to design more flexible method entry points to your classes. Providing performance flexibility unfortunately clashes with the "defensive" programming that is (reasonably) used when creating reusable classes. For example, a defensive developer creating a collection class based on an array (e.g., `java.util.Vector`) might provide a constructor that accepts an array and copies its elements:

```
public class ArrayBasedCollection
{
  int arraySize;
  Object[] array;
  public ArrayBasedCollection(Object[] passedArray)
  {
    arraySize = passedArray.length;
    array = new Object[arraySize];
    System.arraycopy(passedArray, 0, array, 0, arraySize);
  }
  ...
```

The defensive developer always ensures that elements are copied into a new array so that no external object retains a reference to the internal array and interrupts the logic of the class. This ensures that the new class cannot be inadvertently corrupted. However, this provides inefficient performance. There will be cases when the application coder has created the array specifically to hold the objects, and will discard that array immediately. Developing flexibly with performance in mind directs you to add an extra method that allows the array to be used directly:

```
public class ArrayBasedCollection
{
    int arraySize;
    Object[] array;
    public ArrayBasedCollection(Object[] passedArray)
    {
        this(passedArray, true);
    }
    /**
     * If <copy> is true, the elements of <passedArray> are
     * copied into the a new underlying array in the collection.
     * If <copy> is false, the <passedArray> is assigned directly
     * as the underlying array. This is potentially dangerous:
     * the collection object can be corrupted if the <passedArray>
     * is altered directly by another object afterwards.
     */
    public ArrayBasedCollection(Object[] passedArray, boolean copy)
    {
        arraySize = passedArray.length;
        if (copy)
        {
            array = new Object[arraySize];
            System.arraycopy(passedArray, 0, array, 0, arraySize);
        }
        else
            array = passedArray;
    }
    ...
```

This opens the collection object to potential corruption, but by retaining the original one-arg constructor, you have reduced the chance that the two-arg constructor will be used accidentally. A developer looking quickly for a constructor is likely to use the one-arg constructor, whereas a developer desperately searching through the documentation for ways to reduce the number of copies made from several large arrays will be delighted to discover the two-arg constructor.

Finally, perhaps the most significant way to create reusable code that performs well is for developers to be well-versed in performance tuning. After any significant amount of performance tuning, many of the techniques in this book can become second nature. Developers experienced in performance tuning can produce reusable code that is further along the performance curve right from the first cut. Writing reusable code is one of the few situations in which it is sometimes preferable to consider performance when first writing the code.

Analysis

The analysis phase of development encompasses a variety of activities that determine what functionality you are going to build into your application. These activities include:

- Specifying what the application needs to do (e.g., compress files, display graphic files of type, etc.)

- Identifying major functions and business areas (e.g., compression, display; targeted to the area of graphics files)

- Planning generally how the application will work (e.g., read one or more files, use 2-Ronnies compression if possible, etc.)

- Prioritizing subsections (e.g., the compression component must be completed but can use an alternative compression algorithm, the graphics types XYZ must be supported but the graphics types ABC may be dropped until later, etc.)

- Deciding whether to build or buy (e.g., are there available beans or classes to handle compression and display? How much are they? How much will building our own cost? Do the purchasable ones provide all essential features?)

- Documenting the requirements

The analysis phase does not usually specify either the structure of the application or the technology (e.g., you might specify that the application uses a database, but probably not which database or even which type of database). The analysis phase specifies what the application will do (and might do), not how it is done, except in the most general terms.

Here are major performance-tuning considerations during the analysis phase:

- Determining general characteristics of objects, data, and users (e.g., number of objects in the application)

- Specifying expected or acceptable performance boundaries (e.g., functionality X should take less than M seconds)

- Identifying probable performance limitations from the determined specifications (e.g., function Y is an HTTP connection, and so is dependent on the quality of the network path and the availability of the server)

- Eliminating any performance conflicts by extending, altering, or restating the specifications (e.g., the specification states query Z must always respond within N seconds, but this cannot be guaranteed without altering the specification to provide an alternative default result)

Performance goals should be an explicit part of the analysis and should form part of the specification. The analysis phase should include time to analyze the performance impacts of the requirements.

The general characteristics of the application can be determined by asking the following questions about the application:

- How many objects will there be, and what are their sizes (average and distribution)? What is the total amount of data being manipulated, and how are the manipulations expected to be performed (database access, file access, object storage, etc.)?

- What is a transaction for the application? If there are several types of transactions, define each type. Include details such as the number of objects created, deleted, or changed; the duration of the transactions (average and distribution); and expected transaction amounts (transactions per second), both per person and for the system as a whole. Define how data is accessed and queried for, and how often.

- How many simultaneous users will use the application, and what level of concurrency is expected for those simultaneous users? (Are they accessing the same resources, and if so, how many resources and what type of access?)

- What is the expected distribution of the application? This is, of course, mainly relevant for distributed applications. This applies back to the last point but focuses on the distributed resources that are necessarily used simultaneously.

You can use the answers to these questions to provide an abstract model of the application. Applying this abstract model to a generalized computer architecture allows you to identify any performance problems. For example, if the application is a multiplayer game to be played across a network, a simple model of a network together with the objects (numbers and sizes) that need to be distributed, the number of users and their expected distributions, and possible patterns of play provide the information you need to identify whether the specified application can run over the network. If, after including safety factors, the network can easily cope with the traffic, that section of the application is validated. If the game is unplayable when you put in minimum bandwidths of 28K (lowest denominator modem connection) and latency (network communication response time) of 400 milliseconds, you need to reexamine the specifications.

This type of analysis is part of software performance engineering. The general technique for performance tuning prior to actually testing the code (i.e., testing at the analysis and design phases) is to predict the application performance based on the best available data.* This technique is covered in detail in the book *High Performance Client/Server*, by Chris Loosley and Frank Douglas (John Wiley & Sons).

One of the most significant aspects to examine at the analysis phase is the expected performance gains and drawbacks of distributed computing. Distributing

---

* This is a scientific technique referred to as "successive approximation by the application of empirically derived data." Another name for it is "educated guessing."

sections of applications always implies some performance drawback. After all, network communication is always slower than interprocess communication on the same machine, and interprocess communication is always slower than component-to-component communication within the same process. Good design usually emphasizes decoupling components, but good performance often requires close coupling. These are not always conflicting requirements, but you do need to bear in mind this potential conflict.

For distributed applications, distributed components should be coupled in such a way as to minimize the communication between those components. The goal is to limit the number of messages that need to be sent back and forth between components, as too many network message transfers can have a detrimental effect on performance. Components engaged in extended conversations over a network spend most of their time sitting idle, waiting for responses. For this type of situation, the network latency tends to dominate the performance.

A simple example, showing the huge difference that distribution performance can make to even a standalone applet, indicates how important this aspect is. You might have thought that a standalone applet does not need much analysis of its distributed components. Table 13-1 shows two development paths that might be followed, and illustrates how ignoring performance at the analysis stage can lead to performance problems later.

Table 13-1. Contrasting Development Processes

Applet1 Development	Applet2 Development
Distribution analysis: Applet is distributed using a compressed JAR file.	Distribution analysis: Applet2 is distributed using one or more compressed JAR files. Because the download time may be significant for the expected number of classes, the analysis indicates that the applet should be engineered from the ground up, with minimizing download time as a high priority. To this end, the specification is altered to state that a small entry point functionality of the applet, with a small isolated set of classes, will be downloaded initially to allow the applet to start as quickly as possible. This initial functionality should be designed to engage the user while the remainder of the applet is downloaded to the browser in the background. The applet could be downloaded in several sections, if necessary, to ensure the user's waiting time is kept to a minimum. A secondary priority is for the user to have no further explicit download waiting time.

Table 13-1. Contrasting Development Processes (continued)

Applet1 Development	Applet2 Development
Applet1 functional analysis: Similar for both.	Applet2 functional analysis: Similar for both.
Applet1 design: Simple.	Applet2 design: Requires careful thought about which classes require the presence of other classes.
Applet1 coding: Similar for both.	Applet2 coding: Similar for both.
Applet1 performance testing: Applet takes far too long to download. User testing indicates that 99% of users abandon the web page before download is complete and the applet can start. Unpacking the JAR file and having classes download individually makes the situation even worse. Project may be terminated, or a major (and costly) rewrite of the applet design may be undertaken to allow the applet to start faster at the user's desktop.	Applet2 performance testing: Applet downloads and starts in adequate time. Performance within the browser requires some rounds of tuning.

Table 13-1 shows how important performance prediction can be. The analysis on the right saves a huge amount on development costs. Of course, if not identified at the analysis phase, this aspect of performance may be picked up later in some other phase of development, but the further away from the analysis phase it is identified, the more expensive it is to correct.

Another consideration at the analysis stage is the number of features being specified. Sometimes "nice to have" features are thrown into the requirements at the analysis phase. Features seem to have an inverse relationship to performance: the more features there are, the worse the performance or the more effort required to improve the performance. For good performance, it is always better to minimize the features in the requirements, or at the very least, to specify that the design should be extensible to incorporate certain nice-to-have features, rather than to simply go ahead and include the features in the requirements.

One other important aspect that you should focus on during the analysis phase is the application's use of shared resources. Try to identify all shared resources in this phase, and identify the performance costs associated with forcing unique access of shared resources. When the performance cost is shown to be excessive, you need to specify alternative mechanisms to allow the efficient use of the shared resource. For example, if several parts of the application may be simultaneously updating a file, then to avoid corruption, the updates may need to be synchronized. If this potentially locks parts of the application for too long, an alternative, such as journaling, might be specified. Journaling allows the different parts of the application to update separate dedicated log files, and these logs are reconciled by another asynchronous part of the application.

Design and Architecture

Many design-stage decisions affect performance. These include how long a transaction will be, how often data or objects need to be updated, where objects will be located, whether they are persistent and if so, how the persistency is achieved, how data is manipulated, how components interact, and how tightly coupled subsystems are, as well as determining responses to errors, retry frequencies, and alternative routes for solving tasks.

As I mentioned in the last section, the general technique for performance tuning during the analysis and design phases is to predict performance based on the best available data.* During the design phase, a great deal of prototype testing is possible, and all such tests should feed data back to help predict the performance of the application. Any predictions indicating a problem with performance should be addressed at the design phase, prior to coding. If necessary, it is better to revisit the analysis and alter specifications rather than leave any indicated performance issues unresolved.

At each stage, part of the design objective should be to predict the performance of the application. (Note that when I refer to the design phase, I include both logical and physical design; physical design is often called architecture.) The design phase usually includes determining the target platforms, and any predictions must be tailored to the limitations of those platforms. This is especially important for embedded Java systems (e.g., applets and servlets), environments where a specific nonstandard target VM must be used, and where the target VM may be highly variable (i.e., is unknown). In all these cases, the target Java runtime system performance cannot be inferred from using the latest standard VM, and performance prediction must be targeted at the known system or at the worst-performing Java runtime system. (Alternatively, the design phase may rule out some runtime systems as being unsupported by the application.)

Any decoupling, indirection, abstraction, or extra layers in the design are highly likely to be candidates for causing performance problems. You should include all these elements in your design if they are called for. But you need to be careful to design using interfaces in such a way that the concrete implementation allows any possible performance optimizations to be incorporated. Design elements that block, copy, queue, or distribute also frequently cause performance problems. These elements can be difficult to optimize, and the design should focus attention

---

* See Loosley and Douglas.

on them and ensure that they can either be replaced or that their performance is targeted.* Asynchronous and background events can affect times unpredictably, and their effects need to be clearly identified by benchmark testing.

Shared Resources

Resources that must be shared by several users, processes, or threads are always a potential source of bottlenecks. When a resource is shared, the resource usually requires its various sharers to use it one at a time, to avoid a conflict of states and corruption. During the design phase, you should try to identify all shared resources, and predict what performance limitations they impose on the application. Be careful to consider the fully scaled version of the application, i.e., with as many users, objects, files, network connections, etc., as are possible according to the application specifications. Considering fully scaled versions of the application is important because shared resources are highly nonlinear in performance. They usually impose a gently decreasing performance at their bottleneck as the number of sharers increases, up to a point at which there is a sudden and catastrophic decrease in performance as the number of sharers increases further.

If the performance prediction indicates that a particular shared resource is likely to impose too high a performance cost, alternative designs that bypass or reduce the performance cost of that shared resource need to be considered. For example, multiple processes or threads updating a shared collection have to synchronize their updates to avoid corrupting the collection. If this synchronized update is identified as a performance problem, an alternative is to allow each process or thread to update its own collection, and wrap the collections in another collection object that provides global access to all the collections. This solution was illustrated in "Avoiding Serialized Execution" in Chapter 10, *Threading*.

Failing to identify a shared resource at the design phase can be expensive. In some cases, a simple class substitution of a redesigned class can reduce the performance drawback of the shared resource to acceptable performance levels. But in many cases, a complete redesign of part or all of the application may be needed to achieve adequate performance.

Transactions

The purpose of a transaction is to ensure consistency when using shared resources. If there are no possible conflicts across sharers of those resources, there

---

* For example, in Chapter 10, remember that we considered a load-balancing solution that included a queue. The queue is a potential bottleneck, and care must be taken to ensure that the queue does not unnecessarily delay requests as they pass through.

is no need for a transaction. Removing unnecessary transactions is the simplest and most effective performance optimization for applications that include transactions. So, if you do not need a transaction, do not use one. Most systems that provide transactions usually have a "transactionless" mode, i.e., a way to access any shared resources without entering a defined transaction. This mode normally has better performance than the transaction mode.

When transactions are absolutely necessary, your design goal should be to minimize the time spent in the transaction. If transactions extend for too long and cause performance problems, a complete redesign of a significant part of the application is often needed.

You also need to be aware of the shared resources used by the transacting system itself. Any system providing transaction semantics to your application uses an internal set of shared resources: this is necessary to ensure that the transactions are mutually consistent. These transaction-system internal shared resources invariably have some product-specific idiosyncrasies that result in their being used more or less efficiently. These idiosyncrasies can have a large effect on performance. Many products have a performance-tuning section within their documentation, detailing how best to take advantage of idiosyncrasies in their product (more usually termed "features").

Even where short transactions are designed into an application, the application may enter unexpectedly long transactions in two common situations. The first situation is when bugs occur in the transaction, and the second, when the application user has control over the transaction. Because unintended long transactions can occur, transactions should always have a timeout imposed on them: this is usually fairly easy to incorporate in Java using a separate high-priority timeout thread.

A standard way to convert naturally long transactions into short ones is to maintain sets of changes, rather like undo/redo logs. In this design pattern, changes are abstracted into separate objects, and ordered lists of these changes can be "played." With this design pattern, the changes that occur in what would be a long transaction are leisurely collected without entering the transaction, and then a short transaction rapidly "plays" all the changes. This pattern cannot be used exactly as described if the precise time of a particular change is important. However, variations of this pattern can be applied to many cases.

Locking

Locking is a technique for ensuring access to a shared resource while maintaining coherence of state within the shared resource. There are a variety of lock types, from exclusive (only one sharer has any type of access) to various types of shared locks (allowing any of a set of sharers simultaneous access, or all sharers access to a restricted set of capabilities of the shared resource, or both of these combined*).

Locking can be expensive. Overheads include the locking and unlocking overhead itself; the fact that locks must be shared resources implying extra shared-resource considerations; the explicit serialization of activities that result from using locks; and the possibility of deadlock when two sharers are simultaneously trying to obtain a lock held by the sharer, causing both sharers to "freeze" activity (see Chapter 10 for a concrete example).

These drawbacks mean you should consider locking only when the design absolutely requires it. For instance, locking must be used when there is a requirement for definite deterministic noncorrupted access to a shared resource. To illustrate: a bank account with no overdraft facilities must serialize access to the account and ensure that each deposit and withdrawal takes place without any other activities legally occurring at the same time. The balance accessed for display also needs to be accurate. You do not want to display a balance of $100 at the ATM window, then have the ATM deny withdrawal of $50 because the actual balance is lower due to a check for $55 being processed at the same time. From the bank's point of view, both transactions might go though, and the bank is owed $5 from someone it did not want to lend to. Or the customer is given the wrong information and suffers frustration. To avoid these two situations, locking is required.

Occasionally, locking improves performance by reducing the conflicts otherwise generated by simultaneous access to a shared resource. Consider the situation in which objects are concurrently added to a collection. You can define the addition operation to provide exclusive updates either by locking the update method or by throwing an exception if the update is not exclusive. The lockable update method can be defined easily with a synchronized method:

```
public synchronized add(Object o)
{
   unsynchronized_add(o);
}
```

The exception-throwing method would be a little more complex:

```
public add(Object o)
   throws InUseException
{
   //throws an InUseException if I am currently already in use
   setInUse();
   unsynchronized_add(o);
   setNotInUse();
}
```

---

* For example, one type of write-lock allows read access by multiple sharers to the shared resource, while restricting write access to just one sharer.

The advantage of the second definition is that the locking overhead is avoided during the update.* This definition is suitable for cases where there is unlikely to be much concurrent execution of the add() method: the exception is not thrown very often. But when there are frequent simultaneous updates to the collection, you will encounter the exception more often than not. For this latter situation, your performance will be better if you use the first synchronized implementation of the add() method and explicitly serialize the updates.

Parallelism

For performance reasons, you should try to design parallelism into the application wherever possible. The general guideline is to assume that you parallelize every activity. One of the tasks for the design phase, then, is to identify what cannot be parallelized. This guideline is fairly cost-effective. It is always easy to move from a parallelized design back to the nonparallelized version, since the nonparallelized version is essentially a degenerate case of the more general version. But retrofitting parallelism to the application is often considerably more difficult. Starting with an application designed to work without any parallelism and trying to restructure it to add in parallelism can be extremely difficult and expensive.

Any parallelism designed into the application should take advantage of multiple processors. This can be evaluated in the design phase by predicting the performance of the application on single- and multiple-CPU machines.

Once the application has been designed to run with parallelism, you can decide at the implementation stage, or possibly even at runtime, whether to use the parallelism. A low degree of parallelism (e.g., 5 threads, not 500 threads) almost always improves the performance of an application. But parallelism has overhead that can swamp the advantages. The overhead comes from contention in trying to use shared resources and delays from the communication needed for synchronization. Additional overhead comes from starting extra threads and distributing and coordinating work between the threads (there may also be overhead from caches that deal with twice the data throughput in the same space).

When designing the application to run activities in parallel, you need to focus on shared resources, especially the time spent using these resources. Increasing the time spent exclusively using a shared resource adversely affects all other activities using that resource. For example, the CPU is the most basic shared resource. The more separate threads (and processes) using the CPU, the smaller the time slices allocated to each thread relative to the time spent waiting to acquire the CPU by

---

* In fact, the setInUse() method probably needs to be synchronized, so this pattern is useful only for avoiding synchronizing methods that might take a long time. The long synchronization is replaced by a short synchronization and a possible thrown exception.

each thread. Consequently, the time actually taken for computing any particular activity becomes longer, since this is the sum of the time slices allocated to carry out the computation together with the sum of times waiting to gain a time slice.

And the situation is not linear, but exponential. Consider a CPU where 10% is currently used. If there is a computation that normally takes five seconds when this CPU has no work, then as the CPU can currently allocate 90% of its power to that computation, the computation will instead take just over 10% longer: the actual expected time is $5/0.9 = 5.55$ seconds.

If instead the CPU was 40% utilized (i.e., 60% available), the expected time for that computation would instead be $5/0.6 = 8.3$ seconds. Now look what happens to a 90% utilized CPU (10% available). The expected time for the computation is now $5/0.1 = 50$ seconds. And a 99% busy CPU is going to make this computation take 500 seconds (see Table 13-2). You can see the need to keep spare capacity in the CPU to avoid an exponential degradation in performance.

Table 13-2. Theoretical Computation Time (Single-Threaded) Depending on CPU Availability

CPU % Used	CPU % Available	Computation Time
0% used	100% available	5 seconds
10% used	90% available	$5/0.9 = 5.55$ seconds
40% used	60% available	$5/0.6 = 8.3$ seconds
90% used	10% available	$5/0.1 = 50$ seconds
99% used	1% available	$5/0.01 = 500$ seconds

You can also predict the effect threading can have if you can parallelize any particular calculation, even on a single-CPU machine. If one thread does the calculation using 10% of the CPU in five seconds, and you can fully parallelize the calculation, then two threads (ideally) each take half the time to do their half of the calculation. Assuming that the calculation does not saturate the CPU when running,* then if the two halves run together, each half takes 2.5 seconds on an unutilized CPU. But since there are two threads and each thread takes 10% of the CPU, each thread sees only 90% availability of the CPU. This means that each half calculation takes $2.5/0.9 = 2.8$ seconds. Both calculations run at the same time (that is why the CPU has double the utilization), so this is also the total time taken. Time-slicing adds some additional overhead, but this will leave the expected time well below the three-second mark.

So even on a single-CPU machine, parallelizing this calculation enables it to run faster. This can happen because the calculation considered here is not a pure CPU

---

* CPU availability is indicated in the example since the calculation loads the CPU only by 10%; presumably, there is some disk activity required by the calculation.

calculation: it obviously spends time doing some I/O (perhaps a database query), thus it can be parallelized effectively. If the calculation was number crunching of some sort, the CPU utilization would be 100%, and parallelizing the calculation would actually slow it down.

For example, suppose the number-crunching calculation took five seconds and caused a 100% CPU utilization on an otherwise unworked machine. Running the same calculation on a 50% utilized machine would take 5/0.5 = 10 seconds. So theoretically, if you can parallelize this calculation into two equal halves running together on an otherwise unutilized machine, each half is allocated 50% of the CPU utilization. Each takes half the time of the unparallelized calculation running on a 50% utilized machine (which we just calculated to take 10 seconds), i.e., each parallelized half calculation takes 10/2 = 5 seconds, both running simultaneously. So the total time taken is still five seconds, and there is no overall speedup. If you add in the slight factor due to CPU time-slicing overhead, the total time increases beyond the five-second mark, so it is actually slower to parallelize this calculation. This is what we should intuitively expect for any process that already takes up all the CPUs power.

Now what about the multiple CPU case: do we get a benefit here? Well, for a two-CPU machine, the CPU synchronization overhead may be 5% (this is normally an overestimate). In this case, each part of the parallelized application effectively gets a 5% utilized CPU of its own. For the example, the expected times taken are 2.5/0.95 = 2.63 seconds. And since the two threads are running in parallel, this is also the total expected time taken. See Table 13-3.*

Table 13-3. Theoretical Computation Time Depending on Number of CPUs and Non-CPU-Bound Threads

	CPU % Used	CPU % Available	Computation Time
1 CPU, 1 thread	10%	90%	5 seconds
1 CPU, 2 threads serialized	10%/thread	90%/thread	2.5 + 2.5 = 5 seconds
1 CPU, 2 threads parallelized	10%/thread	90%/thread	max(2.5/0.9,2.5/0.9) = 2.8 seconds
2 CPUs, 2 threads parallelized	5%/CPU	95%/CPU	max(2.5/0.95,2.5/0.95) = 2.6 seconds

However, CPU overhead is increased for each additional CPU, since they all have to synchronize with each other. This means that almost another 5% utilization is added to the overhead of each CPU: in fact, Dan Graham of IBM has determined

---

* In the case of the number-crunching calculation, you have the exact same calculation resulting in 2.63 seconds. So again, as you intuitively expect, the two-CPU machine lets the CPU-swamping parallelized calculation take just over half the time of the original unparallelized version.

that the overhead is multiplicative, so that if two CPUs each have a 5% utilization (0.95 × 100% free) from CPU parallelism, then three CPUs each have a 9.75% utilization (0.95 × 0.95 × 100% free), and four CPUs each have a 14.26% utilization (0.95 × 0.95 × 0.95 × 100% free), and so on. See Table 13-4.

Table 13-4. Theoretical Computation Time Depending on Number of CPUs and Threads

	CPU % Used	CPU % Available	Computation Time
1 CPU, 1 thread	0%	100%	100 seconds
2 CPUs, 2 threads parallelized	5%/CPU	95%/CPU	100/0.95/2 = 52.6 seconds
3 CPUs, 3 threads parallelized	9.75%/CPU	90.25%/CPU	100/0.9025/3 = 36.9 seconds
9 CPUs, 9 threads parallelized	34%/CPU	66%/CPU	100/0.66/9 = 16.8 seconds
10 CPUs, 10 threads parallelized	37%/CPU	63%/CPU	100/0.63/10 = 15.9 seconds
19 CPUs, 19 threads parallelized	60.3%/CPU	39.7%/CPU	100/0.397/19 = 13.26 seconds
20 CPUs, 20 threads parallelized	62.3%/CPU	37.7%/CPU	100/0.377/20 = 13.26 seconds
21 CPUs, 21 threads parallelized	64.2%/CPU	35.8%/CPU	100/0.358/21 = 13.30 seconds
30 CPUs, 30 threads parallelized	64.2%/CPU	22.6%/CPU	100/0.226/30 = 14.75 seconds

Clearly, there are diminishing returns from adding CPUs. In fact, at some point, adding CPUs actually makes performance worse. For example, let's suppose our number-crunching application is fully parallelizable to any number of CPUs, and that on a single unutilized CPU it takes 100 seconds. On a two-CPU machine, it takes 100 seconds divided by 2 (the number of CPUs, which is how many parts you can parallelize the calculation by) and then divided by 0.95 (the factor by which the CPU is utilized by the CPU parallelization overheads), giving 52.6 seconds.

For three CPUs, this time is $100/(0.95 \times 0.95 \times 3) = 36.9$ seconds. So far, so good. Now, let's move on to 20 CPUs. This works out as $100/(0.95^{19} \times 20) = 13.26$ seconds. But 21 CPUs takes $100/(0.95^{20} \times 21) = 13.30$ seconds, actually taking more time. In fact, for this particular sequence, 20 CPUs gives the minimum time. Beyond that, the overhead of parallelizing CPUs actually makes things successively worse, and each additional CPU makes the fully parallelized calculation take longer.

In addition, well before the 20th CPU was added, you reach a point where each additional CPU is not at all cost-effective: 6 CPUs gave a value of 21.5 seconds for the calculation, 7 CPUs reduced that by only a couple of seconds to 19.4 seconds. A 10% reduction in time does not justify the cost of an extra CPU.

The general calculation presented here applies to other shared resources too. In a similar way, you can determine the performance effects of adding other additional shared resources to the application and predict whether the advantages will outweigh the disadvantages.

Note that these are all general predictions, useful for estimating the benefits of adding shared resources. The actual tested results can sometimes differ dramatically. For example, parallelizing some searches can provide a tenfold speedup on a single CPU, because the increased variation in starting points of the solution space means that the probability of one of the searches starting much nearer the solution is greatly increased (see "Threaded Problem-Solving Strategies" in Chapter 10). But this is an exception. The cutoff where adding a shared resource gives a useful speedup is usually quite small, so you can mostly assume that a little parallelizing is good, but a lot of parallelizing is too much of a good thing.

All the calculations we made in this section assumed full load-balancing. Each thread (sharer) took exactly the same share of time to complete its task, and thus the total time was that of any one sharer since they all operated simultaneously. In reality, this is unlikely. If the sharers are unbalanced (as they usually are), the sharer that takes the longest to complete its activity is the one limiting the performance of the system. And the less balanced the various sharers are, the worse the performance is. This is extremely important as the application scales across different workloads. An unbalanced workload means that one resource is used far more intensively than others. It also means that all other parallel resources are being underutilized, and that the overused resource is highly likely to be a performance bottleneck in the system.

Data parallelism

If you have a large amount of data that needs to reside on disk, a typical strategy for improving access and searches of the data is to split up the data among many different files (preferably on separate disks). This is known as *partitioning the data*. Partitioning the data provides support for parallel access to the data, which takes advantage of I/O and CPU parallelism.

The are many data-partitioning schemes. Some of the more popular are:

> *Schema partitioning*
>> Separates the data into logically distinct datasets and allocates each dataset to a separate file/disk.

> *Hash partitioning*
>> Places data in multiple files/disks with location based on a hash function.

Range partitioning

Splits data into ranges, and each range is allocated a separate file/disk; for example, a–c in disk1, d–f in disk2, etc.

Expression partitioning

Uses a logical expression to determine the mapping of data to file/disk. Unbalanced partitioning requires refinement of the expression and repartitioning.

Round-robin partitioning

Allocates data to disks sequentially.

Partitioning schemes work best when used with indexes. Indexes also make searches much faster.

Although your design does not need to support a specific partitioning scheme, it should support partitioning in general if it is relevant to your application.

Scaling

The performance characteristics of an application vary with the number of different factors the application can deal with. These variable factors can include the number of users, the amount of data dealt with, the number of objects used by the application, etc. During the design phase, whenever considering performance, you should consider how the performance scales as the load on the application varies. It is usually not possible to predict (or measure) the performance for all possible variations of these factors. But you should select several representative sets of values for the factors, and predict (and measure) performance for these sets. The sets should include factors for when the application:

- Has a light load

- Has a medium load

- Has a heavy load

- Has a varying load predicted to represent normal operating conditions

- Has spiked loads (where the load is mostly "normal" but occasionally spikes to the maximum supported)

- Consistently has the maximum load the application was designed to support

You need to ensure that your scaling conditions include variations in threads, objects and users, and variations in network conditions if appropriate. Measure response times and throughput for the various different scenarios and decide whether any particular situation needs optimizing for throughput of the system as a whole or for response times for individual users.

It is clear that many extra factors need to be taken into account during scaling. The tools you have for profiling scaling behavior are fairly basic: essentially, only graphs of response times or throughput against scaled parameters. It is typical to have a point at which the application starts to have bad scaling behavior: the knee or elbow in the response-time curve. At that point, the application has probably reached some serious resource conflict that requires tuning so that "nice" scaling behavior can be extended further. Clearly, tuning for scaling behavior is likely to be a long process, but you cannot shortcut this process if you want to be certain your application scales.*

Distributed Applications

The essential design points for ensuring good performance of distributed applications are:

- Supporting asynchronous communications

- Decoupling process activities from each other in such a way that no process is forced to wait for others (using queues achieves this)

- Supporting parallelism in the design of the workflows

Determining the bottleneck in a distributed application requires looking at the throughput of every component:

- Client and server processes

- Network transfer rates (peak and average)

- Network interface card throughput

- Router speed, disk I/O

- Middleware/queuing transfer rates

- Database access, update and transaction rates

- Operating-system loads

Tuning any component other than the current bottleneck gives no improvement. Peak performance of each component is rarely achieved. You need to assume average rates of performance from the underlying resource and expect performance based on those average rates.

Distributed applications tend to exaggerate any performance characteristics. So when performance is bad, the application tends to slow significantly more than in

---

* By including timer-based delays in the application code, at least one multiuser application has deliberately slowed response times for low-scaled situations. The artificial delay is reduced or cut out at higher scaling values. The users perceive a system with a similar response time under most loads.

nondistributed applications. The distributed design aspects should emphasize asynchronous and concurrent operations. Typical items to include in the design are:

- Queues
- Asynchronous communications and activities
- Parallelizable activities
- Minimized serialization points
- Balanced workloads across multiple servers
- Redundant servers and automatic switching capabilities
- Activities that can be configured at runtime to run in different locations
- Short transactions

The key to good performance in a distributed application is to minimize the amount of communication necessary. Performance problems tend to be caused by too many messages flying back and forth between distributed components. Bell's rule of networking applies: "Money can buy bandwidth, but latency is forever."*

Unfortunately, communication overhead can be incurred by many different parts of a distributed application. There are some general high-level guidelines:

- Allow the application to be partitioned according to the data and processing power. Any particular task should be able to run in several locations, and the location that provides the best performance should be chosen at runtime. Usually the best location for the task is where the data required for the task is stored, as transferring data tends to be a significant overhead.

- Avoid generating distributed garbage. Distributed garbage collection can be a severe overhead on any distributed application.

- Reduce the costs of keeping data synchronized by minimizing the duplication of data.

- Reduce data-transfer costs by duplicating data. This conflicts directly with the last point, so the two techniques must be balanced to find the optimal data duplication points.

- Cache distributed data wherever possible.

- Use compression to reduce the time taken to transfer large amounts of data.

---

* Thomas E. Bell, "Performance of distributed systems," a paper presented at the ICCM Capacity Management Forum 7, San Francisco, October 1993.

Object Design

My advice for object design is to use interfaces and interface-like patterns through-out the code. Although there are slightly higher runtime costs from using inter-faces, that cost is well outweighed by the benefits of being able to replace one object implementation with another easily. Using interfaces means you can design with the option to replace any class or component with a faster one. Consider also where the design requires comparison by identity or by equality and where these choices can be made at implementation time.

The JDK classes are not all designed with interfaces. Those JDK classes and other third-party classes that do not have interface definitions should be wrapped by your own classes so that their use can be made more generic. (Applications that need to minimize download time, such as applets, may need to avoid the extra overhead that wrapping causes.)

Object creation is one significant place where interfaces fall down, since inter-faces do not support constructor declarations, and constructors cannot return an object of a different class. To handle object creation in a way similar to interfaces, you should use the *factory pattern*. The factory design pattern recommends that object creation be centralized in a particular *factory method*. So rather than calling new Something() when you want to create an instance of the Something class, you call a method such as SomethingFactory.getNewSomething(), which cre-ates and returns a new instance of the Something class. Again, this pattern has performance costs, as there is the overhead of an extra method call for every object creation, but the pattern provides more flexibility when it comes to tuning.

Design for reusable objects: do not unnecessarily throw away objects. The factory design pattern can help, as it supports the recycling of objects. Canonicalize objects where possible (see "Canonicalizing Objects" in Chapter 4, *Object Cre-ation*). Keep in mind that stateless objects can usually be safely shared, so try to move to stateless objects where appropriate.

Using stateless objects is a good way to support changing algorithms easily, by implementing different algorithms in particular types of objects. For example, see "An Efficient Sorting Framework" in Chapter 9, *Sorting*, where different sorting algorithms are implemented in various sorting classes. The resulting objects can be interchanged whenever the sorting algorithm needs to be varied.

Consider whether to optimize objects for update or access. For example, a "statis-tics-calculating" object might update its average and standard deviation each time a value is added to it, thus slowing down updates but making access of those statis-tics lightning-fast. Or, the object could simply store added values and calculate the average and standard deviation each time those statistics are accessed, making the update as fast as possible, but increasing the time for statistics access.

Techniques for Predicting Performance

Predicting performance is the mainstay of performance tuning at the analysis and design stages. Often it is the experience of the designers that steers design one way or another. Knowing why a particular design element has caused bad performance in another project allows the experienced designer to alter the design in just the right way to get good performance.

Some general guidelines can guide the application designer and avoid bad performance. In the following sections we consider some of these guidelines.

Factor in comparative performance of operations

Different types of operations have widely varying execution times. Some design abstractions decouple the type of intercomponent-communication mechanism from any specific implementation. The design allows the intercomponent communication to be based on a local or remote call, which allows components to be placed very flexibly. However, the performance of different types of calls varies hugely and helps define whether some designs can perform fast enough.

Specifically, if local procedure calls have an average time overhead of one unit, a local interprocess call incurs an overhead of about 100 units. On the same scale, a remote procedure call (RPC) on a local area network takes closer to 1000 time units, and an RPC routed across the Internet likely takes over 10,000 time units.

Applying these variations to the design and factoring the number of messages that components need to send to each other may rule out some distributed architectures. Alternatively, the overhead predictions may indicate that a redesign is necessary to reduce the number of intercomponent messages.

Note also that process startup overheads may need to be considered. For example, Common Gateway Interface (CGI) scripts for HTTP servers typically need to be started for every message sent to the server. For this type of design, the time taken to start up a script is significant, and when many scripts are started together, this can slow down the server considerably. Similarly, if your design allows many thread startups within short intervals, you need to determine whether the architecture can handle this, or if it may be a better option to redesign the applications to use thread pools (see "Thread Pools" in Chapter 10).

Consider the relative costs of different types of accesses and updates

Accesses and updates to system memory are always going to be significantly faster than accesses and updates to other memory media. For example, reads from a local disk can be a thousand times slower than memory access, and disk writes are typically half as fast as disk reads. Random access of disks is significantly slower than sequential access.

Recognizing these variations may steer your design to alternatives you might otherwise not have considered. For example, one application server that supports a shared persistent cache redesigned the persistent cache update mechanism to take account of these different update times (GemStone application server, *http://www.gemstone.com*). The original architecture performed (transactional) updates to objects by writing the changes to the objects on the disk, which required random disk access and updates. The modified architecture wrote all changes to shared memory as well as to a sequential journaling log file (for crash recovery). Another asynchronous process handled flushing the changes from shared memory to the objects stored on disk. Because disk navigation to the various objects was significant, this change in architecture improved performance by completely removing that bottleneck from the transaction.

Use simulations and benchmarks

Ideally, you have a detailed simulation of your application that allows you to predict the performance under any set of conditions. More usually, you have a vague simulation that has some characteristics similar to your intended application. It is important to keep striving for the full detailed simulation to be able to predict the performance of the application. But since your resources are limited, you need to project measurements to come as close as possible to your target application.

You should try to include loads and delays in your simulation that come close to the expected load of the application. Try to acquire the resources your finished application will use, even if those resources are not used in the simulation. For example, spawn as many threads as you expect the application to use, even if the threads do little more than sleep restlessly.*

Graphing the results from increasing various application-specific parameters allows you to predict the performance of the application under a variety of conditions. It is worth checking vendor or standard benchmarks if you need some really basic statistics, but bear in mind that those benchmarks seldom have much relevance to a particular application.

Consider the total work done and the design overhead

Try stripping your design to the bare essentials or going back to the specification. Consider how to create a special-purpose implementation that handles the specification for a specific set of inputs. This can give you an estimate of the actual work

---

* Sleeping restlessly is calling `Thread.sleep()` in a loop, with the sleep time set to some value that requires many loop iterations before the loop terminates. Other activities can be run intermittently in the loop to simulate work.

your application will do. Now consider your design and look at the overheads added by the design for each piece of functionality. This provides a good way to focus on the overheads and determine if they are excessive.

Focus on shared resources

Shared resources almost always cause performance problems if they have not been designed to optimize performance. Ensure that any simulation correctly simulates the sharing of resources, and use prediction analyses such as those in the section "Parallelism" earlier in this chapter to predict the behavior of multiple objects using shared resources.

Predict the effects of parallelism

Consider what happens when your design is spread over multiple threads, processes, CPUs, machines, etc. This analysis can be quite difficult without a simulation and test bed, but it can help to identify whether the design limits the use of parallelism.

Assess the costs of data conversions

Many applications convert data between different types (e.g., between strings and numbers). From your design, you should be able to determine the frequency and types of data conversions, and it is fairly simple to create small tests that determine the costs of the particular conversions you are using. Don't forget to include any concurrency or use of shared resources in the tests. Remember that external transfer of objects or data normally includes some data conversions. The cost of data conversion may be significant enough to direct you to alter your design.

Determine whether batch processing is faster

Some repeated tasks can be processed as a batch instead of one at a time. Batch processing can take advantage of a number of efficiencies, such as accessing and creating some objects just once, eliminating some tests for shared resources, processing tasks in optimal order, avoiding repeated searches, etc.

If any particular set of tasks could be processed in batch mode, consider the effect this would have on your application and how much faster the processing could be. The simplest conceptual example is that of adding characters one by one to a `StringBuffer`, as opposed to using a `char` array to add all the characters together. Adding the characters using a `char` array is much faster for any significant number of characters.

Tuning After Deployment

Tuning does not necessarily end at the development stage. For many applications such as agent applications, services, servlets and servers, multiuser applications, enterprise systems, etc., there needs to be constant monitoring of the application performance after deployment to ensure that no degradation takes place. In this section, I discuss tuning the deployed application. This is mainly relevant to enterprise systems that are being administered. Shrink-wrapped or similar software is normally tuned the same way as before deployment, using standard profiling tools.

Monitoring the application is the primary tuning activity after deployment. The application should be built with hooks that enable tools to connect to it and gather statistics and response times. The application should be constantly monitored, and all performance logs retained. Monitoring should record as many parameters as possible throughout the system, though clearly you want to avoid monitoring so much that the performance of the running application is compromised by a significant amount. Of course, almost any act of measuring a system affects performance. But the advantage of having performance logs normally pays off enormously, and a few percent decrease in performance should be acceptable.

Individual records in the performance logs should include at least the following six categories:

*   Time (including offset time from a reference server)
*   User identifier
*   Transaction identifier
*   Application name, type, class, or group
*   Software component or subsystem
*   Hardware resource

A standard set of performance logs should be used to give a background system measurement and kept as a reference set of logs. Other logs can be compared against that standard. Periodically, the standard should be regenerated, as most enterprise applications change their performance characteristics over time. Ideally, the standard logs can be automatically compared against the current logs, and any significant change in behavior is automatically identified and causes an alert to be sent to the administrators. Trends away from the standard should also trigger a notification; sometimes performance degrades slowly but consistently because of a gradually depleting resource.

Administrators should note every single change to the system, every patch, every upgrade, every configuration change, etc. These changes are the source of most performance problems in production. Patches are cheaper short-term fixes than upgrades, but they usually add to the complexity of the application and increase maintenance costs. Upgrades and rereleases are more expensive in the short term, but cheaper overall.

Administrators should listen to the application users. Users are the most sensitive barometer of application performance. However, you should double-check users' assertions. A user may be wrong, or might have hit a known system problem or temporary administrative shutdown. Measure the performance yourself. Repeat the measurements several times and take averages and variations. Ensure that caching effects do not skew measurements of a reported problem.

When looking for reasons why performance may have changed, consider any recent changes such as an increase in the number of users, other applications added to system, code changes on the client or server, hardware changes, etc. In addition to user response time measurements, look at where the distributed code is executing, what volumes of data are being used, and where the code is spending most of its time.

Many factors can easily give misleading or temporarily different measurements to the application. Distributed garbage collection may have cut in, system clocks may become unsynchronized, background processes may be triggered, and relative processor power may change, causing obscure effects. Consider if anyone else is using the processors, and if so, what they are doing and why.

You need to differentiate between:

- Occasional sudden slowness, e.g., from background processes starting up
- General slowness, perhaps reflecting that the application was not tuned for the current load, or that the systems or networks are saturated
- A sudden slowdown that continues, often the result of a change to the system

Each of these characteristic changes in performance indicate a different set of problems.

More Factors That Affect Performance

The following sections discuss some aspects of the application that may not immediately strike you as part of the performance of the application. But they do affect the user's perception of the application performance, and so are relevant.

User Interface Usability

The application's user interface has a significant effect on the user's perception of performance. The time required to navigate through the user interface to execute some functionality is seen by the user as part of the application's response time. If window and menu navigation is difficult, performance is seen to be bad (and actually, it is bad).

The user interface should support the natural flow of the user's activity; otherwise, you are forcing the user to perform less efficiently. Improving only the navigability of the user interface, even with no other changes to the application, improves the perceived performance of an application.

Training

Training users to use the application is also a performance issue. Without proper training, users may not use the application efficiently, and will then compare the application unfavorably with another application they are comfortable with. Since they are comparing similar functionality, the user immediately focuses on the differences. The main difference, of course, is the perceived performance.

The user never thinks he is untrained. He simply feels that executing some function in your application takes forever, as he stumbles through menu options trying to find what he wants, fills in forms incorrectly, etc. The result is a perception of bad performance.

Note that making help desks available is an essential part of the training program. Training is seldom so thorough that all parts of the application are covered in enough detail, and it is also common for people to forget some of their training. A help desk keeps the users from getting lost and giving up on the most efficient route to solve their tasks.

Server Downtime

If people can't start a piece of software, they can get frustrated, but they don't normally view this as bad performance. Most people would instead get annoyed at the quality of the software. But when servers are not running, this can be perceived differently. Sometimes a server that isn't running is perceived as bad-quality software, but sometimes it is seen as poor performance. If the server stops responding in the middle of processing, this is invariably seen as slow performance. Consider your own response to a stalled download from an HTTP server.

Avoiding server downtime is a robustness issue as well as a performance issue. Servers should be designed to avoid unnecessary downtime and minimize necessary downtime. One issue when running servers is altering their configuration and patching them. If you need to stop a server from running while you make changes, this affects its perceived performance. You must signal it to stop accepting requests and either wait for current requests to terminate or forcibly terminate all requests; either way, this causes interruptions in service to the clients.*

It is possible to design servers that can be reconfigured and patched with no downtime. Designing for reconfiguration on the fly is easier. In this case, you typically have a configuration file. One common solution is for the server to periodically test the timestamp of the configuration file and reread it if the timestamp changes. This solution also provides good security (as presumably, the configuration file can be changed only by authorized persons). Another solution is for the server to recognize and accept a particular signal as a sign to reset its configuration. In most servers using this solution, the signal is an operating-system signal that is trapped. However, Java does not support operating-system signal handling, so if you steer down this path, you need either to install operating-system handlers yourself (using the Java native interface) or use another communication mechanism, such as sockets. If you do use sockets, you need to consider security aspects; you don't want unauthorized persons triggering a server reconfiguration.

Patching a running server is more complex. You need to provide some level of indirection on how the request-processing classes (and all the classes they depend on) are loaded. The most basic solution is to use the configuration file to list names of all classes. Then the server must be built using `Class.forName()` to access and create any classes and instances. This way, providing a new version requires only changing the class names in the configuration (in an atomic way to avoid corruption).

A more sophisticated solution is to use different `ClassLoaders`. Note that any particular class in Java is identified by its package and class name, and by its `ClassLoader`. It is possible to have classes with the same package and class names loaded multiple times in the same VM (whether the implementation is the same or different for those classes) using multiple `ClassLoader` instances. This is easiest in Java 1.2, where there is a proliferation of `ClassLoaders`. A useful classloader for this type of runtime patching is the `URLClassLoader`:

```
//This method gets a new implementation of a RequestProcessor
//every time.
public RequestProcessor getNewRequestProcessor()
{
  URL[] urls = {new URL(...)};
  Class c = RequestServerMain.class;
  ClassLoader cl = c.getClassLoader();
  URLClassLoader xtra_cl = new URLClassLoader(urls , cl);
  c = xtra_cl.loadClass("RequestProcessor");
```

---

* Load-balancing products often provide features that allow server maintenance with minimum downtime.

```
    RequestProcessor proc = (RequestProcessor) c.newInstance();
    return proc;
}

public void processRequest(Request aRequest, RequestProcessor proc)
{
  //Signal to get a new implementation of a request processor
  //by passing a null value in the <proc> variable
  if (proc == null)
    proc = getNewRequestProcessor();
  proc.processRequest(aRequest);
  ...
}
```

In most cases, you will find that a customized classloader is the best solution, especially because you can include consistency checking within that classloader, as well as ensuring atomicity of changes. You can even provide unloading and loading of classes, which is probably the most sophisticated solution available for runtime patching.

Performance Checklist

- Consider performance at each stage of the development cycle.
  - Plan for tuning phases.
  - Leave code tuning until after the code is functional and debugged.
  - Consider how a particular performance change will affect other parts of the application.
  - Identify performance limitations.
  - Eliminate performance conflicts.
  - Consider how the performance scales as the application scales.
  - Consider how the performance scales as the application load varies.
- Determine the general characteristics of the application in the analysis and design phases.
  - Minimize the features in the requirements.
  - Specify performance boundaries and goals.
  - Consider the numbers, sizes, and sources of objects, data, and other parameters of the application.
  - Create an abstract model of the application to identify any performance problems.
  - Design applets to engage the user as soon as possible.

— Identify and focus on the performance costs of shared resources.

— Target decoupling, indirection, abstraction, and extra layers in the design.

— Predict the performance of design elements that block, copy, queue, or distribute.

— Consider alternative designs that bypass or reduce high performance costs.

— Avoid transactions where possible.

— Minimize transaction time where transactions are necessary.

— Lock only where the design absolutely requires it.

— Design parallelism into the application wherever possible. Identify what cannot be parallelized.

— Watch out for too much parallelism. There are diminishing returns from parallelism overheads.

— Balance workloads. Unbalanced parallel activities may limit the performance of the system.

— Split up the data among many different files (preferably on separate disks).

— Support asynchronous communications.

— Decouple activities so that no activity is unnecessarily blocked by another activity.

— Minimize points where parallel activities are forced to converge.

— Design for redundant servers and automatic switching capabilities.

— Consider using batch processing.

— Design more flexible method entry points to your classes, to provide greater performance flexibility when developing reusable code.

• Partition distributed applications according to the data and processing power requirements of components.

— Minimize the communication between distributed components.

— Avoid generating distributed garbage.

— Reduce transfer costs by duplicating data.

— Cache distributed data wherever possible.

— Minimize the synchronization requirements of duplicated data.

— Use compression to reduce transfer time.

- Design objects so that they can be easily replaced by a faster implementation.
  - Use interfaces and interface-like patterns (e.g., the factory pattern).
  - Design for reusable objects.
  - Use stateless objects.
  - Consider whether to optimize objects for update or for access.
  - Minimize data conversions.
  - Minimize the number and size of developed classes for applications that need to minimize download time.
- Constantly monitor the running application.
  - Retain performance logs. Choose one set as your comparison standard.
  - Monitor as many parameters as possible throughout the system.
  - Note every single change to the system. Changes are the most likely cause of performance variations.
  - Listen to the application users, but double-check any reported problems.
  - Ensure that caching effects do not skew the measurements of a reported problem.
- Make the user interface seem fast.
- Train users to use the application efficiently.
- Minimize server-maintenance downtime.

14

Underlying Operating System and Network Improvements

If you control the operating system and hardware where the application will be deployed, there are a number of changes you can make to improve performance. Some changes are generic and affect most applications, while some are application-specific. This chapter applies to most server systems running Java applications, including servlets, where you usually specify (or have specified to you) the underlying system, and where you have some control over tuning the system. Client and standalone Java programs are likely to benefit from this chapter only if you have some degree of control over the target system, but some tips in the chapter apply to all Java programs.

I don't cover operating-system and hardware tuning in any great detail, though I give basic tips on monitoring the system. More detailed information on Unix systems can be obtained from the excellent book *System Performance Tuning* by Mike Loukides (O'Reilly). Another more specific book on Sun's Solaris operating system is *Sun Performance and Tuning*, by Adrian Cockcroft and Richard Pettit (Prentice Hall). A couple of relevant Windows systems books are *Windows NT Performance Monitoring, Benchmarking, and Tuning*, by Mark T. Edmead and Paul Hinsberg (New Riders) and *Windows NT Applications: Measuring and Optimizing Performance*, by Paul Hinsberg (MacMillan Technical Publishing).

It is usually best to target the operating system and hardware as a last tuning choice. Tuning the application itself generally provides far more significant speed-ups than tuning the systems on which the application is running. Application tuning also tends to be easier (though buying more powerful hardware components is easier still and a valid choice for tuning). However, application and system tuning are actually complementary activities, so you can get speedups from tuning both the system and the application if you have the skills and resources.

Here are some general tips that apply for tuning systems:

- Constantly monitor the entire system with any monitoring tools available, and keep monitoring records. This allows you to get a background usage pattern and also lets you compare the current situation with situations previously considered stable.

- You should run offline work in off hours only. This ensures that there is no extra load on the system when the users are executing online tasks, and enhances performance of both online and offline activities.

- If you need to run extra tasks during the day, try to slot them into normal low user-activity patterns. Office activity usually peaks at 9:00 A.M. and 2:30 P.M., and has a low between noon and 1:00 P.M. or at shift changeovers. You should be able to determine the user activity cycles appropriate to your system by examining the results of normal monitoring. The reduced conflict for system resources during periods of low activity improves performance.

- You should specify timeouts for all processes under the control of your application (and others on the system, if possible) and terminate processes that have passed their timeout value.

- Apply any partitioning available from the system to allocate determinate resources to your application. For example, you can specify disk partitions, memory segments, and even CPUs to be allocated to particular processes.

Hard Disks

In most cases, applications can be tuned so that disk I/O does not cause any serious performance problems. But if, after application tuning, you find that disk I/O is still causing a performance problem, your best bet may be to upgrade the system disks. Identifying whether the system has a problem with disk utilization is the first step. Each system provides its own tools to identify disk usage (Windows has a performance monitor, Unix has the *sar*, *vmstat*, and *iostat* utilities). At minimum, you need to identify whether paging is an issue (look at disk-scan rates), and assess the overall utilization of your disks (e.g., performance monitor on Windows, output from `iostat -D` on Unix). It may be that the system has a problem independent of your application (e.g., unbalanced disks), and correcting this problem may resolve the performance issue.

If the disk analysis does not identify an obvious system problem that is causing the I/O overhead, you could try making a disk upgrade or a reconfiguration. This type of tuning can consist of any of the following:

- Upgrading to faster disks

- Adding more swap space to handle larger buffers

- Changing the disks to be striped (where files are striped across several disks, thus providing parallel I/O, e.g., with a RAID system)

- Running the data on raw partitions when this is shown to be faster

- Distributing simultaneously accessed files across multiple disks to gain parallel I/O

- Using memory-mapped disks or files (see the section "Cached Filesystems (RAM Disks, tmpfs, cachefs)" later in this chapter).

If you have applications that run on many systems and you do not know the specification of the target system, bear in mind that you can never be sure that any particular disk is local to the user who is using the application. There is a significant possibility that the disk being used by the application is a network-mounted disk. This doubles the variability in response times and throughput. The weakest link, whether it is the network or the disk, is the limiting factor in this case. And this weakest link will probably not even be constant. A network disk is a shared resource, as is the network itself, so performance is hugely and unpredictably affected by other users and network load.

Disk I/O

Do not underestimate the impact of disk writes on the system as a whole. For example, all database vendors strongly recommend that the system swap files* be placed on a separate disk from their databases. The impact of not doing so can decrease database throughput (and system activity) by an order of magnitude. This performance decrease comes from not splitting the I/O of two disk-intensive applications (in this case, OS paging and database I/O).

Identifying that there is an I/O problem is usually fairly easy. The most basic symptom is that things take longer than expected, while at the same time the CPU is not at all heavily worked. The disk-monitoring utilities will also tell you that there is a lot of work being done to the disks. At the system level, you should determine the average and peak requirements on the disks. Your disks will have some statistics that are supplied by the vendor, including:

- The average and peak transfer rates, normally in megabytes (MB) per second, e.g., 5MB/sec. From this, you can calculate how long an 8K page takes to be transferred from disk; for example, 5MB/sec is about 5K/ms, so an 8K page takes just under 2 ms to transfer.

- Average seek time, normally in milliseconds (ms), e.g., 10 ms. This is the time required for the disk head to move radially to the correct location on the disk.

---

* The disk files for the virtual memory of the operating system; see the later section "RAM."

- Rotational speed, normally in revolutions per minute (rpm), e.g., 7200 rpm. From this, you can calculate the average rotational delay in moving the disk under the disk-head reader, i.e., the time taken for half a revolution. For example, for 7200 rpm, one revolution takes 60,000 ms (60 seconds) divided by 7200 rpm, which is about 8.3 ms. So half a revolution takes just over 4 ms, which is consequently the average rotational delay.

This list allows you to calculate the actual time it takes to load a random 8K page from the disk, this being seek time + rotational delay + transfer time. Using the examples given in the list, you have 10 + 4 + 2 = 16ms to load a random 8K page (almost an order of magnitude slower than the raw disk throughput). This calculation gives you a worst-case scenario for the disk-transfer rates for your application, allowing you to determine if the system is up to the required performance. Note that if you are reading data stored sequentially on disk (as when reading a large file), the seek time and rotational delay are incurred less than once per 8K page loaded. Basically, these two times are incurred only at the beginning of opening the file and whenever the file is fragmented. But this calculation is confounded by other processes also executing I/O to the disk at the same time. These overheads are some of the reasons why swap and other intensive I/O files should not be put on the same disk.

One mechanism for speeding up disk I/O is to stripe disks. Disk striping allows data from a particular file to be spread over several disks. Striping allows reads and writes to be performed in parallel across the disks without requiring any application changes. This can speed up disk I/O quite effectively. However, be aware that the seek and rotational overheads previously listed still apply, and if you are making many small random reads, there may be no performance gain from striping disks.

Finally, note again that using remote disks affects I/O performance very badly. You should not be using remote disks mounted from the network with any I/O-intensive operations if you need good performance.

Clustering Files

Reading many files sequentially is faster if the files are clustered together on the disk, allowing the disk-head reader to flow from one file to the next. This clustering is best done in conjunction with defragmenting the disks. The overheads in finding the location of a file on the disk (detailed in the previous section) are also minimized for sequential reads if the files are clustered.

If you cannot specify clustering files at the disk level, you can still provide similar functionality by putting all the files together into one large file (as is done with the ZIP filesystem). This is fine if all the files are read-only files or if there is just one file that is writeable (you place that at the end). However, when there is more than one writeable file, you need to manage the location of the internal files in your system as one or more grow. This becomes a problem, and is not usually worth the effort. (If the files have a known bounded size, you can pad the files internally, thus regaining the single file efficiency.)

Cached Filesystems (RAM Disks, tmpfs, cachefs)

Most operating systems provide the ability to map a filesystem into the system memory. This ability can speed up reads and writes to certain files in which you control your target environment. Typically, this technique has been used to speed up the reading and writing of temporary files. For example, some compilers (of languages in general, not specifically Java) generate many temporary files during compilation. If these files are created and written directly to the system memory, the speed of compilation is greatly increased. Similarly, if you have a set of external files that are needed by your application, it is possible to map these directly into the system memory, thus allowing their reads and writes to be speeded up greatly.

But note that these types of filesystems are not persistent. In the same way the system memory of the machine gets cleared when it is rebooted, so these filesystems are removed on reboot. If the system crashes, anything in a memory-mapped filesystem is lost. For this reason, these types of filesystems are usually suitable only for temporary files or read-only versions of disk-based files (such as mapping a CD-ROM into a memory resident filesystem).

Remember that you do not have the same degree of fine control over these filesystems that you have over your application. A memory-mapped filesystem does not use memory resources as efficiently as working directly from your application. If you have direct control over the files you are reading and writing, it is usually better to optimize this within your application rather than outside it. A memory-mapped filesystem takes space directly from system memory. You should consider whether it would be better to let your application grow in memory instead of letting the filesystem take up that system memory. For multiuser applications, it is usually more efficient for the system to map shared files directly into memory, as a particular file then takes up just one memory location rather than being duplicated in each process.

The actual creation of memory-mapped filesystems is completely system-dependent, and there is no guarantee that it is available on any particular system (though most modern operating systems do support this feature). On Unix systems, the administrator needs to look at the documentation of the mount command and its subsections on cachefs and tmpfs. Under Windows, you should find details by looking at the documentation to set up a RAM disk: this is a portion of memory mapped to a logical disk drive.

In a similar way, there are products available that precache shared libraries (DLLs) and even executables in memory. This usually means only that an application starts quicker or loads the shared library quicker, and so may not be much help in speeding up a running system (for example, Norton SpeedStart caches DLLs and device drivers in memory on Windows systems).

But you can apply the technique of memory-mapping filesystems directly and quite usefully for applications in which processes are frequently started. Copy the Java distribution and all class files (all JDK, application, and third-party class files) onto a memory-mapped filesystem and ensure that all executions and classloads take place from that filesystem. Since everything (executables, shared libraries, class files, resources, etc.) is already in memory, the startup time is much faster. Because it is only the startup (and classloading) time that is affected, this technique is only a small boost for applications that are not frequently starting processes, but can be usefully applied if startup time is a problem.

Disk Fragmentation

When files are stored on disk, the bytes in the files are not necessarily stored contiguously: their storage depends on file size and contiguous space available on the disk. This noncontiguous disk storage is called *fragmentation*. Any particular file may have some chunks in one place, and a pointer to the next chunk that can be quite a distance away on the disk.

Hard disks tend to get fragmented over time. This fragmentation delays both reads from files (including loading applications into computer memory on startup) and writes to files. This delay occurs because the disk header must wind on to the next chunk with each fragmentation, and this takes time.

For optimum performance on any system, it is a good idea to periodically defragment the disks. This reunites those files that have been split up, so that the disk heads do not spend so much time searching for data once the file-header locations have been identified, thus speeding up data access. Defragmenting may not be effective on all systems, however.

Disk Sweet Spots

Most disks have a location from which data is transferred faster than from other locations. Usually, the closer the data is to the outside edge of the disk, the faster it can be read from the disk. Most hard disks rotate at constant angular speed. This means that the linear speed of the disk under a point is faster the farther away the point is from the center of the disk. Thus, data at the edge of the disk can be read from (and written to) at the fastest possible rate commensurate with the maximum density of data storable on disk.

This location with faster transfer rates is usually termed the *disk sweet spot*. Some (commercial) utilities provide mapped access to the underlying disk and allow you to reorganize files to optimize access. On most server systems, the administrator has control over how logical partitions of the disk apply to the physical layout, and how to position files to the disk sweet spots. Experts for high-performance database systems sometimes try to position the index tables of the database as close as possible to the disk sweet spot. These tables consist of relatively small amounts of data that affect the performance of the system in a disproportionately large way, so that any speed improvement in manipulating these tables is significant.

Note that some of the latest operating systems are beginning to include "awareness" of disk sweet spots, and attempt to move executables to sweet spots when defragmenting the disk. You may need to ensure the defragmentation procedure does not disrupt your own use of the disk sweet spot.

CPU

Java provides a virtual machine runtime system that is just that: an abstraction of a CPU that runs in software. These virtual machines run on a real CPU, and in this section I discuss the performance characteristics of those real CPUs.

CPU Load

The CPU and many other parts of the system can be monitored using system-level utilities. On Windows, the task manager and performance monitor can be used for monitoring. On Unix, a performance monitor (such as *perfmeter*) is usually available, as well as utilities such as *vmstat*. Two aspects of the CPU are worth watching as primary performance points. These are the *CPU utilization* (usually expressed in percentage terms) and the *runnable queue* of processes and threads (often called the load or the task queue). The first indicator is simply the percentage of the CPU (or CPUs) being used by all the various threads. If this is up to 100% for significant periods of time, you may have a problem. On the other hand, if it isn't, the CPU is underutilized, but that is usually preferable. Low CPU usage can indicate that your application may be blocked for significant periods on disk or network I/O. High CPU usage can indicate thrashing (lack of RAM) or CPU contention (indicating that you need to tune the code and reduce the number of instructions being processed to reduce the impact on the CPU).

A reasonable target is 75% CPU utilization. This means that the system is being worked towards its optimum, but that you have left some slack for spikes due to other system or application requirements. However, note that if more than 50% of the CPU is used by system processes (i.e., administrative and operating-system processes), your CPU is probably underpowered. This can be identified by looking at the load of the system over some period when you are not running any applications.

The second performance indicator, the runnable queue, indicates the average number of processes or threads waiting to be scheduled for the CPU by the operating system. They are runnable processes, but the CPU has no time to run them and is keeping them waiting for some significant amount of time. As soon as the run queue goes above zero, the system may display contention for resources, but there is usually some value above zero that still gives acceptable performance for any particular system. You need to determine what that value is in order to use this statistic as a useful warning indicator. A simplistic way to do this is to create a short program that repeatedly does some simple activity. You can then time each run of that activity. You can run copies of this process one after the other so that more and more copies are simultaneously running. Keep increasing the number of copies being run until the run queue starts increasing. By watching the times recorded for the activity, you can graph that time against the run queue. This should give you some indication of when the runnable queue becomes too large for useful responses on your system, and you can then set system threshold monitors to watch for that level and alert the administrator if the threshold is exceeded. (One guideline from Adrian Cockcroft is that performance starts to degrade if the run queue grows bigger than four times the number of CPUs. See Chapter 15, *Further Resources.*)

If you can upgrade the CPU of the target environment, doubling the CPU speed is usually better than doubling the number of CPUs. And remember that parallelism in an application doesn't necessarily need multiple CPUs. If I/O is significant, the CPU will have plenty of time for many threads.

Process Priorities

The operating system also has the ability to prioritize the processes in terms of providing CPU time by allocating *process priority levels.* CPU priorities provide a way to throttle high-demand CPU processes, thus giving other processes a greater share of the CPU. If you find there are other processes that need to run on the same machine, but it wouldn't matter if they were run more slowly, you can give your application processes a (much) higher priority than those other processes, thus allowing your application the lion's share of CPU time on a congested system. This is worth keeping in mind. If your application consists of multiple processes, you should also consider the possibility of giving your various processes different levels of priority.

Being tempted to adjust the priority levels of processes, however, is often a sign that the CPU is underpowered for the tasks you have given it.

RAM

Maintaining watch directly on the system memory (RAM) is not usually that helpful in identifying performance problems. A better indication that memory might be affecting performance can be gained by watching for paging of data from memory to the swap files. To clarify the term *paging*: most current operating systems have a virtual memory that is made up of the actual (real) system memory using RAM chips, and one or more swap files on the system disks. Processes that are currently running are operating in real memory. The operating system can take pages from any of the processes currently in real memory, and swap them out to disk. This is known as paging. Paging leaves free space in real memory to allocate to other processes that need to bring in a page from disk.*

Obviously, if all the processes currently running can fit into the real memory, there is no need for the system to page out any pages. However, if there are too many processes to fit into real memory, paging allows the system to free up system memory to run further processes. Paging affects system performance in many ways. One obvious way is that if a process has had some pages moved to disk and the process becomes runnable, the operating system has to pull back the pages from the disk before that process can be run. This leads to delays in performance. In addition, both the CPU and the disk I/O subsystem spend time doing the paging, reducing available processing power and increasing the load on the disks. This cascading effect involving both the CPU and I/O can degrade the performance of the whole system in such a way that it may be difficult to even recognize that the paging is the problem. The extreme version of too much paging is *thrashing*, in which the system is spending so much time moving pages around that it fails to perform any other significant work. (Beyond this, you would be likely to have a system crash.)

As with runnable queues (see the previous section "CPU"), a little paging of the system does not affect performance enough to cause concern. In fact some paging can be considered good. It indicates that the system's memory resources are being fully used. But at the point where paging becomes a significant overhead, the system is overloaded.

Monitoring paging is relatively easy. On Unix, the utilities *vmstat* and *iostat* provide details as to the level of paging, disk activity, and memory levels. On Windows, the

---

* The term *swapping* refers to moving entire processes between main memory and the swap file. Most modern operating systems no longer swap processes; instead, they swap pages from processes, thus the term "paging."

performance monitor has categories to show these details, as well as being able to monitor the system swap files.

If there is more paging than is optimal, the system's RAM is insufficient or processes are too big. To improve this situation, you need to reduce the memory being used by reducing the number of processes or the memory utilization of some processes. Alternatively, you can add RAM. Assuming that it is your application that is causing the paging (otherwise, either the system needs an upgrade, or someone else's processes may also have to be tuned), you need to reduce the memory resources you are using. Chapter 4, *Object Creation*, provides useful recommendations for improving application-memory usage.

When the problem is caused by a combination of your application and others, you can partially address the situation by using process priorities (see the previous section "CPU"). The equivalent to priority levels for memory usage is an all-or-nothing option, where you can lock a process in memory. This option is not available on all systems and is more often applied to shared memory rather than to processes, but nevertheless it is useful to know. If this option is applied, the process is locked into real memory and is not paged out at all. You need to be aware that using this option reduces the amount of RAM available to all other processes, which can make the overall system performance worse. Any deterioration in system performance is likely to occur at heavy system loads, so make sure you extrapolate the effect of reducing the system memory in this way.

Network I/O

At the network level, many things can affect performance. The *bandwidth* (the amount of data that can be carried by the network) tends to be the first culprit checked. Assuming you have determined that bad performance is attributable to the network component of an application, there are more likely causes for the poor performance than the network bandwidth. The most likely cause of bad network performance is the application itself and how it is handling distributed data and functionality. I consider distributed-application tuning in several chapters (notably Chapter 12, *Distributed Computing*), but this section provides lower-level information to assist you in tuning your application, and also considers nonapplication causes of bad performance.

The overall speed of a particular network connection is limited by the slowest link in the connection chain and the length of the chain. Identifying the slowest link is difficult and may not even be consistent: it can vary at different times of the day or for different communication paths. A network communication path can lead from an application, through a TCP/IP stack (which adds various layers of headers, possibly encrypting and compressing data as well), then through the hardware interface, through a modem, over a phone line, through another modem, over to a service provider's router, through many heavily congested data lines of various carrying capacities and multiple routers with differing maximum throughputs and configurations, to a machine at the other end with its own hardware interface, TCP/IP stack, and application. A typical web download route is just like this. In addition, there are dropped packets, acknowledgments, retries, bus contention, and so on.

Because there are so many possible causes of bad network performance that are external to an application, one option you can consider including in an application is a network speed-testing facility that reports to the user. This should test the speed of data transfer from the machine to various destinations: to itself, to another machine on the local network, to the Internet service provider, to the target server across the network, and to any other destinations appropriate. This type of diagnostic report can tell your users that they are obtaining bad performance from something other than your application. If you feel that the performance of your application is limited by the actual network communication speed, and not by other (application) factors, this facility will report the maximum possible speeds to your users (and put the blame for poor network performance outside your application, where it belongs).

Latency

Latency is different from the load-carrying capacity (bandwidth) of a network. The bandwidth refers to how much data can be sent down the communication channel for a given period of time (e.g., 64 kilobits per second) and is limited by the link in the communication chain that has the lowest bandwidth. The *latency* is the amount of time a particular data packet takes to get from one end of the communication channel to the other. Bandwidth tells you the limits within which your application can operate before the performance becomes affected by the volume of data being transmitted. Latency often affects the user's view of the performance even when bandwidth isn't a problem. For example, on a LAN, the latency might be 10 milliseconds. In this case, you can ignore latency considerations unless your application is making a large number of transmissions. If your application *is* making a large number of transmissions, you need to tune the application to reduce the number of transmissions being made. (That 10-ms overhead added to every transmission can add up if you just ignore it and treat the application as if it were not distributed.)

In most cases, especially Internet traffic, latency is an important concern. You can determine the basic round trip time for data packets from any two machines using the *ping* utility.* This utility provides a measure of the time it takes a packet of data to reach another machine and be returned. However, the time measure is for a basic underlying protocol packet (ICMP packet) to travel between the machines. If the communication channel is congested and the overlying protocol requires retransmissions (often the case for Internet traffic), one transmission at the application level can actually be equivalent to many round trips.

If, for instance, the round trip time is 400 ms (not unusual for an Internet link), this is the basic overhead time for any request sent to a server and the reply to return, without even adding any processing time for the request. If you are using TCP/IP and retransmissions are needed because some packets are dropped (TCP automatically handles this as needed), each retransmission adds another 400 ms to the request response time. If the application is conversational, requiring many data transmissions to be sent back and forth before the request is satisfied, each intermediate transmission adds a minimum of 400 ms of network delay, again without considering TCP retransmissions. The time can easily add up if you are not careful.

It is important to be aware of these limitations. It is often possible to tune the application to minimize the number of transfers being made by packaging data together, caching, and redesigning distributed-application protocol to aim for a less conversational mode of operation. At the network level, you need to monitor the transmission statistics (using the *ping* and *netstat* utilities and packet sniffers) and consider tuning any network parameters that you have access to in order to reduce retransmissions.

TCP/IP Stacks

The TCP/IP stack is the section of code that is responsible for translating each application-level network request (send, receive, connect, etc.) through the transport layers down to the wire and back up to the application at the other end of the connection. Because the stacks are usually delivered with the operating system and performance-tested before delivery (since a slow network connection on an otherwise fast machine and fast network is pretty obvious), it is unlikely that the TCP/IP stack itself is a performance problem.

---

* *ping* may not always give a good measure of the round trip time because ICMP has a low priority in some routers.

NOTE   Some older versions of Windows TCP/IP stacks, both those deliv-
           ered with the OS and others, had performance problems, as did
           some versions of TCP/IP stacks on the Macintosh OS (up to and
           including System 7.1). Stack performance can be difficult to trace.
           Because the TCP/IP stack is causing a performance problem, it
           affects all network applications running on that machine. In the past
           I have seen isolated machines on a lightly loaded network with an
           unexpectedly low transfer speed for FTP transfers compared to
           other machines on the same network. Once you suspect the TCP/IP
           stack, you need to probe the speed of the stack. Testing the loop-
           back address (127.0.0.0) may be a good starting point, though this
           address may be optimized by the stack. The easiest way to avoid the
           problem is to ensure you are using recent versions of TCP/IP stacks.

In addition to the stack itself, there are several parameters that are tuneable in the
stacks. Most of these parameters deal with transmission details beyond the scope of
this book. One parameter worth mentioning is the maximum packet size. When
your application sends data, the underlying protocol breaks the data down into
packets that are transmitted. There is an optimal size for packets transmitted over
a particular communication channel, and the packet size actually used by the stack
is a compromise. Smaller-size packets are less likely to be dropped, but they introduce more overhead, as data probably has to be broken up into more packets with
more header overhead.

If your communication takes place over a particular set of endpoints, you may
want to alter the packet sizes. For a LAN segment with no router involved, the size
of packets can be big (e.g., 8KB). For a LAN with routers, you probably want to set
the maximum packet size to the size the routers will allow to pass unbroken.
(Routers can break up the packets into smaller ones; 1500 bytes is the typical maximum packet size and the standard for Ethernet. The maximum packet size is con-
figurable by the router's network administrator.) If your application is likely to be
sending data over the Internet, and you cannot guarantee the route and quality of
routers it will pass through, 500 bytes per packet is likely to be optimal.

Network Bottlenecks

Other causes of slow network I/O can be attributed directly to the load or configuration of the network. For example, a LAN may become congested when many
machines are simultaneously trying to communicate over the network. The potential throughput of the network could handle the load, but the algorithms to provide communication channels slow the network, resulting in a lower maximum
throughput. A congested Ethernet network has an average throughput approximately one-third the potential maximum throughput. Congested networks have

other problems, such as dropped network packets. If you are using TCP, the communication rate on a congested network is much slower as the protocol automatically resends the dropped packets. If you are using UDP, your application must resend multiple copies for each transfer. Dropping packets in this way is common for the Internet. For LANs, you need to coordinate closely with the network administrators to alert them to the problems. For single machines connected by a service provider, there are several things you can do. First, there are some commercial utilities available that probe your configuration and the connection to the service provider, suggesting improvements. The phone line to the service provider may be noisier than expected: if so, you also need to speak to the phone line provider. It is also worth checking with the service provider, who should have optimal configurations they can demonstrate.

Dropped packets and retransmissions are a good indication of network congestion problems, and you should be on constant lookout for them. Dropped packets often occur when routers are overloaded and find it necessary to drop some of the packets being transmitted as the router's buffers overflow. This means that the overlying protocol will request the packets to be resent. The *netstat* utility lists retransmission and other statistics that can identify these sorts of problems. Retransmissions may indicate that the system maximum packet size is too large.

DNS Lookups

Looking up network addresses is an often overlooked cause of bad network performance. When your application tries to connect to a network address such as *foo. bar.something.org* (e.g., downloading a web page from *http://foo.bar.something.org*), your application first translates *foo.bar.something.org* into a four-byte network IP address such as 10.33.6.45. This is the actual address that the network understands and uses for routing network packets. The way this translation works is that your system is configured with some seldom-used files that can specify this translation, and a more frequently used Domain Name System (DNS) server that can dynamically provide you with the address from the given string. The DNS translation works as follows:

1. The machine running the application sends the text string of the hostname (e.g., *foo.bar.something.org*) to the DNS server.

2. The DNS server checks its cache to find an IP address corresponding to that hostname. If the server does not find an entry in the cache, it asks its own DNS server (usually further up the Internet domain-name hierarchy) until ultimately the name is resolved. (This may be by components of the name being resolved, e.g., first *.org*, then *something.org*, etc., each time asking another machine as the search request is successively resolved.) This resolved IP address is added to the DNS server's cache.

3. The IP address is returned to the original machine running the application.

4. The application uses the IP address to connect to the desired destination.

The address lookup does not need to be repeated once a connection is established, but any other connections (within the same session of the application or in other sessions at the same time and later) need to repeat the lookup procedure to start another connection.*

You can improve this situation by running a DNS server locally on the machine, or on a local server if the application uses a LAN. A DNS server can be run as a "caching only" server that resets its cache each time the machine is rebooted. There would be little point in doing this if the machine used only one or two connections per hostname between successive reboots. For more frequent connections, a local DNS server can provide a noticeable speedup to connections. *nslookup* is useful for investigating how a particular system does translations.

Performance Checklist

Some of these suggestions apply only after a bottleneck has been identified:

- Tune the application before tuning the underlying system. This is especially pertinent to network communications.

  — Limit application bandwidth requirements to the network segment with the smallest bandwidth.

  — Consider network latencies when specifying feasible application response times.

  — Aim to minimize the number of network round trips necessary to satisfy an application request.

- Constantly monitor the entire system with any monitoring tools available. Monitoring utilities include *perfmeter* (Unix CPU), *vmstat* (Unix CPU, RAM, and disks), *iostat* (Unix disks), performance monitor (Windows CPU, RAM, and disks), *netstat* (network I/O), *ping* (network latency) and *nslookup* (DNS lookup and routing).

  — Keep monitoring records to get a background usage pattern.

  — Use normal monitoring records to get an early warning of changes in the system usage patterns.

  — Watch for levels of paging that decrease system performance.

  — Watch for low CPU activity coupled with high disk activity and delayed responses. This may indicate an I/O problem.

---

* A session can cache the IP address explicitly after the first lookup, but this needs to be done at the application level by holding on to the InetAddress object.

- — Monitor for retransmissions of data packets.
- — Ensure the CPU runnable queue does not get too large.
- — Aim for average CPU utilization to be not more than 75%.
- Consider spreading extra computation loads to low activity times.
  - — Run offline work in off-peak hours only.
  - — Time all processes and terminate any that exceed timeout thresholds.
- Consider upgrading or reconfiguring parts of the system.
  - — Doubling the CPU speed is usually better than doubling the number of CPUs.
  - — Consider striping the disks (e.g., RAID disks).
  - — Add more swap space when there is no alternative way to increase the memory available to the application (or to reduce the application's memory usage requirements).
  - — Test to see if running on raw partitions will be faster.
  - — Look at mapping filesystems into memory for speedier startups and accesses. But be aware that this reduces system memory available to applications. For multiuser applications, this is an efficient way of sharing in-memory data.
  - — Move any components from network-mounted disks to local disks.
  - — Ensure that system swap files are on different disks from any intensively used files.
  - — Cluster files together at the disk level, if possible, or within one big container file.
  - — Defragment disks regularly if applicable to your system.
  - — Move executables or index files to disk sweet spots.
  - — Consider altering priority levels of processes to tune the amount of CPU time they get.
  - — Consider locking processes into memory so they do not get paged out.
  - — Partition the system to allocate determinate resources to your application.
  - — Consider tuning the maximum packet size specified by the TCP/IP stack.
  - — Ensure that your TCP/IP stacks have no performance problems associated with them.
  - — Consider running a local caching DNS server to improve the speed of hostname lookups.

15

Further Resources

Books

Algorithms in C++, Robert Sedgewick (Addison Wesley)

The Art of Computer Programming, Donald Knuth (Addison Wesley)

Concurrent Programming in Java, Doug Lea (Addison Wesley)

Data Structures and Algorithm Analysis in Java, Mark Weiss (Peachpit Press)

High Performance Client/Server, Chris Loosley and Frank Douglas (John Wiley & Sons)

Inside the Java 2 Virtual Machine, Bill Venners (McGraw-Hill) (see *http://www. artima.com/insidejvm/resources/*)

Introduction to Computer Performance Analysis with Mathematica, Arnold O. Allen (Academic Press)

Java Distributed Computing, Jim Farley (O'Reilly)

Java Threads, Scott Oaks and Henry Wong (O'Reilly)

Performance Engineering of Software Systems, Connie Smith (Addison Wesley)

Sun Performance and Tuning, Adrian Cockcroft and Richard Pettit (Prentice Hall)

System Performance Tuning, Mike Loukides (O'Reilly)

Windows NT Applications: Measuring and Optimizing Performance, Paul Hinsberg (MacMillan Technical Publishing)

Windows NT Performance Monitoring, Benchmarking, and Tuning, Mark T. Edmead and Paul Hinsberg (New Riders)

Writing Efficient Programs, Jon Louis Bentley (Prentice Hall)

Magazines

Dr. Dobb's Journal (*http://www.ddj.com*)

Java Report (*http://www.javareport.com*)

Java Developer's Journal (*http://www.JavaDevelopersJournal.com*)

Javaworld (*http://www.javaworld.com*)

Java Pro (*http://www.java-pro.com*)

Byte (*http://www.byte.com*)

New Scientist (*http://www.newscientist.com*)

IBM Systems Journal (*http://www.research.ibm.com/journal/*) (see Volume 39, No. 1, 2000 — Java Performance)

The Smalltalk Report (*http://www.sigs.com*)

URLs

O'Reilly (*http://www.oreilly.com*)

Java (*http://www.java.sun.com*)

Perl (*http://www.perl.com*)

Pavel Kouznetsov's *jad* decompiler (*http://www.geocities.com/SiliconValley/Bridge/ 8617/jad.html*)

IBM alphaWorks site (*http://www.alphaworks.ibm.com*)

Vladimir Bulatov's HyperProf (*http://www.physics.orst.edu/~bulatov/HyperProf/*)

Greg White's ProfileViewer (*http://www.inetmi.com/~gwhi/ProfileViewer/ ProfileViewer.html*)

JAVAR experimental compiler (*http://www.extreme.indiana.edu/hpjava/*)

Jalapeño server JVM (*http://www.research.ibm.com/journal/sj/391/alpern.html*)

Java supercomputing (*http://www.javagrande.org*)

Java supercomputing (*http://www.research.ibm.com/journal/sj/391/moreira.html*)

Web robot guidelines (*http://info.webcrawler.com/mak/projects/robots/robots.html*)

Web robot guidelines (*http://web.nexor.co.uk/mak/doc/robots/guidelines.html*)

GemStone application server (*http://www.gemstone.com*)

Profiling metrics (*http://www.research.ibm.com/journal/sj/391/alexander.html*)

Bill Venner's discussion of optimization (*http://www.artima.com/designtechniques/hotspot.html*)

Doug Bell's article discussing optimization techniques (*http://www.javaworld.com/jw-04-1997/jw-04-optimize.html*)

Classic but old Java optimization site (*http://www.cs.cmu.edu/~jch/java/optimization.html*)

Rouen University String Matching Algorithms site (*http://www-igm.univ-mlv.fr/~lecroq/string/*)

Generic Java (*http://www.cs.bell-labs.com/~wadler/gj/*)

Profilers

Many of these profilers have been reviewed in the various magazines listed previously. You can usually search the magazine web sites to identify which issue of the magazine provides a review. Often the reviews are available online. The profiler vendors should also be happy to provide pointers to reviews. The annual "best of Java" awards includes a section for profilers (see the *Java Developer's Journal*).

Intuitive System's OptimizeIt! (*http://www.optimizeit.com*)

KL Group's JProbe (*http://www.klgroup.com*)

CodeWizard for Java from ParaSoft Corporation (*http://www.parasoft.com/wizard*)

eQASE Auditor from eQASE LLC (*http://www.eqase.com*)

PureLoad from PureIT AB (*http://www.pureit.se/products/pureload*)

SilkObserver from Segue Software, Inc. (*http://www.segue.com*)

SockPerf from IBM alphaWorks (*http://www.alphaworks.ibm.com/tech/sml*)

TrueTime/DevPartner Java Edition from Compuware Corporation (*http://www.compuware.com/numega/*)

Visual Quantify by Rational Software (*http://www.rational.com/products/vis_quantify/index.jtmpl*)

Segue Solutions' SilkPerformer (*http://www.segue.com/html/s_solutions/s_performer/s_performer.htm*)

Metamata Debugger (*http://www.metamata.com/products/debug_top.html*) (some people list this as a profiler, though it looks like a plain debugger to me)

Optimizers

PreEmptive's DashO optimizer (*http://www.preemptive.com*)

TowerJ environment (compiler & runtime) from Tower Technology Corporation (*http://www.towerj.com*)

TowerJ review: (*http://www.javaworld.com/javaworld/jw-10-1999/jw-10-volano_p.html*)

JOVE (*http://www.instantiations.com/jove/*)

Condensity from Plumb Design (*http://www.condensity.com*)

High Performance Compiler for Java from IBM alphaWorks (*http://www. alphaworks.ibm.com/formula/*)

JAX size optimizer from IBM alphaWorks (*http://www.alphaworks.ibm.com/tech/jax/*)

jres resource manager and compressor from IBM alphaWorks (*http://www. alphaworks.ibm.com/formula/*)

Jshrink size optimizer from Eastridge Technology (*http://www.e-t.com/jshrink.html*)

SourceGuard (*http://www.4thpass.com*)

Index

A

accept( ) (ServerSocket), 281
access control, 68, 103, 311
  avoiding, 77
  caching, 302
  canonicalizing objects and, 107
  costs of, 379
  load balancing and, 280
  native methods and, 232
  optimizations and, 368
  queues, 282
  serialization and, 221, 224, 228
  sorting and, 239
  synchronization and, 257
  variables and, 172
adaptive optimization, 72
Adder classes, 268
advantages of Java, 2
algorithms, 293
  array matching, 150
  Boyer-Moore string search, 154
  bubblesort, 294
  collection comparisons, 151
  compression, 234
  conversion
    overhead of, 46
    to strings, 126
  for data structures, 295
  dependency on data, 152

  inefficient, 96
  network access, 401
  Neubert's flashsort, 251
  optimizing compilers and, 73
  performance checklist, 333
  quicksort, 154, 237, 252, 294
  read-ahead, 10, 204
  recursive, 195
  scaling behavior, 250, 294
  scavenging, 25
  sorting, 237, 249
  stateless algorithm objects, 378
And operators, 177
append( ) (StringBuffer), 128
applets, 364
  design of, 378
  tuning performance and, 366
  user interface thread in, 258
applications
  distributed, 15, 363
    batching, 346, 348, 352
    bottlenecks, 335, 376
    caching, 344–346, 351
    compression and, 350
    garbage collection, 354
    measurements of, 16
    monitoring, 337–339
    multiplexing, 354
    optimizations, 364, 376–377

About the Author

Jack Shirazi is an independent consultant. He was an early adopter of Java, and for the last few years has consulted mainly for the financial sector, focusing on Java performance. Before using Java, Jack spent many years tuning Smalltalk applications.

Jack's early career involved research in theoretical physics and bioinformatics. Jack has publications in the field of protein structure and is proud to have contributed to some of the core Perl5 modules.

Colophon

Our look is the result of reader comments, our own experimentation, and feedback from distribution channels. Distinctive covers complement our distinctive approach to technical topics, breathing personality and life into potentially dry subjects.

The image on the cover of *Java™ Performance Tuning* is a stopwatch. Unlike traditional clocks, which track the continuation of time through the minutes and hours of a day, the stopwatch measures elapsed time over short intervals by allowing the user to start and stop it. This is particularly suited to sports: stopwatches (also known as chronographs) were common at English horse races as early as the mid-seventeenth century. However, a stopwatch like the one pictured on the cover is prone to human error: its exactness is limited by the reaction times of the person holding it. Although more precise photographic-electric timers appeared as early as 1892 and were used experimentally in the Olympic Games in Stockholm in 1912, the Olympics continued to rely on handheld stopwatches until 1960 in Rome, when the transition was officially made to electric timers.

Emily Quill was the production editor and proofreader for *Java™ Performance Tuning*. Mary Anne Weeks Mayo was the copyeditor for the book. Jane Ellin and Nancy Kotary performed quality control reviews. Nancy Williams provided production assistance. Nancy Crumpton wrote the index. This colophon was written by Emily Quill.

Hanna Dyer designed the cover of this book, based on a series design by Edie Freedman. The image of the stopwatch is from the Stock Options photo collection. It was manipulated in Adobe Photoshop by Michael Snow. The cover layout was produced by Emma Colby using QuarkXPress 4.1, the Bodoni Black font from URW Software, and BT Bodoni Bold Italic from Bitstream. Alicia Cech and David Futato designed the interior layout, based on a series design by Nancy Priest.

Text was produced in FrameMaker 5.5.6 using a template implemented by Mike Sierra. The heading font is Bodoni BT; the text font is New Baskerville. Illustrations that appear in the book were created in Macromedia Freehand 8 and Adobe Photoshop 5 by Robert Romano and Rhon Porter.

Whenever possible, our books use a durable and flexible lay-flat binding. If the page count exceeds the maximum bulk possible for this type of binding, perfect binding is used.

 # *More Titles from O'Reilly*

Java

Java Cryptography

By Jonathan B. Knudsen
1st Edition May 1998
362 pages, ISBN 1-56592-402-9

Java Cryptography teaches you how to write
secure programs using Java's cryptographic
tools. It includes thorough discussions
of the java.security package and the Java
Cryptography Extensions (JCE), showing
you how to use security providers and even implement your
own provider. It discusses authentication, key management,
public and private key encryption, and includes a secure talk
application that encrypts all data sent over the network. If you
work with sensitive data, you'll find this book indispensable.

Java Distributed Computing

By Jim Farley
1st Edition January 1998
384 pages, ISBN 1-56592-206-9

Java Distributed Computing offers a
general introduction to distributed computing,
meaning programs that run on two or more
systems. It focuses primarily on how to
structure and write distributed applications
and discusses issues like designing protocols, security, working
with databases, and dealing with low bandwidth situations.

Java Network Programming, 2nd Edition

By Elliotte Rusty Harold
2nd Edition August 2000
760 pages, ISBN 1-56592-870-9

Java Network Programming, 2nd Edition,
is a complete introduction to developing
network programs (both applets and
applications) using Java, covering everything
from networking fundamentals to remote
method invocation (RMI). It includes chapters on TCP and UDP
sockets, multicasting protocol and content handlers, and servlets.
This second edition also includes coverage of Java 1.1, 1.2 and
1.3. New chapters cover multithreaded network programming,
I/O, HTML parsing and display, the Java Mail API, the Java Secure
Sockets Extension, and more.

Java Security

By Scott Oaks
1st Edition May 1998
474 pages, ISBN 1-56592-403-7

This essential Java 2 book covers Java's
security mechanisms and teaches you how
to work with them. It discusses class loaders,
security managers, access lists, digital
signatures, and authentication and shows
how to use these to create and enforce your own security policy.

Java Threads, 2nd Edition

By Scott Oaks & Henry Wong
2nd Edition January 1999
336 pages, ISBN 1-56592-418-5

Revised and expanded to cover Java 2, *Java
Threads, 2nd Edition* shows you how to take
full advantage of Java's thread facilities: where
to use threads to increase efficiency, how to
use them effectively, and how to avoid common
mistakes. It thoroughly covers the Thread and ThreadGroup classes,
the Runnable interface, and the language's synchronized operator.
The book pays special attention to threading issues with Swing, as
well as problems like deadlock, race condition, and starvation to
help you write code without hidden bugs.

Database Programming with JDBC and Java, 2nd Edition

By George Reese
2nd Edition August 2000
352 pages, ISBN 1-56592-616-1

This book describes the standard Java
interfaces that make portable object-oriented
access to relational databases possible, and
offers a robust model for writing applications
that are easy to maintain. The second edition
has been completely updated for JDBC 2.0, and includes reference
listings for JDBC and the most important RMI classes. The book
begins with a quick overview of SQL for developers who may be
asked to handle a database for the first time, and goes on to
explain how to issue database queries and updates through
SQL and JDBC.

O'REILLY®

TO ORDER: **800-998-9938** • *order@oreilly.com* • *http://www.oreilly.com/*
OUR PRODUCTS ARE AVAILABLE AT A BOOKSTORE OR SOFTWARE STORE NEAR YOU.
FOR INFORMATION: **800-998-9938** • **707-829-0515** • *info@oreilly.com*

Java

Creating Effective JavaHelp

By Kevin Lewis
1st Edition June 2000
188 pages, ISBN 1-56592-719-2

JavaHelp is an online help system developed in the Java™ programming language. *Creating Effective JavaHelp* covers the main features and options of JavaHelp and shows how to create a basic JavaHelp system, prepare help topics, and deploy the help system in an application. Written for all levels of Java developers and technical writers, the book takes a chapter-by-chapter approach to building concepts, to impart a complete understanding of how to create usable JavaHelp systems and integrate them into Java applications and applets.

Java Native Methods

By Alligator Descartes
1st Edition November 2000 (est.)
300 pages (est.), ISBN 1-56592-345-6

Although Java offers the promise of platform-independent programming, there are situations where you may still need to use native C or C++ code compiled for a particular platform. Maybe you have to tie some legacy code into a Java application. Or maybe you want to implement some computationally intensive methods for a performance-critical application in native code. *Java Native Methods* tells you everything you need to know to get your native code working with Java, using either Sun's Java Native Interface (JNI) or Microsoft's Raw Native Interface (RNI).

Java Internationalization

By Andy Deitsch & David Czarnecki
1st Edition November 2000 (est.)
350 pages (est.), ISBN 0-596-00019-7

Java Internationalization shows how to write software that is truly multilingual, using Java's very sophisticated Unicode internationalization facilities. *Java Internationalization* brings Java developers up to speed for the new generation of software development: writing software that is no longer limited by language boundaries.

Java Performance Tuning

By Jack Shirazi
1st Edition September 2000
446 pages, ISBN 0-596-00015-4

Java Performance Tuning contains step-by-step instructions on all aspects of the performance tuning process, right from such early considerations as setting goals, measuring performance, and choosing a compiler. Extensive examples for tuning many parts of an application are described in detail, and any pitfalls are identified. The book also provides performance tuning checklists that enable developers to make their tuning as comprehensive as possible.

Learning Java

By Pat Niemeyer & Jonathan Knudsen
1st Edition, May 2000
726 pages, Includes CD-ROM
ISBN 1-56592-718-4

For programmers either just migrating to Java or already working steadily in the forefront of Java development, *Learning Java* gives a clear, systematic overview of the Java 2 Standard Edition. It covers the essentials of hot topics like Swing and JFC; describes new tools for signing applets; and shows how to write networked clients and servers, servlets, JavaBeans, and state-of-the-art user interfaces. Includes a CD-ROM containing the Java 2 SDK, version 1.3.

The Java Enterprise CD Bookshelf

By O'Reilly & Associates, Inc.
1st Edition November 2000 (est.)
622 pages (est.), Features CD-ROM
ISBN 1-56592-850-4

The Java Enterprise CD Bookshelf contains a powerhouse of books from O'Reilly: both electronic and print versions of *Java Enterprise in a Nutshell*, plus electronic versions of *Java in a Nutshell, 3rd Edition*; *Java Foundation Classes in a Nutshell*; *Enterprise JavaBeans, 2nd Edition*; *Java Servlet Programming*; *Java Security*; and *Java Distributed Computing*.

O'REILLY®

TO ORDER: **800-998-9938** • *order@oreilly.com* • *http://www.oreilly.com/*
OUR PRODUCTS ARE AVAILABLE AT A BOOKSTORE OR SOFTWARE STORE NEAR YOU.
FOR INFORMATION: **800-998-9938** • **707-829-0515** • *info@oreilly.com*

Java

Java Servlet Programming

By Jason Hunter with William Crawford
1st Edition November 1998
528 pages, ISBN 1-56592-391-X

Java servlets offer a fast, powerful, portable replacement for CGI scripts. *Java Servlet Programming* covers everything you need to know to write effective servlets. Topics include: serving dynamic Web content, maintaining state information, session tracking, database connectivity using JDBC, and applet-servlet communication.

JavaServer Pages

By Hans Bergsten
1st Edition November 2000 (est.)
450 pages (est.), ISBN 1-56592-746-X

JavaServer Pages shows how to develop Java-based web applications without having to be a hardcore programmer. The author provides an overview of JSP concepts and illuminates how JSP fits into the larger picture of web applications. There are chapters for web authors on generating dynamic content, handling session information, and accessing databases, as well as material for Java programmers on creating Java components and custom JSP tags for web authors to use in JSP pages.

Java and XML

By Brett McLaughlin
1st Edition June 2000
498 pages, ISBN 0-596-00016-2

Java revolutionized the programming world by providing a platform-independent programming language. XML takes the revolution a step further with platform-independent language for interchanging data. *Java and XML* shows how to put the two together, building real-world applications in which both the code and the data are truly portable.

Enterprise JavaBeans, 2nd Edition

By Richard Monson-Haefel
2nd Edition March 2000
492 pages, ISBN 1-56592-869-5

Enterprise JavaBeans, 2nd Edition provides a thorough introduction to EJB 1.1 and 1.0 for the enterprise software developer. It shows you how to develop enterprise Beans to model your business objects and processes. The EJB architecture provides a highly flexible system in which components can easily be reused, and which can be changed to suit your needs without upsetting other parts of the system. *Enterprise JavaBeans* teaches you how to take advantage of the flexibility and simplicity that this powerful new architecture provides.

Developing Java Beans

By Robert Englander
1st Edition June 1997
316 pages, ISBN 1-56592-289-1

Developing Java Beans is a complete introduction to Java's component architecture. It describes how to write Beans, which are software components that can be used in visual programming environments. This book discusses event adapters, serialization, introspection, property editors, and customizers, and shows how to use Beans within ActiveX controls.

In a Nutshell Quick References

Internet in a Nutshell

By Valerie Quercia
1st Edition October 1997
450 pages, ISBN 1-56592-323-5

Internet in a Nutshell is a quick-moving guide that goes beyond the "hype" and right to the heart of the matter: how to get the Internet to work for you. This is a second-generation Internet book for readers who have already taken a spin around the Net and now want to learn the shortcuts.

In a Nutshell Quick References

AOL in a Nutshell

By Curt Degenhart & Jen Muehlbauer
1st Edition June 1998
536 pages, ISBN 1-56592-424-X

This definitive reference breaks through the hype and shows advanced AOL users and sophisticated beginners how to get the most out of AOL 4.0's tools and features. You'll learn how to customize AOL to meet your needs, work around annoying idiosyncrasies, avoid unwanted email and Instant Messages, actually understand Parental Controls, and turn off intrusive advertisements. It's an indispensable guide for users who aren't dummies.

ASP in a Nutshell, 2nd Edition

By A. Keyton Weissinger
2nd Edition July 2000
492 pages, ISBN 1-56592-843-1

ASP in a Nutshell, 2nd Edition, provides the high-quality reference documentation that web application developers really need to create effective Active Server Pages. It focuses on how features are used in a real application and highlights little-known or undocumented features.

Perl in a Nutshell

By Ellen Siever, Stephen Spainhour & Nathan Patwardhan
1st Edition December 1998
674 pages, ISBN 1-56592-286-7

The perfect companion for working programmers, *Perl in a Nutshell* is a comprehensive reference guide to the world of Perl. It contains everything you need to know for all but the most obscure Perl questions. This wealth of information is packed into an efficient, extraordinarily usable format.

Web Design in a Nutshell

By Jennifer Niederst
1st Edition November 1998
580 pages, ISBN 1-56592-515-7

Web Design in a Nutshell contains the nitty-gritty on everything you need to know to design Web pages. Written by veteran Web designer Jennifer Niederst, this book provides quick access to the wide range of technologies and techniques from which Web designers and authors must draw. Topics include understanding the Web environment, HTML, graphics, multimedia and interactivity, and emerging technologies.

Webmaster in a Nutshell, 2nd Edition

By Stephen Spainhour & Robert Eckstein
2nd Edition June 1999
540 pages, ISBN 1-56592-325-1

This indispensable books takes all the essential reference information for the Web and pulls it together into one volume. It covers HTML 4.0, CSS, XML, CGI, SSI, JavaScript 1.2, PHP, HTTP 1.1, and administration for the Apache server.

How to stay in touch with O'Reilly

1. Visit Our Award-Winning Web Site

http://www.oreilly.com/

★ "Top 100 Sites on the Web" —*PC Magazine*
★ "Top 5% Web sites" —*Point Communications*
★ "3-Star site" —*The McKinley Group*

Our web site contains a library of comprehensive product information (including book excerpts and tables of contents), downloadable software, background articles, interviews with technology leaders, links to relevant sites, book cover art, and more. File us in your Bookmarks or Hotlist!

2. Join Our Email Mailing Lists

New Product Releases

To receive automatic email with brief descriptions of all new O'Reilly products as they are released, send email to:
listproc@online.oreilly.com
Put the following information in the first line of your message (*not* in the Subject field):
subscribe oreilly-news

O'Reilly Events

If you'd also like us to send information about trade show events, special promotions, and other O'Reilly events, send email to:
listproc@online.oreilly.com
Put the following information in the first line of your message (*not* in the Subject field):
subscribe oreilly-events

3. Get Examples from Our Books via FTP

There are two ways to access an archive of example files from our books:

Regular FTP
* ftp to:
  ftp.oreilly.com
  (login: anonymous
  password: your email address)
* Point your web browser to:
  ftp://ftp.oreilly.com/

FTPMAIL
* Send an email message to:
  ftpmail@online.oreilly.com
  (Write "help" in the message body)

4. Contact Us via Email

order@oreilly.com
To place a book or software order online. Good for North American and international customers.

subscriptions@oreilly.com
To place an order for any of our newsletters or periodicals.

books@oreilly.com
General questions about any of our books.

software@oreilly.com
For general questions and product information about our software. Check out O'Reilly Software Online at **http://software.oreilly.com/** for software and technical support information. Registered O'Reilly software users send your questions to: **website-support@oreilly.com**

cs@oreilly.com
For answers to problems regarding your order or our products.

booktech@oreilly.com
For book content technical questions or corrections.

proposals@oreilly.com
To submit new book or software proposals to our editors and product managers.

international@oreilly.com
For information about our international distributors or translation queries. For a list of our distributors outside of North America check out:
http://www.oreilly.com/www/order/country.html

5. Work with Us

Check out our website for current employment opportunites:
www.jobs@oreilly.com
Click on "Work with Us"

O'Reilly & Associates, Inc.
101 Morris Street, Sebastopol, CA 95472 USA
TEL   707-829-0515 or 800-998-9938
      (6am to 5pm PST)
FAX   707-829-0104

International Distributors

UK, EUROPE, MIDDLE EAST AND AFRICA (EXCEPT FRANCE, GERMANY, AUSTRIA, SWITZERLAND, LUXEMBOURG, LIECHTENSTEIN, AND EASTERN EUROPE)

INQUIRIES
O'Reilly UK Limited
4 Castle Street
Farnham
Surrey, GU9 7HS
United Kingdom
Telephone: 44-1252-711776
Fax: 44-1252-734211
Email: information@oreilly.co.uk

ORDERS
Wiley Distribution Services Ltd.
1 Oldlands Way
Bognor Regis
West Sussex PO22 9SA
United Kingdom
Telephone: 44-1243-779777
Fax: 44-1243-820250
Email: cs-books@wiley.co.uk

FRANCE

INQUIRIES
Éditions O'Reilly
18 rue Séguier
75006 Paris, France
Tel: 33-1-40-51-52-30
Fax: 33-1-40-51-52-31
Email: france@editions-oreilly.fr

ORDERS
GEODIF
61, Bd Saint-Germain
75240 Paris Cedex 05, France
Tel: 33-1-44-41-46-16 (French books)
Tel: 33-1-44-41-11-87 (English books)
Fax: 33-1-44-41-11-44
Email: distribution@eyrolles.com

GERMANY, SWITZERLAND, AUSTRIA, EASTERN EUROPE, LUXEMBOURG, AND LIECHTENSTEIN

INQUIRIES & ORDERS
O'Reilly Verlag
Balthasarstr. 81
D-50670 Köln
Germany
Telephone: 49-221-973160-91
Fax: 49-221-973160-8
Email: anfragen@oreilly.de (inquiries)
Email: order@oreilly.de (orders)

CANADA (FRENCH LANGUAGE BOOKS)

Les Éditions Flammarion ltée
375, Avenue Laurier Ouest
Montréal (Québec) H2V 2K3
Tel: 00-1-514-277-8807
Fax: 00-1-514-278-2085
Email: info@flammarion.qc.ca

HONG KONG

City Discount Subscription Service, Ltd.
Unit D, 3rd Floor, Yan's Tower
27 Wong Chuk Hang Road
Aberdeen, Hong Kong
Tel: 852-2580-3539
Fax: 852-2580-6463
Email: citydis@ppn.com.hk

KOREA

Hanbit Media, Inc.
Chungmu Bldg. 201
Yonnam-dong 568-33
Mapo-gu
Seoul, Korea
Tel: 822-325-0397
Fax: 822-325-9697
Email: hant93@chollian.dacom.co.kr

PHILIPPINES

Global Publishing
G/F Benavides Garden
1186 Benavides Street
Manila, Philippines
Tel: 632-254-8949/637-252-2582
Fax: 632-734-5060/632-252-2733
Email: globalp@pacific.net.ph

TAIWAN

O'Reilly Taiwan
No. 3, Lane 131
Hang-Chow South Road
Section 1, Taipei, Taiwan
Tel: 886-2-23968990
Fax: 886-2-23968916
Email: taiwan@oreilly.com

CHINA

O'Reilly Beijing
Room 2410
160, FuXingMenNeiDaJie
XiCheng District
Beijing, China PR 100031
Tel: 86-10-66412305
Fax: 86-10-86631007
Email: beijing@oreilly.com

INDIA

Computer Bookshop (India) Pvt. Ltd.
190 Dr. D.N. Road, Fort
Bombay 400 001 India
Tel: 91-22-207-0989
Fax: 91-22-262-3551
Email: cbsbom@giasbm01.vsnl.net.in

JAPAN

O'Reilly Japan, Inc.
Yotsuya Y's Building
7 Banch 6, Honshio-cho
Shinjuku-ku
Tokyo 160-0003 Japan
Tel: 81-3-3356-5227
Fax: 81-3-3356-5261
Email: japan@oreilly.com

ALL OTHER ASIAN COUNTRIES

O'Reilly & Associates, Inc.
101 Morris Street
Sebastopol, CA 95472 USA
Tel: 707-829-0515
Fax: 707-829-0104
Email: order@oreilly.com

AUSTRALIA

Woodslane Pty., Ltd.
7/5 Vuko Place
Warriewood NSW 2102
Australia
Tel: 61-2-9970-5111
Fax: 61-2-9970-5002
Email: info@woodslane.com.au

NEW ZEALAND

Woodslane New Zealand, Ltd.
21 Cooks Street (P.O. Box 575)
Waganui, New Zealand
Tel: 64-6-347-6543
Fax: 64-6-345-4840
Email: info@woodslane.com.au

LATIN AMERICA

McGraw-Hill Interamericana
Editores, S.A. de C.V.
Cedro No. 512
Col. Atlampa
06450, Mexico, D.F.
Tel: 52-5-547-6777
Fax: 52-5-547-3336
Email: mcgraw-hill@infosel.net.mx

O'REILLY®

O'REILLY[®]

O'Reilly & Associates, Inc.
101 Morris Street
Sebastopol, CA 95472-9902
1-800-998-9938

Visit us online at:
www.oreilly.com
order@oreilly.com

O'REILLY WOULD LIKE TO HEAR FROM YOU

Which book did this card come from?

_____

Where did you buy this book?
- ❏ Bookstore
- ❏ Direct from O'Reilly
- ❏ Bundled with hardware/software
- ❏ Other _____

- ❏ Computer Store
- ❏ Class/seminar

What operating system do you use?
- ❏ UNIX
- ❏ Windows NT
- ❏ Other _____

- ❏ Macintosh
- ❏ PC(Windows/DOS)

What is your job description?
- ❏ System Administrator
- ❏ Network Administrator
- ❏ Web Developer
- ❏ Other _____

- ❏ Programmer
- ❏ Educator/Teacher

❏ Please send me O'Reilly's catalog, containing a complete listing of O'Reilly books and software.

Name _____ Company/Organization _____

Address _____

City _____ State _____ Zip/Postal Code _____ Country _____

Telephone _____ Internet or other email address (specify network)

Nineteenth century wood engraving
of a bear from the O'Reilly &
Associates Nutshell Handbook®
Using & Managing UUCP.

POST CARD

PLACE
STAMP
HERE

|||||

NO POSTAGE
NECESSARY IF
MAILED IN THE
UNITED STATES

BUSINESS REPLY MAIL
FIRST CLASS MAIL   PERMIT NO. 80   SEBASTOPOL, CA

Postage will be paid by addressee

O'Reilly & Associates, Inc.
101 Morris Street
Sebastopol, CA 95472-9902